JOHN

MAKING THE FUTURE WORK:

JOHN

DIEBOLD

Unleashing Our Powers of Innovation for the Decades Ahead

International Authority on Management and Technology

Simon and Schuster   New York

SIMON AND SCHUSTER and colophon are registered trademarks of Simon & Schuster, Inc.

Designed by Jennie Nichols/Levavi & Levavi
Manufactured in the United States of America

10 9 8 7 6 5 4 3 2 1

Library of Congress Cataloging in Publication Data

Diebold, John, date.
  Making the future work.
  Bibliography: p.
  Includes index.
  1. Industrial management—United States. 2. Public administration
—United States. 3. Industry—Social aspects—United States. 4. Industry and state—United States. 5. Twentieth century—Forecasts.

I. Title.
HD70.U5D53   1984   302.3′5   84-13889

ISBN: 0-671-45657-1

The author is grateful for permission to use excerpts from the following works:

Autograph Notes for Political Speeches by Abraham Lincoln, Springfield, Illinois, 1858, an original manuscript owned by the Pierpont Morgan Library, New York. The author is grateful to Herbert Cahoon, Curator of Autograph Manuscripts.

From Know-how to Nowhere—The Development of American Technology by Elting E. Morison, copyright © 1974 by Basic Books, Inc., Publishers. Reprinted by permission of the publisher.

Politics and Markets: The World's Political-Economic Systems by Charles E. Lindblom, copyright © 1977 by Basic Books, Inc., Publishers, and reprinted by permission.

"Why Westway is Right" by William S. Woodside, *New York Times,* August 1, 1983, copyright © 1983 by The New York Times Company. Reprinted by permission.

Statecraft as Soulcraft copyright © 1983 by George Will, Simon and Schuster.

"Toward a Pluralistic but Coherent Society" by John Gardner, Executive Seminar Readings, day 2, week 6, the Aspen Institute for Humanistic Studies, Inc., 1983.

Knowledge and Decisions by Thomas Sowell, copyright © 1980 by Basic Books, Inc., Publishers, and reprinted by permission.

(Continued on page 465)

Acknowledgments

As with any undertaking of this kind, there are myriad individuals who, over the years, have contributed both in general and in specific to the development of my ideas and to the final form of this manuscript. I can do no more in these acknowledgments than to try to thank those who have been most specifically helpful—often very extensively so. And while there is only one person who is ultimately responsible for the form of this manuscript, ideas that were long in gestation would never have turned into the reality of a finished book without the invaluable and full-time help of Catherine Marenghi of the Diebold Group, Inc., and the encouragement and guidance of my editor, Patricia Soliman, vice-president and associate publisher of Simon & Schuster. Nor would these ideas have been brought to Patricia Soliman's attention had it not been for my friend Eden Collinsworth, publisher, Arbor House.

The first time I put any of these ideas on paper was at the instigation of Ed Kosner, then editor-in-chief of *Newsweek*, who encouraged me to produce a "My Turn" column. Ed Klein, then a senior editor of *Newsweek*, was the individual with whom I worked most closely in the final form of that piece. The next big step in the development of the ideas was a Trueman Wood Lecture on April 17, 1980, to the Royal Society of Arts, London, to which I have been elected a Benjamin Franklin Fellow. I want specifically to thank Christopher Lucas, Secretary of the Royal Society.

Several friends, colleagues, and family members have been kind enough to read, critically comment upon, and annotate portions of the book, and in some cases the entire manuscript. Specifically I would like to thank Liesa Bing, William and Ruth Diebold, William Stockton of *The New York Times*, and Martin Wassell of the Institute of Economic Affairs in London, each of whom read and commented on the entire manuscript. Individuals who read single chapters—sometimes more than one chapter—included:

VETOES AND PRIORITIES: Peter C. Goldmark, Jr., executive director, Port Authority of New York and New Jersey; Robert C. Holland, president, Committee for Economic Development; Elmer Staats, former comptroller general of the U.S.; Stephen Stamas, vice-president, Exxon Corp.; Annmarie Walsh, president, Institute of Public Administration; Frank A. Weil, Esq., Wald, Harkrader & Ross. SHORT TIME HORIZONS: Roy Ash, former director, Office of Management and Budget; Dr. William O. Baker, former chairman of Bell Laboratories and now chairman of Rockefeller University and the Andrew W. Mellon Foundation; Fletch Byrom, former chairman of the board, the Koppers Co.; Lewis Young, editor in chief, *Business Week*. THE MISRULE OF LAW: John Beerbower, Esq., Cravath Swaine & Moore; Judge Marvin E. Frankel, Kramer, Levin, Nessen, Kamin & Frankel. UNLEASHING INNOVATION IN PUBLIC SERVICES: Graham S. Finney, president, the Conservation Company and chairman of the Philadelphia Planning Commission; E. S. Savas, professor of management, Baruch College/City University of New York. TALENT AS CAPITAL: Sidney Harman, chairman, Harman International Industries; Lewis H. Young, editor in chief, *Business Week*. MANAGING FOR SOCIOPOLITICAL CHANGE: John Gardner, chairman, Common Cause; James A. Perkins, chairman, International Council for Educational Development. LABOR IN TRANSITION: Robert C. Holland, president, Committee for Economic Development. THE INFORMATION AGE: Dr. William O. Baker, former chairman of Bell Laboratories. THE BIO-REVOLU-

TION: Joan Diebold; Rod Nichols, executive vice-president, the Rockefeller University.

An even wider group of friends, acquaintances and colleagues were kind enough to respond to my initial outline and precis of the book with specific comments and suggestions. Some of their ideas were incorporated into the book, and some were equally helpful by leading us to other materials that provided good case examples. Of those who helped in this manner, in addition to those already named, I would like to mention: G. Wallace Bates, president, the Business Roundtable; Dennis Bonney, vice-president, Standard Oil Company of California; Joseph L. Bower, professor, Harvard Business School; Frank Cary, chairman of the Executive Committee, IBM; Edward E. David, Jr., president, Exxon Research and Engineering Company; Isaiah Frank, professor, School of Advanced International Studies, Johns Hopkins University; James Henry, president, Center for Public Resources, Inc.; Reginald H. Jones, chairman emeritus, General Electric; Gerry Laubach, president, Pfizer, Inc.; Ian MacGregor, chairman, National Coal Board; David Mathews, president, Charles F. Kettering Foundation; Hans Merkle, supervisory board chairman, Robert Bosch GmBh; Newton N. Minow, Esq., Sidney & Austin; Gerald A. Pollack, coordinator, international economics, Exxon Corp.; George T. Scharffenberger, chairman, City Investing Co.; Lionel Stoleru, former minister of the French government; Mason Willrich, vice-president, Pacific Gas & Electric Co.; William S. Woodside, chairman, president and chief executive officer, American Can Company; Richard Wool, Public Affairs Division, Pfizer, Inc.; and Ralph Weindling, vice-chairman, the Diebold Group, Inc.

In addition, several individuals shared with me their invaluable expertise on specific questions: Jill Abramson, senior reporter, *The American Lawyer;* Leo Cherne, executive director, Research Institute of America; Alfred D. Chandler Jr., Straus Professor of Business History, Harvard Business School; Gerald Edelman, Nobel Laureate and head of Laboratory of Developmental and Molecular Biology, Rockefeller University; Robert W. Galvin, chairman and chief executive officer, Motorola Inc.; Peter Gwynne, managing editor, *Technology Review;* Charles Hugel, president, Combustion Engineering; Michael Rice, of Michael Rice Media; Arthur Schlesinger, Jr., Albert Schweitzer Chair in the Humanities, City University of New York; Gus Tyler of the International Ladies' Garment Workers Union, and my friend of twenty years; Daniel Yankelovich, chairman and cofounder of the Public Agenda Foundation; John A. Young, chairman, Executive Committee, Hewlett-Packard Company; and Walter Zinn, corporate director, Combustion Engineering.

These acknowledgments would not be complete without thanking my staff at the Diebold Group, Inc., including: Nelson Smith, my assistant at the Diebold Institute for Public Policy Studies, Inc., who was most helpful during eleventh-hour revisions; my tireless secretaries, Katherine Martin and Ruth Evans; Susan Landstreet, director of administration; and Aneck Sanchez, word processing supervisor, who oversaw the massive word processing effort.

For Vanessa

Contents

Part 1 The Need for a New   13
             Scheme of Things

  I. *Why Things Don't Work Anymore,*
       and What We Can Do About It   15

 II. *Vetoes and Priorities*   43

III. *Short Time Horizons*   79

 IV. *The Misrule of Law*   120

Part 2 Tapping Human Potential   149

  V. *Unleashing Innovation in*
       Public Services   151

 VI. *Talent as Capital*   193

VII. *Managing*
       for Sociopolitical Change   236

VIII. *Labor in Transition:*
       Facilitating Change in Jobs   270

Part 3 Moving Toward the Future   303

      Foreword   305

 IX. *Technology Outrunning Policy:*
       The Information Age   308

  X. *Technology Outrunning Policy:*
       The Bio-Revolution   360

XI. *A Guiding Vision*   388

Notes   423

Selected Bibliography   439

Index   449

ONE

THE NEED FOR A NEW SCHEME OF THINGS

Major strides in science, applied through the arts of technology and modern management, have given us the keys to unlock a truly golden age in human history. And in some ways they have. Yet, with the cornucopia of material wealth and knowledge that has characterized the last two centuries, the keys we forge seem increasingly to be those to Pandora's box rather than to a golden age. How to construct a new scheme of things?

Why Things Don't Work Anymore, and What We Can Do About It

Having grown up in an age when problems were thought to have solutions, I find it quite natural to approach the important predicaments of our day with an interest in helping to solve them. That may be a tall order, but the experiences of my life lead me to believe that we need not accept many of the considerable negatives of our present situation. If nothing else, I want to make a start by clarifying just what I believe these problems are, for, by and large, they are not the crises that dominate the headlines.

This is a book about big societal problems, but addressed from the standpoint of *process*, *function*, *structure*, and *management*. Since I have spent my adult life directing a professional firm whose bread-and-butter business is helping large institutions—public as well as private—work better, I have looked to the examples encountered in the course of several thousand assignments as a guide to ways in which we might tackle some of our country's systemic ills and unleash the energies and imagination of our highly creative society. One thing I have certainly learned in working thirty years with the best managed and most successful organizations in the world is that one should concentrate one's time and effort on getting right the structure and process, not on solving a sequence of crises—which is what

15

we have been doing on a societal level. Good people working within the right structure and process will be able to anticipate trouble long before it escalates to crisis proportions.

And trouble is the name of our era. No other period in history so eminently deserves to be characterized by the Chinese character that simultaneously represents crisis and opportunity as do the post–World War II years.

By the time I was in college, in the 1940s, it had indeed become Henry Luce's "American Century." World leadership was unquestionably ours—no one ever thought twice about it. But the realization that the times were changing came especially early to those of us who spend a good deal of time abroad. It began to be evident in the most tentative manner, coinciding with the popular outlook in the States that all material things had been achieved and that we must learn to look beyond work to give life meaning—the first rumblings of a social revolution that would explode in the 1960s.

By now we can no longer take U.S. preeminence for granted; indeed, evidence of our faltering leadership comes across loud and clear in recent years:

▷ The U.S.'s becoming a debtor nation should not have shocked regular newspaper readers or TV news viewers who tracked development of the $60-billion-plus annual U.S. trade deficit— but incremental change is rarely viewed in advance in quite these terms, even if it is the inevitable and worsening result of declining U.S. competitiveness.

▷ The long-awaited new subway cars that were to have replaced New York City's forty-year-old vehicles failed their first performance tests in February 1984, delaying the city by an additional four to six months from putting the cars into operation. The front-page *New York Times* headline read, "First Cars for IRT Made by Japanese Fail 30-Day Tests." But the subhead and story indicated that the Japanese had done their job just fine— the failure was caused specifically by the door switch and brake systems made by two *American* companies.[1]

▷ A Public Agenda Foundation study indicates that most U.S. jobholders see no connection between the quality of their work and their compensation. "Only 13 percent of the U.S. work force believes that they would benefit more from their own hard and effective work"—so out of step are our motivation systems in large organizations with the workplace reality and outlook of employees.[2]

▷ The 1983 collapse of the Mianus River Bridge in Greenwich, Connecticut, focused attention on our national infrastructure, and we learned that we have 253,000 substandard bridges, 1.3 million miles of roads in need of immediate repair and, at 1984 rates of repair and maintenance, a thirty-two-year, $324 billion repair backlog.[3] "As General Motors has discovered, some streets in Queens are rougher than the rough track on which it tests buses."[4]

▷ Official estimates say there are 40,000 homeless in New York City, but the city's housing policies continue to decimate the housing stock. Peter Salins, chairman of the Urban Affairs Department at Hunter College, said public-assistance programs, rent regulations, the system of adjudicating landlord-tenant disputes, and economic factors all contribute to the "ecology of housing destruction."[5]

▷ By 1983, in comparison with other nations, the U.S. had dropped to forty-ninth in literacy, eighth in longevity, eleventh in per capita income (as a proportion of GNP), and nineteenth lowest in infant mortality, according to the Population Reference Bureau in Washington, D.C.

And it has all happened while I and my contemporaries watched—during our adult life in a country that remains the envy of the world for our political freedom and human as well as natural resources. The extent to which this change in the state of our nation and way in which we view ourselves as well as conduct our affairs has come across in our national consciousness—which I think is encouraging as a prelude to corrective action—was reflected recently in an excellent sports book, *UPSET: Australia Wins the America's Cup:*

▷ On September 26, 1983—for the first time in 132 years—the United States team lost the America's Cup. What really happened that day at Newport, R.I.? John Marshall, the sailtrimmer of the American yacht, said *Liberty* was a "creative failure": "It's more of an endemic American problem of not reaching far enough, not taking large enough risks, and not having the structure to permit or encourage that. . . . The Australians won the America's Cup because they had a more creative design, a radical design—a risk-taking design, but a successful one."[6]

Many of these problems bedevil other advanced societies. My European friends are much concerned these days with the "European disease." But the form and many of the problems themselves are uniquely American.

While I am fond of quoting Charlie Brown (not my friend the AT&T chairman but the "Peanuts" philosopher) to the effect that "There is no problem so big that it cannot be run away from," I think that any further dodging of the real dilemmas of our society will bring us into the arms of that other comic-strip curmudgeon, Albert, in "Pogo," who observed, "We has met the enemy and it is US!" While I hesitate to overdramatize this situation, the alternative to making our vital institutions work is something we must avoid at all costs—moving toward an increasingly authoritarian government of either right or left. Individual liberty, not simply the quality of life, is at stake.

Our late twentieth-century propensity to focus on symptoms rather than on root causes results in technofix—applying increasingly expensive Band-Aids to our condition—and does so too late in the day to provide satisfactory solutions. We need to make the institutions of our society capable of dealing with life in the advanced industrial world in which we live, or we are going to expend increasing resources in coping with a stream of ever more demanding emergencies.

Don't get me wrong. The need for action on today's crises is urgent, whether they be unemployment, urban decay, public education, international competitiveness, energy dependence, environmental pollution, or you name it. But we had better recognize that crisis management is self-defeating when it excludes attention to what in this book I refer to as our "real problems." These are part of the very machinery with which our society manages itself and the processes by which we cope with the "you-name-its" as they come along. An example of what I mean by a "real problem" was described by David Stockman, director of the U.S. Office of Management and Budget, in a recent interview. Several of his predecessors have used virtually the same words in reflecting to me their own frustrations with what I consider to be one of our key systemic problems:

> There is a breakdown in the Congressional machinery.
> There are 100 gantlets and 1,000 vetoes on Capitol Hill. You simply can't sustain any kind of policy through that process, whether it's the conduct of foreign affairs, the shaping of the budget or the management of the fiscal affairs of the nation, because there are 180 subcommittees with overlapping jurisdictions and huge staffs. All of these actors want to get in the process, and as a result, everybody has their hooks on everything.[7]

I recognize that entire books could be devoted to each of the many and diverse issues I raise in this volume and that I cannot do full justice to any of them. Nor is it my intent to do so. My real purpose in this brief space is to attract the attention of our society's best thinkers and movers to these, the central dilemmas of our day. If I can lift the level of debate or even shift its focus, I will feel the effort is worthwhile.

I became interested in the systemic, or process, problems of our society not only through the realization that it was becoming harder year by year to get both large- and modest-scale undertakings accomplished but by firsthand observation of just how difficult, and often impossible, it was to apply the excellent new technology at our disposal to really important endeavors, such as education. Veto points to new initiatives appeared at every turn, so that one of the great revolutions in education that should have taken place has yet to happen. (Transportation, the running of cities, and improved delivery of medical and other social services are some other areas ripe for technological revolutions.)

In addition, I encountered increasing frustration at our inability to anticipate, in public as well as private planning, foreseeable changes in the future that are already in the pipeline: the imminent U.S. labor shortage, for example. I know of no better illustration of the kind of mind set that resists the inevitability of tomorrow than a Charles Addams cartoon from *The New Yorker;* I obtained the original drawing and have it framed behind my desk. It shows a moth emerging from its cocoon, and below, on the ground, one caterpillar says to another, "You'll never get *me* up in one of those things!"

The absence of distant early-warning systems, combined with the problem of ever larger organizations stifling the creativity of their employees and putting a premium on the "Don't rock the boat" syndrome, seemed to me to be contributing to our inability to make imaginative use of much of the technology with which I was working. The more I began to study these changes, the more acutely conscious I became of the disjunction between the needs and values of our times and the ways in which our public and many of our private institutions were structured and managed.

While some of the needed changes are complex and difficult to achieve, many are eminently doable and lend themselves to experiment on a local and modest level. For example:

▷ Corporations have an important and a direct financial stake in the cost and quality of public services in the communities in which they have plants or large offices. Not only is the tax rate affected but the desirability of working in the community and the quality of life for employees and their families are translated in part into salaries and wages. The delivery of public services is labor-intensive and necessarily high-cost. Usually, too, there is little in the way of advanced technology because there is no "demand pull," which is usually provided in for-profit organizations. It is this advanced technology that results in lower cost.

My point is that corporations have the opportunity to foster privatization experiments in such communities—in other words, providing essential services for profit. This has already been tried in many, often isolated and unreported cases, which I later address in more detail. In practice, privatization has generally resulted in lower-cost, higher-quality services, ranging from fire protection to trash removal to education and day care. Privatization for selected public services is far from the full answer to their improvement. Indeed, a central thesis of this book is that a new relationship between government and the private sector is essential. But injecting competition and other free-market principles into the delivery of public services can at least start the ball rolling.

Similarly, the mass media could take a small step in the right direction by focusing attention on the unfortunate short-term thinking that leads to so much trouble in both public and private sectors. There are journalistically effective opportunities in showing where legislators, government officials, and businesses have acted to our long-term detriment by focusing exclusively on the immediate present. Such stories are notable for their absence in the press.

I hope I will not seem cynical when I add that a major value of such press attention will inevitably be that it will help change the focus of our political leaders—for all too often their "leadership" consists of looking over their shoulders, at the polls, to see which way the troops are moving and then adroitly positioning themselves at the head of the column. If educating the electorate is the way we can get politicians to focus on long-term strategy, I am all in favor of starting with the public rather than the "leaders." I have great faith in the common sense of the common man and in the vision of a new generation of leaders. And with outstanding leaders, the ability to act depends on what Abraham Lincoln called *public sentiment:* "In this age, and this country, public sentiment is every thing. *With* it, nothing can fail; *against* it, nothing can succeed."[8]

While many of the thorny systemic problems I discuss in this book involve all kinds of good new thinking, policy analysis, and research, they are very much within our control—once we recognize the key role they play in making our society workable. In addition to illustrations of the *problems*, I have tried throughout to show promising examples of *solutions*, partial solutions, or at least directions in which we might move.

The Widening Gap

It seems to me that for the better part of this last half century there has been a widening gap between what is possible in the improvement of mankind's condition through utilizing the means at our command and what it is we are actually able to turn into reality. From the everyday frustrations of ordinary life through to the virtual impossibility of undertaking major national initiatives (except in the worst national crises), it is simply much more difficult to get things done than it was only a few decades ago.

At the end of his beautifully written and all-too-brief book *From Know-How to Nowhere: The Development of American Technology*, Professor Elting E. Morison of the Massachusetts Institute of Technology goes straight to the heart of the matter:

There were, of course, temporary injustices, local inequities, episodic horrors, but on the whole the movement was in a favoring direction. Those who had plodded their weary way, in 1800, through the short and simple annals of the poor, came, as time passed, into possession of automobiles, telephones, television sets, air conditioners, credit cards, fringe benefits, oil heat, major medical contracts, electric lights, old-age annuities, snowmobiles, and the 40-hour week. It was all done in the space of 150 years. By any standard, it was astounding.

It shows what can be done when human energy is released and mobilized by the power of an attracting vision, a general scheme that made it fit the times so well. When a bridge, a light bulb, a steel beam, or a telephone wire was understood to serve the progress of human affairs, men were set free to seek out many kinds of invention. While men had the opportunity by taking thought, working hard, and pursuing every kind of main change, to improve their own station, they had confirming evidence that they were also increasing the general welfare.

And now it appears that the thing has been overdone. Even before we have sufficiently increased the standard of living of a single person, we are in trouble . . .

So how to proceed with the construction of a new scheme?[9]

How to proceed indeed? Considering the means that science has given us to apply through technology the extraordinary knowledge of our day, things should be otherwise.

While today we have all kinds of conveniences and luxuries, and while statistics show (until recently at least) that we all enjoy a better quality of life—and we are certainly vastly better off than in the historical past—I think we all correctly experience a sense that things just don't work any longer the way they should.

National Purpose

Would more formal national goals help? It has long fascinated me that the successive efforts at formulating national goals never seem to have worked, as in Eisenhower's case. But I suspect there is a more basic reason and that it relates to what Charles Schultze, former director of the U.S. Budget Bureau and now of the Brookings Institution, aptly assessed as follows: "Not only do our social ends or values conflict, but being quite subtle and complex, they are exceedingly difficult to specify. We simply cannot determine in the abstract our ends or values and the intensity with which we hold them. We discover our values and the intensity we assign to them only in the process of considering particular programs or policies. We articulate 'ends' as we evaluate 'means.' " [10]

We cannot go about choosing objectives for society in the abstract; it is only by continuous, rigorous analysis of the consequences and costs of alternative routes that we can make decisions. It must be part of the everyday process. But our processes must be designed with the reality in mind that the way in which they function determines the goals we reach. And it is here one finds the most important role of management in the future.

I can't help but believe that some organized and ongoing assessment of alternative futures and the demands of these on our society would be useful, so that in the daily prioritization that occurs, for example, in the Congress's ongoing choice of budget alternatives, there is some consideration of the longer-term and perhaps far more important needs that are not at the moment exerting pressure. We need as well, I believe, some coordinating mechanism to ensure that 23 government programs, activities, and regulations are all pulling in the same direction and that the incentive/disincentive signals that they inevitably send out will be consistent with the considered policy objectives that have been set.

Some of what seem to be the most intractable of our systemic problems arise from our laudable desire to carry democracy into all of our undertakings. This, coupled with our equally admirable concern for protection of individual rights via the courts, creates a situation in which positive initiatives for the public good seem unimaginably difficult today. Indeed, even the most minor undertakings are regularly thwarted or at best delayed for years, often by those with the best intentions. Ted Sorensen succinctly describes the problem as "political gridlock":

> The result is all check and no balance. It is almost as if this country's policy-making process were being shaped not only by the Constitutional laws on legislation and regulation, but also by the physical laws of force and counterforce. "Gridlock" is the new term applied to the urban traffic tangle in which lines of waiting vehicles blocking intersections in all directions become so long and unyielding that ultimately no one can move forward or backward. Washington in the past 15 years, with each party and each faction within a party checking the other, with each house of Congress blocking the other, with each branch of government curbing the other, and with myriad special-interest groups on the left and right delaying and belaboring them all, has increasingly been in a state of political gridlock.[11]

Yet, as I illustrate in the following pages, there are fascinating experiments and models, often isolated or unknown outside a small circle, which show promising avenues for solution: for example, corporations in the food industry involving activists early in the planning process to work out together the question of chemical additives in foods—rather than waiting until products are on the supermarket shelves to exercise a veto or boycott. Similar approaches for avoiding roadblocks to new plant and facility sitings lend themselves to controlling or mitigating vetoes in other activities of our society. Alternatives to litigation and

24

innovations in conflict resolution can help undo at least part of the mischief we have made for ourselves with the glut of lawyers we have all helped create.

Likewise, there are many promising experiments by large organizations to encourage innovation—for without doubt, overcoming the dead hand of bureaucracy, public or private, is clearly one of our greatest challenges. On the positive side, it is necessary to foster innovation, as I develop in the chapter "Talent as Capital." But it is equally necessary to make life more human. What could better personify the Kafkaesque experience we all undergo more and more frequently in dealing with maddening bureaucracies in ever larger organizations than the following:

▷ In March 1984, TV and radio news stations played a chilling tape-recorded conversation between a Texas ambulance dispatcher and a man seeking emergency medical attention for his mother. The man explained that his mother was having trouble breathing and may have been dying. The nurse dispatcher insisted on asking detailed questions on the woman's medical history and repeatedly demanded to speak with the man's mother—a physical impossibility. Her insistence on following procedures apparently took precedence over saving a life. While the man and the nurse argued over the course of several minutes, the elderly woman died.

One important word of caution. While I use many case examples in every chapter to illustrate the various problems, this book is concerned with *process*, not with any of the specific issues that I use as examples. Redefining the role of government; some of what I call "political inventing" or "institutional inventing" in the design of new public as well as private institutions; mechanisms for prioritization and making trade-offs; and some restructuring of the relationships among the existing institutions in our society— these are the focus of this book. (One of the reasons for choosing multiple and diverse cases at the beginning of each chapter to illustrate the problem is to minimize the quite natural tendency the reader would otherwise have to assume that a particular chapter is about a particular case problem used as an illustration.)

A Pandora's Box

Each age is justly proud of its accomplishments, and so it is with ours. Major strides in science, applied through the arts of technology and modern management, have produced a society in which, for the first time in human history, wealth and leisure have not been confined to the fortunate few. They have given us the keys to unlock what should have been a truly golden age in man's history—and to some extent they have. Yet while we have unquestionably benefited in innumerable ways from the cornucopia of material wealth and of knowledge that have characterized these past two centuries, the keys we have forged increasingly seem to be those to a Pandora's box rather than to the gates of a utopia.

Our political and governmental institutions were far-sighted innovations in the eighteenth century; they served as well in the nineteenth, and have been modified a lot in the twentieth—but the nature of our problems, as well as their solutions, has altered dramatically. The essential elements of our government were brilliantly conceived, the structure well planned, and the balance has sturdily met the test of time—for the greater part of two hundred years. We have carried some ideas to excess (usually with the best intentions), and it surely would not surprise the Founding Fathers to find that the system needs some adjustment. I am only sorry that Madison, Hamilton, Jefferson, Adams, Franklin, and Washington are not around to help us!

The more I read of the history of the first industrial revolution, the more struck I am with the extraordinary contrast between that age and ours. With a relatively simple technology and the most rudimentary tools, our forebears took on Herculean tasks—throwing rail networks across unexplored continents; moving half a nation from farms to factories, offices, and cities; telescoping the workday to seven or eight hours from what had previously extended from dawn to dusk. It was then that Macaulay could correctly write: "The history of England is emphatically the history of progress." I don't think that could be said any longer of England or the U.S. or any other industrialized country. In fact, Robert Nisbet's sobering study *History of the Idea of Progress* reaches the very opposite conclusion: "Everything now suggests . . . that Western faith in the dogma of progress is waning rapidly in all levels and spheres in this final part of the twentieth century." [12]

In response to my comments on the heroic scale of nineteenth-century enterprise you may counter with: "But today we are more concerned with protecting the worker and individual rights, protecting the consumer, monitoring our impact on the environment, and otherwise ensuring general welfare before we embark on grand schemes and regulating their conduct." Yet it is precisely in attempting to improve these aspects of our world that our society has shown the least ability to apply the knowledge we possess. Undoubtedly life today is in many ways vastly better than it was a hundred years ago. What I am suggesting is that it is pertinent to ask ourselves why it is not *a great deal* better, considering the means at our command.

Many of the steps taken toward introducing more democracy into the political process, in the United States at least —from the selection of candidates to committee assignments and legislative procedures in the Congress—have defeated their objectives by making it virtually impossible except in the worst crisis to achieve forward motion. Looking back on his Senate days, John Kennedy described Senator George McGee standing in a virtually deserted Senate chamber mumbling a speech from a few handwritten notes and, on being asked what he was going on about, saying, "Oh, nothing at all important." And—to quote President Kennedy—". . . and Grand Coulee Dam was built!" For better or worse, things don't happen like that anymore in this country.

▷ Consider a simple anecdote that brought home to me in human terms the problem I am addressing: the building of what was to have been an integrated memorial library and school of public administration named for President Kennedy. It was announced while the public horror at his murder was still fresh, and widespread contributions were subscribed. Yet it took more than fifteen years to turn even as modest an undertaking as this into what is only a pale simulacrum of one half the plan into reality! Not even in the home city and state of one of our   **27** most powerful political families was it possible to get agreement among some fourteen political districts to an alternative site for a rapid-transit car yard in order to make room near Harvard for the library and school. A decade and a half passed, with other problems arising and the project dropping in scope every few years as inflation soared and various kinds of opposition developed, until today it exists, but only as a shadow of the original concept.

Unfortunately one does not have to look long for far more important and dangerous examples of our collective inability to cope, through needed initiatives, with the demands of our age.

While there are major problems unique to each country, it does seem to me that most of the real problems of making an advanced society work are common to all industrialized countries and in part to many developing ones as well. Professor Charles E. Lindblom of Yale has stated it succinctly in his important study *Politics and Markets: The World's Political-Economic Systems:* "Boldly conceived major new democratic alternatives have not yet been designed. They may never be, even if their design may some day become necessary to the survival of polyarchy. Yet new forms seem urgently necessary. In the United States, many citizens fear that social problems are running far ahead of government. We are losing control."[13]

The incentives we often unconsciously build into our system are frequently at odds with the very results we are trying to achieve. For example, the "Don't rock the boat" incentive in all bureaucracies is diametrically opposed to the spirit of innovation we need to cope with new exigencies. In addition, the boundaries of problems have changed dramatically. Physical demarcations, often based on the speed at which information could travel, have expanded from county lines appropriate to travel by horse, to federal boundaries in the age of railroads, to global ones for the era of jets and telecommunications. Yet often our machinery for handling the problems is keyed to yesterday's smaller political boundaries.

Our problems themselves have been transformed from individual issues to extremely complicated and interconnected syndromes—often with unexpected side effects. For example, low mortgage rates in the 1920s and 1930s were as much responsible for the population shift to suburbia as was the advent of the automobile—with the unintended side effect of urban blight in the 1960s and 1970s.

Major shifts in our value systems further exacerbate the problems—from the desire, heightened by the media, for instant gratification to a decline in moral fiber and values; from the absence of strong political leaders to the push for greater democratization in both public and private organizations; from the "me first" generation to the "you-name-it" crisis of the moment. A good case could be made that we have already squandered much of what my French friends call our "patrimony." But I am too much the optimist to believe we are faced with an irreversible process.

As with most things, the difference between a healthy, vigorous society and one that is sliding downhill consists of a lot of small elements taken together. A slight increase in the productivity of each one of us, sustained for a few years; a series of relatively minor changes in the incentive structure leading to individuals' retiring earlier or later; a small increase in the savings rate—these make the larger difference. Great progress takes place at the sustained margin. As former Secretary of Commerce Peter Peterson has pointed out, between 1870 and 1950 the annual rate of growth of productivity of the U.S. exceeded those of the UK, West Germany, and Japan by only 0.6 to 0.8 percent. Yet that fractional difference maintained for eighty years produced the colossus Henry Luce was writing about.[14] When these incremental moves work in a negative manner, as was true for most of the seventies, great damage can be done even to a country as inherently strong as ours.

Rethinking the Role of Government

While I believe we need to redefine the role of government, I deplore what I consider to be an unfortunate tendency in recent years to view our relationship in a "they vs. we" manner. While an adversarial relationship has undoubtedly developed in many important parts of our society—not least of which are significant portions of the business/government interface—it is only by a mutually supportive interplay between government and the private sector that we are going to be able to make our society work. This is certainly not new—but "more government" or "less government" is not the answer. Some rethinking of the *role* of government, together with a little of what I call "political inventing," is what is wanted. An example of what I mean by both can be found in what may seem an unlikely place—agriculture.

▷ One of the great success stories of American technology happens to be that of agriculture. Not only has it permitted us to shift from 40 percent of our population engaged in farm work as late as 1900 to 3 percent in 1980 but it provides a consistently crucial element in our exports—one of a handful that keep us afloat in terms of international competition. Few accounts of U.S. technological leadership even mention this enormously powerful engine of agriculture.

This transfer of scientific knowledge through technology to practical application by the ultimate entrepreneur of the free enterprise system, the farmer, was brought about in large part by a series of innovative political moves late in the last century and early in this. In more recent times, starting with the farm-support programs of the thirties, there has been a major transfer of real wealth as well. But the knowledge and technology transfer mechanisms of which I speak had already been in place and functioning for many decades by the time they were supplemented by the money transfer. The creation of the land-grant colleges and the Agricultural Extension Service were the key elements.

By creating institutions for agricultural research and education on the one hand and, on the other, a system for transferring this knowledge to the user through county agents, a powerful and creative interplay of science, government, and the private sector was made possible. The process was started by Abraham Lincoln during the Civil War. Today we are the beneficiaries of this system—as are the Soviets and others around the world who rely on our agricultural exports for providing the margin of survival.

At roughly the same time all this was going on in our own **30** society, the Meiji Restoration was occurring in Japan—in part a reaction to Admiral Perry's opening of Japan's feudal society to the West. The restructuring of the interface between government and population set in motion the most successful existing case study of industrial development—other than our own nineteenth-century example. The heart of the Meiji Restoration was the creation of a whole series of new institutions and relationships, which have led in successive stages to today's Japan. Too often Western focus is on the most recent, albeit dramatic and successful, post–World War II phase of this century-old process.

The "Issue" of Industrial Policy

A recent example, both of the need for and difficulty of finding new ways of coping with some of our problems—and of the never-ending revival of proposals for the one demonstrably ineffective solution, namely, a new government agency—is evident in the debate over what is being called "industrial policy." The declining economic competitiveness of some of our industries, the staggering increase in our balance-of-trade deficit, and the well publicized successes of foreign economies (especially the Japanese) in catching up with or surpassing us in new technologies, while at the same time seeming to drown us in autos, video recorders, and other staples in our own markets, has understandably resulted in much flailing about, especially during the recent recession.

The need to "do something" has been felt by all, most poignantly by politicians. Just what that "something" should be is so elusive that the old standby "government should . . ." is all too readily pulled off the shelf. That "something" most commonly takes the form of a proposal of a government agency to subsidize new industries and perhaps prop up the old. Those of us who shy away from looking to still more government find it hard to believe that this will be any sort of "solution." As much as our society often likes to indulge in what I call "creative forgetting"—looking back on a fictitious past of totally free enterprise with no government intervention—the reality has been a government/private-sector interplay right from the beginning. For examples of the most creative form of this interplay, I strongly recommend a reading of Alexander Hamilton's "Report on Manufacture":

> In countries where there is great private wealth, much may
> be effected by the voluntary contributions of patriotic
> individuals; but in a community situated like that of the
> United States, the public purse must supply the deficiency of
> private resource. In what can it be so useful, as in prompting
> and improving the efforts of industry? [15]

At times the relationship between government and private enterprise has been destructive, as in the late 1960's and 1970's; but it has always been an interplay. What I think we need today is a conscious re-assessment of the relationship and the forging of a new partnership appropriate to the times.

More to the point, one of the leading liberal economists, Charles Schultze, has written: "But the one thing that the American political system cannot do well at all is to choose among particular firms, industries and regions, coldbloodedly determining, on grounds of economic efficiency, which shall prosper and which shall wither. The government often adopts policies that have the indirect consequence of harming various groups. But the American political system's equivalent of the Hippocratic Oath is, 'Never be seen to do direct harm.' " [16]

The study of industrial policy is one in which my brother, Bill, did much of the intellectual groundwork. It evolved in part from his early work in the forms of a Bilderberg paper, contributions to a Trilateral Commission report, and a book. It developed through debate among thoughtful people in the policy community. Industrial policy was unfortunately turned into a partisan political issue because of the obviousness of the problem on the one hand and the attractiveness of a sweeping proposal (especially one involving large public expenditures) on the other. Yet Charles Schultze's comments have a strong resonance, perhaps especially for those who do not so frequently find themselves in harmony with many of his policy proposals!

But the paradox remains. It does not seem to me to be a
question of whether government should get involved in the

private sector. It already is! For many of us what the whole issue comes down to is whether we would not be better off if this de facto nonstrategy were more rationally reviewed periodically or on a continuing basis. Yet before this can happen we need to know a good deal more about the processes that are in play. I suspect the heart of the matter is how to create mechanisms to ease the transition of labor from dying or faltering businesses to emerging "sunrise" industries.

In contrast to the easy nonsolution of proposing that government throw money at the problem, the development of a useful solution is going to take a good deal more knowledge than we have. That statement may not have the political appeal candidates seek, but it's the reality. I know just how difficult it is to formulate useful recommendations in this area, not only from my brother's longtime effort on the intellectual side of the issue and from many professional assignments from various governments but, in my own case, as a result of grappling with the problem for the past two and a half years as a trustee member of the Committee for Economic Development committee on industrial strategy. As we concluded in that report:

> To bolster the performance of *all* sectors of the economy, the challenge now is developing concrete, constructive public policies to enable the economy to adapt better to emerging trends with less delay, fewer inefficiencies, and less contradictory actions. Future policies should focus on how to provide individuals with the skills to be flexible in the labor markets of the future and how to motivate investors and managers to shift labor and capital resources smoothly toward expanding markets and away from less competitive ones. . . .

> Neither further government involvement in the economy nor new policies or institutions designed to steer the economy in some predetermined direction will increase U.S. competitiveness. Rather, the most effective, and perhaps the only successful, path to increased U.S. international competitiveness is through (a) placing significantly more reliance on pre-market forces and (b) reforming necessary government interventions to provide an economic

environment which stimulates innovation in the private sector and helps resources adapt to changing competition.
Increased interference with the market economy will weaken it further, harming business, workers and consumers alike.[17]

However, how to produce this kind of solution is the task to which much of this book is devoted. Getting informed public debate so that there can be meaningful participation in the political process and innovative proposals is all part of the process changes that are needed. None of this is easy.

Today, when the Japanese experiment is bearing fruit at a prodigious rate in the industrial sector (although not without its own recurrent problems), and our economy continues on a roller coaster, it is all too fashionable in the U.S. to propose that we copy the Japanese system. No advice would be worse! When my firm is called on to aid foreign governments in the formulation of technology and industrial strategies and assist U.S. and foreign corporations in their strategy formulations, the last thing we would think of doing is copying the tactics of a competitor. Studying the behavior of all the players in any game is a prerequisite, but to win one's strategy must be based on one's own strengths, with a clear understanding of weaknesses and unique competitive advantages.

Much of Japan's obvious strength is in national industrial policy, consciously arrived at and executed by highly competitive private, not nationalized, firms. When MITI concluded in the 1960s that Japan would not be able to compete internationally in the textile industry in another decade because of its wage scale, Japan moved its textile industry to lower wage areas in the Pacific basin, replacing it with electronics manufacturing. There was much internal resistance, but the change took place much earlier and at less national cost than in the U.S. One can only admire such a supple society!

Yet, while we can learn a great deal from some Japanese techniques (including the fact that such fashionable and successful managerial techniques as quality circles were indeed invented in the U.S. but not adopted here until the recent rush to copy "Japanese techniques"!), many of them depend on long-established cultural conditions unique to Japan. For example, the relative freedom enjoyed by Japanese companies to introduce new technologies once the "consensus" discussion is completed is due not only to the consensus process itself but to the fact that the prestige and income of an individual Japanese is determined by seniority and schooling. The quid pro quo of the lifelong employment practices of the large firms is the employee's readiness to embrace rather than resist new techniques. Not only is there no worry over unemployment due to technological change but there is also an understanding of the importance of that change to maintain the employment.

We can learn much from studying the Japanese, just as we can learn from studying highly centralized planning processes such as those in the Soviet Union, eastern Europe, and even France. The Japan story, incidentally, is by no means an unqualified success. For example, I can recall that MITI took an exceptionally strong stand against Japan's engaging in international competition in the automobile industry! It was only by the private firms' successfully ignoring the strong MITI "guidance" that Japan's current success was scored in the automobile field.

Any realignment of U.S. industrial strategy must start with its focus on our own often unique strengths: our ability to innovate—sometimes known as Yankee ingenuity and already apparent at the time of Alexis de Tocqueville's first visit to this country in 1835—and our cultural characteristics, including the willingness to tolerate failure and the stubbornness and stamina that encourage a "try, try again" mentality. (In neither Japan nor Germany would it be easy for someone to leave a large company, find venture capital to start a new business, fail in that business, and find it possible either to rejoin his former employer or to enter another large company without an almost ineradicable blot on his record.) In addition, we have the enormous strength imparted by our highly educated population and our job mobility, which is often overlooked in light of the obvious need to improve our educational system and to provide better mechanisms for mobility. We have *extraordinary* strengths, and it is from an understanding of these that our own policies must be formulated. But that is getting ahead of myself.

What This Book Is Not About

It would be foolish to go on at any length about systemic problems *not* commented on in this book, but I do want to make clear that I recognize there are many. And we are going to be forced to cope with some of these quite soon. For example, we not so gradually lowered the age at which people were forced to retire, even as we prolonged the potential for economically useful lives. Not only has this been a big element in our Social Security dilemma but it has also increasingly denied us the efforts and talents of too many of our most gifted and dedicated citizens. What began as a humanitarian effort to ensure a few years of respite in our later years has, without much policy thought, turned into a forced decade or more in a retirement community—and a state burden. Even in line-management posts, where the strongest case exists for forced departure from key positions—before the negatives of age in the helmsman endanger the organization—we find overwhelming evidence that people age at quite different speeds.

I gave an eightieth-birthday dinner for Jack McCloy at my home a few years ago, and it became clear that, in spirit and common sense, he was the youngest man at the table —even though no one was within a calendar generation of him. As he is often fond of saying, "Since I'm a lawyer, I can just hang out my shingle indefinitely!" Yet if he had been a corporate executive or a civil servant, he would have had to retire before much of his remarkable career had unfolded. The same could be said of some of the men with whom he worked, such as Churchill and Adenauer. (The good news here is that dramatic shifts in demographics are going to force us to allow those of our older citizens who wish to continue to work to do so.)

Nor is this book about economic policy, art and culture, ethics and morality, the relationship between the President and Congress, education per se, religion, or many other things. Nor have I discussed the critical problem of our savings and investment rates, the national deficit, or the international value of U.S. currency—which, even if we get everything else right, can still bury us.

Nor, despite the international orientation of my firm or

my personal interests, does this book intend to address anything but American problems and propose solutions appropriate to that scene. After thirty years of extensive professional practice abroad, advising heads of corporations, cabinet members, and heads of state, I am only too aware that what works in one country can be totally negated by cultural differences in another. Nor do I discuss the needs of international agencies, as important and interesting as they are to many of our domestic problems. Yet I have from time to time introduced case examples from foreign countries where they offer insights into our own condition.

In discussing information technology, I do so in the context of some of the questions it raises for us when technology in several areas outruns policy. I do not address the important ways in which computers offer a means of materially improving the analysis of problems and decision making in public agencies, businesses, and other areas of society. We have already at our disposal an undreamed-of analytic capacity, which is increasing yearly in quality and ubiquity. What we do with it is a different matter. "Computer" decisions and analyses are all too often crutches on which unimaginative, carelessly formulated, and empty policy decisions lean for support. That, however, should not obscure the fact that if we can get our policy formulation process right, we will find at our disposal extremely powerful tools. The fact that our tools have currently outpaced our artistry is neither new nor need it be discouraging. Rather, it represents an unprecedented challenge.

I hope that the problems I have chosen to concentrate on in this book are sufficient in number and variety to make just *one* point: that we must get our policy *process* right and that it is doable, despite the fact that it will take some doing.

American Solutions

Redefining the role of government in the U.S. is going to involve institutional innovation as original as the agricultural example I cited earlier. It will not be brought about by the current tendency to treat government as the enemy, but   **37** neither is it a case of looking to government to solve all of our problems. Indeed it is, in part, because government has assumed so many roles in our lives that the backlash of public resentment at government per se has resulted. Part of the answer here is redefining the role of government—emphasizing its capacity for broad-brush policy analysis and formulation while decreasing its direct role in operations and detailed regulation.

Everything I have learned about management in a lifetime of study and practice teaches me the importance of placing decision making as close as possible to the problem, hence delegation. I have also observed the stifling effect of the difficulty of innovation in large organizations. The only managerially workable method of handling large organizations (and the U.S. society is certainly a large one) is for top management (read "the federal government") to create the conditions that allow the constituent elements to express initiative while protecting the rights of all. The problem starts with Congress. Too much time is devoted to detailed discussion of how broad policies will be carried out, when organizations one-thousandth the size could not succeed in centrally promulgating such procedures. Not surprisingly, this often leads to precisely the opposite of what is intended. For example, today at the height of universal concern over the ability of the U.S. to move into new technologies and industries and out of dying ones, we find such ludicrous examples as:

▷ The IRS rule for tax-deducting educational expenses. In practice it allows an unemployed steelworker to deduct the cost of training to provide even more skill in a field in which there are no jobs—but will not allow the deduction for training in a new skill in which there *are* jobs!

▷ Rule 861 of the IRS Code states that research and development expenditures of U.S. multinationals can be deducted only in proportion to the U.S. business of that multinational to total world business. Since other countries do not allow the allocation of U.S.-conducted R&D to the subsidiary in their country, the result is the movement of research work that would otherwise be conducted in the U.S. to other countries.

38

▷ The Food and Drug Administration interpretation of the perfectly reasonable statute prohibiting all unapproved drugs from travel in interstate commerce results in forbidding the bulk shipment of basic materials for drugs from U.S. plants to overseas plants in countries where the drug is allowed. One result is that U.S. companies must either abandon the export opportunity or build plants overseas—and shift jobs. Since the FDA's interpretation of how it should perform its regulatory role has resulted in much of the world's adopting drugs some years before they are permitted in the U.S., a large percentage of U.S. pharmaceutical company R&D has shifted away from the U.S.

All this occurs at a time when there is a general agreement within the Congress and the administration that precisely the reverse is in the national interest!

One of the most interesting and least discussed aspects of the new institutional relationships that will develop in the U.S. is the "post-multinational corporation." Post-MNCs could well incorporate some of the characteristics of Japanese and Hungarian trading companies as it becomes necessary both to compete with commercial arms of other countries pursuing quite different national objectives and to find ways of helping smaller firms sell abroad as international trade becomes more important to the U.S. economy. Similarly, in their efforts to encourage maximum entrepreneurial activity, MNCs will increasingly experiment with new forms of ventures in which venture managers, key scientists, and creative people will be partial owners and in which the MNC will provide not only the venture capital but perhaps the trading company and other functions. Gradually new forms of genuine post-MNCs will emerge.

A problem U.S.-based MNCs increasingly face is competition with foreign firms that are in reality extensions of governments. Most American MNCs ask no more of the U.S. government than to be left free to compete, rather than receive special assistance. Yet it is clear that part of the working out of a new pattern of government/private-sector relationships is in this area, just as encouraging exports by the great preponderance of middle-sized firms that are not so oriented is going to be necessary if we are to overcome increasingly disadvantageous trade imbalances.

There are a lot of things government should do that it doesn't, or doesn't do to the extent or in the way it should, such as: follow-up evaluation of the consequences of laws or executive orders, compared with the expectations or the problems when the laws or executive orders were passed, and rethinking and coordination of actions on all three levels of U.S. government (federal, state, and local). In general, it is imperative to have a reordering of machinery and a focusing not only on the future but also on what in this book I shall call the "proper role of government"—namely, minimum operation (which large bureaucracies usually do not do well) and maximum attention to the creation of environment and conditions that will unleash the energy, imagination, and concern of the individuals and the institutions that make up our society. For example, rather than having government decide that a particular kind of technology is needed (unless, of course, it is needed for a specific legitimate government purpose), I would far rather see government focus on the things it needs to do to create conditions that allow bright young people to pursue what they see as important scientific or technological opportunities.

The individual problems are enormous. How do we handle the insatiable demands for medical services? When General Motors pays more for employee health care than for the steel in its automobiles, as it already does, what do we do? How do we improve the savings rate and channel those savings into productive investment? How do we build an effective way for moving workers from dead-end jobs to those with a promising future and in the process eliminate the political pressure to prop up dying industries? (In the end this causes the greatest hardship to precisely those individuals who are supposed to be helped by it, since they have been allowed to reach middle age or beyond in a skill for which there is no real need.)

Our problems are not unique. In their own way they beset the advanced industrial societies of Europe and Asia. Redefining the role of government is part of the solution, but only part. The real solutions involve all of us in our roles as individuals, parents, church members, job holders, and voters. Myriad actions are needed, and I have tried to suggest a number of them in the "straw-in-the-wind" examples of experiments, partial solutions, or promising proposals at the end of each chapter. We need to learn from many sources —not only from the Japanese but from the Hungarians and the Chinese (who have made the most effective and largely market-oriented departure from the Marxist system) and from the approaches that have demonstrably not worked (in most of Eastern Europe and the Soviet bloc). (Incidentally, the title of this book was *not* inspired by the famous Lincoln Steffens tribute to Russia, "I have been over to the future, and it works." See *The Autobiography of Lincoln Steffens*, 1931.)

My point is that the solutions for this country must be uniquely American, just as we need an overarching vision of the objectives of society which is unique to our own time and culture. None of the myriad pieces of the solution can fall into place, nor will the system itself perform effectively in handling the continuous flow of new and unexpected problems, unless it has that vision. And the idea of over-arching vision must transcend rhetoric. All manner of grand schemes are regularly proposed but are doomed to failure or neglect without a key ingredient: *leadership*. An abused concept currently, leadership in its most basic sense—vision coupled with the ability to communicate and educate —is essential to any great undertaking.

I was born into the tail end of an age of which I still have memories, characterized by long hours of work (my own company began thirty years ago with five and a half days as the normal work week for the first decade of our corporate history). Air conditioning was the exception for most of us; unshielded lights and oil-soaked wooden floors were the norm in factories, which were cold in winter and unbeliev-ably hot in summer. (It was in these working conditions that I first began thinking about automation.) To extrapolate the emotions and relations of management and labor, of right and wrong, to today is as wrong as it is an accepted stereo-type. The extraordinary change that has taken place is far less, I am sure, than what I have as yet lived through and what my children will experience as they move what the Europeans are already calling the Third Industrial Revolu-tion. Getting us through this transition and maintaining a semblance of liberty will be no small task.

Today, and for at least the immediate future, might not our vision be centered on the task of making our increasingly complex advanced industrial society work? Making the structures and processes of our society workable and creating the new relationships necessary to make it happen may not seem on the grand scale of a "vision"—but I think it is grand enough, grander than any we have recently been able to provide.

II Vetoes and Priorities

*In our admirable desire to ensure democracy in all
our decision processes, we have created literally
hundreds of places where we can thwart initiative with
a veto. In doing so we have rarely created what I shall
call trade-off mechanisms—ways of moving ahead
despite all the negatives of a particular course of
action. The result is our present-day world where
everyday life becomes difficult, imaginative initiatives
are rare, and our increasingly precious resources are
squandered as priorities are set by crises.*

Case:
Pork Barrels and Striped Bass

On December 15, 1973, a section of the elevated West Side
Highway in Manhattan collapsed under the weight of a dump truck
and a passenger car, injuring both drivers. Public alarm over the
incident accelerated the momentum behind a proposed new West
Side Highway project—later known as Westway—which had been
officially launched two years earlier by Governor Nelson A. Rockefeller and Mayor John V. Lindsay.

At a time when New York's financial future was imperiled, the
Westway seemed to represent a symbolic road to economic reju-
venation. The reasons to move ahead were compelling: new construction jobs, reduced air pollution, a sorely needed auto route, a
stimulus for business investment, and the certitude of some $2
billion in federal funding. And in 1978 Governor Hugh L. Carey and
Mayor Edward Koch agreed on an expanded Westway plan that
included renovating the city's West Side and laying out a new state
park (to be created by landfill) along the Hudson River.

Meanwhile momentum was building in another camp. In 1974
Action for Rational Transit and other plaintiffs sought a permanent

43

injunction against an interstate system on the city's West Side. Opponents argued for the so-called "trade-in option," whereby federal highway funds would be exchanged for money to renovate the city's mass transit system.

Who was right? Someone who has been close to the issue and also a longtime friend provides some useful insights. William S. Woodside, chairman and chief executive officer of both the American Can Company and the Regional Plan Association, detailed the findings in an in-depth study by the Regional Plan Association in conjunction with Battelle Laboratories. On August 1, 1983, he wrote in an Op Ed piece in *The New York Times:*

> The proposed highway for the West Side of Manhattan, known as Westway, will provide a much-needed auto link between midtown and downtown, produce one-eighth the air pollution of a surface road, provide 93 acres of parkland on the Hudson River, pay for a new solid-waste disposal plant and a new bus garage, and renovate the city's West Side—all at little cost to the city. . . .
> Construction of Westway and related developments on the landfill would create nearly 100,000 man-years of employment and add nearly $3.4 billion to the gross regional product. . . . By comparison, trading in Westway for transit dollars would create about 21,400 man-years of employment and add only $1.1 billion to the gross regional product.

Taking strong exception to the Regional Plan Association's findings was John B. Oakes, former senior editor of *The New York Times.* He argued in a *Times* Op Ed piece of November 30, 1983, that the Westway was good for the New York politicians, construction unions, realtors, and bankers who were backing the plan "in typical pork-barrel fashion." But, he added, it would be harmful to practically everything else: "to the economy, for which it would constitute virtually an open-ended drain on federal, state and city treasuries; to the environment, on which it would impose immeasurable new burdens; and to New York City's mass transit and local street systems, which it would deprive of about $1.5 billion in 'trade-in' funds." Oakes suggested an alternative to Westway: "There is obvious need for a reconstructed boulevard-parkway along Manhattan's lower West Side. Such a thoroughfare, comparable to the Thames Embankment or to the Shanghai Bund, could be constructed relatively easily, in far less time and at a fraction of Westway's cost of $1 *billion* per mile."

44

By the time these words appeared in print the Westway had been tangled in red tape and lawsuits for a dozen years and had already rung up a tab of $200 million—even though three New York City mayors, three New York State governors, and four federal secretaries of transportation had approved the project. And yet, the sources of the multiple veto points that have blocked Westway are far more complex than is possible to describe here. Indeed, it was not merely a case of Westway's backers versus Westway's opponents. An argument could be made that even Westway's supporters had effectively blocked progress on the project by refusing to compromise on a very costly design.

Perhaps the most frustrating roadblock came in September 1983: the Army Corps of Engineers announced that before it could grant the project a permit it needed at least two years to assess the environmental impact of the Westway on a small nonvocal but politically influential constituency—the Hudson River's striped bass.

Case:
The Coal Slurry Pipeline

Back in the early 1960s President John F. Kennedy had proposed legislation to guarantee rights-of-way for coal slurry pipelines. The pipeline idea is simple: crushed coal is mixed with equal amounts of water to produce a heavy liquid—slurry—which is then pumped through underground pipelines to industrial areas. Once at its destination, the mixture is spun in a centrifuge to remove most of the water and is used in the normal way to fuel power plants.

The concept is a proven one. Between 1957 and 1963 the Ohio pipeline successfully carried 1.3 million tons annually along a 108-mile route from coal mines on the Ohio–West Virginia border to Cleveland. The Black Mesa Line, still in operation, pumps 4.8 million tons annually from northeastern Arizona to Las Vegas, 273 miles away.[1]

But a far more ambitious pipeline was proposed in the early 1970s by Energy Transportation Systems, Inc. (ETSI): a transcontinental pipeline to run from the coal-rich Powder River Basin in Wyoming to industrial areas in the Southeast. Proponents of the scheme say the pipeline could, at full capacity, carry 30 million tons of coal a year at about three-quarters of railway costs and with less havoc to the environment. The then governor of Wyoming, Stan Hathaway, and the state legislature supported the original ETSI scheme, as did utilities, coal companies, consumers, and labor.

Subsequent oil shocks would prove how prescient Kennedy's plan was. Yet, ironically, it was around the time of the Arab oil embargo of 1973–74 that the slurry pipeline started running into major roadblocks. The three camps that opposed the pipeline were summed up as follows in an October 1982 *Technology Review* article:

> The objections, which have yet to quiet down entirely, fell into three basic categories. Railroads complained that the pipeline would unfairly take away a vital part of their business—and thereby force them to increase freight charges for customers shipping products other than coal. Environmentalists complained that the pipeline system might cause a variety of ecological aggravations. And a coalition of interests in Wyoming and surrounding states argued that the pipeline—and others that would inevitably follow it—would remove precious water from the region.[2]

At the present time (1984) construction of the pipeline has already been delayed ten years. After two oil crises, only two slurry lines have ever been laid down in the United States. The Ohio pipeline, mentioned earlier, was itself terminated by railroad opposition after six years of successful operation. The only other line, the Black Mesa, in Arizona, is the property of the Southern Pacific Railroad. And two decades after Kennedy's proposal, federal legislation to clear rights-of-way was still stymied in Congress.

Case:
Nuclear Shutdown

On February 1, 1972, a consortium of sixteen New England utilities set out to build a nuclear power plant at Seabrook, New Hampshire. Ground breaking, it was thought, would take place in 1975, and the first of two generating units would be ready for operation by 1979; the second was scheduled to open in 1981. Public Service of New Hampshire, with ownership of 35.6 percent of the project, estimated the cost of building both units at $1.175 billion.

What with hearings before the appropriate state agencies, a year passed before application was made to the Atomic Energy Commission for a construction permit. Because numerous state hearings were demanded, and because the federal Environmental Protection Agency required time to assess the intake system and other design factors, it was not until July 1976 that the Nuclear Regulatory Commission (successor to the AEC) actually issued the construction permit. Immediately upon that approval, a slew of appeals were filed, challenging the utilities' right to build the plant.

A month after the NRC action, the Seabrook site was visited by six hundred antinuclear protestors; 18 were arrested. Three weeks later, 1500 protestors attempted to enter the site, and 176 were arrested. As many as 2000 demonstrators occupied the plant site in the spring of 1977.

While the protests were focusing media attention on the Seabrook site, the tempo of legal action stepped up. The New England Coalition on Nuclear Pollution won a suspension of the construction permit on September 30, pending NRC review of the environmental effects of the fuel cycle. On November 5, NRC relented upon deciding that the environmental effects of the fuel cycle were small. But four days later, the EPA announced its initial decision revoking approval of the plant's cooling system design. After two months' time, Public Service of New Hampshire decided to reduce the level of construction activity at Seabrook until EPA issued a final decision on the cooling system.

In June 1977, the EPA reversed its earlier decision and decided that the intake and cooling systems represented the best technology available. But within two weeks the Seacoast Anti-Pollution League and the Audubon Society petitioned the U.S. Circuit Court of Appeals to reverse the EPA. The court said it wouldn't act just yet, but that SAPL/Audubon could file the same request again after the NRC acted to lift the suspension it had imposed on construction two months earlier.

The appeals, filings, and reversals mounted—and the delays caused mounting bills as well. New Hampshire voters, prompted by the Clamshell Alliance and other antinuclear groups, began getting restless about the prospect of expensive nuclear energy. A new governor, Hugh Gallen, was elected in November 1978 and, at his urging, the legislature adopted a measure forbidding PSNH from adding construction costs to the current rate base. In retaliation, PSNH's board directed its management to reduce its share in Seabrook ownership from 50 to 28 percent.

As work proceeded in fits and starts, expenses became astronomical. Inflation and high interest rates boosted construction costs geometrically higher than original estimates. The sixteen cooperating utilities began to look for ways out of the Seabrook mess. By early 1984, Public Service of New Hampshire said the eventual cost of building both units would be $9 billion—*if* they were actually built at all.

On March 30, 1984, eleven years to the day after PSNH had first asked the federal government for permission to build the plant, its owners voted to cancel Unit 2—if the New Hampshire utility could find help recovering the $293 million it had already sunk in the reactor. At this juncture, Unit 1 was 73 percent complete, at a cost of $2.5 billion. PSNH stared bankruptcy in the face. Robert Backus, a Manchester attorney who had represented the Seacoast Anti-Pollution League, said: "It looks to me like Public Service is going to beat the Long Island Lighting Company to be the first utility to take refuge in Chapter 11."[3]

While Seabrook was struggling to be built, the rest of the U.S. nuclear industry was in similar shape, with no new plants commissioned since 1978. Even before the incident at Three Mile Island in March 1979, delays in plant construction had pushed nuclear plant financing into the stratosphere. Plants begun in the late sixties and early seventies—a time of relatively low inflation and 3 percent interest rates—were running into trouble as inflation soared and the price of borrowing climbed into double digits. As oil prices dropped following decontrol, and electrical demand entered a recession-era slough, the original rationale for nuclear energy began to look less and less persuasive.

Meanwhile, other nations have pushed ahead with nuclear power—a technology in which the U.S. was the innovator. Keeping reactor costs at less than half the U.S. levels, and finishing plant construction in an average four years' time, France kept to its schedule of providing 70 percent of its electricity from nuclear power by 1990. Japan, even with its uniquely painful experience of atomic energy, put nuclear power plants on-line in an average seven years' time, and now expects the bulk of its twenty-first century electrical power to come from nuclear fission.[4]

In all these, and many more, instances, the citizen is exercising a power once reserved for heads of state: the power of veto. There is no better illustration of the type of problem we need to solve to make our society work than the de facto veto power we have busily been building into our political structure and institutionalizing at virtually every level.

The word "veto"—Latin for "I forbid"—carries an imperious connotation. In the United States Constitution it is reserved for the President of the United States. Yet in its most profound sense, the democratization of the veto, of the right of the people to talk back and to back their talk with power, has been the essence of free societies from the Magna Carta to the Constitution of the United States to the Charter of the United Nations. Sometimes de jure, sometimes de facto, the proliferated and dispersed veto is the means whereby the parts can protect themselves against the whole, whereby minorities or even individuals can withstand the edicts of the "common will."

Yet the veto also teaches us the limits of democracy and that it is possible to carry a good thing too far. The real issue in the three cases I cited above is not whose side has greater merit—Westway's supporters or the striped bass, coal-burning utilities or environmentalists, nuclear supporters or nuclear foes—the issue is one of *process*. However you feel about breeder reactors or the lowly snail darters, there has to be some way for our society to make up its mind on important issues and then to move ahead, not wasting time and other national resources in procrastination. Otherwise, conflicting viewpoints cancel each other out, resulting in societal paralysis—and we all pay for the waste.

Professor Charles Lindblom describes the problem very well in his study *Politics and Markets:*

In one of the main traditions of democratic thought, government has been conceived of as presiding over constant redistribution of benefits like wealth and power.

The emerging peril to the survival of polyarchy is that vetoes are cast not simply against proposed redistribution but against proposed solutions to collective problems. A veto of a redistribution—say, of new school budgets—is disappointing to some groups. A veto of a solution to a collective problem— say, of an energy policy—may put society on the road to catastrophe.

A failure of policy-making leaves the entire society in peril. One person's loss is now every person's loss.[5]

How do we straighten out the processes of government so that we can balance opposing viewpoints, set priorities, and move ahead—despite all the negatives you can think of for a particular course of action? I think we need three things:

1. A way to bring into account *all* the factors in a decision process—pros and cons, costs and benefits, risks and rewards—and evaluate them fairly and impartially.

2. A way to relate each issue to other demands on our resources and to assign priorities. Even with our nation's enormous resources, we cannot have everything at once—although Congress seems unwilling to face this fact.

3. A way to settle an issue—and *keep* it settled!—by making a trade-off among existing alternatives and then setting a time limit for possible vetoes.

The fact that I am not alone in my growing concern over the number of veto points in our society was brought home to me forcefully some years ago in a conversation with my good friend Elmer Staats, then comptroller general of the United States (a fifteen-year presidential appointment, which is, appropriately, the longest such statutory appointment in our country). "There are a hundred places in this town where you can stop initiative, and no place where a trade-off can be made in the national interest," he told me. Staats, having been appointed by Truman, was frustrated by the knowledge that the supposedly democratic veto was being used to throw a monkey wrench into the works, to block progress—and worse, it had not always been so.

For example, who would vote for the Tennessee Valley Authority today? (I beg the indulgence of those readers who feel that TVA should never have come into existence. That is not my point. Perhaps I should go back to the projects of Hamilton or to other less well known examples, which do not restoke political fires even now still smoldering!) By at least one account, the achievements of TVA's first forty years include a tenfold increase in the area's per-capita income, electricity in 98 percent of the homes, and three million acres saved from erosion. Today, however, the project would not get off the engineers' drawing boards. Mark Shields, in a *Washington Post* editorial, offers some cutting but instructive speculation on what would happen if TVA were proposed today: "First, there would be a generation of

lawsuits over the proposed dislocation of the unfuzzy cater-
pillars, and allied birds and bunny matters. These opponents would be joined by that swelling group of pervasively
pessimistic public officials who sincerely believe that nothing, at least nothing non-Japanese, works."[6]

From the numerous conversations I had with David Lilienthal, the original administrator of TVA, before he died,
it is clear to me that he had that extraordinary freedom of
action that once went hand in hand with the creation of new
public agencies. But TVA today is a pale shadow of its
former self.

I think the main reason that TVA would not happen today
is that our political leaders have become overly concerned
with technical details, fine legal points, and other minutiae
instead of looking to broader social goals. The focus of political and particularly congressional debate should not be
on the myriad operating details of departments and projects
but rather on national priorities and the *processes* of government. Just pick up a copy of the *Congressional Record* and
you will see what I mean. It is incredible that we operate as
well as we do—and it's a real tribute to our much maligned
public servants.

The Founding Fathers' Vision

In his Federalist Paper No. 10 James Madison laid down
the theoretical foundation for the desirability of the pluralist
society, which, in effect, encourages multiple vetoes. The
"seeds of faction," he stated, are "sown in the nature of
man." Factions reflected interests—primarily, although not
exclusively, economic. If in any given society some one
interest group (faction) represented a homogeneous majority, it would not simply wish to govern but would go beyond
that to outlaw any minority that held a contrary opinion, on
the ground that to oppose the majority was to oppose truth
and virtue and goodness. Hence, continued Madison, it is
most desirable to construct a society in which no one interest group, standing by itself, is a majority. It is best to have
a large and complex federation of states, such as the Constitution envisioned, in which every interest group is a minority and in which government is conducted by a majority

that is a coalition of minorities, followed by new coalitions of realigned and recombined minorities.

Not satisfied with laying the socioeconomic foundation of such a pluralist society by bringing the diverse elements of the thirteen colonies together into one nation, the Founding Fathers proceeded quite consciously to construct a political form that would further fragment power. The states would have certain powers reserved to them. The legislature would be divided into two separate houses, elected in different ways and at different times. The President would have the power to veto acts of the legislature. The legislature, by a special majority, could override the veto. The courts would be manned by people who had the approval of both executive and legislature. Individuals would enjoy a Bill of Rights to safeguard certain liberties against all external power.

Although the United States Constitution is peculiar to one country, the pluralist concept prevails in one form or another in every major democracy in the world. The power and presence of different interest groups are respected: farmer, banker, industrial worker, manufacturer. Religious and ethnic minorities dare not be disregarded. Regions are recognized to be special entities with special needs. In all those cases in which an administration rules through a coalition government—which is the case most of the time—the prime minister must include many "factions" in his cabinet, and he must pay heed to their particular claims, no matter how parochial.

Indeed, the most convincing case against socialism—in its pristine form, based on government ownership of the means of production—is that such a system, even if it started out with democratic intentions, would end up as a tyranny because it would abolish the economic basis for polycentric power. Without pluralism, totalitarianism would sooner or later take over.

The Dangers of Pluralism

The pluralism that exists in the Western world today is more than an accident of history; it has been promoted as a civic virtue. Yet pluralism carries its own pains, especially when it runs amok, when each interest group thinks and acts as if it were "it" and all else were naught or near naught. The central nervous system, the government, develops a severe disorder when each limb and organ tries to do its own thing without regard to the rest of the body politic.

Democracy, as we have seen, has its limits. Upholding the rights of the many, carried to the extreme, leads us to the brink of anarchy. Abraham Lincoln's understanding of this truism emerged in the slavery debate surrounding the Kansas-Nebraska Act. The principle in question was whether the new territory should be free to establish or ban slavery as it pleased. While Lincoln might have tolerated slavery if it were confined to the South—where he saw it headed for certain extinction—he would not sanction a law that would broaden the territory of moral indifference.

In his articulate *Statecraft as Soulcraft* George Will offers this historical insight into Lincoln's thinking:

> It was concerning that territory that Lincoln made himself the greatest American. He did so by insisting that there are limits to popular sovereignty. The crucial premise of the Declaration of Independence is that people can make a nation by making the acceptance of an idea a political act. Lincoln said: you cannot have it both ways. You cannot repeal the Missouri Compromise and retain the Declaration of Independence. Either slavery shall be forever barred from the territories, thereby placing it on a path to certain eventual extinction, or the nation can no longer pretend to rest on the bedrock principle that "all men are created equal."
>
> Lincoln's point was that fidelity to the Declaration requires placing some questions beyond the reach of majorities, and thus placing some values above popular sovereignty . . .
>
> Lincoln believed there can be closed questions in an open society. Indeed, a society that has no closed questions cannot count on remaining an open society.[7]

Guarding the Turf

In an essay appropriately entitled "Toward a Pluralistic but Coherent Society" my friend John Gardner—who has thought a lot about the veto problem and with whom I have discussed many of the problems detailed in this book—describes the frustration of a society in which just about anyone with the will to do so exerts a veto: "To comprehend the paralysis of government as the policymaker experiences it, imagine a checker player confronted by a bystander who puts a thumb on one checker and says, 'Go ahead and play, just don't touch this one,' and then another bystander puts a thumb on another checker with the same warning, and then another and another. The owners of the thumbs—the interest groups—don't want to make the game unwinnable. They just don't want you to touch their particular checker."[8]

The predicament of a government that wishes to govern among special interests that insist on immobilizing action on their turf is, of course, no recent problem of a pluralist society. After James Madison described the inevitable sources of faction, he noted: "The regulation of these various and interfering interests forms the principal task of modern legislation and involves the spirit of party and faction in the necessary and ordinary operations of the government.[9]

The difference between the eighteenth century, when Madison wrote, and the twenty-first century, into which we are speedily moving, lies in the incredibly increasing complexity of our present civilization. When the Constitution was written, one part of the nation might very well go its own idiosyncratic way without seriously affecting what was happening elsewhere. The nation had not yet been so tightly knit by transportation and communication. But today, interdependence is inherent and inevitable. The whole is very much affected by what happens in its parts. As a result, Gardner says, "Our capacity to frustrate one another through non-cooperation has increased dramatically. The part can hold the whole system up for ransom."[10]

Power at the Center

To counter the war of the parts against the whole, it seems logical to strengthen "the whole," to give greater power to government, especially the central government. Over the nearly two centuries that the United States Constitution has been in existence, this trend toward the federal politicization of the society has been a continuous process. Nor has the United States been alone; in Europe the role of the central government in the social and economic affairs of its people is far greater than that in the United States.

But does this accumulation of greater power at the center really create a centripetal counterforce that effectively offsets the centrifugal force at work in our time? John Gardner, after serving as secretary of the Department of Health, Education and Welfare, concluded that "government" was too often a mere façade for extragovernmental groups: the center itself was riding the centrifuge.

> The groups establish beachheads in Congress and the Executive Branch agencies, they get their purposes written into statute, they get their representatives placed on advisory councils and make sure that their trusted friends are appointed to key posts in agencies. In the process the boundary line between government and "interests outside of government" becomes badly blurred. Rather than saying that "government has taken an action in consonance with the wishes of a particular interest group," one might say—with greater accuracy—that the portion of the interest group's network that lies within Congress, the Executive Branch and relevant advisory councils has accomplished an action desired by the whole interest network.[11]

Nor does decentralization—distributing the governmental functions to state and local governments—really solve the problem, according to Gardner's experiences: "If one examines the cluster of interests involved in government health programs (the medical and nursing professions, hospitals, nursing homes, insurers, etc.) the only difference between the decision made at the national and decisions made at the local level is that the interest groups play out their role on a different stage. The program has not necessarily moved closer to 'the people' or the consumer, nor has it escaped the web of the Special Interest State."[12]

Power to the President

If the "center," as presently constituted, is still too weak to withstand the divisive forces that tear at its core, why not move to put more power into the hands of the President, the single figure elected by the "people"? In times of crisis most people (including the traditionally antiauthoritarian

55

Americans) seem ready to accept this solution. The wartime Presidents—Lincoln, Wilson, Roosevelt—wielded unusual powers, internally as well as externally. In the nation's greatest economic crisis, the Great Depression of the 1930s, Roosevelt was entrusted with unusual prerogatives again and again. But in ordinary times the President is rarely allowed to act as if he were "the government." In a pluralist society he is elected by a coalition; he is consequently answerable to diverse and often divergent constituencies. The overriding priority is rarely the same for all. The mandate is never very clear. The President owes too much to too many, and if he recalls his campaign rhetoric, he may discover that he probably owes everything to everyone.

In practice, of course, American Presidents have almost consistently moved to strengthen the White House vis-à-vis that much more fragmented center of power, Congress. This was almost inevitable once the separate states had come together to "form a more perfect union." It was Thomas Jefferson who presciently wrote just six weeks before the inauguration of Washington: "The tyranny of the legislatures is the most formidable dread at present and will be for long years. That of the executive will come in its turn, but it will be at a remote period." Almost two centuries after Jefferson's prophecy Americans were expressing their distress over the "imperial presidency," a concept that had evolved during the war years from Roosevelt to Johnson but that took on an ugly, threatening connotation after Nixon's Watergate.

As America moved into the last quarter of the twentieth century, Congress began to reassert its presence. Without diminishing the scope of the Executive Branch, Congress insisted on an oversight role—including the area of foreign affairs and defense, once considered the special domain of the presidency. Until some new crisis emerges, Americans —and most people of the Western democracies—seem to opt for a head of state (President or Premier) who is both strong and strongly scrutinized.

The Invisible Hand

If, then, the central government is itself pluralized and paralyzed, does the "invisible hand" of the market serve as a more efficient model? The answer, interestingly, comes from the same man who invented and immortalized the term "invisible hand." Adam Smith recognized, in *The Wealth of Nations*, that in an open-market society, very visible hands would invariably try to manipulate the "invisible hand."

Workmen and their masters would inevitably organize, because "the workmen desire to get as much, the master to give as little as possible. The former are disposed to combine in order to raise, the latter in order to lower the wages of labour."[13] Tradesmen inevitably organize as a special interest. "People of the same trade seldom meet together, even for merriment and diversion, but the conversation ends in a conspiracy against the public, or in some contrivance to raise prices."[14] Even a handful could impose its tyranny on a much larger group. "Half a dozen wool-combers, perhaps, are necessary to keep a thousand spinners and weavers at work. By combining not to take apprentices they can not only engross the employment, but reduce the whole manufacture into a sort of slavery to themselves, and raise the price of their labour above what is due to the nature of their work."[15]

Smith did not limit his critique to tradesmen and craftsmen; he was even more excoriating when dissecting the conduct of "merchants and master manufacturers." The chief interest of these "dealers" was "to widen the market and to narrow the competition. To widen the market may frequently be agreeable enough to the interest of the public; but to narrow the competition must always be against it, and can serve only to enable the dealers, by raising their own benefit, [to levy an] absurd tax upon the rest of their fellow citizens."[16]

Smith understood only too well that the open market could—and would—become a rigged market so long as man's self-interest asserted itself in the public domain. In the United States, after laissez-faire had presided over the American economy for about a century, "the people" decided that it was necessary to pass a law to curb the monopolies that had arisen through the manipulation of highly visible hands; the result was the Sherman Antitrust Act. And from that time on, as government moved in to regulate one portion after another of the economy, the challenge to

57

the regulated was how to act politically to regulate the regulators.

Thus antitrust makes the U.S. government the most awesome veto power of all, sometimes—but not always—to the detriment of its own. (See Chapter 7 for examples of this formidable legislated veto power embodied in antitrust.)

The Risk-Free Society

Nowhere are the limits of democracy more painfully clear than in our conscious or unconscious efforts to create a risk-free society. However, as Thomas Sowell reminds us, "Social values in general are incrementally variable: neither safety, diversity, rational articulation, nor morality is categorically a 'good thing' to have more of, without limits. All are subject to diminishing returns, and ultimately negative returns."[17]

For example, would citizens oppose the transport of radioactive materials through their communities if they were aware of the real risks involved—which are negligible? The news media, which could promote a truly widespread understanding of the death risks from nuclear energy, create precisely the opposite effect. The media are generally geared toward publicizing an extraordinary event as if it were ordinary, with little perspective on how the likelihood of such an event stacks up against other contingencies. For example, the most publicized of nuclear accidents, the Three Mile Island incident, was rarely treated within the context of the statistical probability of such an occurrence —which is extremely low. The event was consequently blown out of all proportion and treated as a catastrophe, supposedly illustrative of the dangers of nuclear power— even though it caused no known casualties.

In an address on Britain's BBC television a few years ago Lord Rothschild, founding director of the British government's Central Advisory Council for Science and Technology, reminded his audience that there is no such thing as a risk-free society. He constructively suggested that we need some comparative guide or index of risks. "Far more row is made of the possibility of a major accident at a nuclear power station than about death from influenza," he observed, citing figures to indicate that death from influenza is 550 times more likely than death resulting from a nuclear disaster.[18] And the statistical certainty of a major number of deaths relating to widespread reliance on coal for power plants is almost never mentioned in the U.S. media coverage of energy policy.

The media, then, particularly the newspapers, could do much to promote a better understanding of risk—and discourage ill-informed vetoes—by placing the story of a death or disaster within a proper statistical context. A child may die from a penicillin injection—but how probable is it that such a tragedy will occur? And what are the figures for the number of deaths *prevented* by penicillin?

Trade-off Mechanisms

As tempting as may be a solution of putting more and more power in the hands of a few "wise men" or a benevolent ruler, I believe we must develop other solutions. Political invention of the most innovative kind is needed. Devising trade-off mechanisms that balance our many demands with limited means; that allow holding a course with sufficient constancy to ensure results; and that adjust the political lead time to the reality of economic time are all fundamentally political problems.

Professor Elting E. Morison has put it very simply: "the only way those best interests can be determined, even in a world where knowledge doubles every 10 years and $e = mc^2$, is by the many themselves."[19] He suggests that in moving toward a solution we take as a model the way in which English common law evolved—growing out of a series of decisions or choices in particular cases. The fundamental idea is to start from a particular case, for example, to start with the siting of a single power plant, rather than with an over-all grand energy scheme, and to go about this with the creation of an ad hoc group:

> . . . a sort of committee of public safety fortified by a staff
> competent in the assemblage of all the varied, requisite
> information . . . (formulating the case and presenting a set of
> proposed alternatives for sites, capacities, means of
> production, etc.). . . .

59

A word more about the formulating groups. They should serve as ad hoc committees, called into existence to study a particular situation. They should have the means to obtain all the appropriate evidence that bears on their special problem so that they may proceed to their conclusions in an "unflinchingly rational" way.[20]

I hope that Professor Morison will wish to develop this idea and that this problem will attract considerably more scholarly study as well as innovative experimentation. We simply do not have the kind of trade-off mechanisms we need in this country to make "unflinchingly rational" decisions. Congress in particular is geared toward exactly the opposite—voting along party lines, or according to the perceived demands of constituencies in the home states, rather than according to the strictest cost/benefit analyses. Perhaps the best solution is, as Professor Morison suggests, from "the many themselves": an informed public that makes their wishes known to their congressional representatives. More will be said on model public-education campaigns later in this book.

Lest we believe that the U.S. is alone in its inability to create trade-offs among the demands of politically warring factions, Thomas Sowell offers this sobering example: "Perfectionism among people of diverse political persuasions led to concerted efforts to bring down the troubled Weimar Republic. However satisfying it may have been to believe that 'nothing could be worse' than the Weimar Republic, many of those who contributed to its downfall learned too late in Nazi concentration camps just how much worse things could be."[21]

The alternative, then, to the kind of trade-off mechanisms we need in a democratic society to balance the costs and risks against the benefits of any course of action is a dangerous polarization that leads inevitably to authoritarian government, of either the right or left. The time is ripe for political inventing and reinventing to meet this societal change. The stakes are very high.

The "Rule of Reason"

The need to make social trade-offs in the public interest was illustrated time and time again in the 1970s and early 1980s by public-interest groups, which were able to manipulate the media to rally public support and to use the regulatory and judicial processes to delay or abort large-scale business or government projects. Large corporations seemed to be a particular target of the consumerist and environmentalist camps.

Recognizing this, some large organizations and industries have taken innovative approaches to dealing with opposing activist groups. One approach that has met with success has been to develop a dialogue with the groups to work out mutually acceptable positions, to give each faction political legitimacy, and to arrive at more rational trade-offs between socially desirable and economically necessary alternatives. This approach addresses three systematic problems: (1) there are no effective social or political mechanisms in place for making trade-offs among social and economic values; (2) the courts are ill prepared to make these kinds of judgments because of their highly technical nature; (3) the adversary process is often counterproductive, since both parties frequently agree on the ultimate goals!

Taking the nonadversarial approach, the parties establish agreement on how to deal with conflicts. They may agree to disagree, but the process is maintained. An example was described in a working session of the Diebold Corporate Issues Program:

▷ The National Coal Policy Project (NCPP) was an effort involving leading conservationists and executives from coal-mining and -consuming industries to agree on how coal can be exploited in ways that society can tolerate.

The Project grew out of Dow Chemical Company's long and costly battle with environmentalists over a power plant serving Dow's main operations in Michigan. Both the power companies and the environmentalists resorted to vigorous adversarial tactics. A decade of court battles and hundreds of millions of dollars in expenditures demonstrated that costs in time and dollars could become uncontrollable when issues of environmentalism and economic growth were politicized. Gerald Decker, Dow's Corporate Energy Manager, resolved to find a better way to resolve environmental disputes.

Decker approached Larry Moss, former president of the Sierra Club, and presented his ideas on using the "rule of reason" as a tool to keep coal-related debates from degenerating to an emotional level. Moss agreed to help Decker bring together environmentalists and industrialists for a test of the concept.

The NCPP was formally organized in January 1977, with Decker as chairman of the Industrial Caucus and Moss as chairman of the Environmental Caucus. First, the parties agreed to seek compromise agreements through the "rule of reason," a nonadversarial approach developed by Milton Wessel based on open sharing of information. Second, the NCPP aimed to get widespread support for its recommendations through education and publications. Third, it sought to get its recommendations enacted into law and regulation.

The task forces involved in the NCPP arrived at over two hundred points of agreement! The two sides really agreed on many points all along but weren't aware of it. In fact, middle positions were often preferable to preconceived positions. For example, the current system had the effect of discouraging R&D in new technologies by penalizing innovating companies for their low initial efficiency and higher costs. Both sides agreed that the EPA should grant a limited number of exceptions to compliance with the Clean Air Act to promote and encourage new technologies with a reasonable chance of success.[22]

Inventing Institutions

The eighteenth century was a vintage period for invention of political institutions. Chief among these is the concept of federalism, perhaps the United States' main contribution to political organization in the world. But the strengths of federalism, in preventing the concentration of power, have become a weakness, inefficiently dividing and checking power, sometimes to the point of paralysis. Thomas Jefferson saw our Constitution as an Enlightenment machine of "counterpoises"—a practical attempt to create a political institution to solve problems of power. But Jefferson was also an eighteenth-century empiricist, and, as Garry Wills

62

points out in *Inventing America: Jefferson's Declaration of Independence*, Jefferson foresaw change and wanted even constitutions revised often. Said Jefferson to John Adams: "One of the questions, you know, on which our parties took different sides, was on the improvability of the human mind, in science, in ethics, in government." And, continued Jefferson to Adams: "You possess, yourself, too much science not to see how much is still ahead of you, unexplained and unexplored."[23] That we are today experiencing a need to change some of these institutions is far more a measure of their success than of their limitations.

Examples of what I mean by inventing institutions to deal with new or emerging problems are:

▷ The international financial institutions created at the end of World War II may seem obvious in retrospect, but at the time they required considerable hard negotiation followed by an extraordinary ability to sell the U.S. Congress on the arrangements that had been negotiated—which were not at all of obvious benefit to the U.S. (e.g., firm commitments by the U.S. without obvious return). We should take a certain amount of encouragement from that, not entirely inapplicable, precedent when we today face tasks that require putting what is right and what is needed for the future ahead of demands for immediate gratification.

▷ I suspect that the development of central banking was another example of a way of coping with new needs of the economy for a degree of stability and flexibility in the money system. The growth in the powers of the Bank of England, and, in the U.S., the creation of the Federal Reserve System in 1914 represent two somewhat different ways of arriving at a rather similar solution. There must be other useful examples of invention in the history of financial instruments.

▷ An example of postwar institutional innovation was the creation by President Eisenhower of the National Security Council. Many separate Executive-branch agencies of the U.S. government are responsible for various facets of international affairs. Eisenhower created the National Security Council in order to provide one place where the national interests of our country could be looked at in the broadest sense—from both short-term and long-term standpoints. The role it has played has changed with various Presidents and their advisers, and it is today beginning to be questioned, but the institution has performed the function for which it was intended. An earlier attempt of the U.S. State Department to establish a policy-planning staff in order to provide long-term views against which the short-term day-to-day problems could be balanced has, I think, been less effective in the solution of the task for which it was created.

A presidential commission is also very often a useful way to build coalitions and to overcome blockages to political action. "Under what circumstances is a presidential commission a good way to solve an intractable problem?" I asked Brent Scowcroft after his MX Commission and Allan Greenspan's Social Security Commission had both secured some measure of success in their respective missions. His answer was not entirely reassuring: "When there is no alternative but to bite the bullet and make a decision." He reminded me that there had been two *previous* MX commissions (on one of which he had served), the practical results of which were negligible. General Scowcroft's conclusion after the full evening's round-table discussion we had on this subject was that however valuable presidential commissions might be in the politics of involving a number of constituencies in a process, from the standpoint of otherwise practical results they worked only when action could not be avoided, in which case they could be of some limited value.

While some of the examples I have cited are concerned with foreign affairs, I believe nonetheless that they offer insights into many of the problems in the U.S. that I am suggesting need institutional innovation. An example of a modern American institution in critical need of innovation is the public education system. Over and over, efforts of people of goodwill to do something about public schooling have been frustrated by the multiple vetoes of the many groups that are all desirous of quality education but pursue purposes they have elaborated in the isolation of a special circle of interest. School boards (elected) and school supervisors (usually appointed) are often at loggerheads. Teachers and principals have their own axes to grind. Parents and

taxpayers—though very often they are one and the same—

are not necessarily looking at services and costs through the same eyes. Local businesses have needs, in terms of educated employees, and worry about whether the schools can produce the desired personnel product—even if corporations were to provide the financing.

I am happy to report one positive effort toward overcoming the veto powers of multiple constituencies and working toward a shared educational priority.

▷ The Public Education Fund, founded in 1983, made its timely appearance at a moment when several major national reports assailed public education for its failure to provide proper schooling for American youth. But who was to lead the way? Public education in America, although it may get state and federal funds, is essentially a local matter. Action takes place in the school district, with its many constituencies at war with one another.

The object of the PEF is to provide funds that will help get interested parties together. "The organization of local business and civic coalitions in support of public education," stated Fletcher L. Byrom, chairman of PEF's board, "will be a vital part of any achievable strategy that may emerge from the current national debate about how to improve the public schools." [24]

The PEF does not tell local communities how to run their schools. What it does is encourage communities to muster their creative forces. In six communities nationwide, PEF funds have already helped build coalitions of parents, educators, and business people to develop innovative school programs. Each of these programs is unique, yet they all resemble one another in their priority: to improve public education.

My point in citing examples like this is both to illustrate what I mean by inventing institutions and to suggest that some systematic study be undertaken of our experiences in this process to see what we can learn that is applicable to the problems I am describing. One of the more hopeful aspects of the problems with which I am dealing is that we are starting to see some solid scholarly research in diverse fields which should help to contribute to a theoretical base necessary to effective solutions.

Organizational evolution is another direction in which we can look for solution of some of these problems. A vivid example of what I have in mind is provided by Harvard

Professor Alfred D. Chandler's important study *The Visible Hand: The Managerial Revolution in American Business.* This study does more than trace the history of an institution. It describes the beginnings of a new economic function —that of administrative coordination and allocation—and the coming of a new sub-species of economic man—the salaried manager—to carry out this function. Technological innovation, the rapid growth and spread of population, and expanding per capita income made the processes of production and distribution more complex and increased the speed and volume of the flow of materials through them. Existing market mechanisms are often no longer able to coordinate these flows effectively.[25]

The new technologies and expanding markets thus created for the first time a need for administrative coordination. To carry out this function, entrepreneurs built multi-unit business enterprises and hired the managers needed to administer them. Is there not a public-sector counterpart—both in need and opportunity—to what Professor Chandler has described in analyzing the evolution of the modern corporation?

The Congressional Budget Process

Perhaps this administration and coordination function, for the public sector, is fulfilled at least in part by the congressional budget process. There is no single act that is more decisive in distributing the income of the nation than the federal budget. Each year it determines who gets what and who pays. Logically, the budget should be the product of a coordinated, integrated, well informed intelligence. Yet before the Congressional Budget Act of 1974 the Congress of the United States acted as if the budget had no meaning. It enacted bits and pieces of legislation to raise so much in such a way and to spend so much in some way without considering the relations of the part to the whole. In handling the nation's money in this helter-skelter fashion, Congress was reflecting the fractional claims of the multiple constituencies that make up the society.

The structure of Congress is such that it encourages this sort of grab-bag politics. Each committee is a fiefdom; within each committee are the subcommittees with their separate chairpersons vying for acclaim; within each sub-committee are members building their favor with special constituencies back home. What happens in one house of Congress is repeated in the other. And the Republican and Democrat parties are internally divided. They are more responsive to PACs (political action committees) and other specialized revenue sources than to ideology.

Although the Constitution looked to Congress, especially the House, to be the money-minded agency in the federal government, controlling the purse strings, as did the British Parliament with its heads of state, in fact the legislature yielded to the Executive—the President—to formulate a budget. While he was subjected to the same pressures as those on Congress, at least he was one person, with one head, with a constituency made up of the whole nation and not just some precinct. Such presidential leadership worked in those years when the White House and the Hill were copacetic. But even then the process was sloppy. Congress would vote on the separate pieces of the President's budget, but there was no one keeping a score of how all those separate actions added up. What was needed was a new process. In 1967 a Commission on Budget Concepts recommended that there be a comprehensive, unified budget, around which congressional debate and action could revolve. This proposal was in line with several statements from the Committee for Economic Development, starting as early as 1947 (long before I became a trustee, but at a time when, as a Swarthmore student, I was already becoming an admirer of the organization!). Finally, in 1974, Congress enacted the Congressional Budget Act.

It is significant that the federal government—in particular, Congress—had functioned for about a hundred and seventy-five years without such a mechanism. But those were years when the country was smaller, when government played a lesser role in the economy. After World War II it became apparent to the sensitive that a new mechanism was needed; by 1967 a respected commission recommended such an invention; by 1974 it was law.

To make sure that these good intentions did not get lost in a pit of procrastination, the act laid out a timetable. Beginning with October to December, a time for in-depth analysis of the next year's issues by Budget Committee staffs and the congressional Budget Office, and then going through fifteen additional steps (all timetabled), ending with the following October 1 (the new fiscal year), the act lays out the work flow for Congress.

Although the primary objective of the act is to provide a mechanism for a comprehensive and integrated fiscal policy, located in Congress, it serves other purposes as well:

▷ It compels Congress to define priorities.
▷ It allocates resources in line with these priorities.
▷ It provides a fiscal tool for distribution of income.
▷ It anticipates federal borrowing needs.
▷ It examines the interplay between taxing and spending, on one hand, and the development of the economy as a whole, on the other.
▷ It provides a monitor over federal getting and spending.
▷ It implies the need for sophisticated and realistic analysis of the total economy, the needed assumptions for fiscal programming.

The Congressional Budget Act, of course, does not guarantee a balanced budget. Indeed, there may be moments when an unbalanced budget may be in order, provided we know why and how we are using the unbalance—whether to provide needed initiatives for economic growth or meet a catastrophe or win a war. But even when we seek to balance the budget, more than an act is required. We need far more sophisticated, realistic, and apolitical forecasts on the economy than we have been getting. If our assumptions about the economic future are wrong, our calculations on income and outgo must be wrong. In making such projections about the future, we must also be aware that what Congress does about taxation and expenditures will, in itself, affect the future of the total economy. Although I have high personal respect for various economic advisers to both the President and Congress, I believe it essential that the work of the men and women holding these posts be depoliticized as much as possible, so that their forecasts (assumptions) will be tailored to national need and not to partisan preference.

It also seems to me that "comprehensive" ought to mean "comprehensive," and not just "partial." There are many expenditures made by the federal government that are not publicly admitted to be expenditures. There are "off-budget" items: for fiscal 1984, total spending by off-budget agencies is expected to run to $17 billion. There are credit budgets and capital budgets. There are tax sources running into the multibillions, that do not appear as part of our budget. There is present legislation that calls for the severance of the Social Security budget from the general budget in 1993.

In each instance a case can be made, often very reasonable, to prove that these special categories, although huge, should not be included. But as Alice Rivlin, former director of CBO, pointed out about severance of Social Security: "In the long term . . . inclusion of Social Security in the unified budget does force the Congress to ask the right question: how much can the nation's economy afford for social insurance given competing claims on the economy and given the willingness of tax-payers to pay? Making Social Security a separate entity would unnecessarily narrow this question into 'how high a level of benefits can payroll taxes support?' . . . a question that ignores competing claims, alternative tax sources, and the burden of other taxes."

Rivlin's line of reasoning is worthy of consideration not simply as it applies to Social Security but also as it applies to the many scattered, overt and covert budgets of the federal government. I would like to suggest that we view a coordinated, comprehensive, integrated, and inventive approach not simply as a way to balance our books but, in a much larger sense, as one way to balance the many claims on government in our pluralistic democracy, as a way to recognize "vetoes" and to overcome them by establishing "priorities" that allow creative reconciliation through carefully, perhaps cleverly, conceived trade-offs, formulated with more collective compassion and less partisan passion.

Let us consider three circumstances within our lifetime in which efforts were made (or are being made) to bring diverse elements together to cope with a major societal challenge: (a) a consensus-building approach to siting nuclear plants; (b) a classic controversy between farmers and environmentalists; and (c) the "resolution" of the crisis over Social Security in 1982. Perhaps each of these is instructive in its own way.

Case:
Consensus Building in Plant Sitings

Power plants present a difficult situation for any community. Residents need the power generated, but they are often concerned over environmental spoilage. Utilities can take a combative stance against the resistance of environmentalists and consumer groups, but two power companies adopted more innovative approaches designed to involve the public at the early stages and to anticipate citizens' objections to local plant sitings.

Ontario Hydro, a large Canadian public utility, has established an elaborate and well-staffed process for public participation in its siting plans. The process is in several stages:

1. Selection of twelve locations within a region for the public to consider in order to arrive at two final sites, followed by development of a community profile for each of the twelve locations.

2. Initial talks with political leadership in each community, followed by a public information program and formation of a group of 50 to 70 citizens representing various community interests. Technical training of the group, and election of a steering committee, so they can understand and deal effectively with the issues raised.

3. Selection of factors to be considered and priorities to be assigned among these factors, in evaluating the sites.

4. Determination by Ontario Hydro staff of feasible options, based on the group's recommendations—and possible follow-up activities as the building goes forward.

Ontario Hydro estimates that the cost of this public participation comes to about 0.1 percent of the total power plant investment. But in following the procedures, the utility is able to avert legal actions costing many times that investment. And, although the process adds approximately one year to plant completion schedules, it avoids the wrangling and stoppages that can inflate the delays by many years.

Pennsylvania Power and Light Co., a private utility headquartered in Allentown, has taken a similar approach. It has decided to open its siting process to the public because Pennsylvania has no siting legislation—and therefore, any group that disagrees with some aspect of the siting decision can tie up the process for indefinite periods. Lacking a legal method to mediate between the regional yes and the local no, PP&L has adopted a public process through consultation on siting with a cross-representation of constituencies involved, first at the regional and then the local level. PP&L works to ensure that citizen interests are fairly represented and that participants do a thorough job of evaluation. If the public feels the process has been fair, it is then easier to get political support in the legislature if that route must be taken to override a local community's objections.

In deciding upon a site for a plant at Summerdale, a suburb of Harrisburg, PP&L convened a committee of twenty-six, representing a balance of political, institutional, civic, and social groups: Cumberland County commissioners, West Shore Chamber of Commerce, Enola Sportsman Association, and others, and including eleven area residents. In four months of deliberations, the committee held thirty meetings and field trips. Significantly, when a letter threatening legal action over a particular parcel of land was presented to the president of PP&L, he directed the complaint to the committee—underscoring the seriousness the company attached to the process, and the confidence it felt in the committee's work.

By the end of the process, a sufficient level of trust and teamwork had been established between the committee and PP&L that when the company deemed it necessary to reject a key recommendation of the final report, the committee responded with further willingness to negotiate—and eventually endorsed the company's alternate offer by a 10 to 1 vote.

The Summerdale Public Participation Project and the example of Ontario Hydro demonstrate how blockages can be avoided when corporations demonstrate a willingness to trust the public's good faith, and solicits their participation in decisions that directly affect their lives.

Case:
Farmers vs. Environmentalists

The Snoqualmie-Snohomish Basin, comprising 690 square miles, forms a lush green bracket around the eastern edge of the Seattle metropolitan area. It serves as a wilderness playground for the people of Seattle, and it also has rich farmlands. However, it is vulnerable to floodings. In 1959 the Snohomish River and its two tributaries overflowed their banks. The flood destroyed two small towns, washed away acres of farmlands, and damaged $8 million worth of crops.

The distressed farmers appealed for help, and the U.S. Army Corps of Engineers stood ready to build a protective dam. But the project needed the approval of the state's governor—and that approval was not forthcoming because of strong objections from kayakers who rode the white waters of the upper Snoqualmie River, hikers who tramped through the Douglas fir forests, and environmentalists who saw the dam as a prelude to further urban sprawl.

The result was a deadlock between farmers and environmentalists that lasted fourteen years.

Gerald W. Cormick entered the dispute in late 1973. He was then running the Community Crisis Intervention Center at Washington University in St. Louis. He and an associate, Jane McCarthy, had experience resolving disputes in labor, civil rights, and community areas, and it was thought that their expertise might be applied to the environmental area. Governor Daniel Evans formally appointed them mediators on May 7, 1974. In a series of meetings that followed, many of the parties to the dispute were brought to the negotiating table. Positions were stated and restated, and different sides began to appreciate the concerns of the other sides. After seven months a package agreement emerged. Farmers gave up something: they accepted strong land-use regulations to preserve wilderness areas. Environmentalists gave up something: they agreed to a dam. The agreement was signed by all participants and forwarded to the governor.

How did the mediators overcome the multiple vetoes of farmers and kayakers and arrive at a workable trade-off? The process of mediation, as practiced by Cormick, takes on the air of a conjurer's trick. He defines the process as follows: "Mediation is a voluntary process in which those involved in a dispute jointly explore and reconcile their differences. The mediator has no authority to impose a settlement. His or her strength is in the ability to assist the parties in resolving their own differences. The mediated dispute is settled when the parties themselves reach what they consider to be a workable solution." Mediation differs from arbitration, which has its own formal rules. The process has not been codified, and Cormick virtually writes the rules as he goes along. However, a few guidelines have emerged from the work of his Office of Environmental Mediation of the University of Washington, Seattle—considered the nation's leading mediation organization.

1. There can be no judgments. Unlike an umpire, who must

decide who's right and who's wrong, the mediator makes no judgments. He or she acts as a *facilitator* who gets the parties to a dispute to agree to a resolution. In the Snoqualmie-Snohomish dispute, for example, Cormick never once expressed the view that a dam should be built or should not be built. What he did to break the impasse was to ask all the parties to assume that a dam could *not* be built and then to choose between two alternative flood-control measures. That exercise resulted in a consensus that a dam of some kind had to be built, thereby moving the debate on to the next questions: What kind of dam, and where should it be placed?

2. Compromise must be possible. A mediator has to determine that there is enough flexibility in opposing positions to make a compromise possible. Some disputes are not suited to mediation. For example, in the siting of a nuclear power facility, the disputants may be so firmly entrenched in their opposing views that mediation will not be viable.

3. All parties have to be represented. It is fruitless to mediate in the absence of one of the parties, although every group need not be present at every meeting. During the Snoqualmie-Snohomish discussions Cormick and McCarthy returned frequently to state government officials to report on how private citizens were faring in the negotiations. Thus another function of the mediator is as a messenger.

4. A settlement must be enforceable. Cormick turned down a subsequent invitation to mediate an environmental dispute in Colorado. His investigation revealed that even if a settlement were reached, nothing might happen, because there was no provision for government implementation.

5. Scales must be balanced. The fight must be a fair one. Mediation is not likely to be fruitful if one party has a clear upper hand over the other and seeks only to legitimize its advantage.

6. Participants must have credibility. It is the mediator's responsibility to see that the participants around the table have standing with their constituencies. It is also part of the job to establish networks in a community to reach interested parties who, for one reason or another, are not represented at the table. Their absence might at a later date cripple any agreement reached. One of the common mistakes, Cormick says, is the "Take me to your leader" attitude, the idea that only *one* person can speak for the black community or the Chicano community or whatever. There are many groups, many representatives, and the successful mediator

73

has to send out antennae to seek out those representatives. Cormick and McCarthy, in choosing a panel, had asked several people, "Can you name ten or twelve people who, if they could agree on something, would have stature or influence so that you could reasonably support them in their agreement?"

7. Scapegoats are useful. It's always handy to have a whipping boy—government can often fill that purpose—so that disputants can get off the hook with their constituencies. Sometimes the mediator can be the scapegoat.

8. The process is ongoing. Mediation can build new relationships among the disputants, making it possible for them to work together in the future. And having succeeded at mediation, they will not be afraid to try it again—in another area.

Cormick is concerned about the ethical implications of mediation, and he emphasizes he does not want the process "sold" as a conflict-avoidance mechanism. One cannot have a dispute without a conflict, and Cormick believes that out of conflict comes progress. He also insists that the parties in the mediation process be committed to serving basic principles of justice, freedom, and proportional empowerment.

Most important of all, the mediator must take on a conflict with a vision of a broader public interest. Rather than trying to impose one's own views, Cormick says, the mediator "has an ethical responsibility to ensure that the parties consciously consider the public interest." Hence: the Ethical Mediator.[26]

Case:
Priorities and Trade-offs in Social Security

Unlike the anticipatory approach to averting vetoes in plant citings and the mediation procedures described above was the way in which the government coped with the crisis in Social Security when it appeared in 1982: unless some changes were made in the law or its administration, the fund would soon be bankrupt. The *priority* was clear: something had to be done about future financing and spending. But what?

Ironically, a veto helped shape the outcome. The veto came from that huge constituency that were on Social Security or were about to receive retirement benefits. Their understanding was that through their working lives they had paid into the Social Security fund, and they were not going to be deprived of the benefits on which they had been counting. Initial moves by the administration in May 1981 to reduce benefits—by as much as 25 percent—were looked upon as betrayal or worse. The outcry against even the slightest intimation of a reduction in retirement pay was deafening.

The size of the vetoing constituency was stupendous. In 1982, 36 million beneficiaries were receiving cash benefits: 24 million retired workers and dependents; 8 million survivors of deceased workers; 4 million disabled workers and dependents. No political personality could disregard an electorate of such dimensions. Yet the problem of solvency was real. The Social Security system was born with a birth defect, known to those who were present at the time. It could not, as originally calculated, support itself. The reason was that way back in 1935 it was decided to provide Social Security payment to retirees immediately. This was considered desirable in order to help those too old to work and to assist them with dignity; it was also a means to stimulate the economy. The money for such payments was to come from those who were at work and who were contributing. In short, a younger generation was, in effect, supporting an older generation: sons and daughters were supporting fathers and mothers in a collective way.

The actuaries who worked on the original plan calculated that at a future moment so much would be going out that it would not be possible to meet the payments even with income from the younger generation. So it was proposed that at a given time the government itself should become a contributory party to make the plan tripartite, with income from employee, employer, and from the U.S. Treasury—as it is in many countries.

When the time came, however, neither the President nor Congress was ready to follow this recommendation. So the fund fell into trouble. It also ran into other difficulties. To keep benefits abreast of economic developments, it was decided to make cost-of-living adjustments (COLA) in benefits in line with inflation. So the costs went up. But income did not go up at the same speed, because in the 1970s wages were not keeping up with inflation and because rising unemployment removed millions of employees from the roll of contributors to the fund. Hence there was the obvious imperative to cut benefits or to raise taxes or both.

That was not, of course, the way people in retirement saw it. They did not recognize that the average wage earner gets his or her total contributions back after receiving benefits for one year. Indeed, the average worker retiring (in 1982) receives his or her lifetime contributions, plus interest in about two and a half years.

The fact was, in 1982, that even if the Social Security fund tapped sister funds, such as that for hospital insurance, by "July 1984, interfund borrowing capacity would (have been) exhausted and more money (would have been) needed to get the system through the rest of the decade." The long-range problem was even worse. Starting in 2015, the "baby boom" generation (would) start to retire. The "senior boom" would be so awesome in size that the younger generation simply could not shoulder the burden.[27]

Both the White House and Congress knew that they had a problem—a problem that was getting worse as unemployment rose after 1980. At the same time, both knew that any proposed solution carried great political overtones.

The year 1982 was a political year; the mid-term elections for the House and Senate were on the agenda. President Reagan had reason to fear that the Democrats would seize on his proposed cut in benefits and would turn it into a campaign issue. So he moved to depoliticize the question. He appointed the National Commission on Social Security Reform with fifteen members: five to be appointed by the Democratic congressional leadership, five by the Republicans, and five by the President.

The commission might have met in Republican caucus to make its recommendations. But that would have defeated its purpose. There would have been no agreed-on report. Social Security would have been an issue—perhaps *the* issue—in the 1982 campaign. The idea was (a) to arrive at a consensus that (b) would be mindful of the veto of present and near-present recipients.

To find a consensus formula the commission had to find a political trade-off between the older and younger generations that would be economically sound. Its final recommendations were approved by twelve of the fifteen commissioners; three of the five Republican appointees dissented.

The way in which the burden was distributed between the generations was an elegant exercise in psychopolitics. The older generation—those receiving benefits—was asked to take a six-month postponement of a cost-of-living increase that would have fallen due in July 1983. The commission proposed that this increase in benefits be delayed to January 1984. This one-time act would add $40 billion to the fund between 1983 and 1989.

One of the members of the commission, Lane Kirkland, president of the AFL-CIO, found it hard to swallow this proviso. "One item in the consensus recommendation which I reluctantly accepted is the one-time six-month delay in the annual cost-of-living adjustment," he testified to the House Ways and Means Committee on February 2, 1983. But, he explained, "in an effort to reach agreement the Democratic-appointed members of the Commission reluctantly made concessions from deeply held positions. A bi-partisan agreement insuring the financial stability of social security based on relatively modest adjustment was preferable to the drastic benefit reductions some have advocated."

A second "burden" was placed on present beneficiaries with an income of more than $20,000 a year (excluding Social Security income) if single, or $25,000 a year on joint returns. In such cases, 50 percent of the Social Security benefits would be counted as income for taxable purposes. In accepting this "adjustment" the Democratic conferees were breaking with a long-held principle: "benefits" should not be taxed. But under the pressure to arrive at a viable compromise, the "tax" on what had not been taxed or even considered taxable was reluctantly accepted. There was no great outcry from the vetoing constituency, in all probability because those who were to be taxed were seen as persons in a higher-income bracket. The adjustment was to yield another $30 billion between 1983 and 1989.

The share of the "burden" placed on the younger generation—those who were not receiving benefits—was much heavier. Higher Social Security taxes, already scheduled under the old law, would be moved forward. For instance, the increase of .3 of a percent, slated for 1985, would be moved up to 1984. But for a time the worker who pays this increase will be allowed a refundable tax credit when paying his/her income tax. So, in effect, there is no undue burden for the employees. In the case of the second increase of .5 of a percent, due in 1990, that increase would be moved forward to 1988–89. The "burden" on the worker would be heavier payments for those two years. The yield on this proposal would be $40 billion for years 1983–89.

The more serious "burden" placed on future retirees (those presently working) was a proposed change in the retirement age—from sixty-five to sixty-six. The change was considered necessary for meeting long-term problems after 1990; the short-term solutions—major portions of which we have noted—would cover two-thirds of the anticipated long-term deficit; but one-third still remained.

The Republicans and Democrats on the commission could not reach an agreement on moving retirement age to sixty-six. The Republicans proposed to phase in an increase in the retirement age from sixty-five to sixty-six, beginning in the year 2000, and, after that, to increase retirement age in accordance with a formula based on greater longevity. The Democrats proposed to raise employer and employee contributions by 0.46 percent of taxable payroll by year 2010 (with the employee getting a refundable tax credit) or—as an alternative—increase funds by an equivalent contribution from the general treasury. (In effect, the Democrats were returning to the recommendations made when Social Security was born—namely, to have the government enter the act as a contributing party.)

Congress resolved the deadlock. Retirement age would be phased in from sixty-five to sixty-seven by the year 2027, in two steps. The age would be raised gradually, starting in the year 2000, and would reach sixty-six in the year 2009. The second step, from age sixty-six to sixty-seven, would be phased in between the years 2017 and 2027.

These major provisos do not cover all the adjustments that were contained in the commission's proposals and in the final congressional act. But they are a fair sample of the inventive mind (minds) at work. The priority was established; the vetoes were recognized and respected—in part; there was a second step—Congress—to resolve the differences and make trade-offs.

What is not included in this account were the innumerable exchanges, informal more than formal, one-on-one more than in committees or subcommittees, among the various individual members of the commission. Much of the story is available from private sources and someday might make a marvelous handbook on modes of negotiation, invention, and cooperation and how the process works—or, at least, worked in one significant moment of history.

III Short Time Horizons

All too often our time horizon is short-term, while the key to solving many of our problems is long-term vision and commitment. As a result, our resources are poorly allocated and our efforts at solving problems are continually frustrated by the context in which we operate. In public life we lack the necessary mechanisms: distant early warning systems to help anticipate problems as well as consequences of planned action; built-in reviews of the actual results compared with the original expectations; required debate and periodic reaffirmation of courses of action. In the private sector many of the analytical tools we use, as well as increased institutional ownership of stock, encourage short-term management.

Case:
The Vicious Circle in Semiconductors

Sometimes short-term thinking is inadvertent. However, in the unusual case of the U.S. semiconductor industry, the players have been fully aware they are behaving to their firms' long-term detriment, yet knowingly continue to do so. U.S. chip producers in recent years have shown disturbing signs of losing ground to their Japanese competitors, and the reasons have little to do with scientific and technical inventiveness. Rather, they stem from the two nations' differing attitudes toward short- and long-term prospects.

A key to progress toward new generations of computer technology is the dynamic random-access memory (RAM) chip, a quarter-

79

inch square of silicon real estate stacked with thousands, and lately hundreds of thousands, of memory cells. Each new generation of RAM chips quadruples the capacity of the previous generation, letting manufacturers build smaller, cheaper, more powerful and more reliable computers, calculators, and other electronic devices.

These semiconductor memory devices are the seedbed for research in the nation's vital computer and communications industry. From memories, researchers learn the integrated-circuit technology that is the heart of all computer devices. Dynamic RAM chips are therefore the bellwether for the information technology industry—an industry of vital importance to the productivity and competitiveness of nearly all other industries as well.

Largely tied to the need to show consistently good quarterly performances, U.S. chip makers routinely lay off a large proportion of their work forces as each generation of chips dwindles in market demand—precisely when they should be gearing up for production of the next generation of chips. Japanese companies, taking the longer view, retain the workers and move ahead with the future generations. U.S. chip producers are hamstrung by the need to show a profit, while Japanese makers sacrifice near-term profits for long-term market share. The Japanese are able to do this because their chip producers are small parts of large organizations, while many of the most innovative U.S. chip makers are freestanding, small, young organizations that, in an increasingly capital-intensive industry, cannot maintain a steady level of investment from one product cycle to the next. Over the long term, continuity inevitably defeats the on-again, off-again cycles with which the U.S. industry is saddled.

The irony is that the corporate managers of American chip companies are fully aware of the problem. With the 16K chip, the 64K chip, and, more recently, the 256K model, these managers repeatedly and knowingly geared *down* their investment in the next generation, when they knew it was time to gear *up.* Since each succeeding chip generation demands increasing investments in capital and labor, some semiconductor makers have been squeezed out of the chip race altogether. Industry executives readily acknowledge the deficiencies in the system but insist that they can do nothing to change it in the business climate in which they operate.

Case:
The Emasculation of Bell Laboratories

Over the years, engineers and scientists joining Bell Laboratories were told, in effect, that they could study anything, however fundamental, that had anything, however remote, to do with telephone service. That freedom gave the laboratory the quality of a small, elite engineering college. It also contributed both directly and indirectly to the betterment of AT&T, which ran the facility, and to the benefit of all of us as users of the system. Many of the devices that Bell Labs researchers developed had immediate and direct impact on telephone service. Automatic dialing, microwave communication, voice recording, the solar cell, radio astronomy, lasers, and many computer innovations are advances that emerged from the laboratory at Murray Hill.

But the Bell researchers also discovered vital insights into the world of electronics that promised dividends many years after their discovery. The whole philosophy of Bell Labs encourages genuinely basic research the way no other industrial laboratory could. The transistor is the most obvious and most famous of their discoveries. In 1948, at Bell Labs, John Bardeen, Walter Brattain, and William Shockley combined to develop the device basic to all modern electronics. The three men received the Nobel Prize in physics for their find in 1956. Other Bell researchers have received the same prize for work that at the outset apparently bears little relation to information technology in general, let alone telephone service, yet which, decades later, might make fundamental changes in communications. (AT&T, however, was forbidden to market products resulting from Bell Labs' research and was required to license others to do so.) Arno Penzias and Robert Wilson, for example, became Nobel laureates in physics in 1978 for fundamental work in cosmology. They discovered faint whispers of radiation emanating throughout the universe—compelling evidence in favor of the "big bang" theory of the expansion of the cosmos. The connection with telephone communications was the fact that their receiver could pick up signals containing information as well as evidence of cosmic radiation.

Then came the breakup of AT&T, effective January 1, 1984, as settlement to an antitrust suit brought by the Justice Department more than a decade earlier for precisely this purpose. While Bell Labs remained with its parent company (for which AT&T management deserves the credit), the split plainly meant that its scientists and engineers would serve a smaller constituency. The key change is that the funding stream for Bells Labs' basic research must come from a much smaller organization. Researchers and administrators understandably feared that the extraordinary institution would be irrevocably altered by the split, becoming more like a conventional industrial laboratory devoted to looking five years down the road rather than fifty and concentrating more than ever before on the immediate profit-and-loss potential of product-related research. In short, the focus of this laboratory would shift from the "R" in R&D to the "D."

In the name of antitrust, Bell Labs is almost inevitably going to be hindered from doing what it does best—basic research. "Whatever short-term savings might accrue to the telephone subscriber must be weighed against the subscriber's long-term interests as a citizen of this country," wrote Ed Feigenbaum and Pamela Mc-Corduck in their book *The Fifth Generation.* "Antitrust surely has its purposes, but it shouldn't be a suicide pact between a nation and an industry." [1]

No one can say for sure what the laboratories' fate will be. In the scramble surrounding the breakup of the phone company, no new definition of the institution's mission has yet emerged. A few researchers argued that the laboratories would remain as strong and far-looking as ever—because, with the unleashing of competition, the new AT&T would recognize the need to continue attracting the very best scientists and engineers to its ranks. More usual, however, was the thought expressed by a pessimistic Bell insider: "No more transistors."

Case:
The Water War

When New York City suffered a months-long drought in 1981, a public relations campaign went into high gear to persuade residents to cut down on their use of water. The City Council passed ordinances against overuse of precious water for lawns, Mayor Edward Koch posed for television cameras shaving from a sink in which the faucets had obviously been turned off, and snappy messages encouraging conservation mushroomed on billboards and buses. The campaign successfully reduced water usage. But the irony was that it should not have been necessary. Chronic abuse of the city's water supplies had been evident for many years. Yet the authorities took no notice until the situation had turned into a full-blown crisis.

New York is not alone in its casual attitude toward water supplies. Authorities and users in the arid Southwest, where water is indeed a precious commodity, treat the liquid in almost as cavalier a fashion as their East Coast counterparts. Throughout much of the region, in fact, water costs consumers less than in the soggy Midwest. Successive government policies, aimed at opening up arid regions to farming and settlers, have created a situation in which nature is automatically expected to be bountiful, despite strong evidence to the contrary.

While climatologists warn that changing weather patterns may significantly reduce the amounts of rainfall to be expected in coming years over parts of the United States, local authorities continue to encourage overuse of water by high subsidies. "The shortage [of water in the Southwest] is related to lack of planning to meet forecasted demand," declared geographer Gilbert F. White of the University of Colorado. "It is not basically a shortage of supply."

Water has made the deserts bloom with people as well as plants. Largely as a result of subsidized water from the Colorado River, Arizona's population soared from 750,000 in 1950 to 2.7 million three decades later. A study by the General Accounting Office determined that about one-fifth of the farm acreage in the seventeen western states is irrigated by water whose price to farmers, locked in under forty-year contracts, was less than one-tenth of the government's costs in providing it. Even more disturbing, a succession of interstate and international agreements permits regions bordering the Colorado to draw more than 110 percent of that waterway's typical annual flow each year.

The Colorado has not yet been asked to yield more water than it holds, but the possibility remains!

All too often we deal in the short term, whether it is the techniques with which we analyze problems, the terms of political office, our stock market evaluations of earnings, financial analyses that emphasize discounted cash flow, the medical profession's traditional focus on short-term cures rather than on long-term prevention, or our aversion to saving money and investing in the future. In the process we ignore simple and low-cost moves that, if timely, **83** could avert or ameliorate longer-term problems. Short-term decisions may make sense for the individual manager or politician or investor, but they are bad for our society. They lead to high-cost, crisis-type solutions.

No magic is necessary to alter our structure of incentives and disincentives in a way that makes a manager, whether of a business or a town, act and think in terms of society's long-term interests. In many cases it's simply a matter of perceiving the long term as a reality. It depends on political leadership and the creation of a climate in which we recapture our concern for our children and give credit to decisions that may sacrifice today's gratification to tomorrow's benefit. Learning how to make this change in our decision processes is a very real problem that I do not hear many people discussing.

I think we could learn a good deal by studying the way in which other societies, including some in different periods of history, have managed to achieve a longer-term view in the resolution of problems. In the private sector, I suspect that one possible explanation for the generally longer-term view taken by German and Japanese firms as opposed to the short-term view taken by many U.S. businesses lies in the way in which each society finances business. In addition to what seems to be longer-term perspective in many product development and investment decisions, I have again and again seen both German and Japanese concerns pay much higher prices for acquisitions that are important to long-term market positioning purposes or for specific R&D capability than are typically considered appropriate by U.S. firms. There are undoubtedly other and perhaps more important forces at work—such as the expectations of longer-term employment with the same firm and the realization that one will be living with the results of decisions for a long time—and they had better be right for the long term!

However, we in the States have a habit of looking at things in a very short time frame. It is partly a function, I think, of our being a young nation. We have little past, and we proceed as if we had very little future. We have no vision to match that of, say, the architects of the Strasbourg cathedral, which took four centuries to complete. It is unusual for our leaders to plan beyond our own lifetimes, let alone
beyond our great-grandchildren's lifetimes.

This was not always so. The time perspective of the Founding Fathers matched that of their European counterparts, who in the same period were laying out the parks that could not achieve their planned effect for a century or more. Often in wandering through the parks and grounds of great European houses and palaces I have wondered what it was —whether greater expectation of continuity in the conditions of life or something more subtle—that led to so much present effort for future benefit. Yet the vast projects of the nineteenth-century industrial revolution were launched amid a universal environment of change, and much of the investment was focused on the future.

My French friends often make the profound yet simple observation that we don't design American cities as if our descendants will live there for centuries to come; we don't plant trees with the thought of creating the tree-lined *grands boulevards* of some decades or even centuries hence. I am very fond of the story of former French President Charles de Gaulle (also attributed to Konrad Adenauer), who asked his gardener to plant trees to create a certain shade effect. "But, Générale," the gardener protested, "the effect you have in mind cannot be achieved for forty years!" To which de Gaulle replied, "Well, then, you had better start this afternoon!"

A Complex Age

One reason why short time horizons are such a problem in our own age is that as systems become complex—and advanced industrial societies are enormously complex systems—lead and lag times become more crucial and sometimes phenomenally long. Among the worst cases are our all-too-frequent perceptions as to the need for particular specialties in education. Invariably, it seems that the cohorts of the originally desired specialists arrive on a scene in which there are no longer jobs for them!

Our political policy processes seem incapable of focusing on a problem—energy, for example—until the lights go out in New York City or the gas lines form at each corner. Corrective action requires years, and economic corrective action often requires decades. We have a strong and robust economy and have been able to swallow high-cost jerry-built "solutions" to a number of major problems. But even with the resources of the U.S., we are finding it is all catching up with us.

Decisions are increasingly likely to be wrong, because more and more of them relate to the direction of complex systems. A failure in one part of the system (in the welding of the huge pots necessary for nuclear power plants, for example) can degrade the performance of an entire industry (in this case, the production of electric power, as it did in the early 1970s in the northeast quadrant). Lead times are such that errors often cannot be remedied in time to avoid widespread damage. (Additional coal-burning capacity could not be added to the generating plant because the coal-mining companies had not made the capital investment necessary to increase their production. And even if the coal could be got out of the ground, the railroads did not have the hopper cars to carry it from the minehead.) Compounding the difficulties created by long lead time is the danger of a long lag time, delay in learning or realizing that something has gone wrong until long after the failure has occurred. (Those in charge of building nuclear power plants —not to mention those responsible for providing electrical energy—did not find out about the inadequacy of the pot welders almost until the day the first pots were to be delivered.)

The relationship between timely decision making and adequate information is by no means limited to decisions involving long time horizons. Yet in the perspective of time frames involving no more than a decade, wrong decisions are even more probable and devastatingly more costly, because of the scale and intricacy of our systems. Great difficulties must be overcome if we are to achieve foresight adequate to our needs, and respectable authority suggests that it cannot be done: "Our political system," argues a National Academy of Sciences report, *Technology: Processes of Assessment and Choice,* "simply cannot address itself intelligently and vigorously to problems that are essentially speculative and remote in time."

How Long Is Long-Term?

Not long ago I was a guest in a magnificent old palace in Rome. As we went in to dinner each room revealed even more splendor than the last, filled with great Renaissance sculptures and with paintings three high on the brocaded walls. I asked, "Prince, your family has always lived in this palace?" Laughingly he replied, "Oh, no, not always—only since the sixteenth century."

By contrast, our own definition of "always" might be anything from a day to fifty years—any span of time that will fit into our lifetimes. Thomas Sowell defines "time horizon" more precisely as "the time required for benefits or costs to reach the vanishing point as influences on present decision making," and he offers the following illustrations:

> Time horizons are subjective. They vary not only from one individual to another, but from one socioeconomic class to another, among ethnic groups, or among age groups. Ironically, older individuals may have longer time horizons than younger, more impetuous individuals, even though younger people objectively have more years ahead of them.
>
> But older people's plans often extend well beyond their own life span, as in decisions made for their children's well being—the preservation of an estate, or in extreme cases, suicide by parents who consider themselves a "burden" to their children (once generalized among Eskimos)—or the older person's time horizon often includes concern for their own good name after death which serves as motivations for decisions concerning philanthropy, religious conversion, or a place in history.[2]

What legacy are we preserving for our descendants? What "good name" will we leave behind?

Having started my firm in the room in which I was born (and still regretting that I no longer occupy that house), I may be particularly sensitive to these issues, but I cannot help believing that we would all do our jobs better if we knew we had to live with the consequences in a direct personal manner. My Japanese friends tell me—for I always ask how they are able to take the long-term view in their decisions—that they know as young executives that they will have to live with the decisions they are then making, and they see to it that they are as right as anybody can reasonably foresee for the long term.

There is no question that times have changed and our culture is different from when Osbert Sitwell could begin the first volume of his autobiography: "Coming of a family that now lives within three miles of the room wherein I now write for at least seven hundred years, I have never experienced that sensation of being separated from the working classes, in the way in which the city-bred, middle-class poets of the proletarian movement continually proclaim themselves to feel cut off."[3] Yet in today's world, where electronics and jets condense time and space, we all do live within sight of our own past—even if we refuse to see— and certainly within sight of the consequences—as Rachel Carson first made so many of us aware.

Lead and Lag Times

Short-term thinking discourages facing up to problems until they become crises. For example, as discussed in the previous chapter, economists had warned for several years that the nation's Social Security system was drifting into trouble. As successive Congresses approved ever more liberal benefits and the size of the labor force supporting those benefits started to dwindle, the warnings became more dire. But not until analysts pointed out that the system was in grave danger of going broke within a few years did Congress actually take notice. At that point cries of crisis echoed across Capitol Hill.

The political process encourages the short-term view in many areas:

▷ In 1972, for example, a budget-conscious Congress persuaded the National Aeronautics and Space Administration to drop its costly plans for a reusable spacecraft that would orbit and return to the earth in its entirety and substitute a no-frills design and program without much of the inbuilt redundancy that had made the *Apollo* moon-landing program successful. At $10 billion the new program seemed a bargain. Six years later the problems started to appear. Because it lacked the careful controls of *Apollo,* the space shuttle started to encounter a series of major difficulties. Its heat-protecting tiles fell off. The main engines failed. Electronic components could not pass verification tests. By the time the shuttle flew into space, it had lost two years of time and had run over budget by billions of dollars.

Nowhere is the discrepancy between lead and lag times more regularly manifested than in our continual inability to handle societal needs related to demographic changes. Social Security is unfortunately only one of many examples.

▷ Colleges of education continued to train large numbers of teachers in the 1970's and 1980's, despite incontrovertible evidence from birth rates that teachers would have fewer children to educate. In the glut that resulted, young, qualified teachers found themselves facing the alternatives of unemployment or retraining for entirely new professions.

▷ Similarly, today we are facing a surplus of doctors in the United States, despite a 1980 report by the Department of Health and Human Services forewarning a glut of doctors in the nation by 1990 if the medical schools did not tighten their entrance requirements. An inflated pool of doctors only increases the nation's $300 billion health-care burden. Despite strong agreement among educators and the medical community that the nation must collectively address the issue, no action has been taken.[4]

Is there any chance we will learn from our past mistakes?

Individuals find it equally difficult to think beyond the next few months. Residents of towns hit by floods, hurricanes, and other natural disasters almost always return to their shattered homes despite strong odds that disaster will strike again. A survey by sociologists at the University of California, Los Angeles, revealed that most residents of earthquake-prone regions would refuse to leave their homes even if they knew that there was a fifty-fifty chance an earthquake would rumble through the region within forty-eight hours. Only if the chances of the tremor were rated at 80 percent would they flee.

The Media: The Fourth Estate

What is the cause of this propensity for short-term thinking? I suspect that the mass media have more than a little to do with it. Television, radio, electronic information services, newspapers, and other printed news media, all taken together, form an institution, one that has a powerful impact on every citizen's view of the world.

What is less widely recognized is the power that the press holds over our nation's leaders. "Every morning in Washington our leaders begin their day by reading a Press Summary (prepared separately by each department . . .)," says Michael Ledeen in a recent issue of *The Public Interest.* "That this generally *precedes* the reading of the classified Intelligence Summary speaks volumes about the power of the press, for it is the Press Summary, for the most part, that will establish the problems that the government will address during the next dozen hours. Thus the media have truly become the Fourth Estate."[5]

One day, in answer to a complaint about a *New York Times* strike, George Ball, who was then undersecretary of state, responded that he and a lot of other Kennedy administration officials had initially considered it a boon—until on the second day he received a prebreakfast call from the President saying, "Krock's column today is outrageous!" George said, "Mr. President, what column? The *Times* isn't being published." John Kennedy replied in steely tones that he was referring to what was then the Paris edition. From that day on through the end of the strike, a courier brought over thirty or so copies of the Paris edition so senior officials could be prepared with early-morning responses.

Without question, the media play a prominent role in setting the public agenda for discussion and action. But how well equipped are they for this important societal task? I should say at the outset that I have the greatest respect for journals such as *The New York Times*, the *Washington Post*, and the *Wall Street Journal*, even though I often take issue with their editorial positions and emphases on news coverage. Although I spend much of my life traveling both in the U.S. and abroad, I always have all three newspapers sent to me or held for my return. And I still follow the advice of my Harvard Business School teacher General Georges Doriot and try to read the paper with the largest circulation in whatever city I happen to be in. Yet I am certain that even our greatest media institutions could do more to deepen the level of national debate on issues that will affect all of us for many years to come.

What I find most disturbing is the media's ability to *create* crises by focusing national and international attention on the dramatic pictures and headlines of isolated events, when the really important stories of our time are continuing ones that cannot be told in pictures and a few paragraphs. Further insight into this problem is provided by a study published by the Media Institute, in which Nelson Smith and Leonard Theberge define a phenomenon called "media panic": "In a state of panic, an individual's critical faculties are impaired. Time seems elongated, and there is an obsessive focus on the here and now. No amount of information or data can dislodge the sense of anxiety, and in an effort to placate a worried mind, the panic-stricken individual may look for an elaborate or contrived solution for his problem."[6]

This "obsessive focus on the here and now" may lead to a loss of critical faculties, the authors argue, citing as a classic example the coverage of the Three Mile Island accident: "Knowing little about nuclear energy, while knowing a great deal about how to cover a catastrophe, the networks portrayed the TMI incident in terms of their training. The lack of technical knowledge among reporters inhibited their own critical faculties and the result, in organizational terms, was panic—a panic which was communicated to the public."[7]

The most trusted journalist in America, Walter Cronkite, reported the Three Mile Island incident in ominous language: "It was the first day in a nuclear nightmare. As far as we know at this hour, no worse than that" (March 28, 1979). "The world has never known a day quite like today. It faced the considerable uncertainties and dangers of the worst nuclear power plant accident of the atomic age" (March 30, 1979).[8] Even now the incident is described as a "disaster," even though the only human harm known for certain to have been caused by the accident was due to anxiety, not radiation.

Television news in particular walks a tenuous line between entertainment and journalism. It competes for ratings as does any soap opera or sit-com, and sensationalism is what "sells." This ratings race can lead to dreadful distortions. While the war raged in Afghanistan, with hundreds of casualties daily, AP had three reporters generating daily reports from Kabul. But *because there were no pictures*, the AP reports were largely ignored by the networks.[9]

Similarly, I suspect that the arrival of Pershing missiles in West Germany was a "crisis" in 1983—even though their predecessors were in place fifteen years earlier—at least in part because of the availability of dramatic photographs; the powerful pictures of human protest are more newsworthy than the thoughtful debates of scholars, experts, and humanitarians. This is not to say that the massive ferment of public opinion against the nuclear arms buildup is not very real and very sincere. But should we not question a powerful institution—the mass media in general, TV in particular—when its principal business is not ideas but drama?

The result of the media's focus on the sensational is to perpetuate the crisis mentality and short time perspective that make it difficult, if not impossible, for the viewer to form rational opinions and make informed judgments. My friend Fred Friendly, former CBS network news executive and now an articulate author and educator, has said that the role of television is to raise the level of consciousness, and you don't do this only by reporting crises. You have to raise the level of consciousness *before* problems escalate to crises. If this were done, TV could become an enormously powerful force in helping our society focus on problems in adequate time to cope with them more effectively.

It is a difficult problem. The well intentioned tendency of television to present "both sides" of a complex issue— when there might be many more than two sides to consider! —does more to polarize and exacerbate problems that to aid in public understanding of either the problems or their alternatives. Polarization, typically a "point counterpoint" or pro-and-con format, might make for good TV, but it adds to the problem. It is very much more difficult to present the nuances of both problems and solutions, but it is possible; and the value of applying TV to this task can be enormous.

Of the several public policy organizations with which I have been privileged to be associated, one has made me aware of how much can be done—and how much hard and creative work is required—to educate the public on current problems as complex systems of interrelated problems, not as one-dimensional distortions or extremes. The Public Agenda Foundation, on whose executive committee I serve, was founded by my friends Cyrus Vance and Daniel Yankelovich. A large part of its task is to give carefully prepared TV presentation of the nuances of issues. More will be said of their important work later in this chapter.

Corporate Outlook in America

Increasingly prevalent since the mid-1970s is a short time horizon among private business leaders—a time horizon that often does not extend beyond quarterly profits. This surprising failure to recognize the importance of the future and its consequences in making present decisions is largely a function of the "performance" orientation of Wall Street analysts, which is in part the result of business-school teaching and in part flows from the Securities and Exchange Commission requirement of quarterly reporting. By contrast, the generally longer-term view of German and Japanese firms is partly due to the way in which each society finances business. There is a dramatically higher debt-to-equity ratio in Germany and even more so in Japan, and much of the equity is held by the banks.

Very often I have been in private meetings with the heads of giant German companies when there was a call from the chairman of one of the three major German banks. It is not uncommon for the heads of banks and businesses to be in hourly contact with one another! Not only do German banks lend a much higher percentage of a firm's capital than our American business schools even today tell us is appropriate —despite German and Japanese successes with this approach—but they vote much of the equity as well. They are in intimate contact with their customers, and the industrialists in turn are able to explain in a few phone calls that they are about to take actions that will adversely affect results for the next few years but that will materially improve the position of the business over the longer term. No doubt chief executives in the U.S. would like to take the longer view too—and not fear being replaced before the expected results were achieved! As my friend Henry

Rowen, former president of the Rand Corporation, has suggested in our discussions of this difficult problem, the Glass-Stigal Act, in its separation of commercial and investment banking, may have caused as much of the problem as the institutional holding (and abrupt selling if even one quarter looks bad) of stock.

The same forces that have led management to focus on immediate financial results have encouraged firms to diversify into unknown new business areas rather than applying adequate assets and management talent to doing a better job on their existing operations. The ways in which the markets and corporate boards have often judged management performance in recent years have too often led to the increasingly uncompetitive position in which American business finds itself. In a perverse way, management has been just as effective in responding to these incentives as workers have been in responding to a clear lack of management interest in the quality of products and services. It is no accident that Thomas J. Peters and Robert H. Waterman, Jr., authors of *In Search Of Excellence*, have found such a high correlation between management emphasis on excellence and a firm's success.

The American auto industry is a dramatic example of short-sighted management:

▷ In the early 1980s, when Japan agreed to limit its exports of automobiles to the United States to 1.68 million units annually, Detroit's auto makers had the opportunity to tackle the long-term problems of organization that had enabled foreign competitors to drive a huge wedge into their sales. This was the rationale for limiting Japanese imports. Detroit rose partially to the challenge, retooling about fifty plants and rebuilding ninety more. But it was largely a missed opportunity: the American auto makers did little to use the time they had bought to really improve productivity, the major reason for Japan's extraordinary success in the U.S. market of the 1970s.

Similarly, Harley-Davidson won some short-term relief from Japanese competition that the government gave to U.S. motorcycle makers in the early 1980s. However, the company gave few hints of devising long-term strategy to improve its international competitiveness. Such behavior is unfortunately more the norm than the exception. This, in my view, is one of the reasons why even a temporary protectionist approach to industrial policy, so often advocated under varying labels, is dead wrong. The labor force is encouraged to perpetuate outmoded skills, and the "temporary respite" just keeps being extended. The short-term relief has the result of propping up the old without providing incentives to boost productivity and move ahead.

One of the great advantages of being sole stockholder in my own company is that I am free to make long-term decisions. I appreciate just how much more difficult this is in a publicly held company unless the firm has one or more highly profitable and dynamic lines—profitable enough to permit many years of investment in areas that show losses only in the development period. This condition permitted IBM to build an electronic computer business on a solid and highly profitable electromechanical punch-card machine business. Yet it also permitted the Xerox Corporation to dissipate the extraordinary earnings on its 914 copier—also a huge rental base—in all manner of unsuccessful ventures! The long-term view is a necessary but hardly a sufficient condition of success. But it is necessary—and not easy—to restore. In fact, except for our society's need for an overarching vision, I believe it is the most difficult to correct of all the systemic problems discussed in this book.

The Red Queen's Dilemma

Like American business managers, our public officials also face financial incentives that help perpetuate short-term thinking. Public contempt regularly greets the Congress' exercise of its traditional privilege of passing pork-barrel legislation. Especially at the end of congressional sessions, small, temporary coalitions appropriate funds to projects such as water development, military bases, and similar enterprises that satisfy short-term local interest but offer little to the nation in the form of long-term prospects.

The immediate political imperatives cause particular dislocation when they encounter issues that demand long-term continuity and consistency. The nation's infrastructure of bridges, highways, tunnels, water supplies, sewers, utilities, and railways is crumbling as public moneys are funneled where the political leverage is greatest. The problem is one of leadership, and that cannot come only from a Congress that bends to its local constituencies. "The Executive Branch must share responsibility for creating and managing public works more coherently than in the past," wrote Pat Choate and Susan Walters in their important study *America in Ruins*.[10]

The "here-and-now" focus is damaging not only to needed engineering projects but to normal maintenance of existing public works—which is all too evident in the condition of the facilities to which we daily entrust our lives. The collapse of the Mianus River bridge in Greenwich, Connecticut, in June 1983 left three people dead and dealt a shock that reverberated throughout the nation. Yet the real tragedy behind that incident is that the same thing could happen again: subsequent studies revealed that about one-quarter of the nation's 600,000 bridges were structurally deficient.

While federal, state, and local governments can readily find millions to invest in new structures and projects, it seems they cannot come up with the tens or hundreds of thousands necessary for maintaining our nation's infrastructure, which is steadily deteriorating. New York governor Mario Cuomo summed up the situation at a December 1983 conference on infrastructure:

> For many of us—especially those of us in government—
> learning to take the long view will mean a conversion. It will
> mean thinking and acting in a way that is, or has been,
> foreign to government. Since at least the 1930's, almost every
> governor and legislative leader has recognized the need for
> long-range planning. Yet we've remained a government that
> mostly deals with problems on an ad hoc basis, that reacts to
> crises rather than trying to anticipate and prevent them.
>   Because of the failure to plan and because of the resulting
> inability to take preventive action, we find ourselves trying to
> catch up with our problems rather than trying to control
> them: running, like the Red Queen in *Alice in Wonderland*,
> as fast as we can just to stay in place.[11]

Education and Science Policy

Equally ill fitted to the cut-and-thrust compromising of two-year congressional terms are education and science policy.

Both pursuits require firm foundations to guarantee effective results. The first real beneficiaries of Great Britain's Education Act of 1944, which was designed to open up genuine educational opportunity to all students, graduated from college in the early 1960s. The seeds of the *Apollo* spacecraft that transported men to the moon in 1969 were planted in the 1920s through the pioneering work of Robert Goddard.

Yet policymakers continue to regard education and science in the same helter-skelter fashion as other strictly political issues, adjusting budgets in response to the monthly —or daily—rise and fall of political fortunes. Many educators agreed with Harvard President Derek Bok when he protested against the precipitate cuts in student aid announced by the incoming Reagan administration in 1981:

> From a time of extreme liberality—where even the affluent could receive federal largesse—we have suddenly entered an era of severe entrenchment that promises a substantial rise in the cost of higher education for millions of students from low- and moderate-income families.
>
> This rapid swing, of course, reflects an equally profound change from a rational mood of ebullience and growth to a feeling of austerity marked by a widely shared concern that we have been living beyond our means. Such swings in national attitude are inevitable. But those who guide our country should not overestimate the permanence of these moods or exaggerate the degree of change that has actually occurred in our underlying situation. It was a mistake to use the taxpayers' money to offer subsidies to well-to-do college students.
>
> It would likewise be a mistake to move too far in the opposite direction. The United States is still the most powerful country with the largest economy in the world. It has serious problems to be sure, but it is important to be clear about what these problems are lest we prescribe false remedies that merely aggravate our ailments. [12]

Cause and effect were linked more obviously in U.S. policy on science and technology, whose federal support suffered growing erosion from its peak in the mid-1960s. At that time the U.S. was spending 3 percent of its GNP on basic research and development, compared to 1.7 percent by West Germany. By the end of the 1960s the U.S. figure had not only fallen to 2.4 percent but had also dropped below West Germany's proportion. Is it any wonder that West German automobiles had such success in U.S. markets, or that American high-energy physicists must frequently find posts in Europe in order to stay at the cutting edge of their specialties?

Environmental Impacts

The long-term horizon can be a distant one. Only recently have we begun to realize the future implications of the destruction of plants, animals, and peoples. The long-range damage that could be caused by the loss of genetic diversity and the disruption of the earth's delicate ecological balance has rarely been weighed by developers, engineers, commercial hunters, poachers, sportsmen, and others who have contributed, consciously or unconsciously, to the endangerment of species. The rapid destruction of the buffalo and the slower decline of the American Indian occurred because neither individuals nor institutions bothered about the long-term consequences of their actions.

The exact consequences of species depletion can be obscure. Those of other threats over the distant horizon are less so; yet decisions on dealing with the threats are still anchored in the short term. The issues are two forms of climatic change—natural and man-made.

According to a great deal of meteorological evidence, the earth's climate was particularly stable during the first half of the twentieth century. U.S. farmers in particular benefited from that stability. They could plant their crops in reasonable confidence that they would produce high yields in most growing seasons. But in recent years forecasters picked up hints that the climate is entering a more volatile period. No long-range forecaster can confirm the forthcoming climatic stress, let alone predict how it might alter the length of the growing seasons and otherwise affect the productivity of the fertile U.S. prairies in coming decades. Yet agricultural decisions are still being made on the basis of assumptions that the relative prosperity of U.S. farmlands will continue as before.

In the late 1970s, the Carter administration faced a similar potential problem. Preliminary data suggested that the atmosphere might be gradually heating up, due to the buildup of carbon dioxide from the burning of fossil fuels, particularly coal. If the effect is a real one, fertile regions could shift dramatically. Studies of past eras in which the climate was hotter than it is today indicate that the prairies could gradually turn into enormous dust bowls, while more northerly regions, in Canada and the USSR, become more hospitable to crops. One way of delaying the onset of the problem, experts said, would be to reduce the use of coal. That solution presents obvious short-term disadvantages in a world that still remembers the oil crisis of 1973–74. Whether the long-term possibility of agricultural disruption should influence the short-term decisions on energy use remains a matter for debate.

Lack of effective foresight can draw harsh penalties. To wit:

▷ In 1971 the Independent Petrochemical Corporation of St. Louis subcontracted with Russell Bliss, a waste-oil dealer in Missouri, who received a contract to dispose of wastes from the North Eastern Pharmaceutical and Chemical Corporation. Bliss used a mixture of the wastes, which contained the toxic chemical dioxin, and oil to hold down dust at a stable near Moscow Mills, Missouri. Shortly afterward humans and animals around the area began to suffer strange illnesses, presumably as a result of exposure to the dioxin. The eventual result was a $2.68 million settlement by Independent twelve years after the original "disposal" of the toxins. That sequence of events would have been hard to predict. But it's surprising that no one realized at the time that other parts of Missouri had been sprayed with dioxin-contaminated oil. It should have been possible, in the middle 1970s, to alert the public to the kind of danger that led to a federal buyout of the town of Times Beach, Missouri, in 1983.

Similarly, the saga of Love Canal could not have been foreseen in its entirety, but informed, intelligent forecasting could have suggested some of the implications of the toxic wastes buried beneath the small region of Niagara Falls, New York:

▷ Hooker Chemical Corporation buried 21,800 tons of waste on the site between 1942 and 1953 before handing the site over to local authorities. Hooker insisted that it warned the town of possible danger. Nevertheless the municipality built single-family homes nearby. Over the next quarter of a century residents complained that they suffered skin rashes and unexplained illnesses; but the complaints were ignored. Only in 1978, when the wastes started bubbling to the surface and epidemiological studies showed a link between the wastes and residents' health, did the authorities recognize the problem. By then the situation demanded drastic, and expensive, action, including the evacuation and relocation of many residents.

In the interim Hooker had been bought by Occidental Petroleum, which spent millions of dollars on cleaning up the dump—after Hooker itself had spent untold millions of dollars and years of management diversion in handling the problem. (The need to incorporate sociopolitical factors into business decision making is covered in more detail in Chapter 7.)

An even more threatening type of waste, from nuclear power plants, revealed the breadth of information necessary for accurate long-term forecasting. Nuclear engineers have always contended that disposing of radioactive wastes is technologically simple. The wastes have merely to be chemically combined with an inert ceramic or glass and then buried deep in a stable geological region. What U.S. nuclear regulators and industrialists did not predict was public skepticism about that assertion—and the determination of local communities that, however safe they might be, nuclear burial sites should not be located within their own boundaries. As a result the issue of nuclear waste disposal remains one of the most intractable on the political agenda. (In its leasing of disposal rights for European nuclear waste, China may well have sensed the opportunity to capitalize on a realistic view of a risk, as opposed to emotional views turned to political intransigence.)

The problem in many of these situations is the emotional and political difficulty of striking a balance between probable risk and prudent action. We lean toward extremes: of no early action, when some action could head off a potential crisis; and of extreme overreaction when the problem is far advanced. It is hard enough to learn in time about long-lead-time biological dangers. Again, our focus should be on *process*—on building in a review procedure as science provides us with additional insights into the consequences of our continuing industrialization.

Present Impact of Discernible Change

We must also consider the complement to long-term thinking: the process of peering over the time horizon to anticipate the future consequences of present decisions. Many problems simply do not lend themselves to forecasting; no mid-1950s projection could have included an overnight quadrupling of oil prices, or the social divisiveness of Vietnam, or Watergate. But there is a great deal we could know about the consequences of many current actions that we do not really consider when taking them.

Determining the present impact of discernible future change is far from an exact art, much less a science, but it is still far more within our grasp even in fast-changing high technology than it used to be.

▷ In 1963 I happened to talk in succession the same morning with two teams of consultants in our New York office. One was helping one of the largest users of computers at the time, Lockheed Aircraft Company, in planning future strategy with regard to the role of computers in engineering and manufacturing. The other was working with Univac—as it happened, a major Lockheed supplier —on long-term product planning. The problem was that the first team was working with the publicly available forecasts of all the major suppliers. In the several cases in addition to Univac, they did not happen to have access yet to much longer-term and basically different product strategies that other parts of our company were working on for these very companies!

It was that day I decided we all needed a program in which the impact on current planning decisions of the discernible future change in the technology and economics of computers could be addressed. Today the Diebold Research Program has passed its twentieth birthday and has over two hundred clients, major public as well as private, European as well as U.S. users and major manufacturers of computers. Our firm does the staff work, and frequent interchanges—there are working sessions in seven or eight countries each month—do a great deal of good precisely because all concerned are able to incorporate into current decisions discernible consequences of future change.

101

If this is achievable on a private basis, think how much could be accomplished by all the many public and international institutions! Not that this is a perfect solution; but I know from my own experience that, especially in a rapidly changing field, much grief and cost can accrue to all involved where there is little or no attempt to consider the future systematically in current decision making. We need more such efforts in many areas.

Unintended Side Effects

Inherent in all decision making is the problem of unexpected consequences. The more profound and longer-term the decision, the greater the possibility of horrendous side effects, often of greater consequence than the original act.

▷ The British Raj at the turn of the century completed irrigation projects that made the Indus Valley the most prosperous farmland on the Indian subcontinent, but prodigious labors by Pakistani and American scientists have been necessary in recent years to keep the land in use as the salts rise into the soil.

▷ Half a century ago the Welland Canal let the sea lamprey into the Great Lakes, destroying, among others, the shad and the trout.

▷ The attempt to farm intensively west of the hundredth meridian gave America a dust bowl in the 1930s and sent the "Okies" fleeing to California.

But man has more muscle today. He can push harder. On the curve extrapolating the sort of behavior that once made local disaster lies a point at which global cataclysm must be assigned a probability.

Rather technical political decisions, made with the highest motives, may produce frightening consequences when amplified by the pervasiveness of government. Even so earnest and obviously positive a policy as the elimination of corruption from municipal government has turned out to have severely negative secondary effects: bureaucratization has made government more remote and less human, while the imposition of educational standards as employment pre-requisites has made it more difficult for the inner-city dwellers, many of them wholly competent for the jobs, to move into government services.

Unexpected consequences to short-term decisions are by no means limited to domestic or operational aspects of day-to-day government. Following are a few recent foreign-policy examples:

▷ The last-minute modifications and vacillations that characterized President John Kennedy's handling of an Eisenhower/Nixon undertaking that should never have been attempted resulted in a great reinforcement of Castro's popularity, just as President Jimmy Carter's handling of the Iranian rescue attempt inadvertently bolstered the Ayatollah's.

▷ In a demonstration of what my late friend Herman Kahn once described as a propensity to lose nerve *after* a crisis is over, and what Robert Lovett has called "post-crisis decisions," President Kennedy reached agreements giving Cuba a kind of protected status in what must simply have been his understandable sense of relief after having averted the grave possibility of setting off a nuclear exchange in the Cuban Missile Crisis.

▷ President Lyndon Johnson's decision not to impose new taxes to support the Vietnam War in order to simultaneously move ahead with the Great Society programs inflicted incalculable damage, the burden of which we all continue to bear—but not as much of a burden as to those who were supposed to have benefited from the programs.

▷ The U.S.'s post-Afghanistan decision to press our European allies to withdraw from the Soviet pipeline deal (a) didn't work, (b) didn't hinder or hurt the project, and (c) hurt only the U.S., in ways not yet entirely apparent with respect to the alliance.

▷ President Carter's eagerness to see Somoza unseated reflected a remarkable inattention to the consequences of what should have been one of the more obvious "what if" situations.

▷ President Reagan's decision to continue with his tax cuts long   **103** after it became apparent that he was not going to be able to produce comparable cuts in spending will have negative secondary and tertiary effects on all of us long after this book is read.

Unexpected and second- and third-order consequences of public as well as private decisions would make considerably better Ph.D. theses than many titles I read these days!

A principal worry of our age is the destruction we can inflict on others and ourselves through our killing devices, from nuclear weaponry to deadly pesticides. But perhaps the greatest dangers of all are from secondary effects of benevolent enterprises and good intentions.

▷ In the Soviet Union, planners proposed a macro project to redirect the flow of the three great Siberian rivers from the Arctic to the shrinking inland seas of Asia. The gains in terms of hydroelectric power, irrigation, and caviar would have been immense. But the cessation of so much fresh water inflow *could* have changed the salinity of the Arctic Sea. The ice cap over the North Pole is unstable even now—half of the Arctic ice melts every summer—and a saltier Arctic might melt entirely, bringing a new ice age elsewhere on the globe.

▷ International agencies went quite far a decade ago in proposing a dam in what was then called Stanleyville, the Congo, which would back up a lake covering one-tenth the surface of Africa. Irrigation channels from such a lake could make the Sahara a vegetable garden, but the lake would also have changed the climate of the Mediterranean basin and perhaps even the worldwide pattern of absorption and reflection of solar energy.

Unexpected side effects are not the only complication to short-term decision making. There are others as well—cases in which what is best for the individual can be bad for the many.

By now it should come as no surprise to the reader that I am a strong believer in the value of market forces and the desirability, as far as possible, of limiting government action to ensure conditions that allow the market to work. As Professor Garrett Hardin points out in *The Tragedy of the Com-*

mons, each farmer entitled to use an overgrazed pasture will still be better off as an individual if he adds to his herd —until all the farmers together, each of them acting in proper self-interest, destroy the pasture that supports them. This is, of course, a part of the ecological problems and the decision structure we establish to handle it.

And the complications do not stop there. In any complex system the optimum results calculated by component individuals or organizations may not be, in sum, the optimum results for the system as a whole. Thus Boeing could decide (correctly) that its best interests are in building the 747; and the airlines could decide (maybe correctly, maybe not) that their best interests are served by buying the 747. But the owners and operators of ground facilities, subject to different constraints, production problems, finance arrangements, and time horizons, could not make any effective decision at all within the lead time allowed. As a result, passengers for some time had no way to board giant 747s except by climbing outdoor ladders—often after descending from gateways they had to climb!

When the problem with which we are dealing is not just an annoyance but a threat to our environment, there is need for public attention to harnessing the incentive systems built into the market economy. Milton Katz of the Harvard Law School has pointed out that paper mills have been *encouraged* to foul the waters, and power plants to poison the air, because the costs of pollution have been externalized—loaded onto anonymous others—by a "legal order." Relatively minor changes in our legal order (Katz suggested merely the extension of liability under the old law of torts) would internalize these costs to an enterprise and therefore might induce much different behavior through the operation of the self-interest that is the surest and strongest engine of change.

Governments, even democratic governments, can plan for the long term.

▷ The Dutch add farmland by a generation's work for the enjoyment of future generations.

▷ The British and Swedes build new towns over the course of a decade.

▷ We in the U.S. build great dams and road systems and water-ways (although the controlling motive at the time of action is all too often the immediate increases in jobs and real estate value that will accrue to a particular congressman's constituency).

Businessmen clearly prefer quick, safe payouts; when money is tight, short-term interest rates rise above long-term though risks are less in the short term, mostly because demand is greater.

Coordination and Planning

Coordination of decisions within a system is certainly not impossible. However, in the U.S. we are reluctant, on a public level, to get involved in that very act of consideration, otherwise known as planning. It is a thorny dilemma. Those who want no part of planning fear it for the very good reason that it might open the door to government direction of investment (just as with industrial policy).

▷ I had never realized the depth of emotion aroused by the subject until testifying one day before the Joint Economic Committee of the House and Senate. The bill under consideration was the Humphrey-Javits national planning bill. I was one of three witnesses seated in equally spaced chairs in front of the committee's concave bench. I thought my testimony had expressed a considerable caution on ways to keep government coordination from turning into government control. But when Senator Humphrey went on at length about agreeing to modify the bill as I had suggested, the then chairman of General Motors, sitting to my right, moved his chair some distance away from me!

Anything that smacks of public planning is a difficult subject in the U.S. Yet there is clearly need for more coordination, at least with respect to market incentives and disincentives in terms of tax policy, regulations, and so on.

Energy has provided a consistent blind spot for planners. An example is the state of the U.S. Synthetic Fuels Corporation, a government-supported body created in 1980 with the aim of reducing U.S. dependence on imported oil. Shortly after the corporation was formed, the costs of synthetic fuels started to soar, while the price of oil stabilized. In May 1982 Exxon Corporation announced its withdrawal from the Colony shale oil program in western Colorado, one of the major synfuels projects. The withdrawal, taken for compelling economic reasons, led analysts to conclude that the synfuel era was over almost as soon as it had started. Realistic long-range planning might have made a difference.

An even more expensive blind spot may be the reluctance of the U.S. to convert to the metric system, a necessity for a nation that must export to a world that predominantly measures in meters and grams. Conversion efforts have progressed at a pace no faster than a few millimeters per decade. True, wines and carbonated soft drinks now come in liter bottles, occasional gasoline stations measure out their sales by the liter, and the computer industry has largely converted to metric measure. But the efforts of the Department of Transportation to include kilometers with miles on highway signs were stymied by public opposition, the construction industry continues to deal in feet and inches, and retail stores insist on maintaining their old English measurements for fear of customers' disapproval. Would not a longer time perspective indicate that conversion is inevitable—and that "sooner" is less costly than "later"?

Many of the coordination problems we so often consider beyond solution are in fact less difficult than those already solved. What we lack is a *process* within which they can be seized, nourished with information, and grown under controlled conditions to the size they will assume in that future which is the only reality; the present being already gone.

Our opportunities to control information are growing today at least as rapidly as our power to do harm to ourselves and our neighbors. We can make what Herman Kahn has called "surprise-free" projections—predictions of what the world will be like if what we expect to happen does indeed happen. (This is a lot trickier than will be believed by those who read as they run.) Moreover, we can analyze with some confidence what changes in our projections would result from specified "surprises." Ramifications through the system are at least dimly ascertainable for any surprise, and a rough cost figure can be placed on provision for contingencies.

The computer has multiplied the power of our minds as manufactured energy has multiplied the power of our muscles. Even at its present level of development, the computer offers not only ways to answer set questions but ways to develop questions and to find out through interaction with the machine what information is needed but is still lacking to rationalize the decision-making effort. Whatever other national goals we may decide on, the first—because it is necessary for achievement of all the others—must be the development of processes by which the information-handling capacity of the computer is employed routinely to aid the judgment of those in enterprise and government whose decisions affect the lives of others. It can help enormously in taking longer-term consequences into consideration—but to do so we need to restructure our decision processes, and that means to link motivations and incentives to the long term as well as to the short term.

While trout fishing at my country home, my friend John McCloy told me that when he was running Germany, as Allied High Commissioner, he always asked himself a few basic questions before making any decision. That was a period in which some of the most successful decisions of our time were made, and in his role as commissioner McCloy contributed substantially to their formulation. His method therefore bears scrutiny. No matter how high-level the matter and regardless of the subject, he would ask:

1. Does it make sense?
2. Is it fair?

Even on projects of a smaller scale than reconstructing the Western world, we might do well to apply these simple criteria to our routine decision processes.

Institutes of the Future

Can we prevent the future from surprising us? Or must we conclude that the framers of our Constitution were the last group of politicians to take a good long-term view? Consider, for example, the prescient view of John Adams, in a letter to his wife, Abigail, from Paris: "I must study Politicks and War that my sons may have liberty to study Mathematicks and Philosophy. My sons ought to study Mathematicks and Philosophy, Geography, natural History, Naval Architecture, navigation, Commerce and Agriculture, in order to give their Children a right to study Painting, Poetry, Musick, Architecture, Statuary, Tapestry and Porcelaine."[13] George Will's comment on this passage is illuminating: "Adams makes the public-spirited modern man's best case for politics. It is not good, but it makes many good things possible."[14] Can we not, today, duplicate Adams' long-term view—for an institutional framework that embraces our children's and our children's children's destiny?

While, as we have seen, strong emotions and proper skepticism surround the term "national planning," we do need some imaginative political inventing to allow us to evaluate the alternative demands on our limited resources, to assign priorities to those ends, and to create incentives and disincentives so that the play of forces in the marketplace occurs within a framework of politically agreed-on direction.

One example of the type of initiative I favor is a series of what I have called Institutes of the Future. They would use a diversity of forecasting techniques to indicate the likely consequences of specific institutional actions. To insulate them from special interests, political pressures, and short-term thinking, the institutes would be publicly funded and managed independently of changing governments and one another, subject to the direction of an independent board. The plurality and secure independence of such groups are absolutely essential. Contrary opinions and the means of sustaining them independent of the current political outlook should be encouraged by long-term independent funding.

The current impact on current problems and contemplated legislation of discernible future change would be within their purview—one of the reasons why multiple independent institutions are needed. Most important, the Institutes of the Future must have no mandate to spend money other than in their own direct operations; spending power would automatically make the institutes into congressional honeypots! Instead, their purpose would be to provide a series of constantly updated independent views of the future for the use of policy makers.

Producing distant early-warning systems through Institutes of the Future and building systems into our institutions for considering such intelligence is indeed a formidable task. But it is far more simple than devising viable trade-off mechanisms for prioritizing a set of goals based on the divergent intelligence that will be produced.

The Dangers of Forecasting

In advocating a serious effort in this quarter, I recognize just how dangerous forecasting, let alone analyzing the future, can be. Arthur Clarke's *Profiles of the Future* provides some cautionary examples:

> . . . When gas company securities nosedived in 1878 because Edison . . . announced that he was working on the incandescent lamp, the British Parliament set up a committee to look into the matter . . . The distinguished witnesses reported, to the relief of the gas companies, that Edison's ideas were "good enough for our transatlantic friends . . . but unworthy of practical or scientific men."
> When the existence of the 200-mile-range V-2 was disclosed to an astonished world, there was considerable speculation about intercontinental missiles. This was firmly squashed by Dr. Vannevar Bush, the civilian general of the United States scientific war effort, in evidence before a Senate committee on December 3, 1945. Listen:
> "I say, technically, I don't think anyone in the world knows how to do such a thing, and I feel confident that it will not be done for a very long period of time to come . . . I think we can leave that out of our thinking. I wish the American public would leave it out of their thinking." [15]

Somewhat earlier, Winston Churchill's science adviser, Lord Cherwell, had advised the British government that the V-2 itself was only a propaganda rumor!

Soon after President Eisenhower announced the U.S. satellite program, the Astronomer Royal of Great Britain, when asked his opinion, stated: "Space travel is utter bilge." [16]

Lord Rothschild offers us this perspective on charting the future:

> But futurologists have not always been too successful when peering into the crystal ball. In 1925, for example, Bertrand Russell pronounced that "physical science is thus approaching the stage when it will be complete and therefore uninteresting." It would be a long job to list the advances in physical science since then. J. B. S. Haldane, one of England's brightest and most eccentric scientists, wrote that he was satisfied from thermodynamic calculations that the energy inside an atom could never be harnessed. Similarly, Rutherford did not believe that atom-splitting would ever be put to practical use (or misuse, for that matter). [17]

A CIA report in 1977 predicted that by 1985 the Soviet bloc would "require a minimum of 3.5 million barrels of imported oil every day" and that 1983 production by OPEC countries would be over 40 million barrels daily. As I write, in early 1984, the Soviets are exporting over a million barrels a day, and OPEC production lingers at about 13 million barrels daily.

The Club of Rome report of 1972, with its doomsday scenarios based on a simple extrapolation from a minimum of data, did a tremendous disservice to the concept of rational forecasting. Nevertheless there is a great deal we can and must learn from exploration of the future, and it should play more than a casual role in our public-policy process. In going about this, I suggest that we take an innovative approach to the kind of individuals to set to work on such tasks. Fred Pohl, a leader in science fiction, has said: "It isn't really science fiction's business to describe what science is going to find. It is much more science fiction's business to say what the human race will make of it all. In fact, this is the thing—the one thing, maybe the only thing—that science fiction does better than any other tool available—it gives us a look at the consequences. And it does it superbly." [18]

A full consideration of future prospects requires the kind of speculative imagination—together with what Coleridge poetically called "willing suspension of disbelief"—which can only be found in the realm of science fiction.

In his *Profiles of the Future* Clarke gives a wonderful example in support of the role of imagination in any such work:

> Friar Roger Bacon (1214–1292) imagined optical instruments and mechanically propelled boats and flying machines—devices far beyond the existing or even foreseeable technology of his time. It is hard to believe that these words were written in the 13th century:
> "Instruments may be made by which the largest ships, with only one man guiding them, will be carried with greater velocity than if they were full of sailors. Chariots may be constructed that will move with incredible rapidity without the help of animals. Instruments of flying may be formed in which a man, sitting at his ease and meditating on any subject, may beat the air with his artificial wings after the manner of birds . . . as also machines which will enable men to walk at the bottom of the seas. . . ."[19]

This passage is a triumph of imagination over hard fact. Everything in it has come true, yet at the time it was written it was more an act of faith than of logic. Probably all long-range prediction, if it is to be accurate, must be of this nature.

Coping with the Future

Franklin Delano Roosevelt dreamed up a simple but remarkably effective method of influencing the future. In 1932, during campaign trips, he was struck by the dust bowl of the great plains. Between 1935 and 1942, under a program that he started when he became President, more than 222 million trees were planted from the Dakotas to the Texas Panhandle, in a belt two hundred miles wide which divided the tall-grass eastern prairies from the short-grass western prairies. Over almost half a century the trees have protected humans, animals, and crops from the high winds, winter cold, and summer heat of the plains.

Can our late-twentieth-century institutions apply similarly imaginative thinking to the future? I think that the political process can adopt methods of looking ahead realistically.

▷ Congressional bills, I think, should carry the equivalent of "environmental impact statements"—projecting costs, examining side effects, and raising questions about long-range consequences. A lot can be done via legislative procedures to require a statement of expected consequences to be attached to the bill (produced by the Congressional Budget Office) and a mandatory review of each at specified intervals, with public disclosure of findings. *Ex post facto* review of laws should include a systematic procedure to compare the costs, outlays, and assumptions of the original bills with actual results. Former comptroller general Elmer B. Staats in recent years has called for an annual report to the President on economic/social indicators and trends. My view is that such a report should be submitted every other year—by an entirely fresh staff that does not share the same tired assumptions and prejudices of its predecessors.

Would longer terms for public officials help? For the best of them, clearly yes. Yet how many of our recent Presidents would we have wanted for really long terms? There is no question as to the negative consequences of elected officials' short attention span with respect to vital long-term issues during an election period, not only in the case of Presidents but of congressmen—and "election period" is now at least two years for Presidents.

Former secretary of state Cyrus Vance has observed that during the last two years of the presidency the campaign for reelection and the need to make politically attractive gestures throw our nation's foreign policy into dangerous disarray. With short terms of office, politicians have little incentive to consider the long-term impact of issues or even to worry about problems that are unlikely to surface more than two years into the future. The prospect of short-term political gain frequently obscures inherent difficulties in seemingly attractive programs.

Should the term of the President be lengthened? The most recurrent proposal is that for a six-year term. Ted Sorensen has expressed the following thoughts on this: **113**

Once the Congress, public and bureaucracy know that he will not be President again, will they be less cooperative, rendering him an ineffective "lame duck"? The only full Presidential term in our history known from the start to be the incumbent's last four years in the White House was the second term of Dwight D. Eisenhower. The first President to be affected by the Twenty-Second Amendment to the Constitution, banning a Presidential third term, "Ike," in the view of both contemporary politicians and historians, was no crippled water fowl from January 1957 until January 1961. Even though the opposition party controlled both houses of Congress, his second term was no less effective than his first. After all, his power under the Constitution to conduct foreign affairs, to initiate legislation, to formulate the Budget, to control appointments, to award patronage, to bestow favors and to appeal to the public was undiminished—as it would be for a one-term coalition President. His policies had the same political basis and the same public appeal as ever. If anything, his ability to reach beyond his party was enhanced by the knowledge that he was not speaking as a potential candidate for re-election.[20]

I should think that a good case exists for lengthening the terms of congressmen to four years, but I'm not yet convinced of the benefits of lengthening the terms of others. A lot can be done to lengthen the time span of elected officials by other means—starting with an excellent but difficult opportunity for the media to focus on the quality and time horizon of public decisions and votes.

Recently the U.S. has shown that it can invent new political institutions to predict, and react to, the future. Before the 1974 Congressional Budget Act, no regular mandated procedure required Congress to even think about federal revenues and expenditures or the over-all consequences of congressional actions on spending and taxes. In fact, Congress had no systematic means of knowing how any particular vote would influence the budgetary equation. So Byzantine was the procedure that many bills were not approved until much or all of the fiscal year to which they pertained had gone by. As a result of the 1974 act, Congress can now take a coordinated approach to the budget.

Beyond the advantage of setting up a rational method of

approving the national budget—which has worked satisfactorily if not strikingly well—the 1974 act created a new institution with a long-term purpose. The Congressional Budget Office now serves as Congress' main source of fiscal information, analysis, and mathematics in all budgetary affairs. Its function is to evaluate and inform Congress of the consequences of proposed legislative measures. In addition, it is asked to conduct numerous analyses of current public-policy problems.[21] Answerable to Congress alone, the CBO avoids the short-term proprietary view of the budget that is common inside the Executive branch of government. As a continuing body, it operates outside the constraints of party affiliation and the limited terms of elected office. (More was said on the CBO as a priority-setting mechanism in the earlier chapter "Vetoes and Priorities".)

The substantial growth of the professional staff of the General Accounting Office, which reports to the comptroller general of the United States, who himself reports to the Congress but is appointed by the President for a fifteen-year term, is also noteworthy. Here again, evaluations of government operations and of public-policy programs by an agency independent of the Executive branch of the government allow for more perspective. A similar example would be the gradual development of the analytical staff attached to the Legislative Reference Service. And in the scientific and technical area, the National Academy of Sciences is regularly called on by the government to evaluate public-policy problems.

These examples fall far short of what I believe to be needed in coping with the future. But they do indicate that at least *some* of our institutions are taking seriously the need for the long-term view. I will conclude with a few more detailed case examples of institutional innovation. Each provides a hopeful view of the ability of our institutions, both public and private, to take a longer look.

Case:
Public Agenda Foundation

The Public Agenda Foundation is a unique example of institutional inventing at its finest. Founded in 1975 by Cyrus Vance and

Daniel Yankelovich, the organization's mandate is to foster meaningful debate and dialogue on vital national issues. This is a double task: to help the average citizen make better decisions on important issues and to help leaders in government and business better understand public attitudes. The crucial aspect of its work, as I follow it from their Executive Committee, is its ability to communicate the *complexity* of important issues to the public—rather than polarizing every issue in the "pro vs. con" or "point counterpoint" formats that are so popular with the media, particularly television.

An illustration of the Public Agenda's work is "Health Vote 82," a model communications campaign, in Des Moines, Iowa, on the complexities of one selected issue—the rising cost of health care —over a two-and-a-half-month period. The campaign was a deliberate effort to involve all the community's media outlets, community-wide membership groups, and institutions in a ten-week concentrated discussion of a vital issue that was, at the outset, ill understood. Public Agenda's small staff prepared and distributed public education materials: a thirty-minute film shown on all TV stations, a special newspaper supplement, a brochure, and other print materials designed to help clarify the choices people have in controlling health-care costs. (Although prepared as a "discussion starter," the film, *What Price Health Care?,* was subsequently aired nationally on PBS and honored by the American Film Festival as an outstanding documentary.)

Des Moines area schools, churches, unions, clubs, and other groups sponsored close to two hundred meetings, at which seven thousand to eight thousand citizens viewed and debated the film. The "Health Vote" film was also aired on every local TV and cable outlet. The Des Moines *Register* covered campaign events and published a series of editorials. Virtually every public-affairs program on Des Moines radio or television devoted programs to health-care costs over the course of the campaign.

The results were spectacular. At the culmination of the campaign more than thirty thousand Des Moines residents completed and returned a mail-in ballot on health-care costs—a response six times greater than anticipated. "Before" and "after" surveys made it clear that residents had participated in unexpected numbers and that their knowledge of the issue and their opinions about possible solutions had changed as they became more familiar with the choices available to them. Through the debate process they had reached a workable consensus on steps that can be taken to control health costs. In fact, Des Moines community leaders are convinced that the campaign was largely responsible for recent legislative and other initiatives on health-care costs.

This experiment shows that the public can and will make informed decisions on complex issues. Initiatives, such as that of Public Agenda, to raise the level of public debate demonstrate that the public *can* take a long-term view on issues of vital national concern.

Case:
Monsanto's "Early-Warning System"

The health and environmental hazards inherent in scientific and technological advancement could prove to be risky business to a company such as Monsanto. The giant chemical company has formalized a system to identify unacceptable risks early in a new product's development and to blow the whistle on potential carcinogens—*before* the product goes into production.

At various stages in a product's development the company brings together knowledgeable scientists, doctors, hygienists, chemists, safety experts, epidemiologists, toxicologists, and other experts from within and outside its ranks to conduct technology risk reviews. John Hanley, Monsanto's chairman and chief executive officer, says:

> We try to eliminate all of the possible surprises. At every major stage of research and development, we formally assess the hazards of a new material or process. We look at things like the known or expected impurities of a new product, its expected toxicity (what technical people call "acute" and "chronic" toxicity), foreseeable dangers in disposal, and the ability of customers to use the material properly and safely. So these are our preliminary assessments of the hazards—any effects on the health of workers, users, the public at large, the natural environment, the chain of life.[22]

So successful is the process that "surprises" have been almost eliminated. Several products that were tempting because of the need they would fill were aborted in the early stages by the technical staff.

Monsanto's long-term outlook is also a part of the over-all corporate approach. In 1977 the company established an environmental policy staff and an environmental policy committee, which together form a system of checks and balances to head off crises as new products go forward. The committees provide corporate guidance for managing Monsanto's impact on the environment and act as a "watchdog" internally and an early-warning system externally.

Monsanto's initiative is an instructive example of institutional invention in the private sector. The following example gives me hope that such long-term thinking will not be confined to isolated companies.

Case:
The GM Job Bias Settlement

In October 1983, the General Motors Corporation made a deal with the United Auto Workers. GM agreed to pay $42.5 million to resolve a decade-old complaint charging employment discrimination against blacks, Hispanics, and women. Federal officials called it the largest out-of-court settlement of an employment discrimination case in history.

What was even more unusual, though, was that the settlement was, according to a UAW spokesman, "more prospective than retroactive." [23] Rather than assigning guilt or penalizing General Motors (which did not admit any wrongdoing), the focus of the agreement was to improve present and future career opportunities for women and minorities—both present and potential GM employees. In one unusual provision, GM agreed to provide $15 million in endowments and scholarships to colleges and technical schools, primarily to help GM employees and their families. Minorities and women would be given preference in the distribution of these educational assistance funds.

The company provided an additional $8.9 million for a training program for 250 women and minority employees in white-collar jobs, after which they would be eligible for promotion. In all other training for salaried positions, the company agreed to numerical goals for members of the "affected class": 15 percent for minorities, 25 percent for women.

Several millions of dollars were set aside for back pay and other relief to resolve individual discrimination complaints. However, the principal intent of the settlement was training and career development for women and minority groups at all levels of the company

118

over a five-year period. Rather than focusing on damages, in the form of a purely cash settlement, the agreement aimed at *undoing* damages.

The GM settlement was achieved without long, costly litigation. Had the company gone to court, it would have paid far more than the $42.5 million settlement in lawyers' fees alone. In a more far-sighted approach, the funds went toward improving the future condition of an entire class of working people.

IV The Misrule of Law

The U.S. legal system, the safeguard of individual rights, has become in many ways a roadblock in the efforts to make our society work and ironically, in the process, a roadblock to justice. Costly, complex, and lengthy court procedures further victimize the victims, to the apparent benefit of no one but the lawyers. A system I was brought up to venerate—my father was a lawyer—has grown totally out of hand. For lack of better institutional alternatives, the courts are also deciding complex new societal issues that they are ill-equipped to address, thus further burdening the system. Meanwhile manpower and other national resources are being drained from more productive ventures to feed a mammoth and growing legal apparatus. How do we preserve every citizen's right to a "day in court"—while not perverting that right in a way that makes virtually any undertaking cumbersome? What creative alternatives to litigation can we develop, so as to cure ourselves of this peculiarly American disease?

Case:
The Van Gemert vs. Boeing Case

In March 1966 Boeing placed newspaper advertisements calling for the redemption of certain convertible debentures. Debenture holders had until the end of the month to either redeem their debentures or convert them into stock, worth almost three times as much. By the end of March many of the holders had done nothing, and Boeing took the position that they had lost their right to convert.

William Van Gemert was the first debenture holder to sue, and when other suits followed, they were consolidated into a class action. The judge presiding over the case, the late Sylvester Ryan, who died during the course of this litigation, appointed several lawyers to represent the class as a plaintiff's committee, as is common practice. They were responsible for running the litigation.

Eighteen years later, the case was still droning on, and became one of the twenty-five suits highlighted by *The American Lawyer* in 1982 in a study called "Endless Litigation." Ironically, the case actually got off to a speedy start. Certifying the class, which is often a protracted process, took only three months. Discovery, another ostensible area of delay, took two years, which, by today's standards, is not inordinately long. The case began to drag in 1969 when a breach developed among the plaintiff's lawyers. They couldn't agree on the preparation of a stipulation that Judge Ryan had ordered to gather as many facts as possible in the case to expedite trial. Each lawyer had a different strategy for preparing the memo. The stipulation was not filed until 1971. While the stipulation had taken two years to prepare, the trial itself lasted only three and a half days.

More delay set in after the nonjury trial was over. Judge Ryan, who was old and ailing, took almost a year to issue an opinion, and found for Boeing on all counts. The case went to the U.S. Court of Appeals for the Second Circuit, which eventually reversed the case and remanded it to Ryan for calculation of damages. The appeal was delayed by the fact that the plaintiff's lawyers, still wrangling among themselves, submitted two different briefs and demanded separate oral arguments. It took Ryan another year to take any action on the remand.

Although the merits of the case had been decided by 1976, an entirely new dispute developed among the plaintiff's lawyers over attorneys' fees. This dispute would drag on for five more years. The lawyers also wanted to take their fees out of the unclaimed portion of the award, a move that Boeing opposed. It was this part of the case that went before the U.S. Supreme Court. Presumably the lawyers wanted their fees to be paid out of the unclaimed portion of the award, because they were asking for an amount— over $2 million—that was almost equal to the amount of claims by the plaintiff. As one of the lawyers on the plaintiff's committee conceded, no judge was going to give the lawyers their full fee request if it eliminated the recovery for their clients.

The lawyers, each of whom wanted to give the oral argument, **121** turned the Supreme Court appeal into a travesty. To determine who would do the honors, they resorted to tossing a coin. Because of its many appeals and long delays, Justice Rehnquist sardonically referred to the case as "not merely Van Gemert, but Van Gemert III." The court ruled that the attorneys' fees would be paid out of both portions of the award, unclaimed and claimed, on a pro rata basis.

The last, and still unsolved problem was to locate claimants for the unclaimed portion of the fee award. The Long Island lawyer whom Judge Ryan appointed as special master to carry out this function took more than a year to find fewer than one-quarter of the claimants. Such searches are supposed to take about six months. At the time that this story was reported in *The American Lawyer* in July 1982 no debenture holder had yet been compensated, because the special master had not yet completed his search—more than three years after his appointment.

When *The American Lawyer*'s story appeared, the lawyers in the case, including the special master, had all been paid, but none of their clients had received a dime—even though the shareholders who had filed the class action received a favorable judgment in 1976. The claim amounts to almost $10 million. By early 1984 a new special master had been appointed and more than half of the debenture holders had been paid. However, Boeing's and the plaintiff's lawyers were still arguing over what should be done with the unclaimed portion of the reward.

Case:
The Pine Tar Dispute

On July 24, 1983, the Kansas City Royals were playing a routine mid-season game against the New York Yankees. The Royals were on the verge of winning the game on a two-out, two-run homer that George Brett hit in the ninth inning.

The home run was challenged by the Yankees' irascible manager, Billy Martin, and was disallowed by the umpires, who claimed that Brett had a few too many inches of pine tar (a substance used to enhance a batter's grip) on his bat. So Brett was out, after all, and the game went to the Yankees, 4–3. Then the president of the American League stepped in and reinstated the home run a few days later after a protest was lodged by the Royals.

This meant that the Royals now led, 5–4, and that the game had to be completed.

The Yankees, however, wanted a long-scheduled day off and opposed resumption of the game, scheduled for mid-August. Conveniently, a few Yankee fans had filed suit in New York in protest over the Yankees' plan to charge additional admission for the completion game instead of honoring tickets to the original bout. Ironically, although the Yankees were the defendants in the case brought by the fans, their battery of seven lawyers also opposed the playing of the game and were taking the same side as the fans, arguing that the stadium could not provide the security force needed to protect the fans during the extra inning or so that the game might take.

On August 17, 1983, the Yankees and the fans won the first round of the battle when a State Supreme Court judge issued a temporary injunction preventing the game from being resumed until the merits of the fans' case could be heard. (By that time the baseball season might have long been over!) The next day, after an hour-long hearing in a circus atmosphere, an appellate judge reversed the order and mandated "Play ball!"

The rest is anticlimax. The much debated and litigated Pine Tar Game took exactly nine minutes and forty-one seconds. Four batters batted and four outs were made. The 5–4 score remained the same. George Brett, the player who had sparked the whole affair, wasn't even there for the game.

Clearly, the issue of whether or not to make the Yankees play ball never belonged in the courts and should have been resolved within baseball's own formidable bureaucracy. Instead the matter, like so many others, drifted into the courts, and drifted out, just as aimlessly. In a sardonic postmortem *The New York Times* wrote:

A forest of trees were felled to produce the yellow pads of the lawyers, veins of coal were depleted to light the offices of baseball executives plotting late into the night, and underground seas of fossil fuel were diminished to transport the Kansas City Royals, the New York Yankees, a herd of journalists and a few fans back into Yankee Stadium last evening for a short and peaceful coda to the fabled pine-tar incident . . .

This expenditure of precious natural and human resources took 25 days of jaw-wagging and statement-making that overshadowed everything else that took place in baseball and —at times, it seemed—the globe.[1]

Case:
The Modern-Day Orlando

I had the opportunity to observe, firsthand, the wasteland that our legal system has become in the government's massive antitrust case against IBM, which was dropped, mercifully, in 1982 after thirteen years. I had never even been in a courtroom until the opening day of that trial, when I entered the New York courtroom of Federal District Court Judge David Edelstein. As I observed IBM's lawyers trying, over the course of a decade, to teach the judge the rudiments of the computer business—it must have been the most expensive private education in history!—I often thought of Virginia Woolf's *Orlando* and the legal case that went on and on from Tudor to Victorian times.

During day after day of my deposition, with the Justice Department's lead counsel across from me, assisting lawyers on one side of him and economists on the other, it became apparent that economic reality had nothing whatever to do with the way the case was being tried. For example, my firm had clocked the entry of more than three hundred new companies in the computer industry since the case was filed. Yet in the fairy-tale vocabulary that the Justice Department had advanced and that Judge Edelstein had tolerated, they maintained that at the beginning of the case IBM had only seven competitors—often likened derisively to Snow White's seven dwarfs—and that a decade later the number of competitors had shrunk to five!

My firm was involved in the defense of both IBM and, in that other massive antitrust trial of the century, AT&T, and in both cases I was struck by the utterly foolish way in which industrial policy and other crucial public issues were being decided, often inadvertently. Equally horrendous was the massive tie-up of high-quality human resources: before AT&T capitulated, nearly five thousand people were working full time in the AT&T defense effort. When I asked my now deceased friend Mark Garlinghouse, general counsel of AT&T, what his budget was, he told me he had just finished submitting a five-year budget with a low estimate of $750 million and a high estimate of $1 billion! Tom Barr, the Cravath Swaine & Moore lead partner who was responsible for the superb and totally successful defense in the IBM case, regularly refused to submit a budget, thus giving rise to a favorite joke of

Frank Cary, then chairman of IBM: "Tom has never agreed to submit a budget, but he has always exceeded it!"

For Cravath, the New York law firm that represented IBM, the antitrust case became a cottage industry. Some associates at the firm had spent their entire careers on the case, working out of a special headquarters in Westchester, close to the company's corporate headquarters. According to one estimate, Cravath had an average of twenty-five to thirty lawyers working on the case full time for each of thirteen years.

Even when former attorney general Ramsey Clark filed the case on the afternoon of the last day of the Johnson administration, Justice Department lawyers openly expressed their belief that their case was weak. And as the years went by, it became increasingly obvious that with the growing competition in the computer market, IBM was not killing off the competition. In fact, when competitors filed parallel private antitrust actions against IBM after the government had filed suit, IBM won six out of six of the suits. Still, the Justice Department was unwilling to drop the case —perhaps for fear of seeming to cave in to a corporate behemoth —but not really pushing it toward a decision, either, perhaps for fear of losing. The IBM case droned on through the Nixon, Ford, and Carter administrations, costing hundreds of millions in legal fees and tying up a small army of talented people. And for what?

In a stinging analysis, author Steven Brill has described how seventy days of court time in the IBM case were spent by government lawyers doing nothing but reading depositions into the record. The government refused to let the documents themselves simply be offered into the record, and Judge Edelstein supported the government in this nonsense—just as he accepted virtually every other request of the government and almost no motion of the defense. Judge Edelstein, more often than not, didn't even show up in his courtroom for these bizarre, useless exercises. By 1977, according to Brill, the IBM case had already produced 61 million pages of documents. There were 950 deposition and trial witnesses, and 17,000 exhibits and 104,000 transcript pages were produced during 726 trial days—only to end up, as Brill sarcastically puts it, with the government saying "Never mind" in January 1982.[2]

More than a quarter million pages had been subpoenaed from my own files alone, each examined by counsel on my behalf, by Cravath on behalf of IBM, and by the Justice Department lawyers. **125**

Another quarter million pages were subpoenaed after my deposition—documents I had neither read nor written! I refused to deliver them because they contained confidential information concerning clients who happened to be IBM's *competitors.* (Apparently the irony of revealing this information to IBM and the government, in a case brought supposedly for the purpose of increasing competition in the computer industry, totally escaped the Justice Department and Judge Edelstein!) I had to retain still other lawyers to argue my case (unsuccessfully) for the protection of these documents, and then was forced to drop out of the case to protect the plans of my other clients, many of whom were competing with IBM.

Although its case was weak to begin with and disappeared completely in the end, another problem that crippled the government's prosecution of this massive case was the fact that once a group of Justice Department antitrust lawyers had mastered the basics of the case and had read through the long record, there was a change of administrations and many of them would be gone. When large cases drag on for more than a decade, the delays, the vastness of the case record, and the turnover in lawyers handling these matters can make them almost impossible to resolve.

The IBM case shows us how the largest, costliest cases can be the most empty; the Van Gemert case illustrates how a relatively simple case can be delayed beyond all reason (and, in effect, lose sight of the client's interests); while the infamous Pine Tar battle of 1983 is a perfect example of the many kinds of disputes that don't belong in the courts at all. I point to these instances not because they are exceptional (or because I necessarily side with one litigant or the other!) but because they reveal fundamental institutional problems that are widely representative of what happens in our legal system.

"For many claims, trials by the adversarial contest must in time go the way of the ancient trial by battle and blood. Our system is too costly, too painful, too destructive, too inefficient for a truly civilized people," Chief Justice Warren E. Burger said in his annual "State of the Judiciary" address to the American Bar Association in February 1984. The Chief Justice warned lawyers that they would price themselves out of the market and court stiffer government regulation unless reforms were undertaken from within their ranks.[3]

"Adversariness" is at the very heart of our democracy. It is our sacred right as American citizens to have our "day in court"—to challenge anyone whose actions may harm us and to hire lawyers to press our cause. Yet, important and useful as the adversary system can sometimes be, it has also become inefficient, time-consuming, and vastly expensive.

The cost and delay associated with litigation can discourage or even prohibit access to our legal system. The courts have become miserably overcrowded: activist groups advocate their specialized interests; affluent clients hire the most sophisticated and costly practitioners to represent their causes; class-action suits seem to take on the entire world; there is even a subspecies of man known as "professional litigants," who earn their daily bread by filing malpractice suits and claiming phony damages.

Although the United States has two-thirds of the lawyers on earth and a government-funded legal-services program, the poor cannot be assured of the same quality of legal representation as the wealthy. The Legal Services Corporation, created in the 1960s to provide free legal assistance to the poor, claims there is now only one legal-services lawyer available to help every ten thousand poor people eligible for assistance.[4] The budget for the entire program is $241 million—slightly more than the amount expended by the government on the IBM case.

The organized bar could take an immediate leadership role in promoting *pro bono* work by private practitioners. Unfortunately the Association of the Bar of New York voted down a proposal made in 1981 that would have required all lawyers to do thirty to fifty hours of *pro bono* work a year. Private practitioners repeatedly argue that this kind of work should be voluntary, yet each year finds fewer and fewer lawyers volunteering.

Are we becoming a society in which justice is no longer blind? Even middle-class Americans and small business concerns are finding access to our legal system increasingly prohibitive. In a well reasoned critique of the legal profession, Harvard University president and former dean of the

Harvard Law School Derek Bok has written, "There is far too much law for those who can afford it and far too little for those who cannot."[5]

Disincentives to Efficiency

A great part of the problem is built into the structure of the legal profession: there are no incentives for lawyers to be efficient or to hold down costs. For example, since most corporate attorneys get paid by the hour (with hourly rates of over $175 commonplace), there's a tremendous incentive for lawyers to drag out every possible judicial proceeding. Preliminary motions, pretrial conferences, stipulations, and discovery procedures are common areas of abuse. Discovery, in particular, is frequently used by lawyers as a way to keep the meter running as long as possible and is often employed as a tactic to exhaust the other side into capitulation. Eight years into the IBM case, for example, the government tried to subpoena IBM documents that would have taken 62,000 man-years to produce—at a cost of $1 billion!

Arthur Liman, a respected New York City practitioner, sums up the problems well: "Discovery has become a narcotic for members of our profession. Some litigating lawyers consider themselves almost professionally derelict if they do not ask for every document they can think of, formulate every interrogatory that arouses their curiosity in four different forms—even if they have full knowledge of the answers—and notice the depositions of every possible witness, no matter how trivial or cumulative his role."[6]

While lawyers deserve a large portion of the blame for lengthy delays, it is often poor case management by a judge that is responsible for spiraling costs and endless delay for the average citizen who finds himself in court. Increasingly, too, judges have been willing to turn over significant parts of their cases for management by special masters. This means, essentially, that judges are giving up control of their cases, and lawyers are much less likely to heed orders to hurry along if they come from a special master than they would be if delivered as a tongue-lashing by a federal judge. It is totally within a judge's discretion to force lawyers to end wrongful practices such as discovery abuse, and, fortunately, many judges are forcing attorneys to move cases along more speedily.

The Lawyering "Industry"

Lawyering in this country has become its own industry, bigger than the steel, aluminum, and electric power industries in percentage of GNP. The supply of lawyers in the U.S. has doubled since 1960. There were more than 600,000 at last count, one for every 400 Americans, and over 40,000 attorneys in New York alone. Los Angeles County has more licensed lawyers than in the entire United Kingdom, the fountainhead of case law. This glut of lawyers has contributed to the explosion in litigation we have witnessed over the past few decades.

There is a growing urge to seek redress in the courts for almost everything, from defective products to medical malpractice. Over 22,000 lawsuits are filed every day in the United States, and many drag on for several years. A recent study of the dockets of the federal courts yielded more than 25 cases that were each over 15 years old.[7] In Massachusetts, which at one point had the slowest federal court in the nation, the average life-span of a case was 847 days.[8] If it took that long to resolve simple business problems, American industry would have come to an absolute standstill! And the cost of all this legal profusion has been estimated at $30 billion a year.[9]

While the country cries out for more engineers, biologists, high-quality teachers, creative public servants and business executives, the best and brightest college graduates are flocking to the much higher salaried legal profession. As Bok points out, "A nation's values and problems are mirrored in the ways in which it uses its ablest people."[10] In Japan, a country with a population half our size, 35 percent more engineers are graduated each year. Yet the total number of lawyers in Japan is only 15,000, less than half the number that graduate each year from American law schools. Japan has one-twentieth the number of lawyers we do. And, as Bok argues, this imbalance has clear practical consequences. As the Japanese say, "Engineers make the pie grow larger; lawyers only decide how to carve it up."

When wealth is no longer being created, only redistributed, society loses. The waste is enormous. Humorist Russell Baker, with his characteristic tongue in cheek, has come up with a unique proposal to cure this imbalance. He has called for the exportation of one lawyer to Japan for every Japanese car brought into the U.S.[11]

"Sue First, Ask Questions Later"

Have we become such a litigious society that we have lost our common vision and now stand at cross-purposes with one another? While I believe such a fatal pronouncement is premature, this is the ultimate consequence of our growing tendency to take the adversary approach. Our first impulse has become to sue; we ask questions or seek settlements later. There has been a fundamental shift in our attitude about being involved in lawsuits. A century ago, being sued was considered a public humiliation. Our attitude was closer to that of the modern Japanese, who, in the tradition of *gamon*, believe going to court means losing face. Now, as former attorney general Griffin Bell complained in 1978, "We just sue people and then find out later what we've got on them."[12]

The Japanese example provides a clear window through which to view the differences in the ways that the Japanese and the American culture cope with disputes. In 1982 a Japan Air Lines DC-8 plunged into Tokyo Bay 300 yards short of the runway, killing 24 people. Not one of the families of the victims sued the airline. By contrast, less than 48 hours after a Soviet fighter shot down a Korean airliner with several Americans on board, San Francisco's most celebrated litigator, Melvin Belli, had already filed a $99 billion federal class-action suit on behalf of the 269 people killed. In Japan the president of the airline personally visited each of the families to express his regret and sympathy. Liability settlements were negotiated amicably between the airline and the families.

I've often heard the story of the Japanese couple whose infant drowned while in the care of their neighbors. They took the unusual step of suing the baby-sitters for negligence and received damages on the order of $200,000. However, so ostracized were they by the rest of the community for putting their individual problems above the harmony of the village that they became ashamed and ended up returning all the money—with apologies.

This last example is, by our cultural standards, extreme. Individuals *should* seek redress in the courts when they have been victimized, although the Japanese are remarkably reluctant to do so. For the people who lived along Japan's Minimata Bay, who suffered brain damage and birth defects resulting from mercury poisoning, it should not have taken over ten years to sue the company that had dumped chemicals into their water. Although they had experienced the damage in the 1950s, the victims were so reluctant to go to court they did not receive any compensation until the 1970s.

In place of the Japanese people's hesitancy and stoicism we find in this country the impulse to sue immediately in the hope of getting quick damages. You don't have to look very far to find examples.

▷ A New York attorney brings a class-action suit against General Motors on behalf of "all persons everywhere now alive and all future unborn generations." He charges GM with air pollution and sues for $6 trillion in damages.[13]

▷ An inmate in Tampa, Florida, sues an NBC network affiliate for $3 million over the station's televising of the World Series. The inmate argues that the series shouldn't be called "World" because only American teams are allowed to play.

▷ A young mother, barred from breast-feeding her baby during free time on duty as a firefighter, sues her employer, charging sex discrimination.[14]

▷ Coleco, the manufacturer of popular Cabbage Patch Kid dolls that come with "adoption papers," faces a multimillion-dollar lawsuit from a man who had been an adopted child. The man claims adoption is not a matter to be taken lightly.

Whether the issue is winning welfare benefits for illegal aliens, extending Medicaid benefits to orthodontics, or spraying paraquat on federal lands to kill marijuana plants, it ultimately winds up in our clogged courts.

Beyond the Courts' Realm

Even more troubling than the flood of frivolous cases is the increasing number of complex civil cases that defy rational adjudication. All kinds of complex issues, which the legal system is not equipped to handle, are winding up in the courts. Increasingly the courts are intruding on many types of private decisions.

In the now infamous "Baby Doe" case, a woman on Long Island gave birth to an infant daughter with multiple birth defects that were certain to leave her totally paralyzed and severely retarded. A complicated operation was needed in order to close her spinal column to ensure against potentially lethal infection. After receiving informed medical advice, the parents, both Catholics, decided against the operation. Almost immediately they found themselves the target of a lawsuit brought by a lawyer who specializes in right-to-life cases.

Then the Reagan Justice Department stepped in and subpoenaed the baby's medical records to see if her civil rights had been violated. As the case worked its way through the appeals process, the parents found their painful personal tragedy transformed into an even more agonizing public debate in the courts, with extensive media attention.

A doctor at another New York hospital has admitted that he has refused to remove respirators from brain-dead patients "for fear of being sued." In New York State an intermediate appellate court ruled that it is for the courts, not physicians or families, to decide whether to remove life-support machinery from the terminally ill.

Do we really want judges deciding on such matters of life and death? Increasingly we have looked to them as superhumans who can decide the most personal and highly esoteric technical issues. This cannot be.

High-technology cases dealing with increasingly complex and abstruse questions have been streaming into the courts at a dizzying rate. This trend is placing additional burdens on judges and juries at a time when they are having trouble dealing with more conventional cases. In the fall of 1983, for example, the U.S. Supreme Court took the unusual step of rehearing a case from the previous term. The case, *Sony Corporation* v. *Universal Studios*, pitted the manufacturers of home videotaping against the movie industry. The nine justices were simply unable to reach a decision on the central issue of the case: whether home video recording of movies and television programs is "fair use" or copyright infringement under the highly technical amendments to the federal copyright law enacted by Congress in 1976. So the justices asked to hear oral arguments all over again in a highly unusual replay of the entire case.[15]

Even more frustrating, the very same battle has been conducted in Congress for almost three years. Of course, Congress (or the executive branch of government) is where this kind of policy should be set, not the courts. But the equipment manufacturers and the entertainment industry have both hired so many lawyer-lobbyists to represent them that Congress has been frozen solid, paralyzed, on the issue. As one lobbyist described the situation: "If both Strauss [a lawyer for the entertainment industry] and Boggs [a lawyer for the manufacturers] have held fundraisers for a senator who is up for re-election, you get the classic result —the senator is undecided."[16] Special-interest lawyer-lobbyists have become so dominant, and politicians have become so obsessed with raising campaign money, that legislators seem incapable of taking action independently.

The Supreme Court ultimately ruled in favor of Sony, basically because it could not uphold copyright laws that had not yet been written! The ball was squarely in the court of Congress, which was to be charged with drafting legislation on this complex issue—and would inevitably expend even more time and effort in duplicative waste. (Technology is introducing policy dilemmas of even greater complexity, as will be seen in chapters 9 and 10.)

Juries are also being overwhelmed by technical data. With paid expert witnesses lined up on each side of an argument, it is difficult for juries to decide some cases on more than whim. In one recent antitrust case the judge's instructions to the jury were one hundred forty pages long. The case was almost solely dependent on an esoteric patent-infringement issue that was so technical that the lawyers themselves had struggled to master it. "The result of such areas," a Washington attorney wrote on the editorial page of the *Washington Post*, "depends more on lawyering and on artful or lucky jury-picking than on true merit."[17]

Frankly, I just don't believe that our legal system is well equipped to deal with these new, highly technical categories of issues and demands, including home videotaping, biogenetic developments, or the patenting of new life forms, the latter an issue that went before the U.S. Supreme Court several years ago. Yet the courts make these societal decisions for us, only by default. (Our legal institutions' handling of biogenetic matters is explored further in a later chapter.)

Sometimes the system works. In the recent trial involving the nuclear accident at Three Mile Island, the judge hearing the case was able to make himself expert on the inner workings of a nuclear power plant. His thoughtful and informed questions helped bring a successful settlement in the case, according to the lawyers on both sides.

However, a larger question remains. In cases of great technical complexity with far-reaching consequences—such as the patentability of new life forms, right-to-life issues, and the right to die—do we want a system that is only as good as a handful of its practitioners?

The Spiraling Regulatory Burden

The increasingly technical and arcane matters that come before our courts are prompted, in part, by the array of federal agencies in Washington, which share the blame for our rampant litigiousness. The number of pages of regulations in the *Federal Register* has tripled in the 1970s and is still growing, despite the Reagan administration's commitment to easing the regulatory burden. The Business Roundtable has estimated that this mountain of new regulations has cost America's fifty largest companies $3 billion annually to comply with.[18] In 1979 Sears, Roebuck, on the brink of being sued by minority employees, filed suit itself against the federal government, charging that there were so many conflicting regulations that Sears was forced to disobey at least some of them.

The number of federal agencies has mushroomed in the last two decades, and new regulations keep gushing out of them. Several Washington law firms have established lucrative practices by specializing in the rules and regulations of a single agency. There are lawyers, for example, who do nothing but defend clients in enforcement actions brought by the Environmental Protection Agency. The number of lawyers in Washington has grown much faster than the national average.

A Question of Ethics

The process of lawyering itself has also contributed to problems in our legal process. As economic pressures built up in the legal profession during the recessionary 1970s, law firms became more like businesses than the collegial, public-spirited partnerships of yore. One New York lawyer who practiced at a large firm for decades and then left, one year ago, to start a small, more gentlemanly practice, lamented on the editorial page of *The New York Times:* "Professional success today is measured by profits . . . The growing bottom-line attitude is undermining the professional independence of American lawyers."[19]

There are also increasing numbers of so-called "mega-firms," with well over 300 lawyers in each. At last count, one firm, Chicago's Baker & McKenzie, with branches around the world, had over 650 lawyers. "There is something," wrote Lloyd Cutler, counsel to President Carter and head of one of Washington's most respected firms, Wilmer, Cutler & Pickering, "some notion of colleagueship and professional standards about the practice of law with partners in a firm that is bound to break down when you reach 100 or 200 partners."[20]

The question of professional standards was prominent in a scathing 1983 statement issued by Philadelphia federal judge Joseph McGlynn, who roasted the lawyers in the giant class-action antitrust case against the manufacturers of fine paper. Besides slashing the lawyers' fee requested from $21 million to less than $5 million, McGlynn charged that there had been an organized effort by the lawyers to "generate wasted hours on useless tasks, propagate duplication, and mask outright padding." The judge exposed the grim facts, from small transgressions to massive fraud. One lawyer involved in the case had the nerve to bill his client for three copies of the book *The Brethren,* which he had given as gifts to other lawyers involved in the case. Fifty-one of the lawyers (including twenty-one partners from nineteen different law firms) spent 4500 hours collectively for the preparation of one pretrial memorandum already filed in a companion case. The cost: over $1 million.[21]

One of the most troubling examples of disregard for professional ethics is illustrated by the OPM leasing scandal. OPM perpetrated a $225 million fraud, kiting checks and making fraudulent loans, using phony equipment leases as collateral. In 1980 OPM's executive vice-president confessed the fraud to his lawyers, New York's Singer, Hutner, Levine & Seeman. Yet, using the advice of outside counsel itself, the firm decided it was under professional obligation not to reveal the fraud, because the OPM executive had pledged not to continue his illegal acts. The firm ended up closing additional fraudulent loans worth over $60 million. Other firms also continued closing loans for OPM, even after learning that OPM's directors had been convicted of writing checks on insufficient funds in 1980.

While the legal profession's strict code of professional responsibility, which shields client confidentiality, was part of the reason that Singer, Hutner remained silent about the fraud, the firm also wanted to go on representing the client. By 1980, according to a report prepared on the fraud by a Washington law firm, OPM accounted for more than 60 percent of Singer, Hutner's income, generating over $2.6 million in legal fees. The firm would probably have found it difficult to lose such a lucrative client. Eventually, however, once the continued fraudulent activities were made known to the firm, Singer, Hutner did resign. But the damage had already been done. And other lawyers were more than willing to take on OPM's business.[22]

Client confidentiality remains in force despite a growing public perception that lawyers shield malefactors from justice. In 1982 the American Bar Association's House of Delegates voted down a new code of professional responsibility which would have prohibited lawyers from keeping silent about dishonesty and criminal conduct on the part of their clients. While the issue of client confidentiality is extremely complex, it raises questions of lawyerly ethics that fuel public mistrust. A recent Gallup Poll showed that only 24 percent of those surveyed rated lawyers high or very high for honesty and ethics (and 27 percent rated them low, or very low).[23]

Might not the ABA take a leadership role in restoring the public's confidence in lawyerly integrity?

"Kill All the Lawyers"?

While the problems in the legal process are real and crippling, I would not go so far as to suggest, as Shakespeare does in *Henry VI*, "The first thing we do, let's kill all the lawyers." Besides their important role in safeguarding citizens' rights, lawyers make it possible to execute and enforce contracts and agreements without which conducting business would simply be impossible.

Yet the sheer number of lawyers is excessive, and, unfortunately, we have a market situation in which the supply creates its own demand. (While Lord Keynes successfully debunked the old economic theory known as Say's Law—namely, that supply creates demand—it lingers on in the legal profession!) I know from long experience in business dealings that if anyone walks into a room with a lawyer, everyone else suddenly has to have one too. Is there anything we can do to check the proliferation of attorneys, while reducing our dependence on them, and to encourage law schools to turn out fewer, higher-quality lawyers? First it is important to understand why there are so many attorneys.

A famous bank robber, Willie Sutton, when asked why he robbed so many banks, replied simply, "Because that's where the money is." One can say the same of the legal profession. When most of the major law firms in New York City are offering beginning salaries of $50,000 to newly graduated law students (many of whom have never worked full time), it is not too surprising to find the legal profession so popular. These enormous salaries are often augmented by bonuses and other fringe benefits, such as memberships to exclusive clubs and unlimited expense accounts. At one New York firm it is customary to hand out Christmas bonuses to associate attorneys ranging from $15,000 to $35,000.

The pampering of young attorneys sometimes begins as

early as the second year of law school, when they are hired as summer clerks and treated to extravagant lunches, movie screenings, and other high-priced cultural events. "I'm actually getting bored with eating lobster," one summer associate wrote in answer to a magazine questionnaire about his summer job. As Steven Brill, editor of *The American Lawyer*, warns, "The marketplace seems to be propagating a leisure class of arrogant, spoiled young lawyers."[24]

While some law students still approach the profession with a social vision, they face enormous pressures and temptations to go in the direction of corporate and "hired gun law." With law school debts ranging between $20,000 and $40,000, there is understandably a much greater incentive to take high-paying corporate jobs rather than going to, say, a firm specializing in legal aid for the poor, where the need for lawyers is far greater.

For medical students there is a National Health Service Corps scholarship program which awards grants to those students who agree to practice in underserviced and poor areas for several years. Might not similar scholarships be made available to law students who agree to go into public-service law jobs? Law schools can also fill the gap in legal services by significantly expanding their programs for second- and third-year students. At many schools clinical work is still largely viewed as an extracurricular activity. Since clinical experience helps teach students the actual skills needed for lawyering, including methods of interviewing, counseling, and litigating, clinical courses should be a formal part of the curriculum.

Harvard has a pioneering program called the Legal Services Institute which operates as a mini law firm, offering legal services to the poor of Jamaica Plain, a depressed area of Boston. The institute employs three full-time attorneys, and about a dozen law students spend their entire third year working in the program. The institute services 3000 clients each year and handles more than 300 cases.

A group of reformist law professors are currently urging the scrapping of the Socratic method as the backbone of legal education, claiming that the method of progressive questioning does not really teach students the skills needed for lawyering. Since Chief Justice Burger has repeatedly complained that most lawyers in this country are not competent to handle a trial, this suggestion bears some examination. Stanford University's Lawrence Friedman recently told the *Washington Post:* "I would completely abolish the present system and replace it with a curriculum that was half clinical training and half training in history, sociology, economic and comparative law. It would be a truth-in-packaging thing. Half of the time they would spend frankly and openly learning how to be a lawyer. And the remainder would be spent, frankly, in educating them."[25] The new law school established at the City University of New York has moved in that direction, with a planned curriculum that downplays—although it does not eliminate—the Socratic method and provides a historical perspective on the study of law.

Another creative proposal involves a $2+2$ plan for law students that would stretch legal education to four years. This plan would require two years of law school and two years of apprenticeship under a practicing attorney before admission to the bar, much like the system of medical internships on graduation from medical school. Apprentices who joined large corporate firms would be paid at the same rate as other nonlegal personnel. And firms would be prohibited from billing their work at higher rates. With the incentive of going to a corporate firm diminished, lawyers might be encouraged to train at *pro bono*-oriented firms.

Alternatives to Litigation

I can hardly pretend to have an answer for each of the problems I have described. The explosion in litigation, the glut of attorneys, the increasingly technical problems coming before the courts, the proliferation of federal regulations, and the breakdown of professional ethics could each take several more chapters to explore, let alone resolve. There are, however, some legal innovations that go a long way toward addressing the problems, even solving some of them.

First, there are alternatives to litigation. The most traditional method of alternative dispute resolution is *arbitration*. In several instances citizens have voluntarily given up their right to a "day in court" in favor of this faster, less costly method of dispute resolution.

139

The concept of arbitrating disputes has a long tradition. In the labor field, arbitration and mediation have been used to resolve disputes for decades. Various religious and ethnic communities circumvent a formal legal structure and rely instead on their own community mechanisms. Certain Hispanic and Italian communities, for example, depend on their neighborhood churches for third-party adjudication in a family or community dispute. Neighborhood dispute-resolution centers have also been established in over one hundred American cities. They have resolved all sorts of minor criminal matters, landlord-tenant disputes, consumer complaints, and domestic quarrels that would otherwise have wound up in local police court.

Another approach that circumvents the courts is to provide automatic relief in certain types of cases in order to eliminate long and costly fact-finding inquiries. No-fault automobile insurance is one example, as is no-fault divorce. Probate is another matter that really may not belong in the courts; in England people take care of probate matters themselves. In the U.S. we spend over $3 billion annually on probate fees.

In the field I know best—information technology—new computerized tools have literally transformed the legal profession—and for the better. Data-base services such as Lexis reduce the time and cost of legal research, just as electronic searches replace expensive footwork. And in a "paper-intensive" profession, word processing and office automation tools reduce the time-consuming task of retyping and editing briefs, while easing document storage and retrieval. Several lawyers I know discuss privately the desirability of having "lawyers' buildings," as doctors and dentists do, to pool their resources in computer tools, libraries, and so forth.

The increasing use of paralegals is another constructive way to cut costs. Paralegals, with adequate training, can do routine document searches and can check the citations in briefs, among other useful tasks, usually performed, at far higher cost, by young associate attorneys.

The organized bar has, unfortunately, opposed many efforts to do away with lawyers as expensive middlemen. When legal clinics began opening across the country, offering middle-class Americans a variety of more common legal services, such as divorce and personal-injury representation at more reasonable rates through economies of scale, the ABA charged them with dishonesty.

More recently, the Florida Bar Association sued a former legal secretary who was charging fifty dollars (one-tenth the going rate) to help Floridians fill out forms in uncontested divorce cases. Of course, the bar's resistance to this and any invasion of their turf is easily explainable. However, might not the legal system benefit from the application of that free-market principle, competition? The legal secretary example is especially troubling, since the system of judges and prosecutors that opposed her is made up entirely of lawyers! Have we no mechanism of checks and balances to review the processes of our legal system?

Reducing or Eliminating Litigation

As large corporations move to bring their legal work in-house, litigation is being approached more cautiously, and the legal fees being charged by outside firms are being scrutinized more closely. This trend was also spurred by the recent recessions. In 1976 outside litigation expenses for the Xerox Corporation alone exceeded $25 million. Xerox's in-house counsel, Robert Banks, who stepped into the job that year, has reduced the company's outside legal costs to about $5 million annually. For every case, Banks demands regular reports on actual and estimated costs—monthly for active litigation. He also demands detailed billing information about the number of lawyers who worked on each matter and their hourly rates. Banks also scrutinizes expenses, even asking his lawyers to fly coach class. He does not allow Xerox's outside lawyers to take extra depositions. And, most important, he has his own team of lawyers to handle more of Xerox's legal work.[26]

Pretrial proceedings can also be used more forcefully to compress litigation and forge settlements in potentially protracted cases. In Massachusetts one federal judge requires a detailed pretrial order memo in which lawyers for both sides are forced to summarize all relevant facts, questions, and issues involved in a case. Both parties are required to write down the minimum and maximum figures for which **141** they would be willing to settle. They can often negotiate a settlement on the spot.

In Chicago another federal judge requires pretrial conferences that are attended by the top officers of the companies involved in a civil suit as well as their lawyers. Each lawyer must explain why and how he or she intends to take each deposition or file each pretrial motion and how much these will cost the client. When the executives realize what the case is going to cost, they often negotiate a settlement on the spot. Since judges often dispose of pretrial proceedings altogether by leaving them under the supervision of federal magistrates, who rarely have the clout to pressure lawyers into streamlining discovery or curbing other abuses, federal magistrates should be used far less. Judges need to confront these costly and time-consuming abuses directly in order to bring them under control.

A variety of financial options can actually deter litigation. One proposal is that lawyers should be fined for filing frivolous suits. In 1982 a New York federal judge fined one of Boston's most respected litigation firms, Hale & Dorr, for pursuing a frivolous stock-fraud suit by forcing the firm to pay the defendants' legal fees. In a Washington, D.C., case, even lawyers were outraged when a firm was found guilty of discovery abuse—and still won a substantial victory for its client—in an antitrust case. When there is lawyer misconduct in a case, the lawyer should be disqualified or penalized. Some lawyers have urged adopting the English rule, according to which the loser usually pays the winner's legal bill automatically. Various financial options should be studied as soon as possible to create financial disincentives to misconduct.

The Holistic View

In a recent editorial in *The New York Times*, Judge Irving Kaufman observed, "It has become fashionable to bemoan the plethora of attorneys and assign this phenomenon responsibility for a host of afflictions."[27] Among these afflictions Kaufman cites: the decline of industry (talent is diverted from entrepreneurship to law); the trade deficit (Japan has fewer lawyers); the crime rate (judges' and lawyers' chicanery allows malefactors to go free); and even problems in professional sports (lawyer-agents induce players to abandon established clubs to obtain greater recompense elsewhere). I agree with Judge Kaufman that "it would be overly simplistic to blame these problems entirely on lawyers."

The legal process does not exist within a vacuum. It is deeply affected by the way our other institutions work, or don't work. We must realize that no proposals for legal reform can cure the litigious nature of some elements of modern American society. Without some sense of community purpose and shared goals among citizens in this country, problems within our troubled legal system will, undoubtedly, persist. (The need for an overarching societal vision is a problem I explore in greater detail at the conclusion of this book.)

Our society's propensity for litigiousness is not a legal but a social phenomenon, as attorney Jethro Lieberman has observed. "It is born out of breakdown in community," he has written, "a breakdown that exacerbates and is exacerbated by the growth of law." A society that is saturated by law and is dominated by the culture of lawyers promotes rather than resolves disputes for profit and inclines, as Lieberman puts it, "toward a belief that in the absence of declared law anything goes. No restraint of common prudence, instinctive morality or reflected ethic need deter or function." [28]

Yet I am hopeful that experimentation and institutional inventing in this area will help reduce litigation in our society and thus lessen all the attendant wastefulness in human and capital resources. One such invention is the Center for Public Resources, a not-for-profit organization in New York that collects and disseminates information about alternatives to litigation. It sponsors seminars that allow lawyers to exchange information about the alternative litigation methods they have tried, including litigation management, minitrials, the unfortunately named "rent a judge" programs, and dispute prevention.

CPR has also established its own Judicial Panel of prominent thinkers. Since its inception in 1982, panel members have included Archibald Cox, Harvard Law School professor; Griffin Bell, former attorney general; G. Wallace Bates, president of the Business Roundtable; Marvin Frankel, one of the panel's many former federal district judges; Sol Linowitz, former U.S. ambassador to the Organization of American States and conegotiator of the Panama Canal Treaty; and many other "high-profile" figures.

James Henry, president of CPR, describes "the potential of the Judicial Panel for facilitating collaborative problem-solving in complex, multi-party disputes—areas where the requisite goal must be problem-solving, rather than resolution of a legal issue." Henry went on to cite examples of cases that were ripe for the Judicial Panel approach: nuclear power questions, major contractor/utility disputes, social issues, and copyright violations. In each of these areas, Henry says, "it struck me that little would be accomplished by costly litigation, when indeed the parties need to sit down in the spirit of collaborative problem-solving and resolve some very complex and difficult issues."[29]

While CPR's approach is relatively new, I believe it holds great promise. Its problem-solving approach suggests commonality—tackling an issue of mutual concern whose solution requires the combined forces of the parties involved—rather than litigation, which fosters confrontation and assumes that one party has wronged the other. It is also refreshing to know that CPR is made up of lawyers, who are taking the initiative for reform from within. Following are a few additional and more detailed examples of this type of institutional innovation at work.

Case:
Fresh Thinking from a Retired Judge

The dispute between Parsons & Whittemore, Inc., a large construction company, and Dade County, Florida, over the construction of a garbage plant was the kind of altercation that could have tied up the courts for years. The contract, worth more than $90 million, made the dispute significant, and the subject matter was highly technical. Nearly a decade of relations between the two parties were, in the words of Larry Lempert, who wrote about the case in *Legal Times,* "memorialized in thousands of documents." Expert witnesses were lined up on both sides.

Rather than have the case tied up in the courts, P&W's lawyers, Washington's Wilmer, Cutler & Pickering, filed an arbitration demand in 1981. Under the arbitration agreement between Wilmer and Dade County's firm from Miami, Greenberg, Traurig, Askew, Hoffman, Lipoff & Quentel, discovery was compressed to only sixty days.

The dispute revolved around whether P&W had lived up to its contract with Dade County to complete the garbage plant on time. During the blitz period of discovery, P&W took only twenty-seven depositions and Dade took twenty-two, as well as a great number of interrogatories, document requests, and requests for inspection. The county had four lawyers at the Greenberg firm working full time on the case. At Wilmer, Cutler, three lawyers and one paralegal worked on P&W's case. Even though the timing of the case was compressed, neither side responded by throwing more lawyers into it. After discovery, evidentiary hearings lasted only five months. Two months later a signed arbitration agreement awarded P&W $100 million, the construction price of the plant, plus interest. Lawyers on both sides agreed that arbitration resolved the dispute far more expeditiously than the courts could have done. "A panel whose only calendar is the calendar of this case," one of the lawyers told *Legal Times,* "provides a flexibility you won't find in court."[30]

The key figure in running the arbitration was a retired federal judge. He used a number of innovations that contributed to the success of the outcome:

▷ He divided the evidentiary hearings into two phases to simplify the proceedings and minimize confusion and delay. The first dealt with the question of completion of the facility, the second with other contractual disagreements, according to *Legal Times.*

▷ He limited briefs to 10 pages in the first phase and 15 pages in the second, restoring the true meaning of the word "brief"!

▷ Unlike procedure in courtroom litigation, each exhibit did not have to be introduced individually. This moved along the process of handling over 20,000 pages of exhibits.

▷ The retired judge and the other arbitrators traveled often to the plant, gaining firsthand knowledge that helped them cut down on testimony.

As a footnote to this successful arbitration case the American Arbitration Association says it handled more than forty thousand arbitrations in 1982. The trend toward arbitration, and the excellent use of such resources as retired judges for arbitrators, make this one of the most promising alternatives to costly, time-consuming litigation. Yet it is no surefire solution. I sit on the board of one company that has spent well over $1 million on outside legal fees in pursuing a contract arbitration (and successfully, I am happy to report!). I wonder how long *Van Gemert* v. *Boeing* might have taken if the parties could have submitted to arbitration—although the method is rarely, if ever, used in class-action disputes.

Case:
Lawyers for Free

At a time when lawyers are coming increasingly under fire for being too costly and therefore beyond the reach of all but the wealthy, pro bono work for the poor has been breaking new ground.

Because of legal-aid cutbacks under the Reagan administration, the Legal Assistance Society in El Paso, Texas, was forced to cut its staff and eliminate a whole category of cases—in this instance, it chose to cut divorce cases. A group of local lawyers feared an epidemic of legal problems in its poor community, and they took action: they pressured most of city's nongovernmental lawyers to take on two *pro bono* divorce cases per annum for the poor.

Similar efforts to step up existing *pro bono* programs for the poor have occurred in Nebraska and Minnesota, while some states like Mississippi are seeing such efforts for the first time. And private lawyers in many areas have been pressing ahead to fill the void in legal-aid cutbacks: Cy Vance has been lobbying hard with law firms and corporations to double voluntary pro bono work in New York City.[31]

Critics of these and other efforts to make up for federal legal-aid cutbacks charge that they encourage the current administration to abrogate its responsibility to the poor. The efforts to date, indeed, do not come close to making up for the cutbacks. Yet, at the same time, I am confident that private-sector law firms have already made a contribution and will continue to approach free work to the poor in imaginative new ways.

One of these is a Canadian approach called Interest on Lawyers' Trust Accounts, or IOLTA. Lawyers pool together their advance fees and other funds held on behalf of clients in a single statewide or regional account, and the interest is earmarked for legal aid. A voluntary IOLTA project in Florida raised $2 million in its first two years of operation and is expected to raise $2.7 million this year. California instituted a mandatory IOLTA program in 1983, and projected it would raise $6 million in its first year.

"The bottom line is that 1,000 people who otherwise would have been shut out of the courts have been served," said Irma Jaime, the project coordinator in El Paso. "That's good news for everybody."[32]

Case:
Executive as Judge: The Minitrial

In July 1977, seventeen representatives of TRW, including the lawyers, sat down around an oversize conference table in Century City in Los Angeles to try to figure out a way to speed along a complicated patent dispute with the Telecredit Corporation. The complex lawsuit had already consumed more than two years of increasingly rancorous pretrial maneuvering and legal fees of nearly $500,000 each. Telecredit, a company with sales at the time of some $8 million, had accused TRW of infringing on a number of patents for its computerized credit-card and check-authorization machines. The company was seeking an injunction and $6 million in damages. TRW denied the infringement.

Discovery and demands for documents consumed two years. Delays were also caused by the judge in the case, to whom the complicated patent issues were totally unfamiliar. TRW lawyers finally entered into negotiations with Telecredit's cofounder to try to find a strategy to speed things along. They hit on the concept of the minitrial. They agreed that each company would submit its case to a third-party expert who would act as an adviser, not as a judge. The minitrial itself was governed by an eight-page set of rules that called for a two-day-long secret hearing, in which each side had four hours to present witnesses and argue its case to the neutral experts and to the top executives of both companies. The rest of the time was devoted to rebuttals.

Immediately after the final rebuttal the lawyers in the case met privately and carved out a settlement. TRW agreed to pay for a   **147** license against certain credits, and Telecredit agreed to get new patents from the Patent Office. Only three months had elapsed from the time the minitrial idea was first broached to the settlement. Through the minitrial the two companies also saved lawyers' fees estimated at $1 million.

Development of the minitrial technique has been largely credited to Eric Green, who pioneered this first and most celebrated minitrial while working under the chief litigator at Munger, Tolles & Rickerhauser of Los Angeles. Green is now one of the lead partners in EnDispute, Inc., which has sponsored several innovative alternative dispute-resolution techniques in addition to the minitrial.[33]

Since the TRW-Telecredit minitrial, EnDispute has used the technique successfully in many other cases, including the 1983 suit of *American Can* v. *Wisconsin Electric Power Company*. EnDispute, with offices in Washington, Los Angeles, Chicago, and San Francisco, charges up to one hundred fifty dollars an hour. It also helps clients identify matters on their dockets that are ripe for alternative dispute resolution. The minitrial system can work, as a Telecredit patent lawyer put it, when companies such as TRW and Telecredit can assume a "negotiating rather than a battle stance."

TWO

TAPPING HUMAN POTENTIAL

We need large organizations, both public and private, and we need the kind of management that can attract and keep the best and brightest of our young people to work in them. The modern business enterprise is an institution that already works exceedingly well, although it faces major new challenges as societal values change, manpower needs shift, and a new wave of international competition opens. Studying ways to use proven business principles in society in both resource allocation and innovation and to infuse market principles into public bureaucracies can be useful only as we struggle toward a workable system. The goal is to "get right" the role of both business and government in our society and to build a new relationship between them, so that our native human creativity and imagination can be let loose upon our societal problems.

V

Unleashing Innovation in Public Services

Many of the most important activities of our society—education, public transport, housing, the running of cities—are characterized by their labor-intensiveness, lack of reliance on technology, and an incentive structure that discourages innovation and risk taking with a "don't rock the boat" mentality. Consequently the cost of public services spirals steadily upward, while the quality and range of services declines. No amount of reorganization or new management technique is going to reverse this continuing erosion in the quality of important areas of our lives. Could the injection of market forces into public-service delivery release the energy, imagination and drive of our human resources and change this gloomy trend?

Case:
The Rocky Road of Public Transit

When John D. Simpson stepped down as president of the New York Transit Authority in August 1983, he summed up the demands of a job in the public sector as too much—if not altogether impossible—for any single person. "I've already given it everything I've got," he wrote in his letter of resignation.

The public transit users of New York City may have felt that they had been taking everything that the system could give for too many years. Just a few hours after Simpson's resignation announcement a subway train jumped the tracks at a station in the Bronx, the year's twelfth derailment. More than five hundred trouble spots had been identified throughout the system where trains were forced to crawl at a few miles per hour for the safety of passengers.

Riders on the New York transit system fared no better above ground than below it. In 1982, after years of freezing in buses with malfunctioning heaters in winter and broiling inside vehicles with defective air conditioning in summer, the long-suffering passengers greeted a fleet of new buses with skepticism. The attitude was justified. The buses, built to specification by the Grumman Aerospace Company of Long Island, broke down even more frequently than the old fleet had. Eventually transit authorities gave up on the shiny new vehicles. They pulled them out of service and substituted old surplus buses from Washington, D.C. The Washington buses generally managed to deliver passengers to their destinations, but the malfunctioning of temperature controls continued to increase and the reliability of service continued to dwindle—while the fares continued to rise.

Even the best intentions of transit officials failed in the face of intractable problems presented by public service. In the late 1970s, for example, the Washington Metropolitan Area Transit Authority —another transit system that has fundamental problems in delivering adequate service—made a major effort to solve the problem of bus air conditioners that didn't work. Technical experts concluded that an important source of failure was overwork: when passengers opened the windows, the air conditioning units could not cope with the overload and broke down.

The transit authority's solution was simple and completely ineffective. It ordered permanent seals on the bus windows. Inevitably some air conditioners continued to fail. As a result, passengers were trapped in high summer in greenhouses without any possibility of summoning up a refreshing breeze. Public complaints became too vocal to ignore. The transit authority ordered the buses back to the manufacturing plant to be refitted with windows that opened.

My friend Steve Savas, in his book *Privatizing the Public Sector,* identifies the inefficiency in public transportation, the same inefficiency that is the root cause of the ballooning of government in general: spending more money and employing ever more people to do the same work, with no improvement in the quality of service. Savas writes:

Because the great preponderance of passenger trips occur during rush hours, few bus drivers are needed between those two periods. "Split-shift" scheduling using part-time drivers makes obvious sense; instead, some drivers for the New York Metropolitan Transportation Authority drive a total of eight hours a day but are also paid (at over-time rates) for a four-hour Mediterranean-style break at midday.[1]

By way of contrast, Westchester County, New York, has a publicly owned bus system that is considered to be the most efficient in the state. However, it is managed and operated by *private* companies. The companies get a flat fee for their services as long as they meet certain standards—otherwise their profit diminishes. The Westchester system features articulated buses and a computer system that tracks buses by way of sensors at bus stops. The vehicles are actually older than the MTA's, but they are so well-maintained that their breakdown rate is only one per 5000 miles—compared with the MTA's rate of one breakdown per 800 to 1000 miles. And the cost? The Westchester system operates its buses at a cost of $3.21 per mile, less than half the MTA's rate of $6.64 per mile.[2]

How does one change the incentive structure in public transportation to promote the application of modern technology and more efficient allocation of human resources? How do we encourage risk taking and experimentation toward finding totally new ways of providing public transit?

Case:
The Blank Check for Health Care

A feverish elderly patient suffering from bronchitis was admitted to a New York hospital one night. During her nine-day stay she received $575 worth of intravenous injections, $657 worth of electrocardiograms, and $994 worth of laboratory tests. Medicare paid almost her entire bill, which amounted to $9065.10. Yet in the judgment of an experienced physician, the woman could have been treated adequately with X-rays, a single electrocardiogram, and antibiotic treatment in the hospital for a maximum of two days.

The case was not an isolated one. A major cause of the burgeoning national medical bill, most analysts agree, is the fact that subsidies of health care by Medicare, Medicaid, and private insurance give patients an illusion that they are receiving something for nothing and present doctors and hospitals with a blank check. In the twenty-one years from 1960 to 1981 the medical-care bill of the United States soared from $27 billion to $275 billion. During the decade up to 1981 the cost of an average stay in the hospital rose from $670 to $2119, appreciably above the rate of inflation, despite improvements in care that should have reduced the cost of those stays.

Medical technology is the major factor in driving up medical costs, according to Stanford University economist Victor Fuchs. While doctors' fees for office visits rose by an average of 8.9 percent annually during the 1970s, the yearly increase in hospital costs consistently exceeded 10 percent in the same period. Some of the technology is expensive and new—CAT scans, for example—but much takes the form of simple lab tests, often ordered for no other reason than that health-insurance payments will cover them automatically.

Physicians should not bear the brunt of the blame. According to Karen Davis of the Johns Hopkins University School of Public Health, the system through which insurance companies and the government automatically reimburse doctors and hospitals for any and all procedures encourages medical inflation. At present, according to Dr. Uwe Reinhardt of Princeton University, the consumer actually pays no more than thirty cents of the health-care dollar directly. Medicare and Medicaid account for about 40 percent, and private insurance for the remainder. One consequence of this is steeply rising bills for the basic providers of health care. Medicare and Medicaid today account for 9 percent of the U.S. federal budget.

General Motors in 1980 was paying $2029 in health insurance for each of its employees. As a result, $315.23 of the cost of a new GM car that year was accounted for by employee health care—more than the cost of the steel in the auto.

Case:
Low Marks for Public Education

A series of federal reports released in the summer of 1983 told millions of American parents what they had strongly suspected all along: that their children were receiving a poorer education in public schools than had most previous generations. The National Assessment of Educational Progress, for example, determined that more than two-thirds of students between the ages of thirteen and seventeen spent less than one hour per day on homework; most of the others did not do homework at all.

The University of California, whose students predominantly represented the elite of their high schools, saw the percentage of its freshmen enrolled in remedial English courses rise from below one-third to one-half between the late 1960s and early 1970s. Students' scores on the Scholastic Aptitude Test, one of the more consistent methods of comparing academic achievements across generation gaps, fell steadily throughout the 1970s, before appearing to stabilize in 1983.

The public schools did not decline in academic aptitude alone. In the inner cities the school system was an all-too-common target, torn asunder by arguments over busing, racial tensions, and crime. Student violence against teachers and other students combined with teachers' ambivalent attitudes toward their careers. The quality of schooling took on the character of the decayed urban landscapes around them.

Even in suburbia, whose school systems had attracted much of the white flight from urban desegregation, solid academic achievement all too often took second place to controversies concerning drugs, lack of discipline, and the need to offer students large numbers of electives. No wonder that growing numbers of educators retired from their vocation suffering from a newly named syndrome: teacher burnout.

The problems were not solely the fault of local school districts. By congressional mandate, the federal government has a central role in funding, creating and disseminating the education research that could make all the difference in advancing the quality of public education. Yet according to a federally funded study released in January 1984, the government has spent more than $560 million on education research in the last twenty years that, for the most part, has failed to reach the classroom. "We found three subcultures that don't talk to each other—researchers, educators, and policy makers," said Kent Lloyd, one of the report's authors and former undersecretary at the Education Department. Lloyd is the Washington director of the Center for Leadership Development of Los Angeles, the private organization that conducted the study.[3]

Many parents who had staunchly supported the idea and prac- **155** tice of public-school education began to think the unthinkable. How could they rework their family budgets in order to send their children to private schools? Frequently they decided that the sacrifices in lost vacations, fewer consumer goods, and a generally poorer standard of living were justified by the benefits of private education.

Evidence of the problems in public education can be readily found in New York City, not because New York is worse than other public systems but, on the contrary, because it is relatively open to scrutiny. As Steve Savas points out:

> In the New York City school system, during a period of constant pupil enrollment, a 50 percent increase in the number of teachers and the addition of one paraprofessional for every two teachers produced only a slight decrease in class size. Instead, classroom time was reduced for teachers, and some teacher duties were delegated to paraprofessionals. It is by no means obvious that the result was better teacher preparation and better pupil education.[4]

While teachers, parents, school board members and other elected representatives disagree on the causes of the public schools' problems, all recognized that the system of public education was in trouble. As the National Commission on Excellence in Education put it, public schools in America were threatened by a "rising tide of mediocrity."

My earliest memories are of saying goodnight to my father in the study he and my mother shared and asking why he too didn't go to bed. He would reply that he still had a lot of work to do for the Weehawken (New Jersey) Board of Education, which he chaired for many years—and which I learned much later had produced a quality of public-school system in line with the standards I found continued at Swarthmore College and Harvard Graduate School. While pursuing what today must seem like a small-town private legal practice, my father spent six to eight hours a night as an unpaid public servant, working at different stages of his life for a wide variety of public enterprises. It was thus that I was brought up with the ideal that improving public services, by way of what was even then called "mod-

156

ern management," was the highest contribution one could make—in an environment in which one neither questioned nor thought of personal gain.

I therefore approach the problem of public services from something of a Puritan starting point. I am appalled by the poverty of human imagination and spirit applied to what I consider the most important aspects of our lives—such essential human services as health-care distribution, education, the running of cities—and, in contrast, the high energy and imagination we devote to producing what seem to me to be less important material products.

If the proverbial man from Mars were to alight one day on planet Earth and spend a few days roaming the streets of any industrialized city, he would, I believe, be struck by the contrast between two distinct phenomena:

1. The store windows are crammed with all manner of diverse and low-cost goods—hand-held calculators, portable TVs, clothing made from synthetics, computer-driven sewing machines—all indicating advanced technical ability.

2. In contrast to the richness and diversity of material goods, the really important things in an earthling's life are treated shabbily: streets are unclean; roads, bridges, and public buildings are crumbling; the educational system is so unsound that the average passer-by, when asked for directions, communicates poorly in his own native tongue . . .

The Martian would return to his spaceship perplexed by the paradox: Why does a society with such scientific capability and the ability to translate it into consumer products that are efficiently manufactured and distributed throughout the population, fail abysmally to apply that knowledge to other areas of life which it ought to value more highly? The same society that can extend its reach, by robot arms, to touch the surface of distant planets—and master this technology within a few decades—cannot manage with equal efficiency to run its cities, care for its sick, educate its children, and perform other essential public services.

The problem with public services is twofold. On one hand, they do not fulfill the tasks specifically assigned to them. (It is unfortunately not an exaggeration to say that if the money spent in supporting many levels of welfare bureaucracies had been given to poor people over the last thirty years, they would by definition no longer be poor.) Nor, on the other hand, do public services operate well on the level on which, I believe, government should operate: setting social goals, charting future directions, looking to the future with a sense of vision and purpose, while delegating the actual "running of the shop," the detail work, to those who are closest to the task.

It is my conclusion from thirty years as a practitioner in management, and more years than that as a student of public as well as industrial administration, that we need to modify drastically our public-service delivery systems. The three principal tasks that I believe need to be undertaken are:

1. Provide a motivation and incentive system that encourages risk taking and puts a premium on effective innovation. The object is to attract the best people in any generation to public service—and then not to lose them because they become so frustrated with their inability to make needed changes and/or to get ahead.

2. Modify our system to create a "demand pull" (as opposed to a "supply push") to allow science and technology to be applied in the delivery of public services. Today, except in national defense, technology plays only a peripheral role, and this omission is the cause of much of the high-cost, labor-intensive character of the services today.

Periodic attempts to push technology through this system have failed. (Nixon's technology program was only one of a series of bad examples. These efforts have tried to find civilian applications of space or military technology—all too often the real purpose of justifying a federal space-program expenditure by emphasizing the "spinoff" value of the technology. It doesn't work.) The reason science is successfully applied in the private sector and in national defense is that the focus is not on the technology and finding an application for it (the procedure used in virtually all of the government technology programs) but rather on achieving some desirable goal and then, as in the case of defense, setting a reward for reaching that goal. In the private sector the market sets the reward.

3. Focus the delivery process on *results* or *output*. Most
158 measures of the efficiency of public processes focus on

input or process measures (how many tons of garbage moved per hour, per man, or per truck, etc.). But the real measure is: Are the streets clean? When it comes to the other end of the public-services spectrum—Is the child educated?—we have hardly made a start. It may take many years of research even to begin to approximate this most difficult of all problems. But, in between, where most public services surely fail, it certainly should not be beyond the imagination and capacity of our society to devise measures of output. Once we have them, we can value the desired result and let public as well as private organizations compete to achieve it.

Despite all the problems I have cited with large bureaucratic organizations, I am the first to applaud the results that exceptional and dedicated public officials have been able to achieve by hard work, imagination, and leadership. One such example is Robert McNamara, who brought dedication, great talent, and many new concepts, as well as analytical teaching, to his job. Another shining example is Herb Sturz, who became chairman of New York's City Planning Commission in 1980. Described by *The New Yorker* as "a social reformer with somewhat catholic interests," Sturz became well known for his work in reforming the city's bail system, which led to reform of the entire federal system in the Federal Bail Reform Act of 1966. His more recent credits include the creation of the Transitional Community Placement program, which promotes health care for the elderly in their own homes rather than in nursing homes. This imaginative program provides humane care to the elderly, while reducing costs to the city.[5]

But surely the public sector should not have to depend on heroic performance by exceptional managers. And time and time again I have seen gifted private-sector managers take public positions, only to grow quickly frustrated by their inability to produce the kinds of results they realize should be possible. The fact that there have been significant successes by public servants is a far greater tribute to them than is often recognized, since they are operating within a system that is essentially flawed. What this book is about is changing the system so that the incentives can be put in place to attract exceptional people to public service and to reward their exceptional performance.

The trouble with the incentive structure of any bureaucracy, public or private, is that there is no system for providing rewards commensurate with the cost of failure from taking risks. An administrator's rank and income relate directly to the number of staff reporting to him or her, not to the quality of services rendered to the public. This creates the incentive for bureaucracies to grow ever larger, at ever-inflating costs, with no corresponding increase in services.

With no competition to keep managers on their toes, talent is focused on internal politics and self-aggrandizement, rather than service to the public. It is a problem inherent in any monopoly. And as long as government is the monopoly provider of a third of our GNP, nothing will change, despite periodic efforts to clean house and the isolated efforts of some exceptional, gifted and hardworking administrators and public servants.

Introducing Change

I approached my studies of public administration at Swarthmore with great idealism and admiration for such exceptional public servants as David Lilienthal and his general counsel, Robert Sessions, both of whom conducted seminars in which I participated as a student. It therefore came as a real shock to me some years later to find my niece, Beatrice, herself a product of the liberal influence of Swarthmore, giving up her work as a social worker in New York City. She resigned in total disgust because so much more money was spent on the bureaucracy than on the clients.

This took place at a time when, in my own work, I was closely studying several examples of the difficulty of introducing change in various levels of government. Having come to the conclusion that the Luddite fears that had greeted computer technology in the 1950s and early 1960s were misbegotten (not to belittle the very real problems that I do address in Chapter 9), I started to focus the work of our operating foundation, The Diebold Institute for Public Policy Studies, Inc., on what clearly seemed to me to be the really big problem facing society: namely, how to encourage conditions that would foster the continued innovation and development in these technologies and, equally important, apply them to the one great area of society that has benefited from them the least—the delivery of public services, which determines much of the quality of our lives.

Gradually I became interested in a series of isolated examples in which private, for-profit organizations were delivering public services at a far lower cost than their public-sector counterparts. Some of the examples unearthed by the Diebold Institute included:

▷ *Day care:* Florida's Dade County (Miami) had reduced by one-third the cost of child day-care centers by turning them over to for-profit operators.

▷ *Garbage collection:* In Bellerose, New York, a private company performed trash removal, for profit, at a cost of $72 per family per year. In nearby Queens, with the same kind of housing, the same service performed by a municipal work force, reaping no profit, cost $209 per family per year.

▷ *Fire protection:* The Rural Metro Fire Department provided Scottsdale, Arizona, residents with high-quality fire protection at roughly half the cost per capita of regular fire departments in nearby cities. The cost was also 25 percent less than the nationwide average for fire protection.

▷ *Auto towing:* New York City's police department charged motorists $65 to reclaim their cars after they had been towed. The fee just covered the department's cost. Subsequently the department put part of the work up for bids. It awarded a contract to the low bidder, who charged $30 per car, made a profit, and returned the rest of the $65 fine to the police department. The only other bidder on the contract offered a price of $34.75 per car.

▷ *Parking garages:* Rochester, New York, contracted out all its parking garages, saving taxpayers roughly $276,000 annually.

We discovered other examples in the areas of health care, housing, snow removal, street-light maintenance, and administrative services.

It was then that the Diebold Institute began to conduct studies of privatization, and I became and remain enthusiastic as to the possibility of injecting competition and market forces into the public sector to improve the effectiveness of public administrators. In addition, the institute sponsored scholarly studies, such as the book *Alternatives for Delivering Public Services* by former Columbia professor E. S. Savas.[6]

What became clear to us in the course of this work is that there are several stages in which a society can attempt to benefit from privatization:

1. The contracting out of a service or the running of an institution, by a town, city, or state on a monopoly basis.

2. The licensing of several organizations, either public or private or in combination, to provide the same service in competition (which usually gives better results than the above).

3. Creation of a truly competitive market, with the only public-sector role being the monitoring of the quality and safety standards of the service itself.

What the Diebold Institute work showed was that there are many hundreds of examples of innovative approaches to providing public services on a profit-making basis. Of course, any radical change in a centuries-old form of institutional relationships is bound to require time, patience, and experimentation. So it is with privatization. Any novel approach is going to require a kind of "greenhouse" over it for some years to protect it during its difficult growth phase and to emphasize that the approach is, in fact, an experiment. Otherwise criticism can kill the approach before the problems are worked out.

The many successful examples we found were isolated cases. What was needed, it seemed to me, was to focus the spotlight of public opinion on an alternative to public-service delivery that seems to work—and then to put some hard work into understanding what is necessary to get these ideas off the drawing boards and more widely applied. Our institute put a great deal of effort into focusing public attention in this area in the 1970s. I think that today there is a

much wider understanding of the alternatives to public-

service delivery than there was a decade and a half ago—
due in part, I hope, to our early work.

Public-vs.-Private Paradox

It is a paradox of our society that many public services were
originally taken over by government because of a conviction
that they were so important they should be made available
to as many citizens as possible at uniform quality. Yet today
it is low-cost, technologically advanced, and widely available consumer goods, produced by the private sector, that
homogenize our society and give it its dynamism. Meanwhile critical public services remain labor-intensive, low-
technology, high-cost, and inefficient, with the built-in certainty of continuous cost escalation and a decline in the
quality and range of services a community can offer.

The remedy lies not in trying to force technology and
modern management through the system—which is like
pushing on a string—but to create the "demand pull" that,
in the private sector, leads to innovation and high productivity. It is the dynamic of competitive markets and feedback
controls through profit—not corporate form or management
technique—that makes private business the most efficient
innovator and resource allocator that man has ever discovered.

The challenge in public services, then, is to develop effective methods to define the end results we want (output
as opposed to input measures) and then create the incentives to innovate in order to achieve them by harnessing the
motive of profit and the discipline of competition, which
Friederich A. Hayek has defined as the "optimum discovery
procedure."

The Collectivist Paradigm

My fear is that unless the advanced industrial economies
embark on that reform of their institutions and processes
which is necessary to harness their sophisticated scientific
and technical knowledge to the solutions of today's problems, people may turn in blind despair to more authoritarian

forms of government. They will be tempted to cede to government what will initially seem limited to economic controls, only to find that the process set in motion escalates to the curtailment of personal freedoms and political liberties.

Economic freedom is the precondition for political freedom. Arguments that attempt to differentiate between them are specious. If we gamble with the former, we put the latter at risk. And experience in modern societies suggests a "ratchet effect," whereby the momentum of government tampering with the market system overwhelms efforts to reverse it.

Every society must have some mechanism for acquiring information about citizens' needs and preferences; for allocating resources to satisfy those preferences; for determining the most effective production methods in use; for introducing incentives to save, invest, innovate, use scarce resources economically; for coordinating the decisions of millions of individual firms and households, so that what is produced is what people want and in the right amounts.

No bureaucracy can coordinate all these bewilderingly complex tasks and comprehend all the knowledge that guides a society. Hence the need for impersonal processes, not dependent on human or bureaucratic judgments, to coordinate individual efforts. The market economy incorporates those processes. And by dispersing economic power, it establishes a countervailing force against the concentration of political power, thereby promoting democracy and personal freedoms.

Ironically, modern Western societies have developed an antibusiness bias, even while they luxuriate in the prosperity and well-being that business has created. The case for competitive private enterprise is strong, but it has gone by default. And the biggest defaulters are those who best understand it: the business community. While business has been winning the economic battle against poverty it has been losing the political battle for the freedom to do so.

The education system and the media have failed to create a widespread awareness of (a) the need for efficient coordinating and incentive mechanisms to ensure that scarce economic resources are employed productively, and (b) the overwhelming superiority of the free market-based economy in meeting that need. Instead, people have come to believe that no problem is too big for government and that collectivist action is both morally good and the most effective method for overcoming the complex problems of an industrialized society.

In recent years, fortunately, the image of government as all-knowing and all-powerful has begun to crack. In several western European countries, like France, the UK and Portugal, industries were extensively nationalized in the interest of keeping large work forces employed. We have now seen those heavy-handed government interventions falter as practical-minded central governments refused to pour good money after bad. The rigidities injected into Western economies by ill-considered and badly managed *dirigiste* policies over the past few decades have borne fruit in a prolonged recession characterized by low growth, high inflation, and high unemployment.

It is this cheerless combination of circumstances that has led to the belated but widespread questioning of the collectivist paradigm. Though the vested interests of collectivism remain strong, they are clearly on the defensive throughout the industrialized world. They are under challenge from growing sections of the intelligentsia, the media, and public opinion generally. Margaret Thatcher and Ronald Reagan were swept to power on a wave of popular disillusionment with bureaucracy and excessive government.

The time for noncollectivists to press home their case has never been riper. I believe the business community should seize with both hands the opportunity presented by public disenchantment with bureaucracy and big government and demonstrate, by practical example, their ethical suitability for helping improve the quality of life.

The problem, to put it simply, is determining what it is that works so well in business and applying it, wherever possible, to the delivery of public services. I am neither for nor against either business or government. However, I am very much concerned with "getting right" the role of government and making it more supple, more responsive, more fitted for its task. It is time for a new partnership between the public and private sectors.

Privatizing Public Services

Potentially, one of the most constructive ways of channeling new-found public interest in lower government spending, while at the same time providing easily understood and attractive examples of the social value of business, is to privatize the delivery of public services—in other words, to allow private enterprise to perform the service—preferably in competition—on a for-profit basis. Already there are numerous—although all too often isolated—examples in the U.S. and Europe of what we would normally think of as public services being supplied for profit by private companies—usually at considerably less cost to the public and with more of a smile than we are accustomed to associate with public services.

The Committee for Economic Development outlined the philosophy in a report issued in 1982:

> Local government has a responsibility to protect the public
> health, safety and welfare, but that responsibility does not
> necessarily require a government's becoming a direct
> provider of services; in fact, in some instances the need may
> be better met by means totally outside of government.
>   Local government should distinguish between the role of
> policymaker and that of service provider and should more
> actively consider alternatives to conventional public-service
> agencies in carrying out their policies.[7]

Privatization spans a wide spectrum of opportunities. There are many public services in which improvements could be achieved simply by allowing public employees to form themselves into groups of entrepreneurs and bid, at existing levels of expenditure, for fixed-term, renewable contracts to perform the services they currently carry out as direct employees. There are very few public employees who, if given the opportunity, would not be willing to produce the same or a higher output than they do at present from their department, within the same over-all departmental budget, but eventually evolving far different operating methods—probably with far fewer people working better and working smarter. Spinning off public tasks to groups of entrepreneurs in this fashion might well be an effective way of getting privatization started in some areas. A first step might be to engage the participation of labor unions in such experiments by identifying the public employees' interests with the interests of efficiently run cities and other parts of the public sector.

One of the very important advantages of privatization is that it affords the consumers of public services a choice—albeit an indirect choice—instead of leaving them with no alternative but to accept what a public monopoly offers. By contracting out services to competitive tender, the public authorities must shop around on behalf of the consumer, as it were, for the least-cost, best-value supplier. Competition is an essential key to improving efficiency, and it does not always have to involve private enterprise. Competition can be effective when the consumers of public service are offered a direct choice—between two or more public enterprises, for example, or between public and private enterprise.

In many instances of privatization, a proportion of such services as garbage collection and snow removal continues to be provided by public employees, while the remainder (typically 75–80 percent) is provided by a variety of competing private contractors. In Indianapolis, for example, five different arrangements are used for the pickup of refuse: municipal service, contract service, voluntary service, free market, and self-service. By stimulating comparisons and competition among the different producers of the services, that approach may well lead to over-all superior service in the city.[8]

Bureaucratic Inefficiency

Why are public services delivered so inefficiently? Several factors spring to mind immediately. By contrast with the private sector, managers in public enterprises can never ignore the political impact of their decisions on a wide range of constituencies. Parents of suspended schoolchildren complain to school board members. Neighborhoods that receive inadequate service set up pressure groups that effectively influence town hall. Hospitals threatened with reduced Medicaid payments for basic procedures lobby Congress directly.

However, these are not the central problems. While I consider it a banality to say, it is nonetheless axiomatic that if any of the various levels of U.S. government had to compete with other service providers, it is a rare case that would not have gone bankrupt long ago. No corporation could afford to be as labor-intensive as the government. No corporation could survive the competition if it were as wasteful and inefficient as the government. In fact, waste will have cost the federal government an estimated $10.5 trillion by the year 2000, according to the President's Private Sector Survey on Cost Control, which released its findings in January 1984. That study, headed by Peter Grace, found that much of that waste could be eliminated simply by applying standard business practices: requiring competitive bidding by suppliers; better record keeping; cutting back sick time to the same level as that in business; and reducing federal pensions while raising federal retirement ages.[9] But the way the system now stands, that simply will not happen. What I am concerned with in this book is *why*?

Government bureaucracies are, almost by their very nature, slow to respond to developing crises and likely to make the wrong responses when the crises become too obvious to avoid. Realistic long-term planning is largely incompatible with the two-, four-, and six-year terms of political office. Yet, despite the helter-skelter changes of political direction over the years, public services today are performed for the most part just as they were in the nineteenth century; they are top-heavy with people and light on technology. Teaching, for example, is generally conducted in fundamentally the same way as it was in the one-room schoolhouses centuries ago.

Some years ago I used a series of fifteenth-century miniature engravings depicting education to illustrate a paper on the potential for applying computer technology to education. While chosen partly for their aesthetic value, they were intended primarily to make a point: they illustrated a period in which the last great technological innovation directly affecting the course of education—Gutenberg's introduction of movable type—took place. The printed book made instruction easier and more widely available. Nonetheless, the technology did little to change the learning *process*, which even today is not very different from the process depicted in the miniatures. Nor will computer technology introduce meaningful changes in the education process, unless we make fundamental changes in the system.

Trimming the Fat

One case in which the voters spoke out—and with more than usual force—illustrates the wastefulness inherent in public-service expenditures. In June 1978 Californians overwhelmingly approved Proposition 13, a measure that limited property taxes across the state to 1 percent of the 1975–76 market value of homes in California. The effect was a rapid cut in property taxes which amounted to 57 percent—and a serious challenge to the public sector to continue somehow to offer services despite the slash. Politicians, economists, and commentators forecast an immediate decline in the quality of fire and police protection and the devastation of California school systems. The city of Oakland laid off a full platoon of police officers in anticipation of financial distress. Los Angeles warned parents that it would have to fire schoolteachers.

Yet disaster never came. Helped, admittedly, by a surprising budget surplus, local governments withstood the blow to their purses without massive layoffs, ruination of the public schools, or rioting in the streets. Oakland rehired every one of the police officers it had furloughed. Los Angeles actually hired new schoolteachers within a year of the passage of Proposition 13. Most important, state and local government employment fell as a result of the measure—just as its proponents intended—but without causing any real decline in the quality of services offered by municipalities.[10]

Over-all employment in California did not drop. Faced with the need to cut fat from their budgets, some local authorities called in the private sector. Los Angeles County, for example, turned drug-rehabilitation programs, security and maintenance services for its recreational facilities, and food programs over to private enterprise. In the first three years those measures saved taxpayers close to $5 million.

The taxpayer revolt symbolized by Proposition 13 was duplicated in other states, like Prop 2½ in Massachusetts, **169** and its spirit was evident in everything from state-mandated caps on local expenditures, to a congressional proposal for a constitutional amendment to balance the federal budget. I must stress, however, that public servants are not bound together in a conspiracy against taxpayers. Everyone, including the public employee, is victimized by a system that delivers poor-quality services at a high cost. In fact, 44 percent of the California families that included public employees voted *for* Proposition 13![11]

A more educated citizenry is coming to realize that public expenditures are no longer synonymous with the public good. The public service "consumer" is beginning to expect government to be smaller, leaner, more responsive, and less intrusive. Yet, unlike competitive enterprises, public bureaucracies are divorced from the feedback mechanisms of the market. Unrestrained by any limits beyond voters' complaints—which can generally be fended off by spending more money—municipal bureaucracies have no incentive to reduce the costs or raise the efficiency of their operations.

It is in the creation of the proper system of incentives and disincentives that lies the only real hope of change in public services.

The Much Maligned Profit Motive

The basis of the incentive system that works so well in the private sector is, of course, profit. Yet people who deliver —and receive—public services have long regarded the profit motive as untraditional, and possibly immoral, when it is applied to such basics as police protection, public education, and medical care. The attitude was summed up by a firefighter in Dover, New Hampshire, after the local council voted to hire a private security firm to run the town's forty-two-man firefighting force. "We're public employees," declared Jack Kenyon. "We work for the people. We don't work for a profit-making company."[12]

Why are people so opposed to profit—a concept so central to our free-enterprise system? Arthur Harrigan, an executive with the International Paper Company, says: "The aphorism 'My mind's made up—don't confuse me with the

170

facts' seems, regrettably, to reflect the attitude of many toward profit. Or perhaps it is just another case of making a virtue out of a prejudice."[13]

That "virtue," according to Harrigan, seems to have derived from such works as *The Robber Barons*, which equate profits with direct theft from the poor. Harrigan goes on to argue that profits are as legitimate as the wages of labor and that no nation—not even Communist nations—could live without it: "Russia, regardless of its professed lack of profit orientation, still looks to us and other developed nations for the technological and managerial leadership that is motivated and sustained by the recognition that profits are a reward for risk and for the innovation of which that risk is the essence."[14]

Public-Private Partnerships

Some local authorities, eager to incorporate the management skills of private enterprise into their operations, have found a compromise in borrowing managers from the world of commerce. Managers lent by private business to the county covering Pittsburgh, Pennsylvania, for example, in its Renaissance II project, achieved a number of material improvements, ranging from flood control to sewage-treatment facilities to park facilities, housing, black community outreach programs, and "bricks-and-mortar" development.[15]

Efficiency in the public sector can often be boosted simply by the introduction or extension of standard management practices, particularly in securing tighter financial controls and better budgetary planning. The help and advice New York's business leaders gave to the City Corporation played a crucial role in saving the city from bankruptcy in the late 1970s.

There are many ways in which to inject better management into the public sector. We have just witnessed an attempt to identify these management principles in the form of the already cited President's Private Sector Survey on Cost Control, or the Grace Commission—an update of the Hoover Commission of the fifties (although less ambitious than that admirable effort). Other examples are:

171

▷ Exchanges of business executives and civil servants to one another's jobs for one-year terms under any of several existing programs.

▷ Periodic management and procedural studies by consulting firms such as our own Griffenhagen Kroeger division (founded 1911), specialists in public administration.

All of these procedures have their value, as do the frequent shake-ups occasioned at the policy level (assistant secretary) by changes of government—but none of them provides the private-sector equivalent of minute-to-minute feedback of market conditions that benefits (even though not experienced as such) the private-sector manager. That is an important reason why generations of managers with reputations for brilliant performance in the private sector periodically come to grief when put into government jobs. (In addition, there are, of course, major differences with regard to the objectives and other "political" elements of public positions. But however much this construct may oversimplify the difference, it is a cardinal difference when it comes to the delivery of public services—and Adam Smith's "invisible hand" is an enormously powerful force.)

No matter how brilliant a manager may be, it is the forces of the market—the discipline of competition and the incentive and feedback control of profit—that make him effective. I feel strongly that the real key to raising the efficiency and productivity of public services lies in devising methods of building market pressures throughout the public sector to the maximum possible extent. The objective must be to develop effective means of defining the end results we want from public services and then to create the incentives to innovate in order to achieve them by harnessing the profit motive and the discipline of competition.

Unleashing Innovation

Public acceptance of profit in various areas of public-service delivery is a major condition for achieving the real potential of privatization. Initially, benefits will come through the more efficient deployment of existing resources of manpower and equipment. Those gains should not be

172

minimized. Ultimately, however, the real potential of privatization lies in unleashing the creativity of private enterprise. If it is confident that it will be allowed to retain the profit it earns in the long term as well as the short, private enterprise can go beyond the *static* efficiency of doing a better job with the existing resources to the *dynamic* efficiency that stems from research and development and investment in entirely new systems.

Instead of remaining wedded to the same labor-intensive methods that have always worked—more or less—private business would, as it does in commercial pursuits, invest in substantial research and development to find radically new and vastly more efficient ways of supplying public services. After all, there is absolutely no technical reason why garbage collection, at least in cities, should not be handled by a system of underground pipes and mechanical conveyors, if not by even more advanced methods of processing. Similarly, if fire service were the responsibility of fire insurance companies, I suspect that there would be, at the very least, major changes in building codes and building materials.

Perhaps the most striking example of the potential of private enterprise to improve a public service through the application of technology is our own national communications system—built largely by AT&T. While we might not think of our telephone system as a public service in the same sense as public education, because government is not the provider, in other countries telephone service *is* provided by public agencies. And, as anyone who has ever traveled abroad can testify, the quality of the U.S. telephone network is second to none. There can be no doubt that AT&T would never have invested the capital to build the satellites, lay the cables, perfect the digital technologies, and create the national and global communications infrastructure—had it not been assured that it could retain a profit commensurate with that continuing investment.

Contracting out public services to private enterprise opens up, therefore, the prospect of immense advances in productivity stemming from a longer-term view that substitutes capital-intensive for labor-intensive methods of delivery. It is folly in our day and age to allow really essential services to remain labor-intensive. Yet that has been the case for all but a few. Even the occasional programs that have emerged to apply science to public service have been very limited and peripheral.

Without the profit motive there is an absence of the "demand pull" incentive which in other areas ensures a continuous application of science, technology, and, most important, innovation. The incentives in government almost always discourage innovation. Our medical system, for example, works on the basis of rewarding its employees when people are sick rather than when they are well.

Employers have shown growing interest in cutting their medical bills by encouraging new forms of health care, such as health maintenance organizations:

▷ HMOs employ salaried physicians who provide a wide range of medical services in a single clinic or in a series of such centers. They have an incentive to hold down hospital use because their subscribers pay a flat fee in advance. If a subscriber has to enter a hospital, the HMO has to pay the hospital costs. Hence HMOs, far more than traditional medicine, practice preventive medicine, encouraging their patients to undertake physical examinations while they are healthy (or think they are), and publicizing the best means of safeguarding health. Partly because of this broad approach to health, HMOs claim that they lower the over-all cost of medical care by anywhere from 10 to 40 percent.

Being a hybrid, part public and part private, health care is a fascinating and important example of the need to get right the incentive/disincentive systems and the institutional structure and process. It is a field in which my firm and I have done a good deal of work, and I know all too well it is too complex and difficult an issue to treat properly within the confines of this book. Yet it remains a challenging example of the potential for injecting competition and free-market forces into a system of burgeoning costs, limited supply, and insatiable demand.

Educating Everyman on the Role of Profit

Probably the most difficult problem in encouraging privatization is that of fostering sufficient understanding of the role of profit to permit firms or individuals to retain what they have earned in improving public services. The danger is that once profit is seen to be made, public opinion will demand that it be taken away, even though services cost less. If that happens, the incentive for continuing, long-term improvement in services will be destroyed.

Even before it receives its first cent of profit from privatization, business faces the problem of convincing the public of its ethical suitability for carrying out public services. Critics argue that in areas such as education and medical care, privatization will inevitably promote elitism among customers and encourage contractors to cut corners. As Albert Shanker, president of the American Federation of Teachers, argued in his opposition to a privatization plan for schools, "The people who are in greatest need stand the greatest chance of being fooled." [16] Critics of for-profit hospital systems contend that medical staffs are all too readily encouraged to order unnecessary but profitable laboratory tests and procedures—doing, in the interest of making money, what staffs of nonprofit medical institutions are now accused of doing through sheer inertia.

Are nonprofit hospitals any better? One dismal example of the not-for-profit sector's performance in health care strikes unfortunately close to home:

▷ In February 1984 my elderly housekeeper was diagnosed as having a tumor requiring immediate operation because of the high probability (which turned out to be a reality) that it might be malignant. She waited seven days for a bed to become available at Lenox Hill Hospital and was understandably on pins and needles, phoning her doctor daily. The hospital phoned her on a Friday and instructed her to be at the hospital within the next two hours. Shortly after being admitted, she was given X rays—and then simply waited all weekend while nothing happened at all.

Tests resumed on Monday, and the operation took place on a Friday—a week after she arrived. A day or so after her operation, and the news that she had cancer, the hospital administrator sent her a letter, saying in part:

"A review of your hospitalization has shown that it was not medically necessary for you to be a patient at Lenox Hill Hospital on 2/11/84 and 2/12/84 (2 days). This determination was made for the following reason: There was no medical necessity for two of the three days prior to initiating workup. Patient was admitted Friday, workup began Monday.

"Your insurance company has been informed of this decision and will make the final determination regarding benefit coverage. Should your insurance company determine not to cover this period of time, you will be held financially responsible."

Was this hospital, in an atmosphere of criticism over excessive medical costs, trying to preempt some of its own charges being disallowed by the insurance company, and transfer them instead to an old woman? Had the hospital been trying to fill an otherwise vacant weekend bed—at the expense of the feelings and fears of human beings?

There is scope for private enterprise to adopt higher standards of self-regulation to avoid or mitigate those types of behavior that give it a bad name. Private enterprise must cut through the suspicions that survive from an earlier age and conduct itself in such a manner that it will be seen to be responsible and caring toward the ills of society. But little of this will happen until private enterprise sees a reason to involve itself in this arena on a large scale.

There is considerable opportunity for business imaginatively to identify itself with the need to tackle effectively major social problems in a way that shows the human face of the private sector and at the same time provide a showcase for private enterprise at work in what are correctly perceived to be the really important areas of life. I believe that private enterprise can and should take more initiatives to demonstrate how, given appropriate incentives, it could use its extensive financial resources to succeed where the public sector has failed—to provide lasting solutions to what appear to be chronic social problems.

This is not to say that government should abrogate its responsibilities or give up its controls. Far from it. By recognizing it is a bad *operator*, and hiving off some of its current responsibilities to competition, government can concentrate on what it has not done well but should be doing: setting goals, not specifying procedures; devising performance measures so results can be judged; and setting an incentive/disincentive structure that will allow profit to be made doing what society wants done, as determined by the political process.

Yet there is plenty of opportunity to make the profit motive of private enterprise work for the benefit of society. "It is not from the benevolence of the butcher, the brewer or the baker that we expect our dinner, but from their regard to their own interests," wrote Adam Smith in *The Wealth of Nations*. More than two hundred years later we are seeing the self-interest of private enterprise turned profitably to the service of the public. At present, privatization operates on such a small scale that it must be regarded as experimental. Nevertheless many of the experiments are working successfully.

The Difficult Example of Postal Service

No one can help being personally struck by the differences between U.S. Postal Service mail delivery and private letter- and package-delivery firms. Even though the Postal Service is no longer a strictly public agency, it should not be considered an example of privatization, for it remains wedded to the labor-intensive, low-technology methods that characterized its former days. Even in the nation's largest cities we can walk into antiquated post offices and find long lines of people, all waiting for human hands to weigh and stamp packages, dispense stamps, take money, and make change from wooden drawers—without even the technological aid of a cash register.

Only now, with the emergence of aggressive competitors in the mail-delivery business, are we beginning to see glimpses of innovation within the Postal Service, including an Express Mail Next Day Service. To understand the full potential of privatization in this area, an examination of a Postal Service competitor, United Parcel Service of America, Inc. (UPS), yields some fruitful insights.

▷ UPS has more than 100 highly automated hubs that can sort up to 40,000 packages an hour. Some of its newer facilities can sort   **177**

60,000 packages an hour. The UPS also has 1000 other operating locations in the U.S., Canada, and West Germany. The UPS can handle more than 6 million prepaid packages daily, 5 days a week, to more than 3 million recipients.

By contrast, the Postal Service has fewer than 25 bulk-mail centers and continues to maintain 40,000 post offices, regardless of whether or not they are profitable. In addition, the UPS can achieve savings in labor costs by relying on large numbers of relatively cheap part-time workers (the company won't say how many, but the number is known to be large). The Postal Service is bound, by labor contract, to use only 10 percent of its work force in part-time work.[17]

UPS began as a messenger service in 1907. However, its customer counters show no signs of age. They are equipped with advanced electronic systems that weigh the package, tally the cost, and dispense a metered price sticker, along with a receipt, while maintaining computerized records. This judicious application of technology lets UPS handle twice as many parcels as the Postal Service and move them faster and more safely. A parcel sent by regular mail from Washington to Los Angeles typically takes eight days to deliver—a rate that makes the pony express alluringly competitive. A UPS parcel would arrive in half the time. In addition, UPS boasts a damage rate of one-fifth that of parcels sent through the mail. Unlike the Postal Service, UPS insures each parcel up to one hundred dollars, keeps a record of each parcel, and makes three attempts to make each delivery. Nevertheless its rates are generally lower than those of the Postal Service. But the clincher comes in the profit-and-loss figures. In 1972 UPS earned an after-tax profit of $77 million; in the same year the Postal Service lost $300 million in its tax-free parcel-post business. (UPS, a privately owned company, rarely gives public accounts of its profits. More recent figures were unavailable.)

If the Postal Service didn't face enough competition from UPS, it faced a more serious challenge from other contenders in another critical area—electronic mail. The Postal Service's troubled Electronic Computer-Originated Mail (ECOM) was off to a faltering start after years of opposition by the Postal Rate Commission.

▷ Under the ECOM system a company generates letters on its own computers—which must be compatible with Postal Service computers—and transmits them via phone lines to Postal Service computers. The Postal Service transmits the mail to specially equipped post offices near the mail's destination, where it is printed out, folded, sealed in envelopes at the rate of 5000 an hour and delivered by conventional first-class mail. The process is guaranteed to take two days.

The concept seemed appropriate enough, but usage was far below expectation. In the first twenty months of operation the Postal Service expected to handle 45 million messages. In fact, it took only 17.5 million.

Critics argued that ECOM was too costly—26 cents for a one-page letter, with a minimum requirement of 200 messages at a time—and too rigid—one could not use company letterheads, inserts, flyers, and so on. Then it was challenged by an electronic mail offering from MCI Communications, Inc., a company that made its fortune by undercutting AT&T long-distance rates. Introduced in the fall of 1983, MCI's scheme works like this:

▷ Senders use their own computer terminals, personal computers, Telex machines, TWXs, word processors or electronic typewriters to generate messages, and will transfer them via modems to MCI, using a toll-free number. If the receiver of the message is registered within the MCI system, the message will go directly to the recipient's "electronic mailbox." But MCI also delivers to recipients outside the system via first-class mail, overnight courier, or MCI postal centers that deliver within four hours of receiving messages.

Initial pricing seemed to favor MCI over the Postal Service. While the latter's Express Mail overnight delivery costs $9.35 per package, MCI charged $6 for overnight delivery of three to five pages to a nonsubscriber—with the added advantage that the message could be sent from the sender's own terminal or computer rather than from the Postal Service. Thus MCI was in a new realm of competition with both the Postal Service and the overnight couriers, which are themselves a product of competition in mail delivery. The largest of the overnight couriers, Federal Express, announced in 1983 an electronic mail service of its **179** own: a national facsimile network guaranteeing two-hour delivery!

Yet for all the ways in which it falls short of the imagination and innovation of private mail-delivery firms, it would be unfair for me not to point out that the Postal Service has unique problems of its own. Its mandate to guarantee universal delivery puts it automatically at a disadvantage with private concerns, which can skim off the most profitable business and leave the rest to the Postal Service. While the immediate future course of the Postal Service looks rocky, the customer is the clear beneficiary of this new competition.

Education, Technology and Business

Education is perhaps the most important—and most difficult—area in which government, as a high-cost, low-productivity operator, might be replaced for many purposes by the private sector. Education represents a crucial area of public policy affecting the environment in which business functions. A greater concern with education is consistent with the trend in business toward a greater sense of responsibility and involvement in the critical social issues of our time.

That is why my firm pursued a series of research studies and analyses, entitled *Education, Technology and Business*, published in 1971. Despite the failures in the schools that were outlined in that study (and recently confirmed by the National Commission on Excellence in Education), at least four trends can be noted, which are close to being convictions, across a broad strata of educators and a growing proportion of the public.

1. Instruction must become more individualized. The requirement that all proceed together at the same pace promotes boredom in some and a sense of failure in others, while wholly failing to develop the potential of each.

2. Education must begin much earlier. Some studies indicate that half of a person's intellectual growth may occur between birth and age four![18]

3. Education must be a continuing process, not an isolated period in one's life. If we are to adapt to accelerating

change in society, education must be radically different and continuing—not a fixed, packaged product.

4. The public should have more options in education. To be required by law to attend a particular school, no matter how tedious its methods, however irrelevant its curriculum, assures the continuation of a school system with limited imagination and a narrow set of perspectives, while further guaranteeing "a rising tide of mediocrity."

Advanced technology and private enterprise both have an indispensable role to play in these undertakings. The problems in the schools are unlikely to be solved without the use of advanced technological tools, from computer-aided instruction (CAI) to televised courses, and the technologies themselves are becoming increasingly applicable to teaching while falling in cost. In addition, technology will bring about fundamental changes not only in *how* we learn but in *what* we learn, introducing a long-overdue stimulus for change.

Private enterprise is already in the education business. If education is understood to include training, business may already be the biggest educator in the land or a close second to government. Its experience in training, especially by electronic means, gives it special qualifications for pioneering more broadly. It is psychologically geared to trying new methods and has no vested interest in the educational status quo. Its focus is on results. Most important, private enterprise stands as a model to the school system in two important respects: its application of the latest technologies to the tasks at hand; and its understanding of the need for research and development to be on the leading edge of the product or service it provides.

Research expenditures are negligible in the school industry's budget. And although, by all accounts, teachers' salaries are shockingly low, salaries make up the lion's share of the school industry's outlays. Bernard Asbell, a consultant with the Carnegie Corporation, makes this observation: "The school industry—which, by most estimates, spends about 85 percent of its budget for salaries, 10 percent for buildings, and scarcely 5 percent for books and papers—invests less than 1 percent in research in how children learn and its own effectiveness in teaching them."[19]

The typical public-sector response to such statistics **181** would be to throw more money at the situation, but the problem is not confined to funding. The problem is one of resource allocation: using technology to replace the repetitive or rote-learning aspects of teaching, while using valuable human resources for what humans do best—stimulating discussion and working with students individually or in small groups.

What I am suggesting is a new role for teachers. Charles Silberman put it well in his Carnegie study *Crisis in the Classroom:* "The new technological devices will free teachers to do the kinds of things only humans can do. . . . The teacher will become a diagnostician, tutor, and Socratic leader rather than a drill master, the role he or she is usually forced to play."[20] Yet this new role for the teacher, within a context of fundamentally new forms of education, will not come about without the investment in research and capital equipment that I have described earlier. What is needed is a public-private partnership to bring the resources and skills of the business community to bear on the mandate of the public sector: to assure quality education for all. This is not another call for voluntarism, private-sector initiative, and decentralization of government, as valuable as all these may be if genuinely pursued. It is a reflection of the need to develop a truly new relationship between the public and private sectors, a need that is much more widely felt than in education alone.

The Voucher Concept

▷ One of the most innovative proposals for a public-private partnership is the voucher plan. It is, in fact, applicable to a wide range of public services and has already been put into extensive practice, examples being the Food Stamp program and the GI Bill.

As applied to education, the voucher plan as envisaged by Professor Christopher Jencks of Harvard would work like this: Families with school-age children would be issued vouchers the equivalent in value of the per-pupil cost of education in their local school systems and redeemable at any participating school, either public or private. This would give parents, regardless of their income, the freedom of choice they do not now enjoy and would break the monopoly of public schools, which might be grossly inferior.

The choices would go beyond the purely public or private school to include a third or fourth alternative, supported by public funds:

▷ *Independent public schools:* created by local school boards as self-governing corporations.
▷ *Family-choice schools:* established as nonprofit private corporations.

Both plans above, supported by Professor John E. Coons at the University of California at Berkeley, would be financed by vouchers pegged at 90 percent of the public per-pupil cost. By Coons's reckoning, the creation of these additional educational options would battle the enormous bureaucracy behind public education; deregulate curriculum and firing and hiring policies; restore choice to families, both rich and poor, while eliminating economic segregation; and provide a marketplace for determining success or failure.[21]

Critics argue that vouchers would allow "unpopular obligations," such as busing and bilingual education, to be circumvented; exacerbate centripetal tendencies—possibly leading to Quebec-style separatism—by allowing people to choose schools made up of distinct ethnic groups or religions; raise troubling questions regarding truth in advertising, certification, curriculum requirements; and make people complacent in the fight for better education for all.

Are vouchers the best, or only, alternative to public education? Whatever the educational alternatives might be, it is certain that the "freedom to choose" would be accompanied by marketlike incentives to improve performance and attract the best students—and teachers. Within the context of educational alternatives in a competitive environment, there would be more opportunity for private corporations, with public guidance, to invest in educational research.

My own impression is that vouchers are superior to government's contracting out services to private firms, because vouchers give the consumer a choice—thus stimulating competition. Vouchers therefore open the way for attracting the heavy R&D expenditures and equipment investment that will be prerequisite to any really fundamental changes in this important field.

It might even be feasible—if there were greater public acceptance of the role of profit—for corporations to run schools as profit-making ventures. An IBM school or a General Electric school is not outside the realm of possibility. And judging from the integrity and innovation that guide these two well run corporations, the prospect is, to my mind, full of promise.

Future Directions

I have said more about education than about any of the other public services that are ripe for innovation only because I see educational reform as the most critical. While I am well aware that I cannot give this crucial issue justice within these brief pages, I hope that my few observations will stimulate meaningful discussion and further experimentation in privatization.

Dynamic privatization shows promise of contributing new solutions to many of society's most intractable problems. Consider its potential in improving our correctional institutions:

▷ Associated Marine Institutes, a private enterprise that operates the Florida Environmental Institute facility for serious juvenile offenders, for example, has put into practice a unique program that increases the privileges of the young offenders based on their good behavior. The youths start their stay at the institution by working at a wilderness camp. Step by step they can graduate through the system to a city job.

The concept of privatization of public service does not stop at the city line. In recent years companies have shown interest in taking over enterprises run by the federal government.

▷ In the furor over the Reagan administration's trial balloon, launched in 1983, for selling government-owned weather satellites, few commentators mentioned that private weather forecasting services, offering specialized predictions for their clients, have competed successfully with the National Weather Service for several years. Even space science, the archetype of the program that demands federal dollars, is opening its ranks to profit-making companies. A Texas consortium started its own launch trials in the early 1980s, and a space platform owned and operated by Fairchild Industries is due to be launched in 1985.

Where the profit motive is incorporated responsibly to address society's needs, even the sky is not the limit.

The Role of Government

In this chapter and elsewhere in this book I have talked about some of the things government should do that it doesn't. For example:

▷ Operate a political structure that focuses on where we are going and, in a democratic manner, resolves the trade-offs between what we can have and what we do have.

▷ Establish institutions that focus on future consequences of present actions.

▷ Regularly reevaluate laws and public programs to compare their results with the intentions that brought them into being.

▷ Operate a democratic trade-off mechanism that fairly states the array of alternatives and allows realistic priorities.

▷ Fund basic research to the extent that there are first-class intellects available at any moment in history.

▷ Do research on how we measure output and performance and then use these results to allow a competitive structure for delivery of public services.

▷ Provide coordination of the thousands of current incentives and disincentives so that a minimum number work at cross-purposes. For example, if we want the work force to be able to train for new jobs in emerging industries, we shouldn't put a tax disincentive to their learning new job skills.

▷ Play a creative role in structuring and financing competition in model projects so that the insights of basic research can be applied in the large new areas that do not yet have markets but that are publicly desirable.

These are a few of the functions of government, not now in place, that seem to me to be necessary if our society is to be made to work. I believe there is much to be gained toward these ends by a new partnership between the public and private sectors. I realize, of course, that I am asking for nothing less than a revolution in the way the American citizen thinks of public service. I am asking that services normally thought of as rightly belonging in the public sector now be considered as the proper concern of private enterprise as well. If business were allowed to make—and retain —a profit in performing essential public services, I believe that it would invest in new technology and new techniques to perform public services in radically new ways.

My principal concern is to stress both the opportunity and responsibility facing business leaders at the present time. As prominent members of the "polis," it is not only necessary but right and proper that they play a prominent role in reshaping the course of the society in which they live and work. The privatization of public services is just one of the ways in which business can make a positive and major contribution.

There are, in fact, many more success stories concerning the privatization of public service than I have told, whether privatization occurred by transferring control of public-service delivery to a private concern or by injecting market principles, such as competition, technological innovation, R&D, and profit, into public agencies. I will close this chapter with a few such case examples, reminding the reader that the most exciting possibilities of public-private partnerships have yet to be seen.

Case:
Privatized Police Forces

The police officer as a paid public servant is a relatively recent
phenomenon; well into the nineteenth century volunteer watch-

men, not police officers, patrolled the neighborhoods to keep order. And although the idea of turning police protection over to private companies is certain to raise eyebrows, the cutbacks in public services across the country will soon make this proposal a necessity.

Reminderville, a small village in Ohio, and an unincorporated surrounding area called Twinsburg Township were threatened with losing their police protection for budgetary reasons. The Summit County sheriff's department had provided basic protection for the small townships in the area. But with public monies running dry, the sheriff announced in 1980 that it would cost Reminderville and Twinsburg $180,000 a year to continue to get emergency-response service and occasional patrol by one car. The village board balked at the price. Corporate Security, Inc., a private security firm, agreed to protect Reminderville and Twinsburg for $90,000 a year—half the sheriff's asking price. In addition, it would offer twice as many patrol cars and a 6-minute emergency response—compared with 45 minutes for the sheriff's department. The village officials would retain authority over hiring, firing, disciplining, and organizing the police force, which would be selected from among trained, state-certified candidates.

The squad cars and all equipment are paid for and maintained by Corporate Security, which also signs the officers' paychecks. The firm runs a no-frills operation: the cars and their radar system were bought secondhand. The firm also saved money on salaries: the nonunionized officers are paid less than typical police forces. On the other hand, the work is less demanding than police work in a large city or even a medium-sized town. The seven-officer force (as of year-end 1982) are young and reportedly glad of the work. With many towns and cities laying off rather than hiring police officers, the private security firm offered a welcome opportunity.

By all accounts the townspeople and officials are pleased with the arrangement. With all costs previously negotiated and fixed, Corporate Security is motivated to keep operating costs low. And, unlike a public force whose future is guaranteed—regardless of the quality of service it provides—the private security firm is motivated to keep up the good work, to assure a continued contract.[22]

Could this experience be repeated in other areas? While police unions and associations pose a major obstacle to privatizing police forces in larger cities, I believe even unions would welcome private management if they were aware of the private sector's potential for better human resource allocation: freeing them for their most important tasks. An experiment in Worcester, Massachusetts, illustrates this point:

▷ In 1976 Worcester began a Public Service Aide program, partially funded with public funds, in which minimally trained civilians were assigned to take over dispatching, report writing, handing out parking tickets, and paramedic duty. Naturally the police officers and their union resisted the idea initially. However, as Captain John Hughes of the Worcester force observed: "The complaints didn't last long, though, when the officers realized that instead of having to detour traffic and take care of injured kids, they could concentrate their efforts on patrolling. In fact, they got pretty dependent on the PSAs."[23]

Worcester's crime rate, which had been among the highest for U.S. cities of its size, plummeted. Not only were police officers freed to patrol more but the very presence of the PSAs—who were hired in addition to, not at the expense of the police—created a supplementary street presence and a deterrent to crime.

A study by William Cunningham of Hallcrest Systems illustrates the problem of misallocated resources that ultimately make public services expensive: he found that 80 percent of the work done by police departments is not crime-related! The police officer's unique skills—handling firearms, breaking up domestic quarrels before they turn violent, catching criminals in the act, and physically fighting crime—occupy a small percentage of the police department's time.[24]

Consequently a wide range of tasks could be turned over to less skilled, lower-paid civilians or private contractors while the higher-paid and skilled police officers would be freed to tackle the jobs they do best. Cunningham found that police chiefs would consider using civilians for the following tasks: parking control, crowd control at large events, bank-deposit escorts, school-crossing guards, public-park patrol, funeral escorts, courtroom security, prisoner transfer, noninjury accident investigation, government-building security, guarding hospitalized prisoners, crime-lab work, on-scene recording of burglary losses and taking reports from crime victims, office and dispatching duties, crime-prevention surveys, parade security, and directing traffic.[25]

I expect that further gains will be achieved through the practical application of technology. There is no technical reason why specially designed robots could not assume some of the life-threatening tasks that human officers now perform.

▷ Might not a robot be useful in a situation in which an armed suspect is believed to be waiting inside a building? Rather than risking a human life, a robot could enter the building and transmit back to the human officers a television picture of the scene inside.

▷ A robot might also be programmed for bomb defusion and other tasks in which life and limb might be threatened but no special human judgment is required.

If the opportunity existed to reap a sustained profit in making cities safer, my guess is that we would see completely new entrepreneurial approaches based on applying scientific insights—in contrast to the real but smaller gains demonstrated by the police examples above, which were achieved by better management alone.

Case:
Computers in the Schools

The small rural town of Forest City, Iowa, has started what may be a revolution in the nation's rural education system: a private business is financing the computerization of the public schools, a college, and even the homes of community residents. John K. Hanson, founder of Winnebago Industries and the mover behind the computer concept, joined education officials in unveiling the $1 million computer education program in October 1983, showing off rows of computer terminals in the junior high and high schools and in the private two-year Waldorf College.

Every student will have access to the computer, beginning as early as kindergarten, and can carry his or her skills out into the work force on the same system in use at Winnebago Industries. Robert Hall, computer coordinator for the 1317-student public school district, said the program provides one computer terminal for every eight or nine students, a ratio he believed to be "unique in the country."

In talking with William Norris, founder of Control Data Corpora-   **189** tion in Minnesota, Hanson became inspired by Norris' dream of having large corporations cooperate with government on education and other societal needs. Control Data's Plato computer-aided instruction system, which was developed at the University of Illinois in the 1960s and is in use at a number of major universities, is the key to the Forest City program. According to a school official, the schools put up about $100,000, Winnebago pays 60 percent of the remaining $900,000, and Control Data is responsible for the other 40 percent.

Assistant U.S. Education Secretary Robert Worthington, who was present at the unveiling of the program, expressed his excitement at the idea of getting a whole community computer-literate. "If this could be repeated in every one of the nation's 16,000 school districts," he said, "there's no question we could improve the quality of education. It'll put them one up on the competition. They'll be about ten steps ahead of the kids who don't have this. Iowa has such a good reputation in education already. To add this to it as well, they will really keep Iowa out in front educationally." And high school science teacher Denny McDonald, who was the first faculty member to embrace the computer program and work it into his class curriculum, said students have accepted computerized learning very well. "It can do some things I can't do, such as graphics," he said, adding that the computers have struck a responsive chord in students who otherwise mentally drift off during classroom lectures.

What's in it for Winnebago? The motor home company employs 2100 people from the area. One benefit it seeks is a more productive work force through a kind of continuing-education program. A unique aspect is the idea of putting computers into the homes of the average Forest City citizens. Winnebago offers a $3000 interest-free loan to employees who wish to buy a computer for their homes. It sold 15–20 terminals in the first week the announcement was published in the firm's newsletter. Although employees initially resisted the idea, many have since jumped on the bandwagon, with the idea that computers are the "coming thing."

Hanson said he considered it a wise investment, because "not only Winnebago, but also the Forest City community at large is dependent on the area to produce a high-quality labor force. What better way to guarantee this than by maximizing our educational potential?" Hanson's goal is to increase the output of each worker from $200,000 a year to $300,000 a year by using computers. "We don't have to work harder, we have to work smarter."

Control Data chairman Norris said he advocates turning over responsibility for education to private business until required changes are implemented and a modernized system is in place. Worthington agreed that a partnership between business and the schools is what is needed for education in the future. He said the Reagan administration wants to turn over more responsibility for education to local and state officials. As part of that philosophy Reagan this year announced an Adopt-a-School program, encouraging business to financially take a public school district under its wing. Hanson, asked if he thought other businessmen would follow his lead and form a partnership with schools, replied, "They'd be damn fools if they didn't." [26]

Case:
Public Service in Denmark

In 1884 the stately Christianborg Palace in Copenhagen, residence of the royal family and the seat of government, went up in flames. One of the onlookers was nineteen-year-old Sophus Falck. Anguished by the tragic destruction of the palace and its priceless contents, Falck is said to have conceived the idea of a rescue corps that could be called on to assist in such crises.

Twenty-two years later, in 1906, Falck realized his old dream by opening the first Falck rescue station in Copenhagen. By World War II, Falck had expanded into road-repair and ambulance services. Having literally grown up with the automobile, Falck was unusually well equipped to provide mobile social services as they were needed. Today the Falck name appears everywhere in Denmark—on fire trucks, ambulances, emergency vehicles, tow trucks, and even on airplanes. In a country whose public sector has grown to gargantuan proportions, Falck is a private organization that turns a real profit on its more than $1 million gross income. and its profits are consistently reinvested in new technology and increasing personnel.

How does such a model of private social-service delivery thrive in a country in which cradle-to-grave welfarism accounts for half the gross national product? "We were there, we were doing the job, and we were doing it better and cheaper than the municipalities could do it," a Falck spokesman explained.[27] Yet Falck's continued success goes beyond the profit-and-loss statement.

Falck workers have earned a national reputation as genuine

public servants. They are carefully trained, and regularly retrained, in a variety of skills, including firefighting, first aid, and other rescue operations. The result is not only an efficient use of human resources but greater job satisfaction for its versatile crew members. Technological resources are also efficiently employed. The company builds, repairs, and maintains its own vehicles, each of which is used for multiple purposes. And an extremely sophisticated communications network further ensures the most strategic allocation of resources possible.

Yet one suspects that the reasons for success go deeper. San Francisco journalist Jon Stewart put it this way:

> Falck employees act as if they are working for the public, and as if the work they are doing—driving patients to the hospital, dousing fires, digging out cars, providing first aid, or repairing home damages—is genuinely contributing to the public welfare, which it clearly is. One reason why such attitudes persist at Falck, one suspects, is that the company has skillfully blended its service and business motives and manners. Falck works as a public servant, but it provides the best possible service by going about it in a rational, businesslike manner.[28]

Denmark has a history of cooperative efforts that are unique to the Danish culture. But it is instructive to remember that this agency started out with no more than the inspiration of a nineteen-year-old man, later augmented by the commonsense business skills of succeeding generations of public servants. How many more examples of for-profit delivery of public services exist, all but unknown except to their beneficiaries, some students of public administration, and a handful of others?

VI Talent as Capital

Human talent is an important part of every corporation's capital, although the balance sheets do not recognize it as such. The task of stimulating creativity, imagination, and innovation in the workplace is one of the great managerial challenges of our age, especially as our economy relies more and more on giant, often multinational corporations. The task is vastly complicated by big changes that have been occurring in value systems and attitudes toward work, although few large organizations have adequately adjusted their systems of managing, motivating, promoting, and paying people. We thus create obstacles to personal performance. Whether it is the big corporations trying to attract and retain the entrepreneurs or government agencies trying to break the lock grips of bureaucracy, there is no chance of gain in innovation, only the risk of failure and forever blotting your copybook, in the "Don't rock the boat" mentality. How to create a human climate conducive to innovation?

Case:
The Dead-End Job

A General Motors plant in Tennessee had an opening for fifty custodial jobs—janitoring, cleaning up, doing routine mainte-nance work. The jobs were without prestige, the sort of openings that might be attractive to older workers who want to spend their last days leaning on a broom. The company notified the union, the United Auto Workers, that these dead-end jobs were open, expecting that maybe some two dozen aging souls might apply. The company could then fill the rest of the openings.

"To the astonishment of both union and management, they received not ten or twenty inquiries, but an overwhelming two thousand applications from men who hold *higher-paying* [author's emphasis], higher-status jobs. Furthermore, most of the applicants are young, vigorous and far from retirement."[1]

The union of course was faced with a problem. Who should get the jobs? The old-timers could be expected to invoke their seniority rights, an ancient bit of mores written into contracts to allow the oldest employee (by employment years) to have the first crack at moving up. But was seniority also to determine who would get a first crack at moving *down*?

Whatever the bewilderment to management and union, the workers were sending them a clear message: wages and prestige were no longer sufficient motivators for putting in a day's work. There had been a shift in the moods and minds of these workers, a change in values that called for a new set of "carrots and sticks."

Case:
The Job-Hopper

"Nobody knows what's expected of him or her; nobody gets rewarded for anything in particular; and morale is horrible." That was how one twenty-seven-year-old woman described her work situation with a West Coast computer company. In her first three months as the company's director of advertising and promotion she had loved the job. Even though her predecessor had left behind a terrible mess, she and her assistant took up the challenge eagerly, working long hours to restore order out of chaos. Her boss, apparently delighted with her performance, gave her two raises in her first ten months on the job. He feared that a competitor would steal her away if he didn't offer this concrete show of appreciation. Yet, somehow, two raises weren't reason enough for this young professional; she was actively looking for another job.

Why? One day she overheard her boss admonishing someone about working too hard, suggesting that it might be "threatening" to others in the department. Suddenly she felt demoralized and stopped putting in extra hours. To her disappointment, no one even noticed. In fact, her two raises were given her *after* that.

Confused and disgusted, the young woman concluded that hard work didn't pay at this company, that rewards were unrelated to one's personal contributions and performance. Meanwhile the company thinks its high turnover rate is due to a competitive job market.[2]

Case:
Journalists Making Headlines

If you were in London on Thursday, January 12, 1984, and hoped to catch the televised news, you were in for a surprise. The British Broadcasting Corporation's main news program was never aired that day; TV journalists had attended union meetings instead of preparing the Thursday news program. In the days that followed, the news program shakily resumed as nonunion TV news readers worked with management staff to produce the shows.

The journalists, known as "current-affairs specialists," were suspended. They were among two hundred members of a National Union of Journalists branch who voted against using desk-top computer terminals instead of their old-fashioned typewriters. Some of the best known names in British television were among those temporarily ousted in the dispute. Britain's national newspapers have had a long history of labor disputes involving resistance to new computer technology. However, this was the first time *television* news had been affected. One broadcasting union officer hinted there might be a series of meetings throughout the country to involve BBC television journalists in other regions.

What was the issue? Computer terminals are already well established among journalists in the United States, Germany, and Japan, so much so that many of these journalists would fiercely resist using anything *but* the computerized equipment. As in the U.S., one might expect some initial resistance to newsroom computerization, based on a misunderstanding of the computer's capabilities or fears of job displacement. But BBC sweetened the deal by offering cash incentives to workers who agreed to use the computers: a $945 one-time payment plus a 2.3 percent salary increase. The union rejected the offer.[3]

The motivations behind the union action clearly go beyond salary considerations. Intelligent, creative people were making a statement about the conditions under which they chose to work. It was a matter of choice—even if it were a misguided choice, for it   **195** ignored a whole new dimension for creativity in journalism—that took precedence even over their professional obligations to get the news on the air.

In *Modern Times* Charlie Chaplin gets caught up in the whirling wheels of a factory in which he is just another gear in the gears. The point of the film is the dehumanizing quality of modern manufacture or, using manufacture as a metaphor, of modern times. From many years of intensively watching modern systems of management I have concluded that it is not only Charlie Chaplin who suffers. So does the productive process. Dehumanization is not only destructive to the person—the employee—but also to the company.

Despite the persistence of the Charlie Chaplin stereotype in our view of technology, the whole thrust of the newer technology in the workplace is to allow greater flexibility in the way work is organized, thus providing a means of magnifying individual creativity when the motivations are right. But the effectiveness of technology can be blunted and its value virtually junked, depending on the outlook of the employees using it.

Dehumanization in the workplace goes far beyond the application, or misapplication, of machinery. Salaries and bonuses may be structured to reward mediocre performance and thus discourage personal initiative. Rigid work hours may be incompatible with the needs of a mother or a father to attend to a sick child. And in thousands of direct and indirect ways, managers may be telling their employees, "You have no voice in this enterprise. You are no more than a gear among gears."

Charlie Chaplin is the most unpredictable gear, because, like all of us in one way or another, he is blessed, or cursed, with free will. Out of boredom he can become angry and throw sand into the machine. He may just lose interest and fail to play his role as a gear. He may report illness when he is not sick, except sick of the work. He may take a drink too many. He can file endless grievances because he is spiritually aggrieved. In short, he is the one gear that can—and ultimately will—gum up the smoothly running mechanism. This is especially so if Charlie was not raised to be a gear. Here I am talking about changing values, about the ways in which modern people differ from their fore-bears. Attitudes to work and personal value systems are changing dramatically, although the various recessions of the 1970s have sometimes disguised the magnitude of the changes. When it comes down to a question of having a job or not having a job, the basic shift in values can be obscured.

The big difference is the desire to be a person in the act —not just a prop. This desire to be creative, to have a say in things, I have found, is a positive factor. I am, of course, aware that if the enterprise is organized like that imper-sonal, insensitive machine in *Modern Times*, the willful "gear" can be a nuisance. But if that same urge to create is viewed as a resource, as a fund of creative capital, then Charlie is no longer an obstacle but an opportunity.

In my experience, however, few large organizations rec-ognize human talent as capital; few have adequately ad-justed their systems of managing, motivating, promoting, and paying people. We need large organizations, yet we are turning off the best and most creative of our younger people from working in them.

The concept of the "company man" or "organiza-tion man" is outmoded. Today's emphasis is on individual self-discovery and expression. Combining this need for self-fulfillment with the fact of working in large organi-zations, both public and private, seems to me a very *real* problem.

Valuing the Human Organization

The lowest epithet ever applied to anyone by my teacher General Georges F. Doriot—who many of us feel was the best teacher Harvard Business School ever had—was the title "accountant." Since my father was at the time writing parts of the CPA exam (and indeed much of this book has been written on the remnants of the pre–World War II larger-than-legal-size yellow pads on which he composed those examinations—an experience that has given me par-ticular pleasure), I was especially attentive to his point that accountants called fixed investments "assets." General Do-riot correctly pointed out that they were mere liabilities, since they locked the owner into technology that would often rapidly be obsolete. And one of the greatest true assets of an organization never appeared on the balance sheet at all—the value of the functioning human organization.

Indeed, the accountants still don't value the human organization, even though it is clearly one of the greatest true assets a business can possess. And this is true not only of a business. One reason for the post–World War II German *Wirtschaftswunder*—economic miracle—was the enormous influx of East German and other Eastern European labor—until the USSR recognized this as well and built their wall. Yet we literally have no financial recognition of the value of our human organizations (except by way of valuations of a profit-making organization, and this is hardly the same thing).

One result is that managers behave differently toward their staff than they might if there were a formally accepted method of attributing value. I have often thought this a considerably more fertile field for Ph.D. theses than many that are filed. Sociologist Rensis Likert is one of the few who address this problem, and he has related the value of a functioning organization in place to a multiple of the dollar value of a year's turnover.

In any event, the crucial difference between the productivity of imaginatively led work forces vs. the run-of-the-mill performances of U.S. organizations has been brought home to us in particularly brutal forms in the increasingly severe recessions of the 1970s and related economic shocks of the 1980s. The problem has become even more complex during this period because of the marked changes in values and attitudes of the American work force, which began in the 1960s and continued—though often disguised by the recurring recessions—during the 1970s. The current status is, however, that no amount of new technology, favorable tax incentives, protectionism, or help from sympathetic presidential administrations can begin to be sufficient to make a U.S. firm internationally competitive in the 1980s without a considerable revamping of organization, personnel, and motivational and compensation policies at all levels.

In some cases this will mean moving to what my colleagues and I have been referring to as the post-multinational form of organization—more akin to the Japanese trading companies, which provide venture capital and distribution for at least partially entrepreneurially owned innovative producers or product developers.

The high-tech world learned long ago that talent is capital —although there is as yet no formal recognition of this in any of our business schools or management systems. Our older large and generally successful firms (even if riding on the momentum of an earlier age) suffer greatly, though they don't yet recognize it, from lack of formal acceptance of talent being capital. The entrepreneurial talent gravitates to the new ventures only later to be sold out, giving liquidity to start again to the venture entrepreneurs. When there is more formal recognition of talent as capital, I think we will see more accommodation on the part of the large MNCs (multinational corporations) to quite new forms, for it will already be easier for them to make such accommodations to the reality many of their CEOs already privately acknowledge.

But the needed accommodations are by no means limited to attracting and keeping the fast-track entrepreneurs. As we saw in the 1960s, many of our most gifted young people decided that they value poetry, or guitar playing, or you name it, more than a traditional career. Their objective was to work in the traditional sense as little as possible in order to be able to spend as much time as possible each year making films or sculpting. Many of these individuals are superbly gifted. The organization, public or private, that structures itself in such a way that it can avail itself of their talent can be ahead of the game.

The same is true of the many highly educated men and women who would like to devote much of their time to raising their children but who could work a few hours a day. This is not only a women's issue any longer, as more and more fathers reject their traditional roles as sole breadwinners in favor of spending more time with their children. The organizations that not only accommodate but seek out and encourage such talent will find that they get some of the best human assets of our age.

Restructuring for the Future

The industrial system that made the Western world rich and powerful was described by C. Wright Mills as follows: **199**

"The most alert hours of one's life are sacrificed to the making of money with which to 'live.' . . . Each day men sell little pieces of themselves in order to buy them back each night and weekend with the coin of 'fun.' "[4] Our technology, our economy, and our society have undergone enormous changes since the implantation of that system, yet Americans still spend their "most alert hours" making money with which to "live." For some, surely, this is a choice, but for an increasing number of people it represents an intolerable sacrifice.

The Western industrialized world has established, and largely maintained, a strict life cycle or pattern. The first two decades of one's life are devoted to full-time education; there is substantial leisure time and minimal responsibilities to family and community. The next four decades are consumed by full-time work, often combined with raising a family; there is very little leisure time, and responsibilities are great and various. The final stage, from retirement on, is characterized by a great deal of leisure time and few responsibilities. However, because of financial worries, due to inadequate pensions, along with the psychological shock of such an abrupt life change, few retirees are able to enjoy this hard-earned "freedom."

Today nearly 80 percent of young Americans go to college or its specialized training equivalent. The conventional wisdom has it that in a progressive democratic society this proportion would continue to rise. However, there are many reasons to suppose this conventional wisdom is unwise. It is not at all certain that for most of the population the years between the ages of, say, seventeen and twenty-three are the most appropriate for the higher-learning process. In many cases those years may be better spent gaining experience in business or other areas of life. Nor is it wise to assume that formal study should stop there. We are living in a society in which technical knowledge incorporated in industry is doubling every fifteen years. At that rate, a fifty-three-year-old who stopped learning at age twenty-three would know only a quarter of what he or she should know.

It seems axiomatic that there should be a more even spread of learning, working, and enjoying throughout the different stages of our lives. This cannot be achieved by a sudden and complete reversal of all our institutionalized patterns, but there are incremental changes that could help us along the way.

Wherever possible, we should begin to change the methods of financing institutions of higher learning. We should move from a situation in which the demand for places is automatically government-subsidized above the supply to a pattern in which competition for students will lead to a wider range of students and stronger educational institutions. A condition of government grants or foundation support for particular universities should be more easily transferable to other institutions for students who feel dissatisfied with the education they are receiving in a specific school.

Business scholarships for retraining employees could be subsidized through the tax system, perhaps even wholly subsidized when the student does not return to the corporation but moves instead to a vital new growth industry. Currently the tax system encourages a citizen, through income-tax deductions, to seek training only in his or her present profession—even if there *are* no jobs in that profession! We could make it easier for older people to enter professional schools or universities: student loans could be made repayable in full for people under thirty but payable in lesser proportions for each decade of age thereafter. Finally, private pension schemes could be restructured so that, rather than forfeiting pension rights on leaving the firm's employ, a person could use the funds as a fringe benefit to finance a retraining period in college.

The Japanese have met the challenge of providing lifelong education through their major corporations. The following are examples of Japan's commitment in this field:

▷ Hitachi Ltd. maintains five institutes devoted to developing engineering skills. The most important of them, the Hitachi Institute of Technology, trained five thousand engineers in intensive one- to three-week courses during the first ten years of its operation. With an annual outlay of $42.8 million starting in 1980, Hitachi has become a major educational institution.

▷ NEC (formerly Nippon Electric Co.) conducted a survey in 1977 in which 50 percent of its engineers reported that their knowledge in the fast-pace computer field grew obsolete within three years. It created the Institute of Technology Education, which is open to all NEC engineers with more than two years' service. "In the age of information technology," says Ykumatsu Takeda, the institute director, "work is permanent lifelong education. The company has become as much an educational institution as it is a place of work."[5]

It should be noted that U.S. corporations, starting with Ford and General Motors but in a major way including IBM, have been the innovators in company training institutes and in lifelong education. As with many other U.S. managerial innovations, Japan picked up and improved on the process just as the U.S. companies were abandoning or downplaying the role of these innovations.

Nevertheless, whether it be corporate education programs like those of the Japanese technology institutes or traditional college courses, changing our learning institutions from monogenerational ghettos into all-age communities might create the conditions for a new culture of greater depth and breadth. One might even hope for a new golden age of art, literature, and music. And by breaking the rigid life cycle of education, followed by work, followed by retirement, we open the possibility of a more vital and productive work force by creating a society that values growth and personal enrichment at all ages.

Changing Values

The whole thrust of our society is toward greater individuality, self-improvement, and better utilization of human potential. This cultural revolution is all but certain to have a continuing impact on the workplace. However, while I am optimistic about the strides our society will make as we learn to unleash that human potential, the years of transition ahead will be difficult for those who adjust to changing values—but catastrophic for those who fail to adjust at all.

In his *People at Work*, Pehr Gyllenhammar, president of Volvo, writes: "People entering the work force today have received more education than ever before in history. We have educated them to regard themselves as mature adults, capable of making their own choices. Then we offer them virtually no choice in our over-organized industrial units.

202

For eight hours a day they are regarded as children, ciphers, or potential problems and managed or controlled accordingly."[6]

Innovative approaches to manpower used abroad have proven highly successful, notably the Japanese system of lifetime employment (in the big companies only) and the German experiments in involving workers in decision making near the work station. Such policies are thought to be key to those countries' "economic miracles." What is significant in both cases is the effective identification of the workers' interests with those of the organization: Japanese employees view themselves as a vital part of a working community; the German workers feel they have as great an economic stake in productivity and profitability as does management.

Against a backdrop of declining productivity we in the U.S. can achieve the same thing—without copying Japan or Germany or duplicating any mechanism that would be inappropriate to our own culture. The challenge is to create a human climate conducive to innovation in both our public and private institutions. Increasing the scope for democracy and independent views in the workplace is something management can do, and it could go a long way toward unleashing the energies and creativity of those who are turned off by yesterday's organizational concepts and practices.

An important caveat: Never presume to know what it is that workers want. Noted industrialist and former undersecretary of commerce Sidney Harman offers an instructive insight into this problem.

A few years ago I visited Volvo, and among others, I spent time at the Skovda Engine plant. There were two—the so-called old plant and a modern new one.

In the old plant we walked into a large room, noisy and dirty as engines were being tested by some fifteen testers wearing ear muffs. In the new plant, the same function was exercised at individual test stations wired to the engines and located outside the noisy room.

I asked my guide, "How in the world do you persuade people to work in that hot, noisy, dirty atmosphere when there are equivalent jobs in quiet, air-conditioned and clean areas?" The answer was immediate: "We don't have a problem. Many people prefer the comradeship and the social environment of the old setting to the antiseptic and isolated positions of the new plant."

The lesson for me was obvious. Don't presume what is best for any worker or group of workers. Don't presume with respect to the conditions which will generate commitment. Ask them. Learn from them.[7]

Multitrack Organizations

To better understand what it is that workers want we must realize that it is not a single ethic or value system that characterizes today's worker. I have observed four distinct worker attitudes, each of which will characterize different types of people, or perhaps the same people at different periods of their lives.

1. The imaginatively lazy. Some people, in both blue-collar and white-collar jobs, will not want to work any more than they have to in order to survive. Ideally they would not work more than a month out of the year if they could make enough money in that month to support what they prefer to do for the rest of the year: skiing, painting, dancing, or any other activity.

2. The upwardly mobile. A large proportion of the population will always be willing to work extremely hard to improve their standard of living. Compared with the 1960s, today a substantial number of people are moving to this camp and regarding work as an important source of satisfaction.

3. Those seeking group enjoyment. An increasingly important incentive for some people is a sense of enjoyable involvement in a friendly work environment. Many people derive their greatest satisfaction from social interaction.

4. Those seeking interesting work. Forms of work that are interesting or fulfilling to the individual will be in increasing demand.

I believe most people really care about their work and don't need to be prodded into doing a good job. Figures of the U.S. Chamber of Commerce support this assessment: nine out of ten workers say it is important for them to work hard and do their best.[8] However, different people require different motivations. What would inspire the imaginatively lazy would stifle the upwardly mobile. Without an understanding of workers' needs managers can create obstacles and disincentives to personal performance. The task for managers is to promote what I shall call "multitrack organizations." Rather than assuming that all workers are driven by the same things, managers could provide multiple motivational systems—based not only on salary and benefits but on flexible hours, interesting work, greater responsibilities, creative outlets and opportunities, and so on—running in parallel, each designed to open creative possibilities to a specific type of worker. The key to all of this, of course, is genuine career counseling for each employee.

An often unrecognized legacy of trade unionism, in its emphasis on "brotherhood" or equality, is the concept of generally equal compensation for generally equal hours (real input). In increasing measure this scheme is inappropriate to today's world. The value of one computer programmer's talent is often out of all proportion to a small army of similarly educated or experienced colleagues—because of his or her *creativity*. The same is true in a different way of other white-collar professionals performing largely unstructured tasks. Yet how little are most of our large organizations able to reflect this often extreme difference by virtue of their own personnel systems. More and more we need hard evaluation of just how well modern-day incentive systems actually unleash creativity and how much difference is accounted for by hours of work and diligence of application.

At the same time, much that makes for success in the workings of our advanced industrial society depends to an increasing degree on imagination and the quality of the intellectual content often provided by only a few workers. The cost and success of a management information system depend more on the quality of programming and system-design talent than on the most sophisticated computer technology. No number of extra hours or added troops makes up for the dedicated ingenuity of one or a few people. The entire development of an advanced product can be similarly dependent. Understanding what motivates, or "turns on," such talent becomes the key to success or failure of an entire enterprise.

Taken to its extreme, the market valuation put on such **205** talent by the venture capital and stock market is a daily reminder of the reality of something I have been saying for years: *talent is capital.* Yet, how many personnel-administration systems recognize this? And how many have grappled with the very real problem of creating a compensation system that recognizes this kind of talent and yet is fair and not discouraging to the rest of the organization? Solutions are not easy. But the search for them should be a priority more commonly than it is in most organizations.

Such are the disjunctions of our transitional age that today, on a single planet, the highly productive Koreans are marching within factory compounds in uniformed platoons to manufacture semiconductors while a Silicon Valley start-up, in the occasionally realized hope that its employees will achieve a chip breakthrough, allows them to enjoy Friday afternoons in company-supplied hot tubs—a sixteenth-century Korean invention!

As much as our high-productivity capital base has allowed these discrepancies, we already see that margin disappearing. More and more we need hard evaluation of just how much of what we do actually unleashes creativity and how much difference is accounted for by hours of work and diligence of application. All too often companies grapple with the problem of providing appropriate motivational systems by crude attempts to give better physical facilities—a fresh coat of paint and piped-in Muzak—or grant a year off, without much understanding of how these unsystematic efforts actually pay off.

More of the Japanese and Korean economic "miracle" is due to longer and harder work than is generally recognized. This is not to say that our society would not be willing to make similar sacrifices and accept a lower material standard of living in return for restoring our nation's economic competitiveness. But before we trade in our hot tubs or any other accouterments of *leisure*, it behooves us to know just how much of the relative drop in living standards may be rationalized in the way I suspect much of the lowest northern European standard of living is so rationalized by my British friends: as a less "materialistic" but fuller, happier, slower-paced way of life.

Certainly, as a society becomes better off, its citizens will want—and expect—to have more leeway to act as they please. We are unquestionably moving toward a more leisurely society. Today it is common to say that Bill Jones is a plumber who likes to fish and play golf. Tomorrow it is more likely we will say that Bill is a man who enjoys fishing and golf and, incidentally, happens to earn a living as a plumber. And if Mary Jones wants to take the day off and go sailing, it should be much easier for her to do it than in the past. This type of behavior might formerly have been regarded as slacking, if not downright sinful, because the absence of one person from the workbench could cause disruption.

It is also true that a more leisurely society may not be merely a luxury but a necessity. As computers and automation assume the burden of vast numbers of jobs that are tedious, dangerous, or otherwise undesirable, there may quite simply be less work to do. The number of "information workers" will no doubt increase—lawyers, educators, consultants, writers, and so on. But it may not be necessary, or desirable, to put everyone to work for fifty weeks a year, forty hours a week. There is no law graven in stone that says the forty-hour work week is inviolable. It may eventually become more appropriate for workers to share jobs and work only half a year or a few months a year consecutively. The new technologies in the workplace, combined with changing attitudes about work, and multitrack motivational systems to accommodate them, will pave the way for a restructuring of the hours and days of our lives.

Yet hot tubs and free time and flexible hours and any of the other perks that are the rightful rewards of creative genius do not produce the genius. Most companies today would grant total freedom to someone like Steinmetz, as General Electric did when it inaugurated its research facility. Yet the campus-style laboratory and company-paid Ph.D. programs rarely unearth great talent if it has not been recognized in the first place. As with most things in life, what we need is the judgment or common sense, but, more than this, the organizational freedom to recognize the exceptional talent and to treat it exceptionally. And we must realize today that it is not the once-in-a-lifetime genius of a

Steinmetz but a whole gradation of talent that we must encourage through an array of alternative tracks, or working conditions.

The New Human Being

We are moving toward a definition of the human being as one who searches for different forms of satisfaction at different stages of life and combines personal goals with the goals of a larger group, whether it be family, community, or corporation. Even the most ambitious young people want to move up the ladder of success *and* pursue satisfying outside interests. The question becomes: What changes can be made to make full use of the worker's talent and drive, both for the workers' sake and for their organizations?

Any company that allows its achievement-oriented workers to feel dissatisfied will be wasting its most precious asset. While my repeated references to talent as capital may sound platitudinous, there is a real value in a human organization, trained and in place, that goes beyond the monetary equivalent of salaries and benefits (which, by the irony of accounting, are treated as liabilities). Obviously, a company starting from scratch is at a disadvantage compared with one that is fully staffed. And the investment that start-up company will make in its people goes far beyond the cost of salaries and wages. That is why I think of human talent as real capital.

Two trends, I think, will work toward the employer's benefit. First, the trend toward payment for modules of work done—rather than for mere attendance at the work site—will mean greater flexibility and personal satisfaction for the worker and greater productivity for the employer. At present the measuring of productivity in the white-collar workplace is an imperfect science. By breaking down office work into more definable tasks, the organization will have a more efficient system of allocating its resources. Moreover, the system of payment for modules of work does not tie the worker to a desk or to a rigid schedule; the work can be performed when the worker is most capable and wherever he or she chooses to do it. Information technology amplifies the worker's options in this regard, so that it will be reasonable for a worker to live in Tahiti and "telecommute" daily to New York.

The second trend is the move toward making work more entrepreneurial for the individual, to allow greater latitude for experimentation while maintaining organizational ties. The most effective way to secure maximum productivity in a highly educated society is to make work more individually interesting. The most successful big corporations will be those that transform themselves into federations of entrepreneurs.

I have some more specific recommendations for the kinds of changes organizations can effect to make work more rewarding and enriching for the individual and more productive for the employer. But first let us examine the seeds of the revolution in human values.

The Seeds of Revolution

How did today's new work ethos come about? A *Zeitgeist* is not without parents; however abstract the spirit of the times may be, its forebears are to be found in very concrete events. As in any great social revolution, there are underlying causes that may be traced back for centuries and immediate ones that are within personal memory. An underlying cause of the new attitudes is a person's resistance to work if the end product is not his to dispose of as he or she wishes: to admire, to use, to peddle in the market. It may very well be that humans found work distasteful even if they ended up as proprietors of their products. If not, then why was God's dictum to Adam that he earn his future bread in the sweat of his brow viewed as the ultimate curse? But where the final commodity did not even belong to the worker, his toil—however necessary—was joyless.

In one of his earlier essays Karl Marx, speaking as the humanist psychologist rather than the economic analyst or revolutionary agitator, described the deep alienation between the worker and his work in the factory systems during the early days of the industrial revolution. In an essay entitled "Alienated Labor" that appeared in the German radical magazine *Vorwärts* about a hundred and forty years ago, Marx wrote:

What then do we mean by the alienation of labor? First, that the work he performs is extraneous to the worker, that is, it is not personal to him, is not part of his nature; therefore he does not fulfill himself in work, but actually denies himself; feels miserable rather than content, cannot freely develop his physical and mental powers, but instead becomes physically exhausted and mentally debased. Only while not working can the worker be himself; for while at work he experiences himself as a stranger.

Therefore only during leisure hours does he feel at home, while at work he feels homeless. His labor is not voluntary, but coerced, forced labor. It satisfies no spontaneous creative urge, but is only a means for the satisfaction of wants which have nothing to do with work. Its alien character therefore is revealed by the fact that when no physical or other compulsion exists, work is avoided like the plague.

Why did a worker put up with such oppressive circumstances? As in every major social institution, so too in regard to work, the crass need to survive was not enough to persuade humans to adjust to the unending tiresome toil; an *ethic* had to be found. In an age of religion the ethic quickly found a theological rationale. It was God's will that man work, no matter how little it served man's needs, because in doing so humans were serving a heavenly purpose. This notion was immortalized by Max Weber, who characterized this divine rationale to sweat for the sake of sweating as the "Protestant work ethic."

Since the secular application of this ethic did not come instinctively to many workers, their employers accepted the responsibility of acting as the Lord's surrogates on earth in enforcing the divine will. Workers were punished for such bad habits as "wandering from one's work station, gazing out the window, washing, whistling, talking with others, swearing, drinking, lateness, and 'seduction.' "⁹

The depersonalization of production that came to mark the next century, from 1850 to 1950, arose not simply from growth in the size of the manufacturing facility but also from the division, subdivision, simplification, and synchronization of the process. The worker was no longer the operator of a machine; he was part of the machine—just another cog, whirling about to the rhythm of the metal monster that ruled him.

The prophet and practitioner of what came to be called "scientific management" was Frederick Taylor, whose system rested on a set of assumptions about working people. "In Taylorism, the working man, often an immigrant, was assumed to be an ignorant, uneducated, unmotivated but physically strong creature who could, oxlike, be forced to do productive work once management, with its superior intelligence, succeeded in breaking work into its simplest components. The worker, then, had merely to be trained in mindless repetitive motions." [10]

Workers did not take readily to this system. Turnover in many large facilities was 100 percent per annum. There almost seemed to be a direct ratio between the degree of "scientism" and the degree of turnover. When the Ford Motor Company introduced the moving belt, workers began to move out.

> Ford's men had begun to desert him in large numbers as early as 1910. With the coming of the assembly line, their ranks almost literally fell apart; the company soon found it next to impossible to keep its working force intact, let alone expand it. It was apparent that the Ford Motor Company had reached the point of owning a great factory without having enough workers to keep it humming.
>
> Ford admitted later that his startling factory innovations had ushered in the outstanding labor crisis of his career. The turnover of his working force had run, he was to write, to 380 percent for the year 1913 alone. So great was labor's distaste for the new machine system that toward the close of 1913 every time the company wanted to add 100 men to its factory personnel, it was necessary to hire 963. [11]

Ford found a solution: high wages. The rest of the auto industry and heavy manufacture in general followed the example. The motivation to work was no longer God but Mammon. Wherever possible, incentive systems were established to relate earnings to output. "Money, money, money" made the wheels "go round." The new *ethic* had invented a robust demonology to replace the old theology.

Time Out

For the worker drawn into this devilish device there was but one respite: free time. Workers bargained for shorter work days, shorter work weeks, more "breaks," more holidays, longer vacations, early retirement. The idea was to work so you didn't have to work—a work ethic that was (is) fundamentally an antiwork ethic.

The system rested on a variety of sticks and carrots, basically the "stick" of firing and the "carrot" of pay. It did not really make the job an activity that found its wellspring in the workers' being. The motivation came from without and from above and not from within. The arrangement was authoritarian and adversarial. Whatever its rewards—and there were (are) many as measured both by earnings and by leisure—the design was depersonalizing and, for many workers, sufficiently depressing to cause much mischief on the job.

Some critics of the system, such as Elton Mayo, held that it was necessary to understand "the worker as a psychological self whose motivation depended upon the fulfillment of social and emotional needs."[12] But such thoughts did not become the basis for significant action until a generation of children born immediately after the Second World War reached working age.

Antiauthoritarianism

The fundamental trait of that generation was its critical, perhaps iconoclastic, attitude toward authority. This antiauthoritarian mood was not limited to the workplace; it applied to all social institutions, from family to government. It was the national expression of a postwar generation growing up.

The years after World War II were "in-between" times, one of those recurrent moments in history when the old order passes and a new order has not yet arrived. The established centers of authority were badly shaken, even shattered, by the war. The great empires—British, French, Dutch, Belgian—were dismembered. New nations, with their own centers of authority, came into being, only to find that their newly asserted authority was challenged within their own borders. Fixed notions of a bifurcated world, divided between capitalism and communism, were scrambled as both systems broke down into a variety of "capitalisms" and "communisms," with variants in mixed economies and mixed politics. Within the traditional great religions and churches of the world new heresies and new heterodoxies emerged.

Into this disorderly world was born a numerous generation of babies. In *Work and Human Values*, a multinational study conducted by the Aspen Institute for Humanistic Studies and the Public Agenda Foundation, Daniel Yankelovich and his associates concluded:

> In the era of peace and economic growth following World War II, many young people had come to take for granted the security that their parents had worked for so strenuously. Instead they began to place great emphasis on what we call the values of "expressivism." These include values such as creativity, autonomy, rejection of authority, placing self-expression ahead of status, pleasure seeking, the hunger for new experiences, the quest for community, participation in decision making, the desire for adventure, closeness to nature, cultivation of self, and inner growth.[13]

In the 1960s the teenagers were very numerous, so much so that when they met with their peers they quite naturally thought of themselves as "the society." In addition, they were growing up in uncertain times, at a moment when the traditional socializing forces were themselves in a state of confusion. Authority surely could not play its traditional role in its customary way.

In the 1960s this challenge to authority expressed itself in the extreme, bordering on anarchy. Opposition to the Vietnam War, personified by "the movement," further polarized the young and the old. The young generation turned riotous—on campuses, at political conventions, in street demonstrations, at rock concerts. The phenomenon was international, running from the University of California to Columbia University, from the Sorbonne to Tokyo, with the most vicious outbreak in mainland China, where the Red Guard, under the aegis of an aging Chairman Mao, went systematically to work to destroy all culture in the name of a "cultural revolution."

In subsequent decades that "generational" chaos waned. But "authority"—at least the traditional authority—had been openly challenged and in many cases openly beaten. **213**

Often institutions made adjustments, introduced reforms in response to the pressures of the young.

The countercultural revolution of the time did not succeed in remaking the world in its own image (for what society can survive without a cultural base?), but it did leave its mark on the traditional culture to produce a new culture or at least a reformed culture. As in the Magna Carta, "authority" was preserved, but in the form of a *shared* authority.

In an essay, "The World of Work," labor leader Gus Tyler notes:

> It can be assumed that the future work force will be more resistant than that of 1950 or 1925 to tight control from above. Our better educated, better paid workers of tomorrow will want to exercise some degree of control over how they perform their tasks. This changed attitude will not necessarily lead to greater friction between workers and managers.
>
> Just as the surge of women into the job market was matched by a vast increase in the kinds of jobs for which women were especially suited, so the recent increase in the number of workers who demand interesting jobs has been matched, at least partly, by a vast increase in the number of such jobs.
>
> It is more and more true that "authority" is derived from knowledge and often resides in the employee rather than the boss.[14]

The New Family

It was predictable that the general challenge to traditional authority would have to affect the customary hierarchical structure of the *family*. For many centuries, going back to Aristotle, the family model, with the father as the dominant and often domineering figure, was used to explain the "natural" origins of kingship. In less grandiose ways the family was seen as the central cell of the body politic—structured, tight knit, ordered. In the post–World War II decades family relations were profoundly altered.

In no small part, this was due to the massive movement of women into the labor market. The war was largely responsible. Some 12 million men were drafted (or volunteered) from civilian life to put on uniforms. The demands for production were great—to meet both civilian and military needs. Women moved into the economy as never before. This shift of women from the home to the work site was foreshadowed for decades. According to the census of 1900, 41 percent of all nonwhite women and 17 percent of white women (many immigrants) were in the work force. Seventy-five percent of the women in factories were immigrants and about 70 percent were unmarried, so the idea of women at work was not new.[15]

But the war turned a trickle into a torrent. When the war started, 25 percent of the women of working age were in the labor market; by the end of the war the percentage had risen to 36. By 1975, a landmark year, more than 50 percent of women above the age of sixteen were in the labor force —"and the percentage has been rising since."[16]

Why did women continue in the labor market, growing in numbers and in percentages, once the war was over and Johnny came marching home again? The answers come in three categories: technical, economic, and cultural. And all three intertwine.

Technology has liberated woman from her traditional chores, including undesired childbearing. She can wash and dry clothes in a machine, so she does not have to scrub, rinse, wring, hang things on a line. She can buy instant food in a can, in a frozen package, in a breakfast-food box, in a take-out shop. She can decide how many children she wants or does not want, and, having had a child, she can throw away the disposable diaper. (In the 1970s alone the average number of children per family dropped from 2.3 to 1.9.)[17]

As a consequence, more women, especially married women, are available for work outside the home. In 1969, 40 percent of all married women were in the labor force; by 1982 the percentage had risen to 55. "The really major changes, however, occurred among those with children, particularly very young children. For example, among those with children under 3 years of age, more than 40 percent work; the corresponding figure for 1969 was only 24 percent. Similarly, about 35 percent of married women with nursery-age children—from 3 to 5 years of age—worked in 1969; today the figure is 52 percent."[18]

In these prosperous times people could afford all kinds of new *services:* radio and TV repairs, hairdos, restaurants, gardening, home maintenance, psychiatrists, nursery schools. With burgeoning governmental expenditures, the nation also underwrote expanding public services, especially at the state, county, municipal, and—above all—school district level. The "civil servant," once a negligible percentage of the labor force, turned up as one out of every five employees in the country.[19]

Measured in terms of the labor force, *services* have been steadily rising and *goods production* steadily declining—percentagewise. In 1950, 49 percent (almost half) of the labor force was engaged in producing goods (mining, construction, manufacturing, agriculture), and 50.9 percent (the other half) in providing services. By 1980 only 31 percent (less than one out of three) was in goods production; 68.9 percent (more than two out of three) was in the service sector.[20]

In this postwar economy the participation rate—the percentage of adults in the labor market—went up from 58.3 percent in 1947 to 62.3 percent in 1977. Prior to that time the participation rate had appeared to be a constant, showing 55 percent over seven successive censuses.[21] This dramatic, historically unprecedented rise in the "participation rate" is, of course, primarily due to the female influx. "During the 1970's, there was a labor force increase of 27 percent, with women accounting for almost 60 percent of that upturn. In the 1980's, with an expected work force increase of 17 percent, women are projected to account for nearly 70 percent of that upturn."[22]

The expansion of the economy made jobs available for women who were available. Indeed, the growth of the service economy provided the kind of jobs that were especially attractive to women with children who did not wish to or could not yet give full time to a job away from home. The service economy offered many part-time jobs and openings "in the neighborhood." In 1950 about 17 percent of the labor force worked part-time—that is, 35 hours or fewer a week. By 1954 that number had risen to 19 percent, and by 1970 to 25.5 percent.[23] One out of every four jobs was part-time.

New Image of Woman

While technology and changing occupational opportunities explain much of the reason why by 1980 women made up 42.6 percent of the labor force (projected to 46.2 percent in 1990),[24] there is still another vector in this dynamic: cultural. It is the woman's new image of herself. "The rapid movement of women into the workforce has derived its strength and permanence from the same sociological needs for a sense of community, identity, and self esteem which drive the work efforts of men in an affluent society," note Levitan and Johnson. "The precedent of wartime labor provided the crack in social mores which kept women at home, and the two more recent women's movement of the 1970's has all but shattered these rigid stereotypes."[25]

Indeed, it can be argued that many of the devices invented to liberate the woman from the home were a response to women's desire to enter the workplace. And it can also be argued that jobs for women, especially in the service sector, became available because entrepreneurs knew that there was a ready female labor force. Whatever the factors, however, behind the movement of women into the labor market, the simple fact is that an overwhelming majority of women are no longer just homebodies. This applies to all income categories. Once women went to work because the husband did not make enough to support the family; there was a strong inverse ratio between family income and women at work. That historic ratio "has weakened considerably amidst growing affluence. The Bureau of the Census reported that almost 60 percent of the women in families with annual incomes of $25,000 or more worked in 1980."[26]

The inpouring of women into the labor market, especially married women with children, has profoundly changed the nature of the family. Once it was the man who was the breadwinner, so that only a quarter of a century ago, 56 out of 100 families had a sole earner—namely, a male. By 1976, however, "the old cliche was applicable to only one family out of three."[27] And the trend toward the two-breadwinner family has continued since.

The economic independence enjoyed by more and more women has given them new standing in the authority struc- **217**

ture of the family. The notion of father as king or, deriva-
tively, of any person as "king," has been on the wane.
Wives and children seek and get a voice in the democratization of the household. The rise in divorce rates is also a
contributory factor in the weakening of the father (or even
the mother) figure as the fixed locus of authority. In the
course of his or her first twenty years a child may now quite
customarily grow up under the "governance" of three or
four or more parents.

From Ox to Oxonian

The typical youth in America is also likely to have tasted
the independence that comes from having his or her own
earnings at an early age. The participation rate of young
people aged fourteen to twenty-four has been going up
steadily, especially among young girls. Their contribution
to family income is significant. "In families with an income
between $7,000–10,000, there are 1.24 breadwinners; in
families of $10,000–15,000 there are 1.58 breadwinners; in
families of $15,000–25,000 there are 1.98 breadwinners;
in families of $25,000–50,000 there are 2.42 breadwin-
ners."[28]

The "kids" pay their "taxes" to support the family and,
as good Americans, seek a form of household governance
in which there shall be no taxation without representation.
Out of this new kind of family arises a new sense of how
institutions are to be governed, a feeling that authority
should be shared. Deeply rooted as this relationship is in
many American homes, it is to be expected that the concept
will not be abandoned at the workplace.

In this modern version of the home there is not only a
dispersion of income sources and of authority but also of
responsibilities. Just as more and more women are expected to work, so more and more men are expected to
share household chores.

[This] rise in the number of families with two or more wage
earners may add to the pressure for more time away from the
workplace in the years ahead.

This push for greater leisure will be partially an outgrowth
of affluence of multiple income families, but it may also

reflect an increasing pattern of husbands and wives sharing family responsibilities. This mutual acceptance of both provider and parenting roles would require an added measure of flexibility in work hours, and these emerging needs in the modern family may well be translated into future demands for paid leisure and shorter or more personalized work schedules."[29]

Women at work are also responsible, in large part, for the rise in the number of young people attending schools of higher learning. The extra household income has gone very largely to pay for the mortgage and for tuition. Simultaneously, public expenditures were expanded for education from kindergarten to postgraduate school. The combined result was to produce wage and salaried employees with ever higher educational attainments. In 1940 the median educational exposure of an employee was 8.7 years—just above the elementary school level; in 1980 (four decades later) that level had risen to 12.7—a college freshman.[30]

This college-bred generation has higher expectations than those of earlier generations: the hours spent in the schools of higher learning are expected to pay off in both monetary and psychic income. If there were enough "interesting" jobs to absorb this generation, the "educated" employee would find a suitable spot in the economy. But a University of Michigan Survey in 1970 found that one in every three employees felt that he had more education than the job required.[31] To motivate these better educated, the job has to be adjusted to tap the potential energies of the modern worker. He is now more Oxonian than ox and has to be treated accordingly.

The New Work Ethic

In the evolution of the work ethic from God through Mammon, the present stage includes humankind. It is an ethic that finds motivation in *being human*—in finding a measure of self-fulfillment at work.

In a six-country study by the Aspen Institute and the Public Agenda Foundation, three kinds of motivation were defined, based on "sustenance" (the need to survive), "material success" (the desire to gather status through income),   **219** and "expressive success" (the urge to be oneself at work). The survey found that for five of the six countries "material success" was the primary drive; Israel, where "sustenance" was primary, was the exception. "Expressive success" was the smallest of the reasons for work in all countries, ranging from 11 percent in the United Kingdom to 23 percent in Sweden.

When the ages of the respondents were factored into the findings, however, it became apparent that there was a shifting of values from generation to generation: "When agrarian society was transformed into industrial society the values of sustenance gave way to the values of material success, and when industrial society was transformed into the welfare state, the values of material success stopped increasing while the values of expressive success continued to grow."[32] For the generation that grew up in an industrial society, with a rising standard of living, reinforced by the practices of a "welfare state," the desire to "express" oneself is of greater significance than it was to previous generations. When this economic basis is added to the sociopolitical dynamic of the postwar years, it is not surprising that motivation of the modern man or woman on the job requires recognition of the worker as a person and a personality.

Interestingly, economic downturn, experienced by the Western world in recent years, has not reversed this trend toward making man himself the center of the work ethic. Economic hardships "have induced a mood of caution and a new respect for the role of industry in creating wealth and jobs. But they have not shaken people's determination to realize their new life values, even if economic viability suffers thereby."[33]

To measure motivation, Yankelovich invented the concept of "discretionary effort"—a producer's variation of the consumer concept of "discretionary income." The assumption is that, on any job, the worker has some leeway on what he does and how he does it. The scope of "discretion" is, of course, not the same on all jobs. In many the worker has no margin for free action or decision; in others the employees may have wide range. According to the findings of Yankelovich, the "amount of discretionary effort in the workplace has greatly increased" because of two factors:

the shift from manufacturing to the service economy; the shift from blue-collar to white-collar employment.[34]

The better educated also tend to hold high-discretion jobs, whether because they end up in such occupations or because, by their presence, they change the job process. Thus 61 percent of white-collar jobs are high-discretion; 48 percent of service jobs; 53 percent of the jobs held by those with some college education. Only 17 percent of those in manufacture have high-discretion positions, 39 percent of the blue-collar workers, and—as might be expected—only 28 percent of those in dirty, noisy, and polluted work-places.[35] In jobs with high discretion, the degree of commitment by the worker is vital to maximum productivity. The Public Agenda study found that about one out of four job-holders felt he or she was working at full potential; almost half say they put in just about enough effort to get by; three-quarters say they could do a lot more than they are doing right now.[36]

The Foundation concludes that the "work ethic"—the worker's commitment to do the best job possible, regardless of pay—is surprisingly strong. In fact, "the work ethic may be growing in strength, especially among the better-educated job holders in high-discretion jobs. The American work ethic is thus one of America's most valuable resources. If correctly utilized, it could provide an important component in an overall effort to revive America's economic competitiveness."[37]

New Technology and Discretionary Effort

Nearly half the work force (44 percent) say they have experienced new technology in their jobs.[38] In theory, advanced technologies can be used to limit the amount of discretion in a job. Karen Nussbaum, director of the "9 to 5" organization representing women in the workplace, points out that word-processing systems let supervisors monitor the precise number of keystrokes performed by individual typists. And complaints are not limited to the steno pool. Middle managers say that new information systems and communications networks let top management keep closer tabs on them.

Yet there is much evidence that new technology can be 221

used to expand rather than limit the scope of workers' actions. I believe that personal computers in particular offer unprecedented new opportunities to unleash individual creativity. Because they are programmable, their uses can be adjusted to the worker's needs rather than the worker's having to adjust to the technology. They extend the capabilities of the individual.

It is significant that the microcomputer revolution that has taken the workplace by storm has not been imposed on the worker by some ruthless technocrats or by any authoritarian external forces. The Diebold Research Program has found that it is the nontechnical professionals who are going out and purchasing personal computers for themselves—bypassing the data-processing departments altogether. This trend is an expression of the worker's need for both self-expression and control over his or her own destiny.

Research by the Public Agenda Foundation indicates an almost unanimous view that technological changes make work more interesting and less regimented. Only 22 percent of the respondents in a nationwide survey said that technology made their jobs more monotonous, while 74 percent found that technology made their work more interesting and less routine. And 55 percent said the changes gave them greater independence in their methods of doing their jobs.[39]

What brings these statistics home to me in human terms is the example of a writer/researcher in my own company. Rather than commuting to work—which in this case would mean a trek from Boston to New York—she works on a personal computer in her home. Her work is easily transmitted in minutes over telephone lines to the computer system at New York headquarters. Far from depersonalizing her work, the computer has made possible a highly individualized work arrangement. It has also enabled her to maintain social and familial ties in her native Boston, avoiding a potentially disruptive move to work in New York City. In this sense the computer may bring an interesting side effect as a stabilizer of social and family life.

Sticks and Carrots

The ancient sticks and carrots to spur commitment are no
longer as effective as they once were. Unemployment, al-

though disastrous for many individuals and wasteful for the society as a whole, is not what unemployment once was when the family had but one breadwinner. Nowadays the head of the family may lose his or her job without precipitating disaster in the household if spouses and children are working. In addition, there is a safety net in the form of unemployment insurance. There is also an informal or "underground" economy of major dimensions (organized crime, "petty" crime that is no longer petty, the cash transaction, barter) that can absorb millions of people. The old "stick" is cracked. And in prosperous times it is useless.

Similarly, the carrot isn't what it was—if we think of the carrot as higher pay. Once a worker has reached a given level of security, he or she begins to think about nonmaterial wants, such as leisure, pleasant surroundings, respect, appreciation as a person: self-realization. Abraham Maslow, in his psychology of being, has popularized the idea of a hierarchy of needs: once the basics are in place (enough carrots to stay alive) and a bit of status is established (better carrots to afford a few luxuries), the menu must change to provide the kind of carrots that will not just stuff a person but will feed the desire for self-fulfillment.

To muster the unused energies of the worker, it becomes necessary to construct a motivational system on those factors that motivate modern men and women, factors that go beyond salary and status—namely, the urge to be a person: unique, creative, and something special.

On Fleximodes

In recognition of the changing nature of the labor force, sexually and psychologically, many companies (large and small) have turned to flexitime. There are "morning" people and "evening" people who, given a degree of flexibility, will make their talents available at their peak hours. There are also many people who can work only part time, whose abilities, if imaginatively organized, can be put to maximum use. The growing number of two-breadwinner families makes flexitime enticing to mothers and fathers who wish to share home-keeping and child-rearing chores.

The direction of technological change supports this growing trend toward "time shifting": voice store-and-forward systems, electronic mail (replete with graphics and voice), teleconferencing, and video recording technologies enhance the opportunity in the years just ahead to shift work to the hours most convenient to the worker.

Flexitime started in Germany, introduced in 1968 by the German aerospace company Messerschmitt-Bolkow-Blohm. Although workers were held to a forty-hour week, they were allowed to choose the hours they preferred. Just so the work process did not fall apart, the company set certain "core" hours that were compulsory and then opened up other hours for personal choice. The idea spread; in Switzerland, 30 percent of the work force is on flexitime. Another form of flexitime is the stretched-out workday and the compressed work week. Some banks and insurance companies, for instance, have put computer operators on a twelve-and-a-half-hour day and cut the work week to three days. Other companies have found it desirable to stretch the work day to ten hours and to limit the work week to four days. Airline pilots have schedules that call for long, continuous hours of work followed by long periods of rest. In working with clients I have found that no one formula applies to all conditions. Each case stands on its own: flexitime for employees requires flexithink for employers.

The "flexi" concept can be applied to more than time, however. There can be flexitask, flexiplace, flexicare (for self and child). Indeed, such suffixes have already been added to the "flexi" root in many places. Flexitask seeks to redesign the job assignment so that the employee can escape undue boredom, learn to do a variety of things, get an overview of the total objective. Many such experiments have been under way in the United States.

▷ Bankers Trust Company of New York introduced a program for their production typists who record stock-transfer data. The program called for a new modular design, embracing related tasks and requiring increased responsibility for work done. "After six months, production rates improved 92% in one section and more than 110% in two other sections. No increase in errors resulted when the checker job was eliminated."[40]

▷ George Washington University Hospital introduced a two-level program: (1) supervisors and food administrators met weekly for one year, studying management theory for application to cases; (2) after time studies for workers in three sections, changes were made in job definitions and duties with new career ladders for promotion. Results: annual savings in costs ran to more than half a million dollars.[41]

▷ Western Union, Philadelphia Bookkeeping Bureau, changed the billing process so that twelve functions were no longer divided among different types of clerks but were shared among twelve bookkeeping clerks. "There was a reduction in percentage of filing errors in relation to total message volume."[42]

▷ Various companies within the Bell System enriched jobs through systematic changes in the module of work, through control of the module, and through feedback. Jobs were reorganized in groups beyond individual jobs ("nesting"). "In one company, a 50% improvement in turnover was reported as attributable to enrichment of individual jobs; where job nesting was used in another company, number of orders typed on time increased from 27% to 100% a half year later." Absenteeism fell; errors fell.[43]

▷ A General Electric plant modified its assembly process so that one operator could follow a unit down the line. Role playing was used to give employees a better grasp of the total process. "Defects per operator were reduced about 50%. Output rose from an average of 25.7 units for nine months before the programs to an average of 46.7 units after."[44]

▷ "A large insurance company," described in a paper by R. Janson, presented at an International Conference on the Quality of Working Life, introduced twenty-five changes, involving greater personal responsibility of operators for their own work, correcting obvious coding errors and their own errors; dealing directly with customers. Productivity rose; errors decreased; ratings for performance rose; absenteeism fell; savings were placed at $64,305.[45]

The positive results I have listed in the cases cited do not mean that every redesign of jobs is bound to be successful. Redesign, like anything else, can be faulty; sometimes the idea is good, but the implementation is bad. But enrichment through redesign is an option that cannot be excluded from management reckoning; there are too many cases in which such innovation has been productive and profitable.

Flexiplace is another alternative. Modern telecommunication makes teletask a possibility. Indeed, it makes it likely to the point of inevitability. An employee, at almost any level, can use a terminal to activate machines, to solve puzzles, to type scripts, to keep accounts, to draw blueprints, to participate in conferences, to receive reports, to issue orders—and can do all this at home or in a variety of locales. This applies particularly to parents who wish to work but need to care for their children. The work can be done, as it increasingly is being done, at home—by telecommuting.

Flexicare is still another variant on the theme. This applies to the diverse benefits—beyond wages—provided for employees, including ways and means to care for small children while parents are at work. Such "benefit" plans, commonly referred to as "fringes," became popular during the Second World War. To hold down wartime inflation, ceilings were set on wage increases; as an alternative, unions asked for "deferred wage payments" in the forms of pensions, health and welfare benefits, life insurance, drug-prescription, and other programs. Many corporations offered parallel plans on their own. Today, such "fringes" make up about 30 percent of the wage-and-salary bill.

These plans have historically treated their beneficiaries en bloc. Certain uniform terms were worked out, making allowances occasionally for minor variations in age, contributions, years worked, and so on. Essentially, however, there were no flexibilities in the system. Yet the case for flexible benefits (flexicare) has a certain logical appeal. A young man or woman might prefer to have higher benefits allocated to child care; someone in his or her sixties might opt for a higher pension; a middle-aged person might choose medical coverage; an ambitious employee might want help with further education.

Ruben Mettler of TRW notes that when the idea was presented to workers, "Eighty-five percent of employees wanted changes in the mix of benefits. The company is spending the same amount for money now for the flexible benefits, but the employees are getting choices, and this is the biggest advantage."[46] As a rule the "selection" is not a free-for-all. Corporations offer a finite number of packages, part of the reason being the difficulty of handling an infinite number of choices. Phyliss Schless of American Can, whose company has had experience with flexible benefits, suggests, however, that "sophisticated computer programs could handle the variety."[47]

As the number of women with small children increases in the labor force, there is increased demand for a fringe benefit to cover child care. Although several companies, early on, set up physical centers within the vicinity of the work site to care for the children of employees, this practice has not caught on. A mother may use the facility when she first gets a job, but after she has a steady income, she is more likely to withdraw the child and place him or her in a neighborhood setting. In a list of recommendations on child care for working parents, an Aspen Institute colloquy proposed:

▷ Paternity as well as maternity leaves.
▷ Subsidies to individual employees to pay for child care.
▷ Subsidies to community care centers or family day-care providers.
▷ Contracts with child-care centers.
▷ Consortiums with other companies to provide care.
▷ Preventive health programs.[48]

The need for flexiprograms and for the encouragement of participation in management and for innovation in tune with the changing demography and values of our work force has not been felt as strongly as might be expected because of the relatively high level of unemployment in the United States and elsewhere. During such depressed periods employees are less than their normal selves. They will put up with irksome conditions because, for the moment, they have no alternative. In such times management also has a greater selection from which to choose its employees and is likely to select those who fit into the old mold. Unemployment masks the real state of employee attitudes. But that won't always be so unless we surrender to the gloomy pros- **227** pect of continuous high unemployment. With recovery of the economy will come return of the value system by which people live in the America of the rapidly onrushing twenty-first century.

Outlook for Unions

Interestingly enough, one of the sectors of the population that has been suspicious of, almost resistant to the sort of innovations I have been discussing appears to be changing its attitude. I refer to the American unions. In a recent evaluation of the union attitude toward "work-innovation" the Work in America Institute noted:

> Despite the benefits unions can gain from work-innovation programs, many of them have a deep anxiety about QWL [quality-of-work-life] and other programs that increase worker satisfaction. The popularity of QWL programs with many non-union corporations has reinforced the feeling among union leaders that keeping unions out is the real "hidden agenda" of quality-of-work-life programs. This concern is not without substance. The QWL process, in one form or another is being abused by some employers as a means of achieving . . . a "union-free environment."[49]

That was written in 1982. In August 1983 the American Federation of Labor–Congress of Industrial Organizations issued a report by its Committee on the Evolution of Work that contained specific reference to "quality of work life." In a positive yet guarded statement the report concluded:

> There are new and growing desires among many workers for recognition of individual dignity and for a job in which the worker is in some way involved and fulfilled. This is a long-standing concern of the American labor movement along with fair compensation, job security, and other conditions of employment.
> Employers usually see "quality of work life" programs as a way to raise productivity and increase competitiveness—and sometimes as a way to fight unions—rather than as a way to increase worker participation in company decision-making. The more than 1,000 QWL programs now under way take many different forms: labor-management committees,

participatory management, employee involved democracy, consultation schemes, quality circles, autonomous work groups, quality of work teams, profit-sharing arrangements, and so forth. Some are within the framework of collective bargaining, some are supplementary to collective bargaining, and some are aimed at circumventing and weakening collective bargaining or preventing union organizing and union recognition. Where QWL is perverted into a management tool or weapon used against workers and unions, skepticism and opposition result. But where QWL programs truly serve worker as well as management interests, unions have cooperated and supported such programs.[50]

Despite its many reservations, American labor recognizes that it can no more dismiss work innovation than it can ignore electric power. They are part of the scene: a new way of acting in response to a new way of thinking.

Responding to Change

Each day is confronted with the only constant in history: eternal change. Products change; processes change; managers change; employees change; the externalities—air, legislation, court decisions, social mores, available capital, infrastructure, business tempo, diet, love for leisure, the rise and fall of markets and nations, sex and age mix, human motivations—all change.

How to respond to today's changing values? There is no single answer. But from an examination of many circumstances I have come to believe there is an attitude that, when properly and pragmatically applied to a specific situation, can often be made to yield surprising results. The attitude may be described subjectively as openness and objectively as participation, especially by employees.

In one sense this suggestion—an openness to encourage participation—seems so obvious that it smacks of the cliché. On the other hand, it is an unnatural form of behavior to many managers. Understandably, the notion is—subconsciously if not consciously—threatening: an implicit challenge to authority; an invasion of reserved turf by the unwashed and unworthy; a democratization of what has been traditionally a hierarchical structure. To many, **229** perhaps too many, participation carries with it the uncomfortable image of the parent learning from the child, of the wise from the ignorant, of the leader from the led, which can only end in creeping indiscipline bordering on anarchy.

And participation does, I believe, have its limits. The West German example of workers participating on corporate boards is, to my mind, nineteenth-century and wooden. It solves nothing to involve people in decision making in areas in which they are not up to the task, either in qualifications or experience. Likewise, top executives would do well to stay out of the day-to-day decisions that take place on the shop floor. From everything I have learned about management in a lifetime of study and practice, both here and abroad, I can only conclude that decision making should reside close to the task. Yet in many instances—real cases—the readiness to invite in the parties traditionally excluded from decision making has proven its positive worth. For troubled companies, cities, even nations, the open mind has opened the door to proven progress.

The following are some real case examples of these participatory techniques in action. One is an approach that Japan, refreshingly enough, learned from the U.S.! It is also one that American industry is relearning.

Case:
"Intrapreneurship" at Convergent Technologies

Entrepreneurship is just as important to large companies as it is to small Silicon Valley start-ups. To kindle the spark of innovation, some large corporations are trying to duplicate the conditions that are conducive to creativity through something my colleagues and I call "intrapreneurship": setting up a small, independent division under the corporate umbrella that is, by all appearances, an entrepreneurial start-up, but is in fact a "company-within-a-company."

In the summer of 1982, thirty-year-old Matt Sanders was charged with starting such a company-within-a-company at Convergent Technologies, Inc., a Santa Clara, California, computer maker that builds high-priced business systems. The company wanted to get into the lucrative market for low-priced personal computers, and do so quickly: Sanders was given a one-year deadline to design, build, and bring to market a new machine. Sanders' group, comprising fifty persons, was code-named "Ultra" after an Allied method of deciphering Nazi communiques during World War II. The name was inspired by the fact that the group was sworn to secrecy; in fact, most of Convergent's parent-based employees never knew of the project until its completion.

Convergent president and cofounder Allen Michels described the approach this way: "You keep things small so you can create a culture, the right culture. . . . You inject a harmonious attitude. You give them the right amount of freedom so that there is no sense of futility."[51] Michels argued that the use of small working units is more productive for Americans than trying to adopt Japanese methods. And the approach was indeed a deliberate attempt to tap one of America's greatest strengths: the creative vitality and risk-taking spirit of its people.

Sanders was given a budget, over which he had total control, and moved out of his comfortable office to a less-than-glamorous one-story building. His first task was to convince the people he recruited that their rewards would be commensurate with those that a true entrepreneur would reap for their risk taking. One clear nonmonetary reward was the opportunity to watch a real product being built day by day and to feel a sense of pride, even ownership —everyone would have a stake in the venture's product.

One year later, on August 23, 1983, Convergent formally introduced "WorkSlate": a portable lap-size computer with built-in software, priced under $895.

Karen Toland, the product's marketing director, felt the machine could only have been built by a small team. "I don't have to go through two department heads and write six memos if something needs to be changed. I just walk across the hall and say, 'Hey, Charlie, this space bar feels like—' and then he fixes it."[52]

Convergent is not the only successful "intrapreneur." Computer giant IBM has at least fourteen "independent business units," working on new technologies like factory robotics. In fact, its extremely successful Personal Computer was conceived by an independent unit in Boca Raton, Florida. Apple Computer created a small group to develop its path-breaking Lisa, an easy-to-use personal computer for the business community. And Timex used the same approach to break into the computer business with its Timex Sinclair 1000, a home computer priced at around $100.

Even the largest and most hierarchical corporations are finding   **231** that this decentralized approach can go a long way toward keeping the entrepreneurial spirit alive.

Case:
No Place Like Home

The word "artist" can mean many things—painter, composer, actor, singer. But when Chris Rutkowski, president and founder of Rising Star Industries in Torrance, California, thinks of artists, he thinks of computer programmers.

Rutkowski believes that programmers, like all creative people, need a special environment and the freedom to work on their own terms. That is why he and nearly everyone else who works for Rising Star, a software research and development firm, are "telecommuters." Of the company's fifty or so employees, only eight work from a central office. The rest include technical writers, programmers, quality-control people, product support staff—and, of course, the company president—all working from their homes on personal computers linked together in a coast-to-coast network.

Why would a company set up shop almost entirely in electronic cottages—while most companies are reluctant to try telecommuting on even an experimental basis?

"When you're working with artists—and the best programmers are, in fact, artists—you can't say, 'Thou shalt be creative from eight o'clock to 12 o'clock.' The best software people often prefer working at odd hours. If you force them into a structured setting, you gain control, but you lose enormously in tapping their creative potential," said Rutkowski, who is also the firm's senior designer.[53]

Rutkowski seeks out the kind of people who "don't fit" in large corporations and become restless in their jobs; typically they leave to form their own companies or become consultants. But companies can help retain creative people by giving them the proper tools and structure. In return, the company gets a happier, more productive employee: by one account, the productivity of at-home workers may be 20 percent to 100 percent greater than for the same workers in an office environment.[54]

Not everyone is suited for the work-at-home phenomenon. One must be highly self-motivated and have a pleasant home environment. An unmarried person living in a bleak studio apartment might well prefer the change of scene and companionship to be found at the corporate office, while individuals with troubled marriages may find working at home only makes their troubles much worse.

But for Rutkowski, the setup is ideal. Speaking from his California home perched eight hundred feet up on a hill, he tells of his three children, his dogs and parakeets, his rabbits, his houseplants—and a "rich, full life in which life-family-job are melded into one." Indeed, working with Rising Star means not just a job but a wholly new life-style and culture.

How well does it work? Rutkowski claims he will put his twenty-six programmers up against a hundred of anyone else's programmers any day.

Case:
Japan Looks to America

In the years following World War II Japan had a bad reputation as the country that turned out shoddy products. As Japan had developed the rudiments of an industrial society by imitating other nations, to whom should it turn for a model to produce quality products? It was quite natural that it should look to the economically and politically powerful and predominant United States.

Way back in the 1940s "behavioral scientists [in the United States] had discovered the potential benefits to morale and productivity of worker participation in decision making." The Japanese turned to America for guidance, visiting American plants and, more important, reading American writings on the subject (in Japanese translation), gobbling up the works of Chris Argyris, Douglas Magregor, Rensis Likert, and "other exponents of participative management."[55] In 1951 "W. Edwards Deming went to Japan to give lectures and workshops on modern statistical methods of quality control . . . At the time, Deming thought he was teaching a methodology to be used by engineers and other management officials."[56] His approach was fundamentally top down.

But the Japanese, who were knowledgeable about the "participative school," wed the perceptions of the behavioral scientists to the statistical approaches of the engineers. "It remained to the Japanese to discover possibilities of involving workers directly in the process of diagnosing problems of quality and production and of devising solutions to these problems."[57] The result: quality control circles.

233

Today the quality control circle is popularly imagined to be a Japanese invention. In reality, the Japanese thought that they were merely imitating common practice in the United States. Robert Cole refers to the interplay as a "creative misunderstanding." By 1979 it was estimated that one in every eight Japanese workers was involved in a quality control circle—a ratio far above that in the United States, from whom the Japanese had learned the practice. In 1982, for example, Toyota received 1.3 million suggestions, an average of twenty-seven from each company employee. Ninety percent of the suggestions were adopted.[58]

Case:
The North Carolina Public Agency

The idea of involving workers in addressing their mission (or chores) as a group, with the purpose of talking about how to do the job better in terms of both output and self-realization, is so contagious that, when the state of North Carolina found itself squeezed budgetwise, it turned to its employees to devise ways to do more with less without taking it out of their hides. In the state offices, a crisis was in formation. "With most government agencies operating in a period of fixed or declining resources, most managers were finding it difficult to live within the budget. Fiscal restraint made it imperative that each government agency boost productivity in order to maintain services."[59] How was it possible to do this in the typically bureaucratic structure that characterizes most governmental bodies?

A special Governor's Commission on Government Productivity, together with the management of Wake County, North Carolina, called on the Productivity Research and Extension Program of North Carolina State University to work with them in developing quality of work circles in the public sector. Essentially, the process was talk therapy—not limited, however, to insight alone; the talk turned to outlook, to what could and should be done. PREP set up a curriculum built around twelve hours of workshop discussions, which started with 185 volunteers (out of a total work force of 1200 employees), followed by significant out-of-class activity. The participants became the core of employee circles that would search out and try to solve problems. The discussion leader became the "captain" of his or her team.

234   The project was independently evaluated by the American Insti-

tute of Industrial Engineers to determine the savings from improved productivity. From an examination of the work of some 39 productivity circles, it was estimated that there were savings of about $151,000 in the first year—approximately $1000 per employee.

"At the close of the project, PREP concluded that government employees at all levels, given the proper vehicle through which to communicate their ideas, can contribute a wealth of knowledge to improve the productivity of their departments." [60]

While the quality circle is not a magical cure-all, it does represent a growing trend toward employee participation in the decisions of the work place. It denotes respect for the worker—a willingness to ask for the employee's opinion.

VII Managing for Sociopolitical Change

The old ways of doing business are vanishing. American management is buffeted by new waves of social and political change—in workers' value systems, consumers' attitudes, government regulations, environmentalists' concerns—all of which have sizable economic consequences. Yet in too many businesses, social/political change continues to be treated as a "non-P&L" item, something that may be important in theory but is handled at a staff level under the rubric of "corporate ethics" or "social responsibility." Until we adjust the ways we motivate line managers—for example, through budgeted nonfinancial performance reviews—and bring the formal management apparatus more in line with today's social and political realities, it is going to be increasingly costly and difficult to operate large organizations productively.

Case:
An Acquisition Gone Sour

On October 23, 1964, when Northwest Industries acquired Velsi-col Chemical Corporation, it thought it was getting a profitable producer of agricultural chemicals. Instead, this was to be a classic case of an acquisition that seemed so right turning out to be wrong, because of changes in public expectations and demands concerning risk and safety, the responsibilities of corporations, and the performance of managers. As Ben E. Heineman, chairman of Northwest Industries, stated, "Had we anticipated [the environmental problems] correctly, we probably would not have bought Velsicol."

Three years earlier Rachel Carson's *Silent Spring* had raised concern about potential environmental damage from the excessive use of DDT, a chlorinated hydrocarbon pesticide similar in manufacture and use to Velsicol's major products. For Velsicol and Northwest Industries, *Silent Spring* was a precursor to years of management turmoil and incalculable legal and regulatory problems.

During the early 1970s Velsicol became a major target of attention for the Environmental Protection Agency, the media, and environmentalists. The company's problems included:

▷ Inadvertent use of polybrominated biphenyl (PBB) in a cattle-feed supplement in Michigan.
▷ A charge that workers at the company's Bayport, Texas, plant had suffered neurological damage from exposure to the chemical Phosvel.
▷ Widespread publicity over the claims that Tris, a major product used as a flame retardant in children's sleepware, was a potential carcinogen.
▷ Serious environmental problems at several plants.

During that period, relationships between the company and EPA were characterized by suspicion and antagonism. A siege mentality spread through the company, and liabilities mounted. At one time, total estimated liabilities amounted to between one-quarter and one-third of the book value of Velsicol! Just as serious was the cost of ruined careers.

Interestingly enough, the young man sent in by Ben Heineman to solve Velsicol's many problems, Howard Beasley, has now become the new CEO of Northwest Industries, Inc.—a sign of the times as to what it takes these days to run a larger corporation.

Case:
High-Tech Secrets and Spies

In the high-speed world of international electronic companies the line between aggressive strategy and illegal actions is often a fine one. On occasion, corporations step far beyond the line. Such was the case in 1982 when U.S. employees of Hitachi, Ltd., the Japanese corporate giant that relies on computers, semiconductors, and communications equipment for about one-fifth of its sales, tried to buy secret information from inside IBM—information Hitachi hoped would give it market advantages in the world of computers.

IBM has more than one-half of the world's market in mainframe computers. As a result, its competitors strive to make their products compatible with IBM's products. To do so, the rivals need the earliest possible information about the design of new IBM equipment. Hitachi, along with another Japanese computer company, Mitsubishi, the American computer firm National Semiconductor Corporation and the latter's National Advanced Systems unit allegedly set out to obtain that information by illegal means.

IBM was told of the attempt, in the middle of 1981, from a Silicon Valley company run by two of its former employees. According to the company, Palyn Associates, Hitachi had bought proprietary IBM information and was seeking more. When investigation set up by IBM confirmed the report, the company took its evidence to the FBI, which agreed to pursue the case with the help of some IBM security officers. In an operation that bore some resemblance to the "Abscam" case, a bureau undercover man met with a senior engineer from Hitachi. The engineer reportedly expressed his interest in obtaining "early information" about IBM products and showed no sense of guilt about the possibility that the information might have to be stolen.

The sting operation led to a series of civil and criminal lawsuits. Hitachi settled the major civil action by agreeing to pay IBM's legal and other costs in the suit, estimated to be in the millions, in exchange for IBM's dropping the suit and allowing Hitachi to continue to use information that IBM contended the Japanese company had stolen. The key part of the settlement, however, was IBM's winning the right to inspect all new Hitachi products, wherever they are produced, when they are shipped to customers in the next five years. In addition, the two companies agreed to an arbitration system to settle future disputes over proprietary technology. The settlement was worked out primarily between an IBM senior vice-president and a Hitachi executive vice-president, a settlement that federal judge Spencer Williams called "far-sighted."[1]

That creative settlement didn't obscure the fact that the whole affair had cast a pall over the international business community. The acquiescence of large companies in industrial espionage, coupled with the willingness of individual employees to give and receive secret information, hardly struck the public as unusual in an age that had already exposed them to Watergate and Abscam. Nevertheless, allegations of corporate gangsterism scarcely provided the most appealing demonstration of the capitalist system in action.[2]

Case:
White Knights and Bullies

From the outside it looked rather like the case of the old woman who swallowed a fly, and then a spider, and then various other creatures of increasing size. Or perhaps it resembled two vipers trying to consume each other simultaneously. William Agee, then chairman of the Bendix Corporation, started the process by making an unexpected bid of $1.7 billion to take over Martin-Marietta. Martin-Marietta wasn't interested, but relying on the old saw that the best defense is a good offense, made its own counteroffer of $1.5 billion to buy a controlling interest in Bendix. Then, when Bendix seemed to be getting the better of the struggle, Martin-Marietta acted as any boy might who is losing a wrestling match to a slightly heavier rival. The company called in a protector, a "white knight," in the form of the United Technologies Corporation.

United Technologies made its own bid of $1.5 billion for Bendix, and agreed to parcel out the acquired company with Martin-Marietta if the bid succeeded. As the struggle continued, it appeared that each side might end up owning controlling shares in the other. Finally Bendix called in its own strongman, Allied Corporation. Allied saved Bendix from take-over by its rivals, but only by absorbing Bendix. After a brief eight days as president of the newly merged company, Agee resigned—but not without tugging on the rip cord of a $4.1 million "golden parachute."

The struggle was played out day by day in the front pages of newspapers—and not only in the financial dailies. What was distressing was that the public was seeing the sight of major corporations and their top officers figuratively scrambling around in a gang fight. The basic dignity of corporate life seemed to have been lost in the race for fast financial rewards.

Certainly the old idea of corporations as institutions that rely on well manufactured goods for their profits was entirely absent from the take-over battle. Contributing to the public's dim view of the whole business was a highly publicized rumored romance between Bendix executives William Agee and Mary Cunningham, who have since been married and have pursued other business ventures. For more cynical members of the general public the whole story confirmed everything that they had suspected about the way in which big business operates.

While the concept of public responsibility and good corporate citizenship was a great thing in *Harvard Business Review* articles of the 1960s, the 1970s brought us successive shock waves in the form of the ITT scandal in Chile, the Lockheed briberies in Japan and Europe, the unscrupulous marketing of Nestlé baby formulas in less developed countries, the Ford Pinto controversy, the Love Canal chemical-dumping story, and innumerable cases of environmental havoc and product defects. It became apparent that some linkage was missing between the "God and motherhood" pronouncements of the corporate chairman and the way managers below actually behaved.

The chairmen and their public-affairs officers had been much quicker to sense change in our society's value systems than they were—or are today—to understand the organizational and motivational changes necessary to get line management, many levels down—and perhaps continents away!—to change its behavior. I have spent years and a great deal of my own as well as client money in studying what seems to me one of the most important and difficult management problems of our complex and difficult age: managing for sociopolitical change in large organizations.

My conclusion is that suitable change can be brought about only through line management, not by adding another staff specialty—such as a public-affairs department or another layer of auditing or compliance-management staff. Senior management should guide line managers and assign
240 to them the primary responsibility for successfully dealing

with social and political challenges. The rewards are enormous, and they directly relate to a company's profitability. The effort should not be viewed as action so much as creation of a climate receptive to the values of a rapidly changing era. The ability to field a new product with a minimum of consumerist backlash; build a new plant with less tie-up of time and capital because of activists; alter production systems with the cooperation, not simply the lack of obstruction of employees—these are the determinants of business success in our age. What is needed is a synthesis of the many until-now separate staffed specialties dealing with human societal and political change and their incorporation in the day-to-day conduct of line management.

An important example of sociopolitical change has been the enormous increase in detailed government regulations that characterized the seventies. Regulation has changed the rules of the game, disrupting the market for capital, products and services, and other resources. Taken together with and emerging in part from the Watergate environment (and it was, of course, from the Watergate hearings that the ITT case emerged) and the justifiable public reaction to successive waves of failure to match rhetoric with performance, an antibusiness cynicism built up.

Much of the problem (and it need not be viewed as such by those who successfully innovate and thus gain a competitive edge for themselves) is a genuine shift in attitudes toward:

▷ Environmentalism
▷ Consumerism
▷ Business morality
▷ Proper government/business relationship
▷ Governance
▷ Participation in decision making

and much more. Coupled with these changes in societal expectations are changes in value systems in the workplace. Simply stated, we have maintained our organizational and motivational systems in an age in which they are less and less pertinent. That isn't what managers like to hear, of course. And there are exceptions. But unfortunately it is more often true of large organizations, both public and pri-   **241** vate, than not. (I have explored in the previous chapter the implication of these changes for personnel policies.) Most organizations retain compensation policies that ensure equal return for mediocre performance, and that applies to line management performance as well.

The difference between a corporate code of ethics and the realities of management behavior was forcefully brought home to me some years ago by the case of a large U.S. corporation, of which I am a board member.

▷ A decade or so ago presidents of the company's subsidiaries (well known retail-store chains) were regularly lectured by our legal counsel on the antitrust laws and the importance of behaving in compliance with them and with the company's clear corporate code of ethics. It was an understandable shock to the board and top management when it was brought out in a subsequent antitrust suit that these same managers literally walked from those lectures to meetings with their competitors and set prices! What was their motivation? The store managers' bonuses depended on the profitability of the chains they ran. Breaking the law, of course, could not be justified by making their bonuses. Something was clearly lacking in the moral climate of the entire industry, for many competitors were involved.

Ultimately it is the responsibility of corporate management to create an internal environment that upholds high standards of ethical behavior. The final irony in the above case was that the leading offender turned state's evidence against his fellow defendants and was granted immunity. And his employer, the corporation whose code he broke, ended up paying the fine!

Changing Values

Extensive changes in value systems and political structures are going on all around us: new attitudes toward work and governance, the emergence of mass movements in consumerism and environmentalism, changed attitudes to business morality, and new layerings of complexity in the business-government interface. These sociopolitical changes have today emerged as vital determinants of corporate profitability and will lead to whole-sale changes in the way we organize and operate large firms.

It is my belief that restoration of productivity in the U.S., and the maintenance of corporate profitability, depend on considerable change in the way large companies are organized and operated. Rather than letting this change be a hodgepodge of responses to social pressures, it should be anticipatory and well thought out—proactive rather than reactive.

For the past several years my firm has conducted major research to analyze, in a systematic way, changes in management practices of large corporations in response to social and political change. The need for new models of corporate management was a major concern to the participating executives, who saw increasing amounts of time, money, and other resources being poured into meeting the demands for change, both internal and external, in the corporation.

The general consensus of this research is that in the future, companies will have to be a great deal more aware of changing social issues than they ever have been in the past, and they must look ahead to integrating social and environmental goals more fully into over-all corporate planning and incentives. So far, however, the responses of large organizations to the new business climate have been largely piecemeal and uncreative. In the meantime the process of government intervention in private economic activity has also so blunted both the rewards for success and the penalties for failure, so reduced the incentives to work and enterprise, that the essential pressures every society needs to pull and push economic resources to where they are most needed have been seriously weakened.

Public Perceptions

How are public attitudes toward business changing? On the one hand, Americans strongly support the free-market system. Studies by the Daniel Yankelovich organization between 1975 and 1977 indicated that more than 90 percent of the public was "ready to make sacrifices if necessary to preserve the free enterprise system." At the same time, 62 **243** percent of respondents rejected increased government control over the economy, 67 percent opposed federal economic planning, and 70 percent regarded profits as necessary.

But, on the other hand, the public in recent years has grown increasingly suspicious of the major practitioners of our free enterprise system—the large companies. In 1968 Yankelovich polled 70 percent agreement with the statement: "Business tries to strike a fair balance between profits and interest of the public." A year later, agreement with the statement fell to 58 percent. In 1970 the proportion fell to one-third, and it continued its downward slide throughout the 1970s—19 percent in 1974 and just 15 percent in 1977. In 1966, 55 percent of the public stated their confidence in corporate leaders; but only 27 percent expressed such confidence five years later, and that diminished confidence also continued to decline.

Big business, as opposed to small business, also earned low grades from the public in recent years in the areas of honesty, dependability, and integrity. Public confidence in large organizations—particularly those perceived as concentrating power where self-interest may lead to corruption —has been falling precipitously. A Yankelovich poll in 1978 revealed that "big business" and "union leadership" ranked lowest of all categories examined in terms of the likelihood of acting in "morally ethical" terms; 55–56 percent of respondents regarded big business as likely to act unethically. In 1974 and 1978 the Roper organization asked the public about possible threats to American society. Big business, with scores of 33 percent and 29 percent, came through as the third biggest perceived villain, exceeded only by big government—which scored 44 percent and 35 percent— and communism.

The public plainly perceives large business organizations in a less than glowing light—a perception that can only harm the operation of business and the American economy over the long term. Yet some large organizations continue to behave in ways that encourage such perceptions: involving themselves in bribery, lobbying for protective controls while proclaiming their allegiance to the free-market concept, and bending the law to avoid payment of taxes. Accurate or not, the image persists that large organizations and their executives are less than perfect role models for young Americans.

The Regulatory Burden

A more important source of sociopolitical change has been the explosion of government regulation. Bureaucrats from federal, state, and local governments are continually peering over executives' shoulders to ensure compliance with a maze of rules. According to a study by Arthur Andersen and Company for the Business Roundtable, the direct incremental costs to forty-eight selected U.S. companies of complying with the regulations of a specific group of federal agencies amounted to $2.6 billion. Of that remarkable total, $1.1 billion went for operating and administrative costs, $0.9 billion contributed to capital expenditures. $0.9 billion brought product modifications, and $0.1 billion purchased incremental research and development. Those figures did not include secondary costs, such as loss of productivity, investment disincentives, and opportunity costs. And they stemmed from just six federal agencies.

Regulation of business is in no way a new phenomenon. It was in 1887 that the U.S. Congress began to pass laws requiring regulation of business by the federal government. State governments followed soon after, and regulatory agencies have been emerging ever since. But what changed the whole climate of American business was a wholesale increase in the formation of regulatory agencies during the 1970s. Each year of the decade saw creation of a major new federal regulatory authority, and the percentage of industries under the agencies of regulation soared from those accounting for 7 percent of gross national product at the start of the decade to those responsible for about 30 percent by the end.

Of course, deregulation efforts were launched in the late 1970s in trucking, railroads, and airlines. And the Reagan administration has made some progress in cutting down at least on new regulations. More importantly, his efforts have changed the regulatory climate. But government regulation is still a massive reality that poses special difficulties for small businesses.

The burden of regulation is changing the financial bal- **245** ance of many large companies. General Motors reported in 1979, for example, that it had the equivalent of 26,000 employees involved in meeting government regulations, at an incremental cost of $1.9 billion. Before its breakup, AT&T maintained a full-time staff of 750 to monitor and report on compliance with equal-opportunity rules alone. General Electric estimated that it spent about 12 percent of its research and development budget on defensive research, aimed primarily at regulatory compliance. In a remarkable counteroffensive, mentioned earlier, Sears, Roebuck and Company sued the federal government, claiming it was impossible to comply with certain government regulations without at the same time breaching other regulations!

Whatever one's attitude toward regulation, there is no denying its soaring dollars-and-cents price tag. The Center for the Study of American Business at Washington University, St. Louis, put the aggregate cost of government regulation in fiscal 1979 at $102.7 billion, up from $79.1 billion in fiscal 1977.

The Quest for a Risk-Free Society

Beyond the absolute costs, new regulation of business in the 1970s introduced a new type of regulation, aimed fundamentally at that type of compliance no company could deliver without spending excessive amounts of money. The principle, espoused by environmental and consumer activists and federal departments, was that companies could manufacture products that presented no risk whatever to the consumer. I believe, in company with most scientists, engineers, and businessmen, that the goal is entirely utopian and has no place in the real world.

Certainly it is possible to engineer systems that are almost entirely safe—automobiles that can withstand forty-mile-per-hour collisions, power plants that give off no measurable pollution emissions, and food additives that present no threat at all to the eating public. But the difference in cost between "safe" and "completely safe" products is enormous.

▷ Du Pont spent $1.2 million to lower particulate emission from a certain plant by 94 percent. Federal regulations, however, mandated an additional reduction of the emissions, to produce a total reduction of 97 percent. The costs of going that final 3 percent to a full compliance amounted to $1.8 million—one and a half times the initial cost for the 94 percent reduction. Was there any practical difference between 94 percent and 97 percent reduction? Du Pont chairman Irving Shapiro didn't think so, nor do I.

The most famous example of the no-risk philosophy is the Delaney amendment of 1958 to the Miller Act of 1954. The amendment requires the Food and Drug Administration to prohibit as a food additive any substance that is found to cause cancer in humans or animals. Thus a compound present in proportions of one part in a billion in foods must be banned if it causes any type of cancer in laboratory rats when fed to them in a proportion, say, of one part in ten.

Even Congress recognized how ridiculous the amendment was when the FDA started moves to ban saccharin under the terms of the amendment. In an experiment at the University of Wisconsin, rats that had been exposed to relatively large amounts of saccharin developed bladder cancers. Under the mandate of the Delaney amendment the FDA had to ban the artificial sweetener in table use and in diet soft drinks, even though researchers had noticed no connection between saccharin use and cancer in humans during almost eighty years of consumption and even though the Wisconsin rats had been exposed to unrealistic amounts of the substance equivalent to that contained in several hundred daily drinks of diet sodas.

Public pressure quickly built in favor of saccharin, however, and eventually Congress passed legislation permitting the FDA to ignore the terms of the Delaney amendment and allow saccharin to remain on store shelves and in diet soft drinks. But the saccharin industry was the only one to escape the clutches of mandatory regulation.

New products in recent years have faced an even more difficult road to the market than such old ones as saccharin. The reason is that regulators have effectively started to apply two different types of regulatory criteria to new and old potential risks. In effect, older products are regarded as innocent until proven guilty, while new products and processes are guilty until proven innocent. A company that wants to bring a new drug onto the market, introduce a new chemical, or license a new power plant must today be prepared to spend millions of dollars in legal fees, assembly of supporting data, and the preparation of environmental-impact statements. Several years ago, for example, Standard Oil of Ohio began the laborious process of securing the approximately 700 permits from 140 different agencies necessary to move oil from tankers at Long Beach, California, to the Midwest. The company finally abandoned the project early in 1979 because of protracted regulatory and litigation difficulties, after having spent more than $50 million.

The U.S. drug industry has suffered particularly severely at the hands of the regulators. Between 1948 and 1962, 641 new drugs were introduced in the U.S.; between 1963 and 1978 only 247 were inroduced. Meanwhile Americans abroad learn of drug treatments that have been approved in other nations years before the FDA is even ready to announce a decision on their efficacy. Admittedly, Dr. Frances Kelsey of the FDA prevented the specter of thalidomide babies in the U.S. by holding up permission to market the drug after European authorities had given it the go-ahead. But against that we must place the number of American lives lost over the past two decades because people were not able to undergo successful drug therapies that had already been approved in other nations.

The regulatory agencies established in the 1970s introduced another new way of thinking into government control of industry. Unlike the older agencies, established in the 1930s, whose scope was industry-specific and whose aim was protection against the rise of cartels or monopolies, the new agencies focus on the quality of life, often assessed as risk to the consumer, and mandate not broad policy—"what to do"—but detailed procedures—"how to do it." Large firms are therefore left with very little choice of how best to ensure consumers' safety. The financial incentives that have traditionally allowed our private enterprise system to run smoothly for the ultimate benefit of the consumer had eroded in this regulatory climate.

I do not believe that the proponents of the all-out risk-avoidance philosophy are inevitably antibusiness. Most are well intentioned but simply indifferent to the economic consequences of far-reaching decisions based on noneconomic criteria. But whatever their motives, the results of their approach are almost always the same.

The Cost of Good Intentions

Regulators do not work in a vacuum. We should remember that democratic governments are rarely leaders of change, but rather are followers and institutionalizers of changes already working in society, sometimes to the detriment of society. While this is assuredly one of the things we would like to change, we must recognize reality for what it is. The key sociopolitical thrusts of the 1960s and 1970s were, I think, embodied in the civil rights and environmental movements. Deriving from these were the women's movement and the programs for worker and consumer protection. At the root has been a basic drive to create a more egalitarian society. However laudable the objectives, the cost of these good intentions has sometimes been horrendous in both financial and social terms. Often their results have been precisely the reverse of the expectations.

Social expectations about the roles of corporations have changed substantially during the past two decades, reflecting the social turmoil of America. The traditional view was a functional one: the corporation provided goods and services to customers, jobs for employees, and profits for owners. Since the early 1960s society has added a whole variety of qualitative features to its expectations of corporations' legitimate duties. For example, in addition to manufacturing foolproof products, they should provide meaningful work and socially responsible earnings. Society anticipated the regulators in demanding that corporations provide not only the substance but also the quality of life.

Economic growth and expanding education aided the institutionalization of these sociopolitical changes in our society. The economy, growing at an unprecedented rate during the 1960s, allowed the luxury of expanding social and economic equality to all our people—or at least gave policy makers that illusion. The educational system, increasingly tied to government, fostered in students heightened awareness of social responsibility and provided a continuing flow of intellectually committed persons for key policy-making positions.

For a variety of reasons, corporate response to changes in societal expectations was slow and reactive. Incidents of corporate malfeasance exacerbated society's perceptions of corporate responsiveness to its new expectations. ITT and Lockheed were just two of the major companies tarred by the brush of new public—and media—interest in the internal details of how companies made decisions. Corporate relations with government and society at large were politicized in ways that corporate executives were unfamiliar with and inept in handling. Activists and bureaucrats learned better than business executives ways of attracting media attention, or mobilizing their constituencies, and of using procedural means to accomplish their goals.

The net result was that public perceptions of what business should do and did became far more closely aligned to those of the activists than of businessmen. Extreme demands, such as those for no-risk products and zero discharge of chemical effluents from manufacturing plants, became the norm. Society developed a strange schizophrenia about industry's use of technology. On the one hand, the products of technology, such as new chemicals, new medical techniques, and nuclear power, were regarded as excessively threatening to the natural order. On the other, industry was regarded as capable of inventing the most imaginative technology possible to satisfy the safety demands of the regulatory agencies.

Sins of Omission

Public perceptions of business achievements also differed widely from reality. In particular, opinion surveys have shown remarkable societal ignorance of corporate profitability. In manufacturing, for example, the public perceives a 33 percent rate of profit as against a reality of 5.2 percent. In the petroleum industry, a perception of 61 percent profit contrasts with an actual figure of 7.2 percent. In automobiles, the perception of 39 percent compares with the reality of 1.9 per cent.

Corporations cannot escape the blame for their poor image in the public's eyes and for the misperceptions that surround the activities of business. Business leaders in general have allowed the public to obtain a negative view of the proponents of the free-market system through omission and commission. The omission concerns the lack of enlightened self-advertisement. The history of recent decades should have taught the business community that if it does not itself fight for the maintenance of a vital, enterprising private sector, no one else will.

Until quite recently business tended to maintain a low profile, allowing itself to be maligned by ignorance, and often malice, in many of the media and other sections of society. Meanwhile government was pouring out massive doses of "public information" about its programs and the benefits it was bestowing on society. Children and adults were being trained to believe that no problem was too big for government to solve and that collectivist action was both morally good and the most effective vehicle for overcoming the complex problems of a modern industrialized society. But business has also dropped in public esteem as a result of its actions. At a time when it could be making rapid headway in engaging public support for expanding the domain of competitive private enterprise and releasing its dynamic, business has undermined its credibility by resisting deregulation, as the airline and tracking industries have done; requesting state subsidies to prop up declining sectors of activity; and petitioning government for import protection at the expense of the consumer.

The problem is that there is too much hankering for the past and too little investment of time and resources devoted to the future on the part of businessmen when addressing the issue of just how much freedom private enterprise should have. Fighting a defensive strategy is inadequate. Social and value-system changes mean that whatever the future holds in store, it will not be the way it was in the past. Employees and the public generally will continue to have new expectations. Businessmen must find new ways to organize and manage. Above all, while seeking to correct the wrong turnings of recent years and reinstitute what was good in the past—such as sound money and a stable dollar —corporations cannot seem to be advocating the past.

Several companies are now acting to overcome bad publicity actively rather than passively. By judicious use of the **251** press and television, and by making their executives available for tough interviews with members of the media, large organizations are realizing the goal of getting their side of the story across to the public. They are also appealing directly to the public. In the process the corporations are showing that they too have a human side!

▷ Procter & Gamble showed the virtues of active public relations. The company was rumored to be dabbling in Satanism, apparently as a result of its moon-and-stars trademark symbol. Instead of ignoring the rumors that were surrounding it, the company met them face on. It called in its consumer center, which took phone calls on its 800 number to hear about, and squelch, the rumor. As a result of the phone calls the company successfully sued a number of individuals for spreading false rumors about Procter & Gamble.

▷ Johnson & Johnson carried out a similar strategy in 1982 during the consumer panic that followed the discovery of cyanide in Extra-Strength Tylenol capsules sold in the Chicago area. A hot line served to reassure potential customers that the company was not only aware of the problem with its products but also taking actions to ensure the general public's safety.

Some companies take even more active roles in their efforts to get their messages across to the public. Atlantic Richfield, for example, periodically supplies more than 115 commercial and over 25 cable television stations with half-hour videotapes in a TV newsmagazine format. Called *Energy Update*, the programs are made available for use in whole or in part. They present the views not only of ARCO and the oil industry but also of nonindustry sources. Among the topics covered have been oil exploration, solar energy, and energy pricing.

In another medium, SmithKline ran a successful "Issues for Action" series, which was published in newspapers and magazines read by policy makers and opinion formers. It contained thoughtful and thought-provoking essays by intellectual leaders and proponents of new ideas. Among the issues the series addressed were taxation, reindustrialization, minimum wages, and innovations in private education.
The prize for fighting back by a corporation, however, must

go to Mobil. In a series of paid advertisements in major newspapers the company has outlined its philosophy of doing business and sought to take on its critics, inside and outside the media, on their own ground of editorial writing. Whether the subject is the windfall-profits tax or corporation support for public television, Mobil has made sure its voice is heard by the general public.

Changing Mood

I have some cause for optimism. Both the public and the activists seem now to recognize that their demands on industry in the decade of the 1970s were overdrawn. Nevertheless business has not geared up to harness the changing mood with the comprehensive strategy and sustained verve that is necessary to forge fundamental long-term change. In the business sector as a whole there remain both an imperfect understanding of the current opportunity and a lack of commitment to a positive program of gathering and coordinating the resources—manpower, institutional, and financial—required for the task. Considerably more is involved than better public relations or, as business seems often to believe, educating the public to understand the role of profit and investment, important though both are.

Business faces an extremely demanding job in trying to alter its public image because of the obvious malfeasance of some sectors of the system. There is scope for private enterprise to adopt higher standards of self-regulation to avoid or mitigate certain types of behavior that give it a bad name. I regard the following as good examples:

▷ The basis of legitimacy of any institution in society depends on its being accountable for what it does and how it does it. Bribery and other scandals in the recent past have created the impression that private enterprise is not fully accountable—and indeed have ended up provoking badly designed legislative controls in some areas. Cannot business voluntarily introduce systematic self-regulation to promote transparency and accountability?

▷ Well publicized instances of senior executives' violation or bending of the law—to evade or avoid personal taxes, for ex-   253 ample—do a great deal to blacken the image of business in the eyes of the average citizen. Cannot corporations do more through their internal procedures to discourage such activities?

▷ There are often sound reasons for price increases in weak markets, but they do give a distinct impression of monopoly. Cannot companies make better efforts to explain those reasons to the general public?

Whither Entrepreneurship?

Corporations must also face up to a different perception of their activities—one that is often true: that the old spirit of entrepreneurship that produced many of the industrial giants of today no longer exists among top management. As Franklin Lindsay, Jerome Rubin, and Richard Cohen wrote in a paper prepared for the Public Agenda Foundation:

> American corporate executives need to begin placing a greater emphasis on an entrepreneurial, as distinguished from an administrative, approach to managing employees and product development. New technologies put a premium on rapid innovation, on a company's ability to come up with new products and processes, to apply new technologies effectively, before they are left behind by others.
>
> One of the most critical tasks is to shorten the elapsed time between basic research and the application of innovations to commercially viable products and processes. This requires more initiative, more creative thought, less job segmentation and more teamwork throughout organizations including front-line supervisors and production workers, who are a vital link in the chain.[3]

Yet the impression persists that many of America's top-level managers are less concerned with technological innovation than with innovations in financial management, mergers, acquisitions, and litigation. Rather than making money the old-fashioned way—by working for it through technology—they seek to enrich their companies by complicated financial manipulations, often at the expense of taxpayers, consumers, or investors. This approach, which

Robert Reich of Harvard University's Kennedy School of

Government has termed "paper entrepreneurialism," is tantamount in many cases to putting friends' money on racehorses rather than into the bank—because the horses are generally strong favorites.[4]

The organizational result of paper entrepreneurialism, according to Reich, is an ever more elaborate system of managerial control of large companies, replete with more rigidly defined rules and procedures and additional layers of staff to devise and monitor them and act as referees when the inevitable conflicts arise. The net result, claims Reich, is a rigidity that makes a corporation less able to make quick decisions and adjust rapidly to new opportunities and situations.

Robert Hayes and William Abernathy put it this way:

> Our experience suggests that, to an unprecedented degree, success in most industries today requires an organizational commitment to compete in the marketplace on technological grounds—that is, to compete over the long run by offering superior products. Yet, guided by what they took to be the newest and best principles of management, American managers have increasingly directed their attention elsewhere. These new principles, despite their sophistication and widespread usefulness, encourage a preference for (1) analytic detachment rather than the insight that comes from "hands-on" experience, and (2) short-term cost-reduction, rather than long-term development of technological competitiveness. It is this new managerial gospel, we feel, that has played a major role in undermining the vigor of American industry.[5]

Political Role

Business is at least beginning to show awareness of the problems of large organizations which stem from government, public perceptions, and companies' own actions. One of the most interesting developments has been a realization on the part of U.S. business leadership that corporations are in politics—in the broadly defined rather than the party sense of the word—whether or not they choose to be. Hence business has a responsibility to help shape social attitudes—particularly as they affect the role of government and labor involvement in business—and not merely to react   **255** to them. Business leadership is no longer standing by, watching from the sidelines as others debate and recast the parameters of its freedom of action.

Business in the U.S. has of course always maintained liaison with government and, from time to time, has lobbied strongly—usually through industry and trade associations. Large corporations have maintained sizable Washington staffs for some years. But what is new is the vigor, the quality, and, above all, the commitment of senior managements to the task of playing a more positive and vocal role in the "polis," the all-embracing political network. There are now numerous examples in which business leaders have so thoroughly mastered the intricacies of specific pieces of proposed regulation that relevant congressional committees have turned to them as experts in order to better understand the consequences of contemplated legislation.

The results have been impressive. Far-reaching proposals for federal legislation—such as that for a major new department of the federal government, a consumer agency —have been defeated as the direct consequence of first-class analytical work demonstrating the negative economic effects that would ensue. Incisive studies carried out by business groups have compelled our legislators to devote more careful consideration than in the past to the potential drawbacks of government interference. This is an altogether new development in the United States. Legislation directing the federal government to tamper with the market which a few years ago would have passed because, most likely, it extolled God and motherhood has either been stopped dead in its tracks or has been substantially modified.

Four Management Tools

Can corporations go further, by responding even more positively to the changing sociopolitical environment in which they must now operate? I believe they can, by applying four new types of management tools.

The first tool is *compliance management*. Our traditional profit and loss statements make no allowances for stating goals such as the measurement of compliance by line management with government regulations or with stated or implied corporate policy. The result is that top management is sometimes caught off guard by revelations of noncompliance, causing both embarrassment and penalties. In order to ensure that there will be no hidden problems and no surprises, a variety of new management tools to ensure compliance are being introduced. They range from new incentive systems for managers in which a set percentage of annual bonuses is given for compliance to complex audits and divisional evaluations. Successful corporations will be those that excel in these compliance-management systems.

▷ Abbott Laboratories provides an excellent example of how to operate in a world of changing regulatory requirements. In the early 1970s the company found that the Food and Drug Administration's application of its Good Manufacturing Practices (GMP) to Abbott's products was subject to widely varying interpretations in different parts of the country. The company was also experiencing some manufacturing difficulties; the combination of circumstances prompted Abbott to adopt a new "compliance assurance" approach. Under the approach, audit teams developed standards based on the FDA's proposed and final GMP standards, the team members' long-term experience with inspection of their plants, and reviews of inspectors' findings at other plants, including those of competitors, obtained through the Freedom of Information Act. The standards used by the teams were thus the most stringent imaginable; however, they retained some flexibility and subjectivity that would have been impossible in the more conventional codified approach.[6]

Ethical standards management is another area not managed under traditional profit-and-loss standards, but it is increasingly necessary in today's world to redefine and affirm the social values the corporation stands for and assure it is in accordance with the prevalent, though perhaps unlegislated, morality. Adherence to basic values is also useful to motivate and cement an organization's team spirit. The traditional model of this type of managment is the successful founder or the top executive, with a broad and humanistic viewpoint on life, who leaves a personal imprint on the organization—such as Irwin Miller at Cummins Engine and Thomas Watson at IBM. Others have introduced more formal from-the-top-down approaches, complementing their ethical codes with videotapes in which the chief executive officer explains the code. Some organizations have reactivated a formal set of values, converting it into a living culture used to make everyday decisions. Johnson & Johnson provides a good example.

▷ Public relations can carry a company only so far in the perceptions of consumers. The message to the public takes on far more credibility if the company plainly operates according to a set of ethical standards. Such is the case of Johnson & Johnson, the manufacturer of medical equipment. The company has a written credo that emphasizes its responsibility to the users of its products, its workers, management, the communities in which it operates, and its stockholders. In the mid-1970s a series of "challenge meetings" suggested by Board Chairman J. E. Burke enabled top executives to think through the corporation's credo and its application to everyday decisions. One result of the meetings is that the credo and the philosophy it embodies are now incorporated into all major decisions. "Is it consistent with our credo?" is a question often asked, not only in decisions but in management reviews. Another result of the meetings was a revision of the credo, bringing it up to date and adapting it more to the international environment.

What was most important, however, was the process of revitalization in the management organization. Managers imbued with the philosophy can more readily act in ways that create support and goodwill for Johnson & Johnson, without the need for more auditors, procedures, and controls.

Value management can play a major role in helping large companies operate effectively in the new world of change. To be successful a corporation needs approaches to develop internally positive attitudes for understanding value changes and identifying opportunities in these for the corporation. The approaches used to manage values vary. Citibank, for example, introduced activists internally. American Express applied an elaborate system of checks and balances through internal consumer ombudsmen.

Finally, large organizations can improve the commonality of interests within them by encouraging *participative management*, such as redesigning the work environment for a worker with changed motivations. Approaches vary from fully participative approaches in which workers are given a plant for which to define values and organization—as implemented in Staley's "old plant" in Decatur, Illinois—to community-change efforts—such as that undertaken in Jamestown, New York—to self-management—such as the Donnelly Mirror plant in Michigan.

Motivating Managers

As the role of the corporation changes from being almost strictly economic to one with broader social as well as economic responsibilities, the systems used to select, develop, and motivate managers will demand rethinking. In the past, corporations have relied on short-term profit and loss as the primary means for guiding and controlling managers.

Success depends on the personal example and initiative of the chief executive officer, who must articulate corporate values and objectives and solicit the active participation of line management, which will formulate and implement social strategy. Changed motivational and incentive systems must be an essential part of the strategy if line management is to be expected to change its method of operation. Otherwise the best conceived social plan is little more than lip service to the requirements of our age and will be perceived as such by the organization.

▷ The St. Paul Companies, an insurer with some 10,000 employees, uses the Hay System to measure the dimensions of the "whole job" of each employee and then evaluates performance in terms of that measurement. Top management sees the company's success resting on two factors: human resources and public issues, particularly those that may impact the company's financial operations.

▷ Control Data Corporation, a major computer-equipment manufacturer with more than 50,000 employees worldwide, encourages performance in nontraditional areas by making them a part of the business. This approach was initiated more than a decade ago by the company's chairman and chief executive officer, William Norris, when the company decided to locate a major manufacturing facility in the heart of a troubled city. Substantial capital commitments were made, imaginative and flexible employment programs were created, and the local, largely hard-core unemployed were hired. The project was an economic and societal success and served as a starting point for a strategy to identify problems and devise profitable solutions to them.

CDC carries out its philosophy of enlightened self-interest by placing great emphasis on career development for all employees. Promotions are generally made from within and are based on competence. Managers who fail to recognize capability or who block the development of subordinates (especially of women and minorities) are themselves punished. Specific employee grievances are handled by an ombudsman service that guarantees exclusion from documentation in employee records. Career goals and corporate goals are thus pursued on parallel tracks.

A challenge to those responsible for designing compensation programs in the years ahead will be to motivate managers to capitalize on all opportunities to improve productivity. The emphasis will be increasingly on results —including nonfinancial goals, such as regulatory compliance, productivity, and human relations—rather than on profit performance alone.

An example of an incentive system that explicitly ties performance in nonfinancial areas to managers' bonuses is the Budgeted Nonfinancial Objectives (BNFO) programs of General Electric and International Paper Company, among others. At International Paper, key elements of the BNFO program have been:

▷ Senior management determines a limited number of nonfinancial areas important to the over-all goals and directions of the company. In one year, for example, technology, management development, and equal-employment opportunity were selected.
▷ Objectives are formulated so that they are results-oriented and challenging, relevant to the business and social goals of the company, well defined, action-oriented, and measurable.
▷ For operating managers, about 35 percent of their incentive is determined by performance vs. BNFOs; for staff

managers, as much as 50 percent of incentive can depend on BNFOs.

The success of the BNFO process at International Paper is illustrated by the fact that BNFOs for strategic planning and government affairs have been eliminated because these activities have become a normal part of the operating managers' responsibilities. They are thus no longer "challenging."

Political and Institutional Inventing

I see some positive evidence of political and institutional changes that indicate recognition of the need to adopt new methods of doing business in the sociopolitical climate of the middle 1980s. Companies—and government—are realizing that the adversary relationships that have developed in recent years will inevitably mean the worst of worlds for society in the broadest sense and are beginning to invent means of coping with the situation to provide best advantages for all the interests involved.

One type of cooperative project provides a model for the best way in which business can organize itself to influence policy in a positive way. The Business Roundtable was founded in 1972 with the express purpose of:

1. Bolstering top-level cooperation between business and government while lessening tensions and antagonisms, and thereby

2. Fostering a healthier economy by increasing business input to public-policy decisions while reducing government intrusion into business.

Membership in the Roundtable is limited to the chief executive officers of about two hundred of the country's larger corporations. The members aim to accomplish the organization's goals by studying a limited number of vital public policy issues, developing findings, and presenting these findings to the government and the public as concrete suggestions for constructive action. By acting in a plainly responsible and nonpartisan way the Roundtable serves to reverse the negative image that corporations have acquired during a period in which the old rules of doing business have been changing at a hectic pace.

An example of ingenious administrative inventing in the public sector is the "bubble" concept adopted by the Environmental Protection Agency. This offers business a way to control air pollutants emitted from manufacturing and power plants at costs far below those of previously standard regulatory techniques. Under the approach, a company is told how much it will be permitted in total emissions from an imaginery bubble surrounding the plant site. Then it is up to company officials and engineers to devise the cheapest, most efficient means of complying with those requirements. Previously the standard regulatory method was for the EPA to mandate specific figures for the maximum emission of individual substances, giving even the most inventive engineers little leeway to save money and improve efficiency. The savings that the bubble concept makes possible are spectacular. Du Pont, for example, spends roughly $136 million per year to meet the EPA's air-quality standards at present. Using the bubble approach, the company estimates that it can achieve the same measure of cleanliness for $55 million. This makes available additional funds for investment in new plant and equipment—a key to maintaining dynamism in the economy.

Another example of an institutional innovation to cope with sociopolitical change is the creation of *early warning systems* to anticipate the impacts of products and operations and the potential impacts of changes in societal values. I believe this capability will be built into our corporations by the 1990s, for defensive purposes if not as a planning aid. Some have already made a start in this direction.

▷ Gillette Company has a product-safety "czar" who must personally review all product-safety data prior to release of a product; he alone can hold up production.

▷ Stop & Shop Companies sponsors a program of regular meetings between local consumer advisory committees and store managers and between consumer leaders and top executives. The program lets Stop & Shop tailor local retail strategies to social and community values—and do so more rapidly than its competitors.

▷ Several companies maintain ombudspersons or employee hot

lines to provide a vehicle for employee complaints or moral turmoil over corporate actions.

The idea behind all these initiatives goes beyond good corporate citizenship. By heading off trouble before it happens, managers' actions have a direct, positive impact on the P&L statement.

Meeting the Challenge

Managing sociopolitical change represents as much an opportunity as a challenge. Senior managers reflecting on these changes usually concentrate on the costs—or record keeping, training, reporting, nonproductive equipment for pollution control, workers' safety, redesigning or recalling products, as well as added R&D costs. The fact that these costs are substantial is unquestionable—although the cost of irresponsible corporate behavior may prove to be much higher! Moreover, some companies have seized on the new regulatory environment as an entrepreneurial challenge.

▷ Hazeltine Laboratories Corporation is in the lucrative testing business, with revenues of more than $43 million annually. It provides, among other things, toxicology laboratories to chemical companies and others who cannot afford them, while providing a source of impartial data.

▷ Electronic Data Services has grown a substantial business by becoming the administrator for the Medicaid program in several states.

I believe, and many of the initiatives I have described in this chapter demonstrate, that it is possible to maintain profitability in an increasingly complex environment. The risk of not acting is all too apparent. If business leaders cannot respond to growing sociopolitical pressures to meet society's new needs, government will intervene and make the process more costly and more punitive. Profitability will be more strictly constrained, if not eliminated. For the chief executive officer, slow response will add even more responsibilities than he or she alone can address, while resulting in a patchwork organization with layers of auditing and compliance staff. This dilution of effort will surely affect short-term profitability as well as long-term legitimacy for corporations.

I have tried to describe in this chapter some of the innovations in the practice of management that are becoming more widespread in the 1980s as a direct result of changes in our society's value systems. The following are some additional and detailed special cases of institutional initiatives to meet the new challenges of running large organizations.

Case:
The Food Safety Council

In the 1970s, innumerable "public interest groups" effectively used the system to achieve their objectives. They were able to manipulate the media to rally public support for their causes and use the regulatory and judicial processes to delay or abort some important business activities. The cost of resolving conflicts in the courts was astronomical, and damage to companies' reputations and public confidence in business was substantial.

In the food industry, vocal activists were making exaggerated demands. As a result, corporations were digging in their heels and government officials were complicating matters with political considerations, creating a messy situation that endangered the credibility of food manufacturers and created the potential for extreme government measures. Uncertainty on the part of the Food and Drug Administration was generally translated into delays in new product introductions, more costly research, and damaging product recalls. Most important, consumer activists had been able to establish a regular liaison with the FDA and had become quite effective in raising their views and concerns with the agency. Interestingly enough, the leading activists became disenchanted with the bureaucratic methods of the FDA. This made possible a unique activist/industry initiative that circumvented government and, in some respects, shows promise for a much wider application across other industries.

The Food Safety Council grew out of a belief that there must be a better way to define society's interests. The council is a nonprofit organization, incorporated in 1976, that enables the food industries and other interested parties to develop methodologies for evaluating the safety of various food products and ingredients. Its aim is to develop a systematic approach to evaluate scientific, social, and economic risks relating to food. The over-all goal is to reduce public uncertainty about food risks to a practical minimum.

The board of trustees, which governs the council, has equal numbers of representatives from both the public and the industrial sectors. Among them are presidents of the Public Interest Center, the Nutrition Foundation, Inc., the American Cancer Society, the National Consumers Research Center, and such companies as Procter & Gamble, General Foods, and Quaker Oats.

The council enables interested parties—government, corporations, scientists, consumerists, and the general public—to come together and develop processes for evaluating food risks. As the cost of legal disputes rises and as narrow or conflicting regulations raise the costs of compliance, new approaches such as creation of the Food Safety Council to deal with product-safety issues open up cost-effective and responsible measures through which companies can resolve their differences with activists.

Case:
Social Policy at Bank of America

Companies are also inventing bold new approaches to the new realities of the business world. In January 1972 the Bank of America created a Social Policy Committee, consisting of eight senior bank officers, as a response to almost a decade of protest against the bank, which had culminated in 1970 with the burning down of one of its branch offices in California. After one year the committee produced a list of priorities highlighting ten issues for immediate attention, resolution of which could provide practical value to both the bank and the affected outside parties. Separate task forces, selected from throughout the company's management ranks, were then set up to deal with each of the issues.

The issue of loan credit practices that discriminated against women illustrates the general approach. The task force consisted of two women and one man whose backgrounds reflected the general intent of "stacking the deck" with people who could identify with and be empathetic to the issue. After five months the group reported that credit discrimination was very much present in lending operations and suggested a series of specific recommendations for changing the situation, including attention to such factors as lending guidelines, procedural review, monitoring, complaints, and credit-reporting agencies.

In December 1973 the Social Policy Committee approved the recommendations, and early the following year they were implemented. Once implementation started, the Social Policy staff set out to test the effectiveness of the new policies. The first test indicated that they were unacceptable. A second round of implementation, including training and indoctrination of staff directly involved with women's credit, improved performance markedly. Now, according to feedback received by the staff, the problem is no longer a serious one.

The Bank of America regards the major benefits from this policy change as internal. One of the major benefits to moving early on the women's-credit issue was the time gained to make the necessary changes in an orderly fashion. For an organization as large as the Bank of America, abrupt catch-up actions can be very costly.

Case:
A Coalition Toward "Clean Sites"

Of all the environmental issues facing U.S. industry, the question of hazardous wastes is one of the most intractable. In the last several years, the public has witnessed a drumbeat of reports on toxic dumps and newly recognized dangers like Dioxin contamination. Chemical companies are now acting responsibly to treat the problem, but remaining toxic waste sites are witness to decades of what might be called "malign neglect."

Government efforts have been remarkably ineffective. The $1.6 billion Superfund hazardous waste cleanup program has been mired in political controversy under its Reagan-era administrator, Rita Lavelle, and its progress has been criticized as painfully slow. Critics claimed the government's program would "drag into the next century."[7]

To get moving on this problem, the Washington, D.C.–based Conservation Foundation conceived the idea of a private company to augment the government effort. Clean Sites, Inc., a nonprofit holding company, would bring together a coalition of environmentalists and business leaders to clean up toxic dumps through voluntary action.

Dr. Louis Fernandez, chairman of Monsanto Chemical Company, has acted as chairman of the steering committee organizing this venture, and he's been joined by the top management from Exxon, DuPont and other companies. Fernandez and his group, together with environmentalists like former EPA administrator Douglas Costle and Conservation Foundation president William Reilly, believe that a private corporation with strong leadership from key industry people will have a better chance of promoting quick action.

EPA's list of cleanup sites numbered more than 500 in early 1984, but the agency estimated that the list would grow to between 1000 and 2000 sites within the next three years. Since government action can deal with only a small portion of that total, it is clear that a private initiative could stimulate effective action on many sites before the companies owning them became subject to EPA enforcement. According to Reilly, this kind of effort is intended to supplement the normal legal channels, not circumvent them: "Continuing, consistent, strong enforcement of Federal law is absolutely essential to make this work."[8]

The key element of Clean Sites is its "mediating branch," which will negotiate cleanup costs among responsible companies, using as leverage the considerable peer pressure brought by members of an industry whose public image has suffered from inaction on hazardous wastes. In addition, a "quality control branch" would determine how to rehabilitate a site, and a "cleanup management branch" would perform the actual cleanup work.

In the background, of course, is the threat of harsh EPA enforcement procedures—but even EPA recognizes that voluntary compliance is a superior solution. EPA administrator William Ruckelshaus has supported the Clean Sites idea. Environmental activists and chemical companies are usually thought of as antagonists, yet both groups recognize the long-term value of a safe, clean environment. When top management can avoid stereotypes and get behind the political labels worn by its public-interest critics, both sides can win.

Key Questions for Top Managers

It would be presumptuous to say that I have arrived at a magic formula for managing large organizations in today's environment. My company's investigations have revealed none. Companies are too diverse in their traditions, resources, risk exposures, and management styles for there to be only one right approach. Our research and reviews of management developments over the last decade do, however, suggest some questions that senior managers can and should ask to examine their strengths and weaknesses with respect to social and political change.

1. Does your board of directors possess sufficiently broad experience to astutely assess your company's operations and strategies? Is it strong enough, personally and procedurally, to oversee your company's actions and provide forthright counsel to management?

2. Is your chief executive's office so structured as to provide him or her with sufficient time to plan strategically, to be the organization's chief spokesperson, to oversee the operations and organization sufficiently to ensure profitable growth and an acceptable level of social performance and responsibility?

3. Does your business plan incorporate explicit as well as implicit goals relating to social/political factors and performance?

4. Does your management compensation system properly motivate managers to balance short-term profitability against the best long-term interest of the company? Are you assured that your compensation plan is not encouraging expedient or even counterproductive behavior among managers?

5. Are you providing training and management-development activities that will enhance your managers' understanding of sociopolitical factors and improve their managerial skills for dealing with them?

6. Does your corporate planning process take into account new opportunities for and threats to your business arising from sociopolitical change? Is the process organized effectively to incorporate line managers in evaluating action options and establishing priorities?

7. Do you have an early warning system that identifies and evaluates trends and changes in the social and political environment?

8. Are your reporting and control procedures effectively monitoring corporate performance in areas of high sociopolitical risk? Do you need a channel of communication to raise employee concerns about this to senior management's attention?

9. What opportunities exist for your company to manage

its human resources more effectively? How can you structure your relations with employees to maximize improvements in productivity and organizational effectiveness by moving decision making closer to the work station?

10. How effective is your organization in dealing with external groups, particularly those that oppose your plans for growth? Are you overlooking opportunities to negotiate with these groups in ways that will both reduce costs and expedite progress?

I am sure that many more questions will come to mind once you start this process. It is not a bad way to begin. As a student of business history I feel confident that the corporation will survive the current demands on it and that it will emerge as a stronger, more valued institution in the years to come. But the survivors will be those organizations that anticipate new developments and formulate thoughtful and appropriate ways to manage change, rather than hastily applying first aid after the events have taken over and the damage has been done.

VIII

Labor in Transition: Facilitating Change in Jobs

We can no longer expect that skills learned in school or in an apprenticeship will last a lifetime. Yet we retain an antiquated concept of the role of formal education as a prelude to, rather than as a continuing part of our working lives. As a result we have inadequate mechanisms to promote continuing education and retraining or to ease labor transitions from dying industries to sunrise industries. By allowing the brunt of the problem to fall on the workers' shoulders—in the form of unemployment—we greatly increase the political pressure to preserve the dying industries and thereby divert resources from the new and growing industries. How can we encourage, rather than block, our transition to the future?

Case:
Shutdown

On July 15, 1983, an era came to a close: the International Harvester Company shut down its Fort Wayne, Indiana, truck-building plant. It was an era that began in 1923 when Harvester moved into the sprawling Romanesque red-brick building that housed 2 million square feet of assembly area. In better times—when oil was cheap and interest rates low—the plant churned out several hundred trucks a day and sealed more than ten thousand pay envelopes a week. It was an institution the townspeople took for granted. It seemed permanent, changeless. Now the truck and agricultural-equipment manufacturer was phasing out truck production in Fort Wayne and consolidating it in Springfield, Ohio, in a last-ditch effort to stave off bankruptcy.

An estimated 800 jobs were salvaged: 300 at the company's Parts Center and 500, mostly white-collar jobs, at its Engineering and Design Center, both of which are separate from the truck factory. But the 2200 workers who lost their jobs with the plant's closing—many of whom were twenty- and thirty-year veterans of the firm—were not so lucky. In a community where unemployment had already reached 10.3 percent, the effects of the closing were swift and severe. As the unemployment rolls swelled, family and health services were strained, and state job-training programs were swamped.

These workers faced the bitter knowledge that their truck-building skills, learned over a lifetime of employment at Harvester, were no longer in demand in an economy shifting away from heavy manufacturing and toward service industries and high-technology "sunrise" industries.[1]

Case:
End of a Newspaper Era

The New York *Daily News* and *The New York Times* were producing newspaper editions in the 1970s by methods that had long been obsolete. Linotypists operated a clumsy old machine that in its time was a great advance over the hand-setting of type but now was a remnant of a bygone era. From the lead lines of type set on the clangorous monster a page was assembled, with great craftsmanship and by hand; a "mat" was made; a plate was made by pouring lead into the mat; the printed page was run by a flatbed or rotary press from the weighty plate. The process was prolix and preposterous.

The publications, in competition with other publications that print by modern means, were hobbled in the race to win advertisers and readers. But the linotypists, the stonehands, and the pressmen were highly trained, skilled, proud, well organized, ready to resist any and all changes that threatened the position they had secured over decades.[2]

Would electronics make their skills obsolete?

Case:
Making the Grade in Retraining

In March 1982, General Motors closed its South Gate, California, plant, putting out of work some 3800 assembly-line employees. Due to generous agreements between GM and the United Auto Workers, some of the employees with more than ten years' service were guaranteed half their regular salary until age sixty-two, if they could find no other work. But if they were to take work at another GM plant—like the night-shift work that soon opened up at a GM plant in Oklahoma—they would lose this "Guaranteed Income Stream." So even the veteran employees had a serious dilemma.

Since there were no other large factories in the area, and since high-tech industry seemed to be where California's future lay, a number of these laid-off employees chose retraining programs that would, they thought, ready them for a new career. Jay Mathews of the *Washington Post* spent eight months with one group of thirty displaced blue-collar workers, who joined a federally funded training program at the Los Angeles Trade-Technical College.

It soon became apparent that "high-tech retraining" is no simple matter. The first problem was that many workers lacked the most elementary mathematical skills which form the basis for more advanced work in electronics. The varying educational levels among the group of thirty caused tensions in the classroom, as more knowledgeable students chafed at the slow pace of their colleagues. In order to get by, at least one student admitted to cheating—but all were under extraordinary pressure.

When it became apparent that the training class just wasn't succeeding in its mission, even the hard-boiled teacher started cutting corners. Since, under the rules of the grant, students not making "satisfactory progress" had to be dropped from the program, the teacher adjusted all the Fs to Ds—and when it was determined that no certificates could be awarded for Ds, the Ds were changed to Cs. The school's electronics department coordinator called the practice "social promotion and grade inflation," and told the teacher, "It will reflect adversely on Trade-Tech."[3]

Later, Mathews reported, when several graduates of Room E221 failed placement tests at Xerox Corp., the teacher heard a Xerox recruiter ask how all these people got As and Bs when they couldn't pass a basic test!

It was a story often repeated. After months of struggle, only a handful of graduates found work. Trained or not, they found the promise of a high-tech job market illusory.

In an age when jobs and international competitiveness depend on the ability of organizations to change rapidly —whether in the application of continually new technologies, developing new products or processes, or changed modes of organization and distribution—there is an obvious premium on easing the retraining for new kinds of jobs and the painless movement of workers to wherever the jobs are. When friction and great personal cost characterize the system, as they do at present in the U.S., the result is not only an unfair burden on some individuals and their families but the understandable, although undesirable, political pressure that all too often leads to propping up dying industries through protectionism. And the inevitable and often dire consequences of protectionism fall on precisely those workers who have been shielded from the need and ability to learn jobs with a promising future.

To follow the U.S. employment picture in the press or on television in the past decade or so, one would be aware of little more than an increasing and recently decreasing level of unemployment. The fact that the U.S. economy has produced *twenty million new jobs* between 1970 and 1980 and that these jobs have been created almost entirely in small- to middle-sized private firms—neither the government nor very large businesses have increased employment during this period—would hardly be apparent. When one couples this job creation with our nation's demographic trends, one must conclude that the big problem in the years just ahead will be a labor *shortage*.

While this does not diminish the central point of this chapter, namely, the importance of ensuring that individuals can make smooth transitions to new jobs, it should nonetheless emphasize for us the importance of looking hard at recent realities, rather than repeating too readily the stereotypes that underlie so much of the literature and so many of the proposals for industrial policy.

We know that industrial robots can take the place of many human hands. Or entire factories might be moved to Mexico or Taiwan, bringing much needed labor cost savings. Or a company, after years of mismanagement, may decide it is time to trim the fat: someone has to be laid off. Such situations are commonplace, a matter of profits and progress.

But what happens to the people?

The "people problem" is more than a hardship to employees and an embarrassment to employers—it is a societal dilemma: Shall the social order move ahead or shall it be mired in a perishing past because "people" stymie progress? Who should pay for progress? The more the cost falls on the individual worker, the greater the political pressure to prop up the dying industries and the greater the ultimate cost to us all.

The U.S. approach to labor dislocation and unemployment is essentially reactive in nature. For example, we apply unemployment insurance as a kind of Band-Aid to the problem, but we have no mechanisms in place to *prevent* large-scale unemployment. It should come as no surprise to policy makers that industries will undergo inevitable cycles of growth and decline and that plant closings will displace workers and create human suffering on a massive scale. Public policy should treat labor transitions as inevitable and be prepared for them with programs that:

1. Encourage continuing education and retraining for new job skills.

2. Give incentives for corporate reinvestment in depressed regions.

3. Recognize that some industries are bound to decline —and should be allowed to do so.

Public outcries that government "do something" become intense when thousands of jobs are wiped out in a single plant closing. But some industries, especially those plagued with bad management, *should* be allowed to die! While the human anguish that comes with unemployment is undeniable, it tends to obscure the larger issue: Given that some industries will decline, what system should government have in place to ease the workers' transitions to new jobs and new skills when their old jobs are obsolete?

Until we learn how to solve this dilemma in a uniquely

American way, we are going to build in political pressures to preserve and protect the old. It is an entirely natural reaction for a person threatened by loss of position (skill value or employment itself) to fight back in any way possible. It is a matter of survival. If the job is a profession, a trade, or a skilled craft that required many years of preparation, loss of the occupation is particularly traumatic. In some cases the layoff becomes a threat to life and health. Research over a thirteen-year period indicates that the suicide rate among workers displaced by plant closings is almost thirty times the national average.[4] Such workers also suffer a much higher than average rate of heart disease, hypertension, and other physical and emotional ailments.

Because the will to survive is both universal and eternal, the compulsion to hold on to one's piece of occupational turf applies with equal force to employer and employee, to master and apprentice. Our present system puts value on the status quo—when the incentives should be structured to encourage change as change becomes crucial in the skill, industry, and geography of jobs. It is for this reason that I have identified labor transition as one of the big systemic problems to concentrate on in this book. In many ways I believe that education and training for new job skills—for that is the heart of what we are concerned with here—is the core of the problem most often described as industrial policy.

The Technological Concerns

Is the progress of technology possible without the pains of massive unemployment?

Although technology is not the sole cause of unemployment, it is a major cause in given sectors of the economy at given times. When production methods are revolutionized in a matter of months, whole industries or their subdivisions can vanish. Huge sectors of the economy are able—as in farming—to increase their rate of output with a mere fraction of the former work force. Production relocates from one continent to another. But unless steps are taken to protect the resultant jobless—the victims of such "progress"—they will protest. They will do it through strikes and restrictive contracts; they will do it—in a democracy—

through political action. If desperate enough, they will resort to the primitive Luddite methods of the machine wreckers or worse.

Very early in my career it was brought home to me that my views on the labor impact of new technology have not always agreed with those of organized labor. My first opportunity to debate the subject presented me with no less an opponent than Walter Reuther; and later, on the international front, I was to pursue the issue with Hans Matthofer of the German Metal Workers Union, who later became Helmut Schmidt's finance minister. When I engaged in my debate with Walter Reuther, in front of our country's principal labor leaders, I was entirely too young to appreciate many of the nuances. But my position has been consistent, and I think the facts have borne me out.

It seemed clear to me at the time that automation was going to be characterized more nearly by the affable Charlie Chaplin of the IBM Personal Computer ads than the dehumanized Charlie Chaplin on the production line of *Modern Times*. But that was not how Walter Reuther and his colleagues saw it, and I have, of course, come to understand that there are two all-too-real human concerns over technological change:

1. There is apprehension and unease among nearly all of us (I lead the pack in this!) at the prospect of change in our personal worlds—certainly in something as basic and as much a key part of our lives as the way we do our jobs.

2. Despite the historical reality of technological change bringing more jobs and better working conditions, there is the well based concern that change in specific jobs at specific times and places can lead to great personal hardship.

Having resisted any direct personal contact with technology—even television!—for most of my professional life, I have a healthy understanding of just how real these concerns can be. And as long as they are a tangible part of our society, is there going to be entirely understandable, if misdirected, opposition to change. It is beside the point that the change may be necessary to protect the income-producing capability not only of the country but of the very people beseeching their congressmen to oppose it. The reality is that we build in pressure for precisely the wrong public policy until we find a way to alleviate both fears.

Despite the important fact that the whole point of the newer technologies is to release workers from the machine pacing of work, the stereotype of mechanization taking command of the workplace endures. Machines are beginning to respond to spoken commands—and to respond in the user's language. When this becomes less costly and therefore more commonplace, in a very few years' time, buttons will push themselves, literally as well as figuratively. Until then, however, learning to work with the new machines—which often requires much less time and attention than learning previous skills—and the apprehension of change will continue to present obstacles to the introduction of productivity-enhancing technologies.

Those who have experienced or at least observed the reality of information technology, especially in its latest incarnation in the form of small, personal computers, realize that machine systems really are *user-friendly*, as the ads say they are, and that the workplace becomes a far freer environment as a result. In any event, time will take care of much of the problem of technophobia, and even the least sensitive social critics will come to realize that the realities of the technological workplace are dramatically different from what many of those who write about it have envisioned.

But time is not going to take care of the other problem—helping the individual make the transition when technology displaces a job—unless we find a new and better transition mechanism. Judging by our experience to date, this is easier said than done. And to date we have a miserable record of well intentioned but misguided efforts to overcome the problem.

▷ *The Comprehensive Employment and Training Act (CETA):* On-the-job training was supposed to have been the program's primary mission, but it degenerated into make-work jobs and revenue sharing for cities.

▷ *The Job Training Partnership Act:* Designed to replace CETA when it expired on September 30, 1983, it focuses on training rather than jobs. But do expensive government-funded training programs work? In what fields does government promote training, and who decides which fields will be "targeted"? Will the program improve the odds of reemployment enough to justify its price tag? Martin Feldstein, chairman of the Council of Economic Advisers and a halfhearted supporter of the retraining program, believes "There's no reason why high-earning people who are displaced can't be left to find new jobs on their own. It's better to target funding toward those who are more disadvantaged."[5]

▷ *The Trade Adjustment Assistance Program:* It provides extra unemployment benefits to people who are permanently or structurally unemployed due to foreign-import competition. But how does one identify a worker displaced by foreign competition—and not by company mismanagement? A study found that 72 percent of the program's beneficiaries ultimately went back to the jobs they had "permanently" lost![6]

It seems to me the solution lies not in direct government subsidy of retraining but in subsidizing the cost of the learning period in *real* jobs with real private-sector employers for those whose skills have been displaced or downgraded—until these individuals are able to pull their own weight in viable industries. The German voucher system is an example of just such an approach. Vouchers equal in value to the difference between a former wage in a superannuated skill and the entry-level wage in a new job allow the burden of retraining for new job skills to be borne by the state, but not in an abstract sense. The worker's wage is being subsidized for a real job in the context of the natural source of employment: private business. It is at least a far better answer than government programs of retraining (for jobs that often don't exist).

Facilitating Change

I remember all too well the first time I testified before the Joint Economic Committee of the U.S. Senate and House of Representatives in 1955. Representative Wright Patman (who had given his name to the Robinson-Patman Act as well as to a number of other important acts) was the chairman. The issue then—as it always is, even in the mildest of recessions—was whether computers and automation were going to cause horrendous unemployment. The burden of my testimony then—as it has been ever since—was that the problem was not net changes in employment but rather that the nature of the jobs would and should change and that we should focus on mechanisms to facilitate the change rather than allowing it to cause undue hardship to particular individuals.

As is true in so many other areas, we should recognize and face up to our failures and not keep assuming that if we throw enough money at old solutions they will finally work. What we need is a system that puts a premium on change and at the same time ensures that the burden does not fall on individuals often ill equipped to deal with it.

As loath as I have always been to advocate more government, I testified in 1963 on behalf of the (subsequently passed) Manpower Act to create an Office of Manpower and Training in the Department of Labor. When I speak of willingness to face up to things that did not work, I certainly feel that this legislation is an example of the recognition of the right problem but application of an inadequate solution.

Of course, it may well be that some sectors of our economy, such as steel and autos, in which wage rates are so many times higher than are internationally competitive, will need to allow for what in finance is called a "soft landing" for those involved—cushioning for a while but also allowing decline or cessation of increases in real living standards. Yet this should be a temporary approach, not intended to shield the industry or worker permanently from international competition.

The assumption underlying much of the protectionist legislation for steel and autos—including the Trade Adjustment Act, and many of the current proposals for industrial policy—is that time must be allotted for industry to adjust to the rigors of international competition. In reality the reprieve is seldom used for retooling plants and "catching up" with the foreign competitors. As a result, the time the industry has bought results in nothing more than a stay of execution. This has been the case in the 1970s in both the steel and auto industries.

As my brother Bill points out in *Industrial Policy as an International Issue*, protectionist trade policies are a way to invoke industrial policy as a reason to excuse a country from its trade obligations.

This is what the special arrangements for textiles and steel amount to. . . . A further accumulation of cases, owing in part to the recession of the mid-1970's and the unsatisfactory recovery from it, would begin to look like a partly rationalized set of exceptions on industrial policy grounds. Another way in which this tendency might express itself is the exceptions to rules limiting the use of subsidies and government procurement. . . . While formal changes and alterations of commitments can only come through GATT, key countries could give assurances as to how they would use the time gained or set standards by which national adjustment programs could be judged.[7]

Once we face the problem of easing the labor transition process rather than seeking the "quick fix" of protectionism, we will find that technological progress is not the demon that everyone feared, destroying jobs on a mass scale. Rather, technology will mean greater resilience and competitiveness for the national economy as a whole.

The Japanese quid pro quo for lifelong employment (at least among the larger companies) is that the content of the work can be changed as rapidly as technology changes and improvements are made in management and organizational methods. But like so much else about the Japanese system, it depends upon a unique set of social values that simply are *not* transferable, whether we wish to apply them in the States or not. Nonetheless, what we can learn from this is that a unique set of circumstances in Japan does indeed facilitate rapid change and that we need to invent our own U.S. equivalent. I am confident it can be done, and I am equally confident it will not at all resemble the Japanese approach.

Two Great Resisters to Change

The heart of the transition problem is finding a way to match our education system to the realities of a world in which skills imparted at an early age simply cannot be of value throughout a working life. In part we have already responded to this reality through many "extracurricular" add-ons from home-study and extension courses to formal sabbaticals from work—even while the "official" educational system remains imprisoned in the nineteenth-century concrete in which it was legislated.

One factor that dramatically increases the need for both continuing and new *kinds* of education is the current information explosion. The amount of information produced doubles every ten years. Half the scientific research done in this country since its founding has taken place in the last eight years. Between 80 and 90 percent of all the scientists in the history of the world are alive today. And with fierce rapidity, research is constantly yielding wholly new fields of knowledge, professional disciplines, and occupations. We need to strike a balance between traditional education (learning the "best of the past") and studies that let us understand the present and cope with the future. It is a reflection of the inability of our educational institutions to respond adequately to the force of change that many of the terms used to identify and describe the new jobs becoming available have little or no meaning to those seeking employment.

The National Science Board has said that "many, if not most, of our social sicknesses are due to failure to anticipate technological and social revolution."[8] Education has been especially resistant to change, being affected by technology but slow to respond. As the Diebold Group, Inc., stated in a position paper some years ago: "Despite earlier optimism on its feasibility and desirability, no really systematic effort has yet been made on the scale required to make the use of technology economic and an integral part of the learning experience."[9] Why, for example, should it have taken forty years after the invention of the talking picture to produce *Sesame Street*, the first really creative audiovisual program designed to help young children learn? Why, even after the introduction of personal computers in the classroom, is there such an appalling void in quality educational software, such that many of the machines are no more than erratic and expensive toys?

Interestingly enough, information technology will change the way in which new skills are learned and will ease us into the kind of continuing education necessary for our era of rapidly changing skill requirements.

▷ A repairman coping with a new product at a remote location can get step-by-step instructions in words and pictures over a remote terminal connected via telephone lines to a machine instructor that never tires of repeating complex steps until they are learned.

▷ An office worker is guided through the process of learning how to use a personal computer by a software program that leads the novice through the procedures and indicates which keys to touch next—representing the first time in history that a machine teaches its operator how to use it!

▷ A General Motors worker uses the Plato system of computer-aided instruction, created by Control Data Corporation, to learn new job skills. GM plans to use Plato to retrain ten thousand workers over the next two years.[10]

▷ Graduate degrees in business education become available through entirely new forms, as in computer courses learned via remote control terminals.

Early in the process of trying to realize concretely some of the potential that electronics holds for education I reluctantly came to realize that the educational establishment is one of the two great reactionary institutions of our society —the other being trade unions—quite in contrast to what my liberal education had led me to believe!

It is precisely these two institutions that concern us here, for what we must do is to establish a system in which change of jobs is not thought of as one-time or unusual but in which it is considered the norm. This requires alteration of many entrenched union concepts. It means, too, recognizing the already achieved reality that most of our education, let alone training, takes place outside of what we still think of as "school." The benefits to us of focusing on the need for such a system will be enormous, for it will allow the kind of continuous change and adjustment necessary to maintain a dynamic and high-productivity and high-income society capable of success in international competition. But changing the process will not be easy. Many societal obstacles exist.

The Unions' Will

One of the great opportunities for the trade union movement to find renewed dynamism and regain a key role in
the U.S. economy has been lost. And we are all poorer for

the lack of it. The opportunity to play a leading part in the continual retraining and education of U.S. labor for even newer and more productive jobs has passed the unions by. The roots of the problem lie deep in the history of trade unionism and not only of unions in the U.S.

In the Middle Ages the guilds that were involved in merchant operations made it the cardinal, generally the sole point in their charters to see to it that "no one who is not of the guild may trade in the said town except with the consent of the burgesses."[11] Even if a trade guild did not have the specific power written into its charter, the guild exercised the power nonetheless. Written permission was omitted because it was taken for granted. Armed with the power to say who had permission to trade, the guilds set forth comprehensive regulations and restrictions to protect their dues-paying members against all competition.[12]

These guilds were controlled by masters, the equivalent of modern employers. To safeguard their turf they placed all kinds of restrictions on apprenticeship, lest the occupation become overcrowded. "The term of training had to run for at least seven years." There were "exorbitant initiation fees and limitations on the number of apprentices per master."[13] Guilds imposed various rules on what could be produced, in what way, by whom, at what price, for what market, and even at what hours. While it was perfectly clear that the guildsmen were writing and enforcing these regulations to protect their privileges as producers, they invariably worked out a rationale to prove that their practices were in the public interest. For instance, in explaining why they outlawed work at night, the spurriers declared: "No one shall work at night by reason that no man can work so neatly by night as by day. And many persons of the trade, who compass how to practice deception in their work, desire to work by night rather than by day; and then they introduce false iron, and iron that has been cracked for tin . . . And then they blow up their fires so vigorously that their forges begin all at once to blaze, to the great perils of themselves and of all the neighborhood around."[14]

Control of the job and the imposition of work rules, it may be inferred from the above, were not the invention of modern unions. The guilds were regulating their occupation as far back as the fourteenth century.

Class Strife

When factories made their appearance, the guilds—based on skills learned through prolonged apprenticeship and hidden from common usage in a shroud of professional "mysteries"—disappeared. Instead of a stream of skilled artisans flowing from apprentice to journeyman to master, there now developed a class division between employer and employee. In this new setting the workers—the employees—set out to protect their jobs and to have a say over work practices.

When "manufacture" (a word derived from "making by hand") turned into a "factory," where machines began to displace hands, workers resisted. It is said that in England the Luddites went on a rampage and demolished the looms that threatened to throw textile workers out of their employment. (In reality, machine destruction had for centuries been a forceful tactic by which to gain concessions from management. Whether the textile workers feared that machines were actually displacing them directly remains unclear.[15]) In subsequent generations, workers organized into unions not only to have a voice in setting hours and wages but also to have a say in hiring and firing (job security) and in working conditions (including who was to do what and how). Many of these arrangements became both calcified and sanctified over time, with resultant waste that came to be known as featherbedding. And lest anyone think that featherbedding is a current invention of the troubled work ethic, it may be edifying to recall the cricism John Stuart Mill directed at unionists way back in 1869.

> All restriction on the employment of machinery or on arrangements for economizing labor deserve moral censure. Some of the unionist regulations go even further than to prohibit improvement; they are contrived for the express purpose of making work inefficient; they positively prohibit the workman from working hard and well, in order that it may be necessary to employ a greater number. . . . It is palpably for the good of society that its means of production, that the efficacy of its industry, should be as great as possible, and it cannot be necessary to an equitable division of the produce to make the efficacy less.[16]

It was not only guilds and unions, however, that tried to stake out their occupational turf; whole nations did the same. Viewed conceptually, "mercantilism" was a system whereby a mother country forbade its colonies from performing certain economic acts because the center of the empire wished to reserve certain occupations exclusively for itself. The British Crown forbade its American colonies to manufacture anything that would compete with and threaten the jobs (income) of England.

Today's trade wars thus have a long if not distinguished history. As Alexander Hamilton wrote in his *Report on Manufacture:* "If Europe will not take from us the products of our soil, upon terms consistent with our interest, the natural remedy is to contract, as fast as possible, our wants of her."[17]

Even when, in the nineteenth century, Britain proclaimed free trade to be its secular religion, it did not allow India to produce textiles to compete with Manchester. In this sensitive area the free traders turned protectionist! And in twentieth-century America the farmer, the symbol of rugged individualism, seeks to protect his livelihood by rules and regulations that curtail output, remove products from the market, and guarantee prices and income.

From a purely cost-effective point of view, all these behavior patterns—of guild masters, of unions, of nations, of farmers—can be proven to be inefficient. Certain practices are pursued not because they are the best way to produce or to serve the consumer but because they protect individuals or groups against real or imagined loss of job or income.

It is the individual's desire to be individually secure—to survive—that must be recognized when any serious innovation is brought into the workplace. If this is ignored, the consequences can be catastrophic, as they so often are when human nature is dropped out of managerial calculations. In the larger equation of society, what may be cost-effective to a given company may not be cost-effective to the community or the nation. The costs are merely transferred from the part to the whole. Thus a company may be able to save costs by cutting its work force. But the additional burden of unemployment to the society may be considerable, especially if the side effects of job loss—physical and mental disorder, crime, violence—are factored into the equation.

Who Shall Pay?

Beyond the dollars-and-cents reckoning there is a moral question. Who shall pay for progress? To introduce a more effective way of performing a task, whether by a new technology, a new work process, a shifting of work from one part of a country to another, or from one country to another, is often a mark of progress. Indeed, it is precisely such flexibility, innovation, improvement in getting the world's work done that make material prosperity possible. The ultimate beneficiary is the society, humankind. But if in the forward movement of the chariot of progress some bodies may be mangled beneath the wheels, should not "society" —the beneficiary—do what it can to minimize the hurt to the victims of progress, even if it carries a cost?

For all these reasons—because it is morally proper, because the disemployment of people can be socially costly, and because disregard for the human factor may be operationally disruptive—many companies have tried to work out ways to change their methods of production and of doing business, with an eye to *smoothing readjustment* for people who can be adversely affected. Sometimes companies do this unilaterally; sometimes management does so in consultation with employees, very often by direct negotiations with unions. A growing body of experience strongly suggests that there are ways to cope with labor pains in a period of rebirth. Consider several significant examples.

▷ One of the earliest efforts to cope with displacement caused by technological change was an agreement written in 1948 to provide for musicians who were disemployed by phonograph records. It called for the "manufacturers of records and other sound reproductions . . . to pay royalties, based on sales" to a trust fund.[18] The accumulated funds would be used to pay musicians to perform at free public concerts or other events.[19]

The arrangement between musicians and record makers seems to be one of those rare occasions in which all parties came out ahead. The record makers gained the right to provide "canned" instead of "live" music. The musicians were paid to perform at a variety of public events. The "people" were treated to music—free.

The efforts of the New York *Daily News* and *The New York Times* to update their printing plants were handled in a similar manner. It is a case I have watched carefully. In 1963 my firm had been asked by Marshall Field to examine the implications of technology for newspaper publishing. Larry Fanning, the principal editor at Field Enterprises, had become fascinated by the things I had been telling him about computers. I reported the results of my firm's work in an address to the American Association of Newspaper Editors in Washington. It was in April 1963—a date I remember vividly because I was sandwiched between President Kennedy, on the last occasion I saw him, and his budget director, Kermit Gordon, who had been my honors examiner at Swarthmore. My message was threefold:

1. That electronics would take over newspaper composition and typesetting, and that electronic video display terminals would be the medium by which reporters wrote their stories and editors modified and formatted text—without "rekeying"—thus eliminating the typesetting or "input" function altogether.

2. That it would be possible to maintain the editorial function centrally and move the press function to the suburbs. In addition, local content could be modified in the suburbs. (A big advantage in all this would be to eliminate trucking newspaper bundles, usually against traffic, to the suburbs, allowing papers downtown to survive in a completely new form.)

3. Longer-term still, a new kind of electronic medium would arise. The image then was of a newspaper popping out on a TV screen, but we foresaw a new medium that merged the best of both traditional newspapers and electronics.

The general responses to all this ranged from "That's impossible" to "Over my dead body!" I was told I simply did not understand the newspaper business. A decade later, of course, the same publishers were inviting me to their new plants to see their electronic composition and, soon after, their color lithography presses.

Newspaper publishers were not alone in their inability to

see that information technology is much more than a new means to perpetuate earlier methods of doing business; it opens up a completely fresh way of doing business. This resistance to change is common throughout business history, and the union workers at *The New York Times* and the *Daily News* were no different.

In 1973 both newspapers negotiated a contract to run for eleven years, an unusual event in itself and especially so in an industry in which contract renewal and strikes came regularly and often. It guaranteed jobs to about eighteen hundred printers employed by the two dailies. In exchange for this unusual "guarantee" the publishers were allowed to "introduce automated printing processes that would do work normally performed by the printers."[20]

Early severance was encouraged. If an employee wished, he or she could leave the company within six months after the agreement was signed and would receive a "termination incentive bonus" of twenty-five hundred dollars.[21] If too many employees rushed to take advantage of this bonanza, so that the publisher would actually have to go out in the market to hire new employees, the publishers could place a limit on the number of employees who could get the bonus.

A key section of the contract revolved around an imaginative phrase entitled "Productivity Compensation." One portion of this section related to wages: "In recognition of their contribution to improving productivity in composing room operations, the employees covered by this Special Agreement . . . shall receive an increase in the pay scale of 1 percent." This fillip to those who were on the job was, however, merely an appetizer for the main dish, entitled "Paid Productivity Leave." This section addressed itself directly to the plight of those who might find that, under the new system, they had time on their hands or who might like to have free time to earn extra income elsewhere while still on the old payroll. "In order to ease the transition from a traditional to an automated composing room operation," read this proviso, "and in recognition of their contribution to increasing productivity in the composing room, the Publisher shall provide to each Guaranteed Employee . . . six months (26 weeks) paid productivity leave."[22] If the employee so wished, he could take a twelve-month leave at

half pay.

The contract provided for the retraining of employees. "In the event a Publisher determines that there is no available composing room work to meet his guarantee to all Guaranteed Employees, the Publisher may offer to any Guaranteed Employee other work which he is competent to perform or for which he can be trained."[23] The contract also made sure that the transfer to the new assignment did not hurt the employee's earnings. "Such Guaranteed Employee will receive no less than the then prevailing straight time wage he would have received had he worked in the composing room."[24]

The parties to the agreement had the sophistication to understand that the whole business of taking people who were set in their ways and retraining them for new kinds of work while guaranteeing their income could cause many conflicts. So they set up a process to deal with the inevitable complications: "It is recognized that training composing room employees for the transition from a traditional composing room operation to an automated composing room will raise questions and problems not foreseen by the parties. Consequently, a Joint Committee on Training shall be formed at each newspaper consisting of two members designated by the Union and two by the Publisher."[25]

The core of this clever and complex contract was the "Guaranteed Employees." They were defined as the "regular situation holders who held situations on May 23, 1974, and who continue to seek and be available for full-time employment in the office" plus "substitutes who were seeking and were available for full-time employment" at a given date.[26] In other words, the object was to take care of those who were in the situation at the time of transition. Such employees—the Guaranteed Employees—were protected during that period of changeover from traditional to modern methods.

In all of the cases I have mentioned so far, the arrangements involved the company and its employees without any outside participation. In some instances the government also enters the action. One such was the contract between the White Farm Equipment Company and the United Auto Workers. The company was closing its plant in Minneapolis and transferring its foundry work to Charles City, Iowa. "To facilitate an orderly closing" of the Minneapolis plant, the "agreement provided some 200 employees of UAW's Local 932 with special early retirement, transfer and retraining provisions."[27] Half of the employees—about a hundred—would be involved in retraining under a joint company-union operation. Because the cost of this program was no minor matter, outside money was sought. The program was ultimately "made possible by a federal grant."[28]

Some Remedies

These innovative patterns for the displaced revolve around some specific technological change or at least a change in the process of doing business, such as moving some operation to another plant or closing down uneconomic facilities. But there are other causes of unemployment—macro, micro, and company-specific. To provide against these contingencies, companies and unions (sometimes management on its own) have worked out ways to ease the ache of job loss. The traditional remedies are:

▷ Severance pay
▷ Supplementary employment benefits
▷ Guaranteed work or income

While most of these concepts have been elaborated to cover the contingency of job loss in a general way, in practice they also serve to smooth transition for workers displaced by planned changes in the work process. The following are several instances.

Guaranteed work or pay is on the rise. A Bureau of National Affairs Survey showed a 50 percent increase from 1970 to 1983.[29] Some agreements specify guarantees by the week, others by the month, and some by the year. Several contracts have actually guaranteed lifetime employment—a truly ambitious undertaking (see the Ford case at the close of this chapter). The contracts vary in the number of hours per week or per month. Thus some guarantee pay for 40 hours of work per week, some for 35 to 38, and others guarantee 15 to 24 hours.[30]

Severance pay is of two types: terminal pay to an individual employee or terminal pay to all employees when the facility shuts down. An individual whose job is terminated may be awarded severance pay in a lump sum when the job ends, or in a lump sum at some later specified date, or on an installment basis. Arrangements whereby employees are given severance pay as a result of a permanent shutdown of the facility are on the rise. In 1979 the Bureau of National Affairs found that only 39 percent of employees surveyed were eligible under severance plans; by 1983 that number had risen to 47 percent.[31]

A wide variety of conditions cover severance. Some employees get severance if layoff runs beyond a given time; some get it because there is no prospect of recall to the job; still others get it because they are on layoff without specified reasons. Some get severance at retirement; and, compassionately, some get it because they are not eligible for retirement. In almost all cases the amount or duration or both of severance are directly related to the earnings of the employee and to the years of service.[32]

Supplemental Employment Benefits, commonly referred to as SUB, are of two types: those that provide benefits only when there is a lack of work and those that run "under individual accounts," where "employees have a vested right to their own accounts and may withdraw the full amount at termination."[33]

The most remarkable aspect of all these arrangements—severance pay, guaranteed pay, and supplemental employment—is their variety. Each plan has its special triggering device, its standards, its exceptions, its eligibility. What they have in common is the desire to maintain income when the normal channels for the flow of income to employees is muddied or blocked.

In addition to these three approaches, a taxonomy of the ways in which companies try to cope with the traumas arising from new processes of doing business would include the following:

▷ Lump-sum settlements for those who choose the cash now
▷ Early retirement
▷ Extended sabbaticals
▷ Reassignment with a guarantee of customary earnings
▷ Transfer to another facility, with help on moving
▷ Retraining

291

These are measures that can be—and are being—used by companies that have the means. Usually they are fairly sizable corporations with sufficient income or reserves to finance relief in what would otherwise be intolerably painful circumstances. In a few cases the government is helpful with funds for training; in most cases the government is not involved.

What can be done in the case of companies that do *not* have the reserves to underwrite the kind of support system I have mentioned is an over-all societal problem of major dimensions. In terms of macroeconomic policy, it may well be necessary to give high priority to encouraging the creation of jobs in new sectors to absorb those who lost jobs in old sectors and, simultaneously, to provide transitional support and training for those who move from one sector or one skill to another.

Whatever the macroeconomic framework may be, however, there is a significant role to be played by those creative concerns that seek to get the best return on every investment dollar and, at the same time, give their employees the best possible deal. Apparently there are more and more companies that operate on the assumption that the two objectives—to maximize return and to optimize employee security—are not only reconcilable but are interdependent.

The Role of Unions

In recent times, the labor unions have been declared all but dead. "We're walking backwards into the 1960's," lamented Anthony Mazzocchi, veteran leader of the health and safety department of the Oil, Chemical and Atomic Workers Union. He charges the labor movement with having "no program, not doing any organization, not having any vision."[34]

Yet it seems to me that unions have a clear role in easing labor transitions. Unions are especially well positioned to assume a central role in the labor dislocation caused by automation, robotics, and other new programmable technologies: the workers who are most likely to be displaced by factory automation are likely to be union members.

Many of the labor leaders and labor intellectuals I met during the late 1950s and early 1960s, when computers and automation were a big fright issue, have remained firm friends ever since. Yet I felt then, as I do now, that unless the unions did a much more basic job of redefining their own mission they would become so reactionary as institutions they would decline.

There are a few exceptions. Joe Burn of the Communications Workers of America and his successor, Glenn Watts, have not only been personal friends but also long-term clients of my firm. The fact that these men have been incorporating studies of the impact of technological change into their union's bargaining strategy is an example of their union statesmanship.

Against this background I was pleased to read the August 1983 report of the AFL-CIO committee on the evolution of work, entitled "The Future of Work." In a section called "Humanizing Technology" the report states:

> Experience shows that technological change can be humanized, that adverse effects can be minimized and cushioned through a variety of arrangements, including advance notice to workers and affected communities, no-layoff attrition, early retirement, supplemental unemployment benefits and severance pay, continuation of health benefits and protection of retirement entitlements, and training-retraining-upgrading opportunities for workers to learn new skills for new jobs with the new technology. These and many other arrangements can ease the transition for workers and local communities hit by job-destroying technological change, plant shutdown, and major layoffs.
>
> Technology must widen the range of leisure-increasing options, increase options for creating and distributing the nation's wealth, and raise new opportunities for widespread citizen participation in political, social and cultural life.

That same report manifests concern about "a labor surplus underclass which does not share these potential benefits from advancing technology." Hence, one of several major AFL-CIO proposals is a macroeconomic suggestion to cut the work week. "To create more jobs and to increase leisure, a reduction of the work week is in order. In the first

40 years of this century the average work week fell from 60 hours to 40 hours. But the standard work week has been unchanged now for almost 50 years. Past and future gains from rising productivity make the [shorter] work week affordable and justifiable and, indeed, necessary." It seems to me, however, that any such move to shorten the work week should be tied to productivity gains, and we are still some ways away from such change.

Meanwhile several unions have been moving to cope with the problem of transition on a lesser, although significant scale. The United Auto Workers (UAW) and the International Association of Machinists (IAM) have been among the most active in promoting technology-related education and training and retraining opportunities for their memberships. In 1982 agreements that the UAW reached with Ford Motor Company, General Motors, and International Harvester there are provisions for training and retraining programs for those currently employed and for those laid off. Special provisions are made for those who are displaced by new technologies or techniques.

The Ford agreement called for the establishment of a National Development and Training Center, where staff on loan from the union and the company would jointly provide training and skills-development opportunities for current and displaced workers. Two projects were launched by the Center in August 1982: the National Vocational Retraining Assistance Plan would provide prepaid financial assistance of up to one thousand dollars to help laid-off workers toward self-directed formal education or retraining; and Targeted Vocational Retraining would offer highly specialized retraining activities designed to develop skills in new or existing occupations in which there are documented worker shortages.

The IAM, as early as 1960, began the practice of preparing a manual of model contract language. Of note are provisions for dealing with in-plant technological change. The IAM model calls for training benefits during working hours at company expense and at prevailing wage rates. It also states that, in cases in which automation substantially reduces the number of jobs associated with a particular task, the training may be in unrelated areas not necessarily associated with new technology.[35]

U.S. Government Role in Easing Transition

In most major industrial societies—with the notable exception of the U.S.—the government plays a prominent role in easing labor transitions for displaced workers. In fashioning a policy for economic dislocation, the U.S. need not reinvent the wheel; Great Britain, Sweden, Germany, and Japan have programs for coping with the adverse effects of dislocation which are far in advance of anything yet tried on a large scale or in a coordinated way in the U.S.

The basic American program is, of course, unemployment insurance. In harsh times the customary system is supplemented by extended jobless benefits, as the Reagan administration provided in 1983. There have also been a handful of federally subsidized programs for the training and relocation of the dislocated, as previously described. On rare occasions the government has undertaken regional development projects in hard-hit areas, such as the massive efforts to assist Appalachia during the years when the coal industry fell into drastic decline and the projects funded since 1977 under the Urban Development Action Grant Program.

In other nations, programs to create new jobs when old jobs are vanishing are common practice. Germany's *regional* programs, focused on the Ruhr, the Eastern Border Zone, and West Berlin, had an average annual budget of $4 billion per annum for the decade 1970–80. Funds came from the Federal Republic and the eleven states. The program encourages industrial development through tax incentives, loan guarantees, low-interest loans, subsidized land and infrastructure, and direct cash grants. Government funding is intended as a lure for funding from banks and local chambers of commerce. During the 1970s regional-program funds represented 15 percent of total German industrial development.[36]

The United Kingdom has a similar approach. An investor who puts money into a distressed area receives an automatic grant of up to 22 percent of fixed assets. That is backed up by subsidies on interest rates, grants for training, and premiums for taking on additional employees.[37]

Japanese labor policy typically places the burden on the company to maintain employment. When a large company closes a factory, it typically finds employment for the affected workers at other company facilities or by building new facilities in the affected region. On occasion the government intervenes by paying companies to maintain employees during a recession. In the case of total bankruptcy the government steps in to ease employment transitions.[38]

Although France has lagged in pursuing such policies, the French government recently set up DATAR, a regional development agency, which has begun to meet with companies to consider ways and means of coping with the problem of labor transitions.

Another technique that is common in other countries is the requirement that employers give *advance notice* if they plan to close a facility, whether this is to happen all at once or over a period of time. "Alone among modern industrial democracies," wrote Ira C. Magaziner and Robert B. Reich, "the United States fails to require major employers to give advance notice before closing a facility and throwing large numbers of people out of work."[39] In fact, in the U.S. we have the shocking situation in which an employee may first learn of a plant shutdown on television or by reading a newspaper—before being notified by his or her employer.

By way of comparison, Sweden requires a 6-month notice where more than 100 workers are involved, 4 months' notice for 26 to 100 workers, and 2 months' notice for 5 to 25 workers. Unions have the right, under Swedish law, to negotiate the terms of the dismissals. In the UK a 90-day notice is required where 100 or more workers are involved, and 30 days' notice for plants employing 10 to 99 workers. In addition, laid-off workers in most foreign industrialized countries can expect benefits amounting to two-thirds of lost earnings up to a year after the layoff.[40]

In Connecticut, the state's AFL-CIO has sought legislation for more than four years to require companies to give advance notice of planned moves or plant shutdowns. Governor William O'Neill, a Democrat, opposed such legislation, believing it would send a signal to industries that Connecticut was "anti-business." In June 1983 a watered-down compromise bill was approved in the state's general

assembly: companies with more than 100 employees would

be required to pay health and medical benefits to its employees 90 days after a plant closing or relocation.[41]

In several countries, law requires more than notification; there are also requirements for severance pay and retraining allowances. This is true in Germany, Sweden, France, Belgium, and Great Britain. The object of such rules is twofold: if the company has to carry some of the costs of worker dislocation, it will think twice before closing; and if all parties concerned have advance warning, they will be in a better position to plan for the coming discomfort.

In Japan, workers are guaranteed *lifetime* employment by the company in return for almost total flexibility from employees. This does not apply to all workers but to the approximately one-third of the work force attached to the most crucial, usually export-oriented, heavy industries. It is possible for Japanese companies to do this largely because the worker's wage is made up of relatively small, regularly stipulated cash payments plus a bonus that may or may not be forthcoming. In hard times the bonus may be reduced or omitted, giving the company a breather until things pick up again for its product or sector. The system also depends on an expanding economy in which the key industries can count on growth. It is important to note that two-thirds of the work force is not covered by such guarantees.

The Japanese economy is also more centrally influenced than in any other industrial democracy. By its ability to direct the flow of capital and research, to provide subsidies, and to protect its "infants," it can—and does—take steps to create new products, new industries and jobs to absorb workers displaced from a declining industry or one that is in a state of "rationalization," where fewer workers are needed to turn out more. However, while the Japanese arrangement is worthy of notice, its appropriateness to other cultures is doubtful.

Transitional *vouchers* represent another useful scheme for helping the displaced. Under this system a displaced worker will try to get a job that will yield his or her customary income. The employer calculates how much it will cost to train the worker and how much the worker is worth to the firm; the voucher is then a kind of subsidy to the employer to make up the difference. Very often the voucher is accompanied by a relocation allowance so that the job search is not limited to one area.[42] West Germany limits the program to workers who have been unemployed for at least one continuous year. In Sweden there is an hourly subsidy to a firm that provides training.

These and similar programs are expensive. But they are probably less expensive than outright unemployment, during which the government must pay for unemployment insurance while the worker is paying no income taxes and contributing nothing to the gross national product. Japan has found that it can pay to subsidize a company to maintain its employees during a downturn. The really difficult question is how to distinguish between cyclical and structural downturns.

The Ultimate Payoff

On balance, many countries have found that vouchers plus relocation allowances and retraining programs can pay off —economically, politically, and socially. I am personally attracted by vouchers plus company-run retraining programs. It seems to me they avoid many of the negative aspects of the European programs that incorporate a built-in cost to change and encourage companies to continue with outmoded processes and products. In the end they have no choice but to rely on government subsidies to sustain employment in a way that saps the vigor of the economy and in the long run hurts everyone involved.

Once we recognize and face the importance of easing the transition process, we will have opened the door to an exciting era in which the innovative strains in the American character will be freed to apply the extraordinary potential of science through what we are also good at, technology. No greater obstacle exists to our benefiting from the cornucopia of science than the fact that we have not yet created a human climate in which change can easily take place. It should certainly not be beyond us to do so—but, as with other problems addressed in this book, society deals with it in a piecemeal form if at all.

A society that neglects the human factor—jobs—in its rush toward necessary and desirable progress runs the risk of seeing its good works destroyed by a dislocated and discontented people. To that end, government can take the initiative in the following areas:

1. It can promote tax breaks and other incentives to companies that reinvest in communities or entire regions after a necessary plant shutdown. As the laws now stand, companies often find tax breaks in shutting down plants—even viable, moneymaking plants.[43]

2. It can promote federal income tax deductions for workers who acquire training in new skills. As the IRS rule now stands, one can deduct only for further training in one's present skill—even if there are no jobs in that area.

3. It can require that companies provide advance notice and even labor-impact statements when massive layoffs are expected, whether resulting from technological change, recession, trade policies, or other process changes.

4. It can provide labor and demographic data from a centralized government clearinghouse. There is now no systematic data-gathering process relating to plant shutdowns, changes in production technology, migration patterns to low-labor-cost countries, or other transitions in labor. With such a clearinghouse, union leaders, management, regional policy makers, and individual workers would gain access to comprehensive information that would enable them to cope more effectively with complex changes in the work place.

Let us consider some other innovative approaches to easing the labor pains of transition.

Case:
The Rhône-Poulenc Scheme

When France's leading chemical manufacturer, Rhône-Poulenc, announced closings of several of its textile and fiber plants in 1978 it promised to find jobs for all its laid-off workers. Faced with the need to eliminate 7000 jobs in three years, the company provided 4000 with transfers or early retirements, leaving 3000 needing new jobs as well as retraining.

Rhône-Poulenc's ingenious scheme would allow its laid-off workers to continue working at the same sites to which they were accustomed—but for a new employer. It decided to lease and sell its surplus plants to new and expanding industries that would provide jobs for its former workers. In addition, it would offer incentives to the companies in the form of financial assistance, marketing support, and production guidance, while offering to invest in them.

Through its subsidiary, the Société Pour la Promotion d'Activités Nouvelles (SOPRAN), Rhône-Poulenc has fostered industrial development. It scouts out firms, both domestic and foreign, that might be interested in setting up shop in former company plants or within the same communities. To assure skeptical companies that its main concern is job creation, not a dominant position in their companies, SOPRAN stipulates that the new partners can eventually buy back SOPRAN shares.

SOPRAN looks for firms with innovative entrepreneurship and promising growth potential. Early takers in the plan include a sports-shoe manufacturer, a mobile-home builder, and an electronic medical-equipment supplier. While its first priority is to find jobs for its former workers, SOPRAN's program will also bring diversification for the economies of the communities concerned. And, as SOPRAN obtains equity in them, it will help diversify the parent company.[44]

Case:
Ford's Bid at Lifetime Employment

In a pilot project developed jointly by the Ford Motor Company and the United Automobile Workers, 3150 of the company's hourly union workers at its Livonia, Michigan, transmission plant became the first auto workers in the United States to be guaranteed lifetime employment. Inspired by lifetime-employment practices at large Japanese companies, the program is expected to be expanded into other company plants. The program will cover 80 percent of the Livonia plant's hourly work force.

While the results of such a program remain unclear, the benefits were immediately recognized by Mike Kokotovich, a forty-five-year-old gear inspector at the plant. The plan had renewed his confidence in his employment and in the economy. "It will give you more incentive to go out and buy something, because you know you'll have a job," he said.[45]

The lifetime-job program was one of the concessions that the UAW won from Ford, and later from General Motors, in return for

labor cost savings during contract negotiations in the spring of

1982. The plan represented a landmark in management's approach to labor; equally, it demanded changes in the union's thinking. To provide stable employment, management needed the flexibility to change job specifications to increase productivity. However, union contracts usually detail tight job specifications, which are antithetical to fluid job adjustments throughout a plant. Perhaps it is this rethinking of labor's needs, on the parts of both unions and management, that will surface as the most important gain from the lifetime-job experiment.

Case:
Getting Into the "Mainstream"

Bethlehem Steel's Johnstown works employed nearly 13,000 steelworkers in 1977, but recession and streamlined foreign competitors cut that number to just 2000 by 1984. For the thousands of men thrown out of work, the blow was not merely economic, but psychological as well. Making steel was not merely a job, it was a way of life and an emblem of masculine pride.

For these men to be told that they weren't worth the $23.00 per hour they'd been making was a severe enough blow; to be told that they'd have to train as computer programmers or sales clerks was a positive affront.

But displaced steelworkers in Johnstown get help from the local branch of Mainstream Access, a sophisticated outplacement service. Begun in 1969 as a counseling service for people leaving the churches, Mainstream was bought in the late 1970s by an ex-seminarian named Richard Pilder and his brother, a psychologist. They transformed it into the fourth-largest outplacement service in the country. Mainstream now offers displaced workers not only job referrals but an entire program of psychological guidance on making the difficult personal transition from blue-collar work to possibly high-tech employment. "What we have to do is to get people to see themselves in another way," says Pilder. "We say put a new frame on yourself."[46]

Mainstream entered the Johnstown picture when Bethlehem sought help in easing the effect of its 1983 cutbacks. Now 40 percent of the Johnstown Mainstream clients are former Bethlehem employees—although most of the rest have been indirectly affected by the Bethlehem decision. The work is funded by the state under grants from the federal Job Training Partnership Act, passed in 1983. The program addresses the personal dimension of economic change.

Inevitably, some of the burden of change will fall on individual workers. According to economist "Adam Smith," "We have always had, in this country, the idea that you should make something of yourself; now we have a generation of workers who will be called on to make something *else* of themselves." Innovative approaches like Mainstream, brought to bear by open-minded business/government partnerships, can lessen the individual pain of unemployment—and some of the political fallout as well.

THREE

MOVING TOWARD THE FUTURE

We are living in an age when technology outpaces our ability to deal with it on a moral and societal basis. Advances in biology and medicine challenge our definitions of life and death, while revolutionary technology in the form of computers and communications raises entirely new questions and makes traditional policy assumptions irrelevant. And through this strange new age we proceed without an overarching vision or purpose. Without an acceptable societal vision of what it is we want, all our splendid science will only lead us closer to a chaotic and menacing future.

Foreword

The reason to explore, even by no more than overflight of the territory, biotechnology and information science in this book is to illustrate the point that quite new problems as well as great amplification of older ones are the inevitable by-product of two of the most socially valuable fields of scientific research of our age. The same is true of other and quite different fields of research, but the two I have chosen should suffice as examples and they are the fields in which I have had firsthand experience.

Aside from atomic physics, these two fields seem to me to be the most important scientific determinants of social change in our times. In both fields the roots of the research have had long histories, but it is only in recent years that the real explosions have started. Certainly at the time when I was first taken through the laboratories at what was then called Rockefeller Institute at age ten by Payton Rowse, who had then not yet received his Nobel Prize (for work done in 1906), there was little reason to think biological science would raise troubling and fundamental questions in humankind's perception of itself, and this was even less so in information sciences. Yet today the most basic human precepts are open to question.

The world of science always poses a broad set of fundamental problems that defy institutional efforts to solve them. They stem from the creative disagreements that make the acquisition of scientific knowledge the dynamic and exciting pursuit it is.

Scientists ply their craft by poking holes in their colleagues' theories, data, and arguments, and then filling in those holes in a more satisfactory way. As a result the **305** scientific community is always drawing closer and closer to the ultimate truth about how nature works, without ever quite reaching that goal. Newton's theory, for example, fitted almost all the observable facts about gravity—but not quite all. Einstein's general theory fitted the observed data better; it extended Newton's theory to the worlds of the very large and the very small—galaxies and atoms—without destroying Newton's basic concepts.

Few people worry about whether Newton's theory, Einstein's concept, or some sophisticated alternative provides the most accurate account of gravitation. And for most of recorded history, the average citizen's life was rarely strongly affected by scientific research. But today some areas of scientific and technological disagreement threaten to affect the man on the street in unprecedented ways. Is the earth's climate changing? What really causes acid rain? How safe is nuclear energy? Can toxic wastes be disposed of safely? The public has a vital stake in the settlement of these new controversies, and we need entirely new procedures and sometimes new institutions to address them.

The point I want to make regarding both information technology and biotechnology is that the processes by which and framework within which we handle many everyday problems—insisting on the fullest and best medical treatment for a relative; gaining access to data from any or all of a multinational firm's subsidiaries—are being changed at the same time. Our prospects are enhanced by the advances in both sciences. It is my objective in the following two chapters to point out a few of the new questions these fields pose regarding the way we organize and operate the institutions of our society.

From the first of what would be innumerable visits to the laboratories and lecture rooms of what is now called Rockefeller University, in which I have been privileged to take part for some years as a member of the University Council, I have been struck by two direct personal meanings of the pioneering work of our biological research establishments:

1. What to me has always seemed the inevitability of the convergence of biology with the field I know best, information technology: first through application of the insights gained in neurobiological research to the organization or architecture of computer-based systems and eventually the

possibility of biological computers formed by "programming" the stuff of life—DNA.

2. The obvious need for students of ethics and philosophy, as well as public-policy analysts, to expose themselves to the work of these scientists and, through firsthand observation and discussion with them, to react to specifics rather than abstract assumptions, and perhaps do some basic research or its equivalent themselves—so we stand a chance of coping with these momentous changes with the help of suitably novel insights.

The former has not yet happened—and at least two of my friends on that faculty who are Nobel laureates have opposing views as to whether it will happen. (I am convinced it will, though I lack totally the scientific qualifications to defend my position.) And thus far I am afraid most of the philosophical and social-theory reaction I've heard makes me less than hopeful that we will match the strides of science with suitable insights that will allow us to cope imaginatively. But we must try.

As with the outer frontiers of information technology, the problem is not only to avoid the undesirable but to encourage the inventions and discoveries. With all too few exceptions, C. P. Snow's two cultures are still far apart.

IX

Technology Outrunning Policy: The Information Age

Technological innovations have often led to changes in society. Seldom, however, have so many fundamental social issues been posed so rapidly as has been the case in the veritable explosion of information technology—computers and communications. The technology is changing far more rapidly than the rules that are supposed to contain it, often leaping over national as well as regulatory boundaries. Dealing as they do with the principal determinant of human organization—information and its communication—this technology promises to change the very fabric of society, and in the process a wide range of the most basic ethical, legal, and moral questions must be faced if we are to make our future work.

Case:
The New Border Wars

It is a bizarre exercise in "data transfer": computer disk packs, containing the data files of a major American bank, are loaded into a station wagon in Toronto. Then the disk packs are driven over the border to the bank's branch in Buffalo, New York, where the files are loaded onto the computer system. Why not transmit the files electronically from Toronto to Buffalo? The reason is that Canada is one of several countries with strict laws regarding trans-border data flows. As a result of the Canadian Banking Act of

1980, all foreign banks in Canada must maintain and process their data within Canadian boundaries.

This is just one illustration of a new barrier that is being erected along national boundaries. It is intended to stop the passage not of political ideas or illegal aliens but of information. The combined technologies of computers and communications make it technically possible to transfer information rapidly and accurately between almost any two points on earth. And many of our most everyday human activities depend on our doing just that, twenty-four hours a day: airline and rental car reservations, credit transactions and credit checks, stock and commodity exchanges, and so on. But many governments are not prepared to tolerate such free movement across their borders, for reasons of politics, privacy, or protectionism.

In consequence, several governments have set up legal limitations on "transborder data flow," in both directions. Brazil, Mexico, Norway, and West Germany protect their information industries by forcing foreign countries to do all their data processing within those nations. The Data Inspektionen, a privacy inspection board in Sweden, told West German computer giant Siemens A.G. in 1975 that it could not electronically transfer personnel files from its Swedish branch to Munich headquarters. Siemens wanted to use its big computers in Munich to process the branch's payroll, but the Swedes protested that the files contained private data on nationality, family, job qualifications, and education that the Germans should not have.[1]

The restrictions apply not only to bits of raw data. Information services, and the people with the skill to provide the services, must also confront the barriers. The Belgian and Canadian governments, among others, place restrictions on commercial visas, making it difficult for U.S. firms to bring their own American specialists into those countries to train indigenous information experts or to repair equipment. Brazil imposes controls over the import of computers and other data-processing and communications hardware. U.S. airlines must overcome political barriers to obtain permission to connect up to the reservations computers in some western European countries.

Many governmental restrictions are aimed at outside companies —particularly American ones—that broadly depend on advanced systems for handling information. The Norwegian government, for example, has not licensed a foreign insurance firm since the 1940s. Major American law firms have been refused permission to open offices in Tokyo. Australia forbids the screening of television commercials that have been filmed overseas. West German regulations require the use of German models in all advertising produced in that country.

This type of limitation is particularly trying to the U.S. for a number of reasons. Despite recent competition from Japan and western Europe, the U.S. remains the world's dominant power in information technology. Its service industries, which largely rely on such technology, have consistently had a positive influence on the U.S. balance of trade. That influence is threatened by the restrictive information policies now being formulated and put into practice by foreign governments. Harry L. Freeman, senior vice-president of American Express, has stated the dilemma: "If we in the post-industrial west are to allow Brazilian steel and South Korean shoes to penetrate our market, our dynamic service industries must in turn be allowed to compete on world markets without unfair and burdensome restrictions."[2]

Further undermining U.S. efforts to obtain genuinely free flow of data across national borders is the fact that no international institution exists to control or encourage movement of information. The General Agreement on Tariffs and Trade (GATT), which protects most of the trading rights of nations, is the obvious model. But no "Information GATT" has yet emerged. Despite U.S. persistence few other countries have been eager to deal with this subject through the GATT machinery. What progress had been made in controlling transborder data flows has been painstakingly hammered out in bilateral negotiations. "In the absence of international agreements that would allow nations to act together to alleviate each others' concerns, they will act alone," explained Royal Bank of Canada chairman Rowland Frazee.[3] The problem with such unilateral approaches is that they will probably produce a Balkanized international information policy—a set of rules so Byzantine that the free flow of information from one point to another around the world will become a politically unattainable goal.

We are living in an age when orbiting communications satellites can serve as Space Age traffic cops for data flows from all over the earth. They are oblivious to national boundaries. What controls are appropriate to a technology that by its very nature transcends national borders? What governing body should regulate transborder information flows? Will we ever see a global information order? What are the societal costs of not having one?

Case:
The AT&T Breakup: In Whose Interest?

As the clock tolled midnight on December 31, 1983, the nation's giant communications company—AT&T—was dismembered—or, if one looks at it optimistically, was unleashed to enter the computer business. Many would argue it had been in that business all along.

Ever since three scientists at Bell Telephone Laboratories invented the transistor in 1948, the distinction between the technologies of computers and communications has been getting fuzzier. The silicon chip lies at the foundation of communications systems as well as at the heart of modern computers. A data terminal for sending information today looks very much like a personal computer that handles information, and the resemblance is more than skin deep. Smart telephones differ from word processors by only a few components.

But while the two technologies were converging in fact, one critical American institution insisted on maintaining the artificial distinction between them. According to the Federal Communications Commission, telephones handled the transmission of data while computers processed data—and ne'er the twain should meet. As the decades passed following the invention of the transistor, and the two technologies inched toward each other, the FCC's effort began to resemble attempts to keep women out of the executive suite because of outmoded ideas on distinctions between the sexes.

Just as women did begin to enter executive jobs in relatively large numbers, so the convergence of computer and communications technologies became a fact too solid to ignore. Under the terms of an antitrust settlement or Consent Decree in 1956 between the Justice Department and the Bell system, Bell retained its regulated monopoly over telephone service in the U.S. in return for forgoing any opportunity to enter the computer business. But in the late 1960s, as the computer business blossomed, Bell had to confront a number of challenges to its monopoly. MCI, for example, won court approval to own and operate a private-line microwave telephone service between Chicago and St. Louis. Rolm Corporation started to market computerized telephone devices that performed better than Bell's. In response, Bell made available communications terminals that seemed to be computers in all but name.

Those episodes set the scene for the U.S. government's recognition of reality—expressed through the deregulation of the computer business to allow Bell's entry, and the farther-reaching breakup of the Bell system into component companies. But the process of Bell's transformation became a political and business nightmare, largely because the U.S. did not possess any rational policy process for dealing with information-technology issues. Congress, the FCC and the courts are all involved, but the process has been largely devoted to radio and television broadcasting on the one hand and regulating what had been until recently a telephone monopoly on the other. In reality, these are today only two of an immensely complex group of issues that are barely recognized, much less understood, by the staffs handling the traditional areas of public policy in communications. We lack altogether the policy machinery for coping with the complexities of a technology that is fast becoming one of the key determinants of international economic competitiveness.

Because of the lack of a clear process for handling U.S. information policy, input for the Bell breakup came from every possible source in Washington—the FCC, the Justice Department, Congress, and the federal judiciary. The Justice Department set the tone on January 8, 1982, when it announced that it had settled a long-running antitrust suit against AT&T, the company that at the time was synonymous with the Bell system. The settlement mandated the divestiture from AT&T of twenty-two local phone companies. AT&T would maintain its hold on the Long Lines division, responsible for long-distance telephone service, Western Electric, its manufacturing arm, and Bell Laboratories, the research and development institution that dreamed up many major technological advances before and after the transistor.

The deregulated entity, dubbed American Bell, would receive in return the opportunity to enter the computer field. Some analysts saw the settlement as a major triumph for the Justice Department; AT&T, after all, had long resisted its breakup into regional pieces. More cynical commentators compared AT&T with Brer Rabbit, who pleaded that the worst thing that could happen to him was to be thrown into the briar patch.

The settlement was just the first movement of a long, jangling symphony, played by a series of different orchestras. Federal

Judge Harold Greene demanded a number of changes from what

AT&T had on January 8 understood to be the pact that gave the money-spinning Yellow Pages and mobile telephone service to the local companies. Then Congress entered the debate. Several congressmen objected to a provision that would demand from local telephone customers a monthly fee for telephone access. Originally, the congressional critics complained, local telephone service had been subsidized by long-distance, to ensure that everyone could afford to own a phone. The access fee chipped away at that egalitarian goal, critics declared, and should be overturned. But if that was the case, AT&T argued, it would have to return to subsidizing local service and hence find itself less able to compete with other long-distance carriers, such as MCI—putting the clock back to pre-1982 days.

Even as midnight tolled on December 31, 1983, marking the debut of America's deregulated telephone service, few customers knew exactly what aspects of their service were being changed and what benefits they could obtain from the new look in information. Telling customers that by 1990 they might be buying their telephones from IBM and their computers from the Bell system drew smiles of amazement rather than recognition.

While computers and communications had finally merged in the eyes of U.S. policy makers, few members of the public could understand just what had happened and what its implications were for them or for the nation as a whole. The only clear lesson is that this is hardly the way public policy should be formulated in as complex and important an area as computers and communications. The really big questions in this matter have yet to be addressed: In whose interest was the dismantling of AT&T effected? Should national telecommunications policy be decided in the courts? Do we want a system in which Judge Harold Greene, for all his competence in expediting a legal case, sets our national priorities in so vital an area?

Case:
Pranks or Theft?

When systems manager Chen Chiu arrived at work on the morning of June 3, 1983, he knew the computer system had broken down briefly the night before. But when he probed further into the matter he found more trouble than he had expected: five unauthorized users had left their electronic footprints in the system. His cause for alarm was considerable: the computer contained the radiation-therapy records of patients at Memorial Sloan-Kettering Cancer Center in Manhattan.

The center notified the police and the FBI, and Mr. Chiu deleted the new names from the list of authorized users. However, evidence of electronic trespassing continued. Systems personnel even left urgent messages in the computer system begging the intruders to stop.[4] To officials at Sloan-Kettering the threat of tampering with its medical records was literally a matter of life or death. However, to the Milwaukee-area computer enthusiasts, or "hackers," who were named by the FBI in connection with the case, the excursion into the hospital system was no more than a playful prank. None of the medical files was actually altered, and the youths claimed that no harm was intended.

To hear one of the practitioners tell it, the joys of hacking take on the quality of a religious experience. "It was like climbing a mountain: you have the goal of reaching the top or accessing a computer. And once you reach the peak you make a map of the way and give it to everybody else."[5] That account came from Neil Patrick, a seventeen-year-old member of the 414s, named after the telephone area code in the group's native Milwaukee. Under normal circumstances Patrick and his friends would have continued to program their computers for sheer fun until they "hacked themselves out" or found jobs in industry. But circumstances were not normal in the summer of 1983.

Patrick became a celebrity who stared out from magazine covers, starred on television talk shows, and appeared as a witness before a congressional panel. The cause of the fame—or notoriety—was the journeys of the 414s through networks of more than sixty supposedly secure computers, including those at the Los Alamos National Laboratory and the Security Pacific National Bank of Los Angeles, as well as that at Memorial Sloan-Kettering Cancer Center. Although the 414s claimed to have entered the computer systems because, as British mountain climber George Mallory would put it, "they were there," the incursions revealed the vulnerability of many business and institutional systems to large-scale computer crime.

Other unauthorized entries also caused more than philosophical damage. A West Coast teenager spirited away a set of new programs from a supposedly secure corporate system 3000 miles away in New Hampshire. An ingenious twenty-four-year-old Connecticut bank employee tapped a leased line between his own bank and a major Boston bank by running a pair of wires down a telephone pole and into his rented basement apartment. He applied for a loan at the Boston bank, intercepted that bank's query to his own employer for credit and employment information, and sent back a glittering rating on himself.

According to the FBI, a group of teenagers led by a fourteen-year-old caused at least $500,000 worth of damage when they sabotaged several computer networks, including a sensitive Defense Department system that serves military computers. Another group caused such informational chaos in the Telemail Service—whose subscribers include at least a dozen Fortune 500 companies—that its owner, the Telenet Corporation, had to close the system down temporarily. Estimates of the cost of the break-ins ranged beyond $100,000.

Hacking is an activity that falls into the twilight zone between legal and illegal use of computer expertise. Many industry insiders take a benign view of hackers. According to Geoffrey S. Goodfellow, a former hacker who made a career as a security researcher at SRI International, hackers consider themselves something of an elite, a meritocracy based on ability. "Hackers can probably best be described as loners looking for someone to appreciate their talents," Goodfellow notes.[6] But for many institutions that use computers extensively the challenge that their systems present to hackers is no different from the enticement that their physical plant offers to outsiders who want to break and enter. Breaking codes over the telephone from a personal computer to rummage around the files of organizations should be illegal, authorities maintain. But states and the federal government have been slow to recognize the threat presented by technology in the form of inexpensive personal computers and youths with the intelligence and irresponsibility to abuse them.

Most hackers condemn the use of their techniques to steal from computer systems or to destroy or damage files inside the hackers' targets. But they see nothing wrong in making unauthorized entry into large systems simply to discover how they work and what they contain. At issue is a fundamental question raised for the first time by the present revolution in computers and communications: Is information subject to ownership in the same way as tangible goods such as jewelry, furniture, and computer terminals? Does the act of reading a computer file constitute theft? And if so, what safeguards can institutions erect against electronic "burglars"?

"The technological revolution, by increasing our control over matter, time and space, shapes the evolution of our economics, life-styles, thought patterns and systems of reference. It will have a positive, or dangerous, effect on unemployment, inflation and growth according to the way in which it is managed." When French President François Mitterrand made the above statement with regard to "the proliferation and interdependence of electronic information systems" at the July 1982 economic summit at Versailles, he was echoing the long-standing recognition of Japan's Ministry of International Trade and Industry (MITI) that information technology is so important it affects the ability of a country to compete in every industry category. A consequence of this is MITI's unique treatment of information technology as the only industry in which no production quotas are assigned! MITI's well-focused policy is in sharp contrast with the U.S.'s cavalier handling of so fundamental a question as the structure of the nation's communications system, as evidenced in the preceding case.

It is a fact that information technology is changing the products, processes, and services of nearly all industries and professions to the extent that it has become a principal determinant of industrial competitiveness. This is to say nothing of the outpouring of personal computers that are changing the fabric of everyday life in homes and in business. Gerard K. O'Neill's statement is equally true of the revolutions in both biotechnology and information technology: "Our success in establishing ourselves in those new markets at a substantial level, before our competitors do, will make all the difference between breaking even—the best we can hope to do in existing markets—and winning the international competition."[7]

Information technology, a two-sided coin combining computers and communications, is no longer the realm of glass-enclosed computer rooms and Space Age video games. The technology that lets us store, process, and disseminate information with astonishing ease has become ubiquitous and everyday: a fact of modern life. It has also become a kind of staple in the American home: microcomputer chips are the "brains" that drive all manner of consumer goods, from automobiles to sewing machines to wristwatches. This same technology controls the gleaming robotic arms that are the nation's best hope for renewed productivity in manufacturing and industrial competitiveness. Giant computers deep in the mountains of Colorado keep tabs on our national security. It is a technology as near as the telephone and as distant as the communications satellites floating in space. And for some, who carry computerized pacemakers implanted in their chests, computers are as fundamental as human life.

The visible artifacts of the electronics revolution—computers linked with sophisticated communications and display devices—are the most obvious but only the smallest of the many ways in which our society is changing.

▷ The incorporation of microcomputers into home appliances not only improves the products' "competitive edge" but it is changing the entire concept of maintenance and service and thus the industry. The Diebold Group is involved in the planning of such new products as an oven that will not only talk to its owner when something is or is not cooked but will automatically dial the computer in the service company when there is a maintenance problem. Following a diagnostic interchange between the oven's computer and the service organization's computer, a maintenance person might ring the owner's doorbell to say, "Good morning, your *oven* called and asked . . ."!

▷ A decade and a half ago one of our German clients, a very large automotive supplier, asked us to help them get into the semiconductor industry. I asked whether this move was for diversification. Their chairman said, "Oh, no, it is essential that we produce the control computers that will play such a key role in determining whether our customers will be able to sell their automobiles." Today's advanced European cars, which contain "trip computers" to signal route changes on highways, already look old-fashioned compared to those in development.

▷ When the supermarket sales clerk moves the can or package across the optical scanner, the pulses in some cases are already fed directly back to the food manufacturer (skipping over two or three levels of warehousing and distribution). This not only makes possible the automatic replacement of goods in   **317** advance of inventory shortage but provides some statistical research on shopping habits (what combinations of goods are bought in what quantities at what moments of which day in specific supermarkets) that has never before been available. It changes completely that parameter of competition in the food and other industries.

▷ The financial service industry has already changed beyond recognition. "Let us put a branch in your living room" is a popular line in one of the ads of the New York Chemical Bank, referring to new home banking services. Is, in fact, a home computer terminal a bank branch? This is no small matter in the states that prohibit off-premise banking! The technology has so far outpaced the regulatory process that it becomes impossible to tell what a bank is! One has only to walk down Park Avenue in New York and observe the consistent pattern of lines forming before automatic teller machines, when human tellers are clearly available, to realize that many people prefer dealing with the machine.

▷ The computer has not only produced an entirely new entertainment industry (video games, which within the industry's first decade became three times the size of the motion picture industry in the U.S.) but is dramatically changing the nature of the movie industry itself. Video-game versions of popular movies, including *Tron* and *Star Wars,* offer moviemakers a new commercial outlet. More important, the ability to create your own story interactively in the newer video games is the precursor of a similar trend in films. Electronic versions of the Czech concept displayed in the Toronto World's Fair will allow an extraordinary range of sophisticated viewer choice.

▷ In publishing, we may expect to see books and magazines published on floppy disks or on information networks. At least one children's magazine is already published on floppy disks (with no hard or printed copy), giving the reader the option of ending stories in alternative ways. I was fascinated to learn at a recent Prentice-Hall board meeting that we were publishing in excess of four hundred new books a year about computers, in addition to delivering what had been loose-leaf tax services via real-time computer systems (the latter being something I had obviously expected for a long time).

▷ The choice of a hotel for business-meeting sites is today as much determined by satellite video-conferencing facilities as by more conventional factors. The ability to bring members of a large sales organization to local motels or hotels for a world-wide video conference is becoming a routine option, as is the ability of an engineering or product development team to save a day or two and the wear-and-tear of travel by a few hours of simple video-conferencing with customers or coworkers in another laboratory.

My assistant, who has worked closely with me on this manuscript, lives and works in Boston, commuting electronically to my New York office many times a day. The ability to sell skis in the near future will be determined in part by microprocessor-controlled safety bindings, programmed to the skier's weight and skiing ability. Push-button-controlled machinery has already been replaced by buttons that push themselves. Keyboards are about to find a strong rival in full-text voice-recognition and voice-response systems. Touch-sensitive video screens on which you call up information by merely touching a portion of a picture or diagram are in daily operation in Disney's Future World. Amputees are able to flex computer-controlled artificial limbs by *thinking*, not pushing their muscles through a harness. Engineers no longer spend months doing detailed drawings as I once did but rotate, turn inside out, or totally redesign complex aerodynamic structures by merely using a light pencil. Astronomers are choosing completely new careers today because of the ability of the computer to do certain kinds of calculation, opening to them entirely new areas of their science. As much as I admire science fiction (I never am sure whether the fiction writers or the scientists should get the most credit!), none of these examples is drawn from my imagination. The everyday work of my firm is helping clients in the planning of these products and in understanding their strategic implications for the organization of business throughout the world.

When we add to all this the stunning increases in productivity and changes in organization and methods produced by what today are the more normal applications of computer and communication systems, the extraordinary impact of **319** information technology on our society can begin to be appreciated. But it is only the beginning.

What I find to be the most exciting part of the future is the convergence that I am sure will take place between work in biogenetics and neuro systems on the one hand and information technology on the other—molecular computers, organized on an architecture drawn from neuro research!

Even today in its early adolescence, information technology has already become, in the course of the post–World War II period, one of the most important industries in the world. Industry lines are being changed, as are career opportunities. Yet, with all our awareness of the home computer and the increasing number of times the life of the average citizen is daily impacted by the computer, just how much realization is there of the profound changes it is producing in our society? Of one thing I am certain, and that is that U.S. public policy is woefully ignorant of both the new questions posed for us by these developments and the impact of these developments themselves on the policy machinery.

Even the most revolutionary and startling technologies are taken for granted by many of us. Virginia Woolf expressed this phenomenon very well in a passage from her novel *Orlando*. Orlando, who is a personification of the spirit of England and who has thus lived for several hundred years, suddenly finds herself traveling from her country house to London on a train, rather than by the horse-drawn carriage she had formerly used.

> Orlando had not yet realized the invention of the steam engine, but such was her absorption in the sufferings of the being who, though not herself, was entirely dependent upon her, that she saw a railway train for the first time, took her seat in the railway carriage, and had the rug arranged about her knees without giving a thought to "that stupendous invention, which had," the historians say, "completely changed the face of Europe in the past twenty years" (as, indeed, happens much more frequently than historians suppose).

Certainly in this day and age we are accustomed to world-shaking changes. Our ability to adjust so well to the revo-

lutionary has the unfortunate effect of our failing to ask
pertinent questions in order to tackle the problems and
issues as they arise.

Two Big Questions

The key policy question that I have not yet heard anyone
ask is why the U.S. is so fortunate as to lead the world in
such a vital industry. What is it that we have done right,
and how can we be sure to preserve or even enhance the
conditions that led to this good fortune? Unlike industries
that depend on the presence of certain natural resources in
a country, the information-technology industry created in
the post–World War II era could have reasonably happened
in any one of a number of countries. However, the U.S. is
where this key industry really "happened."

My guess is that a combination of cultural factors—the
Yankee ingenuity and innovativeness that even De Tocqueville commented on—as well as a spirit of adventure, job
mobility, and the ability to fail and start again with no
stigma attached are part of the answer. Other parts must
surely be the universally high level of education across the
country, the nature of our bankruptcy laws and our tax
structure, the availability of venture capital.

To my mind, we put too much emphasis on the dangers
and negative aspects of any new development, such as information technology or biogenetics, when considering their
societal implications, just as we emphasize what we all too
often perceive as special or even unfair advantages of a
country such as Japan when we address questions of international competitiveness. We would do well to look hard at
our own unique strengths, whether cultural, natural, or policy advantages—at what it is we are doing right—and only
then focus on what may be the negative features of a new
development. As I hope I make evident in this chapter and
the next, there are many reasons for concern over the mis-
use of these new technologies and even accidents involving
them. Yet in both biogenetics and information technology
we lead the world in developments that are truly revolution-
izing humankind. Unlike natural resources, which are God-
given (though they can either be misused or husbanded,
depending on a country's policies), these are developments

that arose from the minds of our people. As must now be apparent to virtually everyone, we can no longer live in the immediate postwar atmosphere and believe that the economic and other supremacies of the U.S. are God-given. We are at a moment in our history when it is essential that we look hard at just why it is that we are ahead in these new areas and, even while we ensure that our public policies shield us from negative impacts, our prime focus must surely be on how to preserve, if not enhance, the conditions that led to this supremacy.

The other big question that information technology poses to me is why we have not been able to do more with it in certain areas than we have. For all our progress in applying information technology to science, industry, business, and the military, we would also do well to ask why, with the potential of information technology, we have not achieved a great deal more than we have in some of the most crucial areas of our society.

Why is there practically no meaningful use of computer-aided instruction in the schools and universities? Why are libraries, in spite of some record-keeping advances, still functioning as they did centuries ago—as storehouses for paper books and paper references? I do not mean to deprecate the many ways in which information technology has made all of our lives a great deal better. But given the enormous capital, labor, and material resources of our nation, shouldn't these advances in schools and libraries be possible—and much more besides? Is this not an area in which public/private partnerships in the form of model programs could serve as a means of aggregating demand for the extensive R&D and software as well as new machine systems?

Only a tiny fraction of public school budgets goes to educational materials, and this is so fragmented through the local school districts that there is inadequate potential for a private firm to invest the amount of money over the decade or more that is necessary to make a real change. (The Winnebago case, at the close of Chapter 5, is a stunning exception.) Is this not an ideal area in which the federal government could perform a demand aggregation function? The private sector would respond as in the case of the space program, and with a far quicker conversion from develop-

322

ment to a sustaining industry. The social and economic consequences of such enhancement of our human capital would be extraordinary. This would seem to me an ideal example of the kind of role government should perform.

Similarly, the application of advanced technologies to running our cities, distributing medical and social services, providing advanced library services, and so on, has the potential for quantum jumps in the quality of our lives and reducing the costs of what are today in all of these areas dreadfully inadequate services. All depend on but are uniquely suited to innovation in public policy and government initiatives.

We are a nation of innovators and entrepreneurs, whose collective genius has made us the world leader in high technology. But our continued leadership is by no means assured. We must eye with concern the growing chasm between what we can and do achieve.

Fresh Conceptual Thinking

The advances that are already bringing about nothing less than a revolution in our cultural, political, and economic institutions have made urgent the need for some fresh conceptual thinking regarding their use. The technology is progressing much more rapidly than the ability of policy makers to understand it and guide its use. Although information technology has already brought about enormous improvements in the human condition, it has also posed new challenges and raised entirely new questions. To whom do we assign ownership and how do we measure the value of such a unique commodity as information? Should we regulate its flow? How should we ensure that secret information does not get into the wrong hands—or, more accurately, into the wrong computers? How should public policy regarding information technology be formulated? Do we in the U.S. need a means of coordinating government policies that relate to computers and communications?

These are only a few of the questions raised by information technology—questions often so novel, complex, and interrelated that they fall into a legal and policy making void. No answers are yet apparent. But since the technology is capable of effecting such profound changes in the fabric of human life, dare we take the considerable risk of allowing policy to be made by default? We have just dismembered the lowest-cost and highest-quality telephone system in the world in such a manner. Perhaps it will prove to be the right thing to have done. But it was certainly not the product of even sophomoric policy analysis aimed at achieving public benefit. We can only guess at the ramifications of this for our industries, our military, and our economic growth.

The shadow of outdated, inconsistent, and inappropriate policies has already been seen. We can only look back with amazement on the government's long-term insistence on the distinction between computer and communications technologies, which kept AT&T out of the computer business until this year. What would have happened if AT&T had been unleashed much earlier to compete in this new industry? Would we have seen a more competitive climate, quite new combinations of computer and communications technologies, and cheaper services for both consumers and business? Would IBM have entered the communications business earlier in the U.S., as it has overseas? Was it necessary to dismantle the Bell system to promote this competition?

What if information technology were recognized at the highest government levels as a strategic economic resource, a catalyst for profound social change, a cornerstone of the nation's security? What if we had a policy machinery that could act on such a realization? What if we occasionally examined the reasons for our strengths in this area and formulated tax and other policy moves according to whether they hurt or helped these innovations? Does the U.S. need a formal information-technology policy?

I can only guess at the answers to these questions. I suspect that what we need is better policy machinery rather than a formal information policy. Despite the strong feelings on all sides of the industrial policy question, few people seem willing to admit what seems to me quite obvious— that, for better or worse, we already have a de facto industrial policy, for government sets an incentive/disincentive structure by its myriad involvements in our economy. I would have thought we would all be better off if this involvement were acknowledged and the incentives and disincentives coordinated more logically. This is especially true in the special case of information-technology policy. One problem is that the industrial policy issue has become so politicized that it is now a code word for government subsidy, trade protectionism, investment policy, and a lot of other things that I strongly oppose, even while I do believe we need coordination and regular review of the many policies that impinge on the development of information policy. My emphasis is thus on the *processes* by which we arrive at public policy. As is true in all the areas I explore in this book, my feeling is that if we get the process right, the necessarily constantly changing substance of policy will take care of itself.

Some of the things we need to do are unique to information technology, and I go into them further in the remainder of this chapter. Others are common to ensuring that we enjoy the benefits of all technologies. In *Stimulating Technological Progress*, a Committee for Economic Development report in the preparation of which I contributed, we stated:

> In our view, stimulation of a higher rate of investment in the economy's productive base will create more rapid technological progress and at the same time have a lasting impact on productivity improvement and inflation control.
>
> Our strategy has three principal elements:
>
> —First, the level of investment in plant and equipment should be raised in order to increase the diffusion of new technology into industrial processes. This would provide the structural change necessary for permanent impact on productivity growth and thereby on the control of inflation. We recommend this be accomplished immediately by removing certain existing tax disincentives . . .
>
> —Second, nonessential regulatory constraints on, and uncertainties inherent in, productive investments should be reduced. This, in conjunction with the improved economic performance that will result from more rapid productivity growth, would create the essential climate in which investment in all phases of technological innovation would be increased as the natural response of the entrepreneurial process . . .
>
> —Third, appropriate tax, patent, and regulatory changes should be made to provide support to foster private research and development. In addition, adequate support of *basic* research should be a high-priority item in the federal budget.[8]

The Japanese Experience

The seeming inability of the U.S. to cope with the policy demands of the new information technology contrasts starkly with the experience of Japan, as has often been the case when that country plays "catch up." Japan's much touted fifth-generation computer project, designed to create machines that can relate to humans in a near-human fashion within a decade, provides a focus for its national industrial policy. Ironically, it is based on audacious new concepts—of *American* origin! Japanese proposals for data flow machines, artificial intelligence, and knowledge engineering were copied almost verbatim from the lectures of American university scientists who had been invited to speak before Japanese scientists in 1979. These scientists had given the same lectures in the U.S., but Japanese policy makers were looking for a way to leap ahead in world markets. As a result, leading-edge work which should have been doable in the U.S. may ultimately be done in Japan.[9]

The difference in approach between the U.S. and Japan does not stem from any lack of brainpower or material resources in the U.S. If Japan has any advantage over the U.S., it is in its clearly articulated industrial policy: a technology-oriented approach that places the computer industry at the nucleus of Japanese industrial development well into the next century. In the United States, by contrast, there is no single authoritative voice heard over the din of incomplete and often conflicting policy statements that affect information technology; no nonmilitary priority-setting body to decide the focus and direction of research in information technology; and no coherent and unified national information policy aimed at assuring the U.S. a solid position at the forefront of innovation.

Although these issues are central to my own and my company's work, I was nonetheless startled on two recent occasions by the quality of senior Japanese officials' awareness of the key elements involved in achieving success in this field. The deputy director of MITI, whom I did not know, asked through the Japanese ambassador if, on quite short notice, he could come to see me on his way back to Tokyo from a meeting in Washington. His opening question was, "Mr. Diebold, what will be the next political problem between our two countries once we get over this 64K RAM issue?" He meant, of course, what would be the next stage of development of silicon chip technology to cause outcries over "unfair" competition?

Shortly afterward I found myself dining in Tokyo with a former foreign minister. I asked about his educational background; it was in electrical engineering! Understandably, he spent the evening asking me extremely detailed questions about the future of information technology. A *foreign minister!* I cannot recall hearing or reading about a top U.S. government official, except in very specialized areas, addressing the future implications of advanced technologies for industrial, economic, and foreign policy. It is usually only when we are deeply in trouble from many years of wrong policies that U.S. political figures give more than lip service to these technologies. In my view, the Japanese deserve high marks as well as all the advantages they have gained through serious study of these key issues.

Throwing Money at the Problem

I am obviously in favor of doing everything possible to stimulate the U.S. computer and communications industries, but, as should be evident from other parts of this book, I am strongly opposed to the idea of government's picking "winners and losers." Just as industrial policy has become politicized and, for too many, a code word for subsidy and protectionism, so too a formal policy vis-à-vis the information-technology industry can all too easily be used as the camel's nose under the tent for those who wish later to do more than enhance conditions favoring innovation.

My consulting firm has spent enough time on behalf of governments in other countries in trying to introduce venture capital and other methods of stimulating innovation in both the information-technology and biogenetic fields for me not to be extremely sensitive to the many ways in which the best intended policies can be turned into government funding of increasingly bureaucratic and out-of-touch losers. Throwing public money at new technologies is no different from throwing it at social and welfare problems. Indeed, even the semiconductor industry provides some vivid examples of the way throwing private money at the problem of innovation in microprocessors leads nowhere. Schlumberger, through its Fairchild subsidiary, has spent perhaps one billion dollars in the unsuccessful attempt to stay ahead in microprocessors. Success has largely gone to the companies doing much more with much less capital (a striking exception being IBM).

The difference between the U.S. system and those of most other countries was brought home to me during a visit in Düsseldorf with Dr. Hanns Martin Schleyer, who was then the head of the German Industries Association, just a few weeks before he was kidnapped and subsequently murdered by German terrorists. Dr. Schleyer was preparing for a U.S. trip the following spring and asked me who in the U.S. he should consider to be his counterpart.

I told him that there simply was none and that he must meet with several organizations, such as the CED, the Business Roundtable, the NAM, the Chamber of Commerce, and the Conference Board. I said that there was still nothing vaguely comparable to his own position as head of the German Industries Association, which, according to the basic law of the German constitution required that German industries be consulted on each piece of legislation before it was introduced to the Bundestad and on its way through the process. Other countries have differing relationships, but in many, such as Japan, through its Keizai Doyukai—CED's sister organization—it is certainly possible and normal for a relatively small number of business leaders to meet in a single room with a small number of government leaders and to arrive at policy.

The Morass in Information-Technology Policy

To understand the argument for coordinating often conflicting U.S. policies, one has only to run through the list of government agencies that have some responsibility for U.S. policy in the information-technology sector:

▷ The Pentagon obviously takes care of military matters and high-technology export controls (together with the Department of Commerce), but the influence it has had on the direction of commercial developments has been confined to a small number of spin-offs of military programs.

▷ The Department of Justice enforces antitrust policy, which is constantly changing.

▷ The Department of Commerce has an Assistant Secretary for Communications and Information, and a National Telecommunications and Information Administration (formerly the White House Office of Telecommunications Policy) that reports to it.

▷ The U.S. Trade Representative reports to the President on matters of high-tech exports and trade in services (transborder data flows and other nontariff barriers).

▷ The Science Adviser to the President, the National Bureau of Standards, and the National Science Foundation are concerned in varying degrees with information technology.

▷ The National Aeronautics and Space Administration has funded telecommunications, sensing and image-processing devices, and long lead-time research on critical components.

▷ The Federal Communications Commission is charged with regulating the converging computer and communications industries.

▷ Congress has overlapping agencies that analyze all of the information-technology industries. It also has its own technical expert agency in the Office of Technology Assessment.

And the list goes on and on. I have not even included the key tax and economic policy players. Plainly, or so it seems to me, the U.S. needs some means of coordinating its policies and priorities in information technology, for the rest of this century and beyond. A necessary starting point is top-level recognition of the vital role of information technology in our national and international economies. I believe that a presidentially appointed panel should study both successful and unsuccessful attempts in countries around the world at formulating policy machinery appropriate to the complexity of the task.

The precedents are abundant, sharply divergent, and by no means limited to Japan. In the UK, for example, a new office was invented in 1982 in the form of a Minister of State for Information Technology, the equivalent of a subcabinet post in the U.S. Brazil, which has formulated policies that are strictly protective of its fledgling computer industry, has what we would call a "computer czar." France ties economic and technological goals with social goals as it attempts to promote, through its World Center, the advancement of computer technology in Third World countries. Korea and Singapore have their own unique policies for putting those countries on the fast track to technological sophistication. Some of these work, some don't. And none can or should be adopted in any wholesale form. But we could certainly learn from a rigorous analysis of what does and does not work in other countries. In particular, we could benefit from studying the conditions that lead to innovation in free-market systems.

Out of this initial study should come recommendations as to ways in which the U.S. policy process should be modified to ensure a minimum of cross-purposes in the activities and policies of the U.S. government as they affect computers and communications. What I am suggesting is not centralized control or regulation of the information-technology industry; what I envision is a clearing away of the regulatory and other obstacles to technological innovation and a coordination of all the disparate government policy mechanisms that are the outgrowth of historical traditions that are less and less pertinent to today's realities. So convinced am I of the need for such comparative studies of national policies that in 1983 the Diebold Institute for Public Policy Studies, Inc., our operating foundation, started a major in-depth study of the information-technology policy processes of nine countries, including Korea, Brazil, and Japan. Our focus is on the consequences of varying policies for the end users, businesses, computer scientists, and other professionals involved in the information-technology field.

There have, of course, been various proposals for government action. The Association for Data Processing Service Organizations (ADAPSO), a group of U.S. software and service vendors, has endorsed a proposal for a National Information Committee to develop an information-technology strategy for the U.S. If formed, the committee would initiate a two-year study to give government a window on information technology in the 1990s, so that government could direct its actions accordingly. Another proposal was outlined by the House Democratic Caucus, favoring an Economic Cooperation Council composed of government, industry, and labor leaders who would advise the government of industrial priorities.[10] These and other positive suggestions have thus far lacked one critical ingredient: presidential commitment. They are also flawed in that they are linked to current developments rather than focused on getting right the process and policy machinery—so that whatever *tomorrow*'s technology and economics may be, we will be able to handle it.

The highest level of leadership will be needed to coordinate the now splintered responsibilities for information technology and encourage technological progress to benefit the U.S. and the rest of the world.

Trade Policy

It is not surprising that a technology already recognized as influencing economic competitiveness in so many industries has begun to appear on the agenda of various trade negotiations. As an example of the kind of issues involved, our high-tech trade balance has been consistently growing and in surplus with all major nations—except Japan, with whom we have a growing deficit. Part of the problem is that the U.S. and its foreign competitors do not always play by the same rules. Our semiconductor industry, in particular, illustrates some disparities.

Between 1977 and 1979 a shortage developed in the market for 16K RAM chips—the chips that at the time had the largest capacity for holding information of any on the market. Seizing its opportunity, Japan shifted its output to 16K chips, at the expense of other items, and cut their prices in the U.S.—prompting charges by the U.S. of illegal dumping. The U.S. Semiconductor Industry Association (SIA), which speaks for many (but not all) of the U.S. semiconductor manufacturers, found prices of 16K chips in Japan to be 30 percent higher than prices charged for the same products in the U.S. After a complaint to the International Trade Commission, Japan dropped the practice, but only after prices, and profits, had been driven down among U.S. suppliers.[11]

The damage was enormous. According to an SIA report, the five top U.S. semiconductor firms suffered a total $39.9 million loss in 16K RAMs in the first nine months of 1982, beyond an aggregate $26.5 million loss for 1981. By contrast, the same firms had garnered a combined profit of $84.9 million in sales of 16K RAMs in 1980. The study blamed this sudden turnaround on Japanese government-subsidized suppliers.[12] All of this is occurring in an industry that is increasingly capital-intensive and dependent on continual new investment at each step of the development curve.

More serious than the immediate dollar losses was the "disinvestment" in the product lines by U.S. firms, according to the SIA. Twelve out of fifteen of the U.S. semiconductor suppliers dropped out of the race to the next plateau of semiconductor achievement—the 64K RAM chip. By extension, they also left the push to the next generation of chips, the 256K chip. In fact, Fujitsu's 1983 announcement of the industry's first commercial 256K chip—beating Bell Labs to the punch—illustrated the success of the Japanese policy.[13]

Of course some U.S. firms were bound to drop out of the semiconductor race—foreign competition or not. However, regardless of whether Japanese practices are "fair" or "unfair," the competitive environment is changing. In the past, U.S. industry has prospered in a market-oriented economy based on relatively free competition. However, U.S. leadership must recognize that the high-technology sunrise industries are increasingly faced with international competition backed by coherent national policies. Competition in high technology is therefore not "pure" competition but is tainted by government intervention and support. The U.S. should not rule out intervention to protect its high-technology industries, but it should take that measure only within the framework of well articulated national goals. In the absence of such goals, the trade actions of the U.S. in other industries in the past have had the unfortunate effect of shielding American businesses and removing incentives to compete more effectively and adapt to changing market demands.

In devising a trade policy for the U.S. information-technology industry, policy makers must recognize once more that the industry presents entirely new problems and characterics, which often fly in the face of experience with traditional industries. Information technology is marked by increasing internationalization, with its attendant diffusion of improved theory and practice. This may lead to an increasing number of shared research and development projects and, in some cases, joint manufacturing and marketing.

Rapid change also characterizes the industry; we should expect that technological developments will continue to outpace public policy and the evolution of regulatory agencies. Even the most responsive U.S. government agencies are often handicapped by their traditionally litigious and adversary attitudes toward industry. This points to the need for frequent updates and reviews as built-in mechanisms in any national information policy. Policy makers must also recognize that the scope of information technology is not limited to any single sector of the economy. It is the key to competitiveness in virtually every industry and service, with ripple effects throughout the national and international economy.

Financial conditions in the U.S. also raise troubling questions. America is unique in the world for its abundance of venture capital. The market encourages a proliferation of small, specialized companies, which personify the American entrepreneurial spirit. While the best of the high-tech start-ups are remarkably profitable, the problems begin as the companies grow more capital-intensive and technology-intensive; the companies find that they are hard pressed to keep up an adequate cash flow or obtain additional capital on attractive terms. Without low-cost capital for research and development, the industry cannot invest for the future as consistently as is needed to stay ahead. The result is a stop-go type of progress through advancing technology which puts the U.S. companies at an automatic disadvantage when they face large, integrated, subsidized Japanese firms. (We have already seen the consequences of this in the semiconductor case at the beginning of Chapter 3, "Short Time Horizons.") One of the implications of this is the merger of developing firms into much larger corporations in which the cash flow of older product lines can be applied to the new needs. This is by no means all bad, but **333** it could be better if intermediary financing were more readily available and if tax laws were more favorable to capital appreciation in R&D–type companies.

American information technology also suffers from a self-inflicted wound: antitrust policies that discourage cooperation among companies in R&D projects. Efforts to restrict monopolistic business practices have traditionally been considered in purely domestic terms, ignoring the international character of the information-technology marketplace. While antitrust laws are designed to *promote* competition, current legislation fails to recognize that foreign computer and communications industries are often nationalized or heavily subsidized and that our own industry cannot effectively compete on an international level under current regulation.

During the *U.S.* v. *IBM* antitrust case the Justice Department consistently argued that foreign competitors should not be considered as being in the computer industry. Of all the extensive idiocy I observed in my decade of involvement in that case, the sight of a federal judge encouraging our Justice Department in such nonsense, at a time when the dominant industry reality was the growth of Japanese competitors, went quite a way to destroying the respect that Clair Wilcox and the Swarthmore economics department had instilled in me for antitrust policy! Interestingly, the U.S. government's claim that Japan was not a competitor in the computer industry was taken as quite an insult by some of my bewildered Japanese friends.

Raising the Level of Debate

Political and media concentration on information technology in the early 1980s has typically highlighted the superficial, reducing high technology to a slogan rather than promoting widespread understanding of what will be a fundamental fact of life in the rest of this century. The advent of the so-called "Atari Democrats" in early 1983 (before they realized the dimensions of the commercial disaster of Atari!) raised the dangerous possibility that information technology would become a political football: a "Democratic" issue vs. a "Republican" issue.

334   Unfortunately, widespread discussion does not equal widespread understanding. We have seen the emergence of "high-tech" as a cliché—a term that has become worn out before ever being understood. More often than not the wrong issues have been debated and the problems misstated or treated out of context. Unemployment, for example, frequently surfaces as the dominant issue in automation: robots displace jobs, the detractors neatly conclude. Such an argument fails to place factory automation within the larger context of information technology, a positive force that stimulates the economy and creates as well as protects jobs.

And in this infamous year of 1984 there has been much discussion regarding the Orwellian nightmare: electronic surveillance, intrusions on personal privacy, the threat of totalitarianism. The question should not be: Can computers be used to abuse privacy and human rights? The answer to that, quite simply, is yes! The real questions should be: How can we elevate the national consciousness of information technology so that society can make the best and most humane uses of computers? How can we, as a democratic society, make decisions and set priorities regarding a technology that will be the hallmark of the decades to come?

Information technology is an ideal example of the more widespread problem discussed in Chapter 3, namely, the need for wide-scale intelligent debate on complex alternatives so that a truly informed public can exercise political judgment. The responsibility of the media and political leaders to do their jobs as public educators is clear. The lack of serious TV coverage of the societal meaning of the computer seems remarkable to me, even in view of the inherent difficulties TV has in dealing with subtle and complex issues.

The Information Age

The sterility of current debate about information technology stems largely from a failure to recognize that the technology is startlingly new in its nature and extraordinarily broad in the sweep of its impact. I believe information technology is the basis of a new age of civilization, the Information Age. Just as the Industrial Age caused mass movements of people from farm to factory, the Information Age will mean profound changes in the way we work and live.

A little more than thirty years ago I wrote a book titled *Automation*. (I was soon credited with having coined the word "automation," although the fact was that I simply couldn't spell the then-accepted term "automatization"!) In that book I made several observations about what was then a fledgling technology, and, to my delight, many have borne the test of time. One of those observations was that, like any important technological innovation, it would bring about three phases of change:

▷ First, you mechanize what you did yesterday.
▷ Second, you find that the task changes; the technology revises *what* you do, not just *how* you do it.
▷ Third, you find that, as a result of this transformation, the greatest change of all occurs in society.

By now we are into the second and third phases, actually doing different work and coping with the resultant societal change. Although these changes are hard to see while we live through them, we must be aware of them if we are to capitalize on them. In the first stage we watch the forward-looking companies seize market share or increase profits by recognizing how the new technology can improve on what they have been doing. It inevitably follows that the entire industry rises to a new level of competition; companies find themselves in new businesses, and their missions change. Finally and most important, these changes do not occur in a vacuum. People move into new occupations and define their work and leisure time in new ways. Social mores adjust to a new reality. And extraordinary opportunities arise as a result, just as they always have when great societal changes have occurred.

So it is with all important new technologies: automobiles, electricity, air travel. All of them radically altered our lifestyles and our economy. Yet I feel information technology will change the world more permanently and more profoundly than any technology so far seen in history and will truly bring about a transformation of civilization to match, and even exceed, that of the industrial revolution. Why?

Dealing as it does with information and communication —the very stuff of human organization and interrelationships—information technology makes it possible to change our thought patterns and values as well as the organization of our society. How can it help but be revolutionary when it introduces change in such a fundamental aspect of life? This is why I wrote in *Automation*, in 1952—two years before the first commercial installation of a computer!— that the greatest impact of the computer would not be mechanizing what we have always done, but fundamentally changing what we do:

> To use the new technology as a speedier means of preparing the same reports that are now prepared and to treat their contents in the same way they are now treated would be a great mistake. What the new tools offer is, in many cases, *an entirely new way of handling business information.*[14]

Information technology is quite different from other business or industrial technologies in that it is an *intellectual* technology. Unlike industrial technologies, from lathes to forklifts, information technology is adaptable to the user's needs, or, more specifically, it is *programmable*. Rather than people having to adjust the task to the technology, computers can be programmed to people's needs. This is perhaps the least recognized and most important characteristic of information technology. It is the precise opposite of the popular image of the machine pacing the human— Charlie Chaplin as gear in *Modern Times*. (While computers are already malleable—or "friendly"—to some extent, the capability for voice interaction and more natural ways of using them in the future will ultimately fulfill their promise as tailor-made human assistants.)

Because computers can be programmed and constantly adjusted, their applications are limited only by the user's creativity and imagination. With communications linkups, they bring information resources from around the world literally to one's fingertips. Information technology thus extends human knowledge and capabilities in unprecedented ways. Computers and communications devices are nothing less than human amplifiers.

National Defense

If our national economy depends on information technology, so by extension does our national security. The fact that a strong defense depends on a strong economy is not lost on the Pentagon. Its Defense Advanced Research Projects Agency (DARPA) has touted itself as a U.S. counterpart of Japan's powerful Ministry of International Trade and Industry (MITI). In addition to sponsoring research projects relating to militarily strategic technologies, including large-scale supercomputer development, DARPA has also assumed the role of a consultant to industry, providing information on factory automation to selected companies.

While DARPA is frequently cited as the only example of U.S. moves to counter the Japanese advances, its role seems to me to be less clear-cut than private initiatives and it raises a host of questions. Do we want the Pentagon to guide information-technology policy? Does it make sense to rely on commercial spin-offs of military technology? Beyond the moral and social questions that swirl around the concept of a military-industrial complex—questions once raised by the President and General Dwight D. Eisenhower—there is the record to consider.

▷ In the late 1970s the Defense Department launched its Very High-Speed Integrated Circuit (VHSIC) program to develop semiconductors to survive harsh military conditions, including nuclear war. In a $200 million program many contracts of a few million dollars each were spread out among several U.S. computer companies. Significantly, several of the nation's leading chip manufacturers chose *not* to participate, some citing the irritants of military bureaucracy and security clearances, and others simply doubting that any commercially viable products would come of it.

▷ By contrast, Japan's Very Large-Scale Integrated Circuit (VLSIC) program of 1976-79 directed $350 million toward clear *commercial* objectives, dividing the funds among a small number of large, integrated Japanese firms. Japan has emerged today as the world leader in semiconductors. Meanwhile, the U.S.'s VHSIC program satisfied the requirements of one customer only—the military.

338

The most sophisticated of my scientist friends in the public-policy community feel that increased military spending often has a *negative* effect on our information-technology position—because it drains good scientists and technicians from basic research and from industrial product development. This is in sharp contrast to the strongly held position throughout the world that our information-technology strength has derived from our military spending. My own experience supports the experience of my scientist friends, and I can cite instances in which defense-related projects have actually hurt competition. The Army Signal Corps selected RCA as its prime contractor to develop a product that proved inferior to integrated circuits. RCA did not sell integrated circuits until several years later than its major competitors.[15]

While I don't believe the military should be determining the economic and technological goals of the U.S., it is clear that national security will depend on a strong economy and a sound technological infrastructure. One of the less well publicized concerns about the breakup of AT&T was expressed by Caspar Weinberger, the defense secretary at the time. The U.S., he argued, needs a strong, reliable, unified communications infrastructure in wartime.[16]

High-technology export control has also emerged as a national security issue. It is one of the most complex areas of public policy relating to information technology, in terms of coming to grips with what is practical as well as what is desirable. For many years there has been an extensive list of goods that cannot be exported to the Soviet Union. In recent years, in response to concerted efforts to circumvent these controls, the U.S. launched Operation Exodus in the Customs Service to prevent critical U.S. technology from reaching the Soviet Union, and it has pressed our allies to assist in this effort. For example, the U.S. asked West Germany to ban its sale to Russia of high-grade silicon, which can be used to make chips for the guidance systems of Soviet SS-20 missiles. And there have been signs of growing support among our allies to stop computer shipments to Russia: in the past year U.S.-built computers en route to eastern Europe and then Russia have been stopped in Sweden, England, and West Germany.[17] In some instances a strong case can be made for the Bucy rule (named after

Fred Bucy, then president of Texas Instruments): "Sell the product, not the process." But can such economic boycott policies ever be enforced?

Meanwhile industry executives complain that the government's East-West concerns make it difficult to export even to friendly nations. In general, our country's interests are not well served if the U.S. restricts the export of technology that the USSR can purchase elsewhere. Does the increased internationalization of the industry mean we cannot discriminate among the countries we wish to help? Do we exclude joint ventures by U.S. firms in other countries? Can we do otherwise? (The Dresser Industries' French experience in the Soviet gas pipeline compressor is evidence that we cannot seek to bind such concerns.)

When the same technology that powers a toy or a wristwatch can also be adapted to weapon systems, how do U.S. policy makers draw the line between national security concerns and the promotion of free trade?

Unique Qualities of Information

Overall, I am convinced that information technology has the capacity to make life more comfortable for individuals, more efficient for businesses, and more democratic for nations. It has the potential for creating societies in which genuine wealth is within the range of larger proportions of people than ever before. But before that happens we must face a series of questions and policy issues that, because of the nature of new technological developments and of information itself, must be dealt with quickly.

The new questions stem in large part from the unique nature of information. Unlike other commodities, its value often increases with use. Information is rarely depleted, although it can be obsoleted. Its value can change dramatically over even short periods of time, and yet there is virtually no methodology for measuring the time value of information—even though time savings may be a company's principal reason for investing in a large-scale computer system. It is, indeed, a basic factor of productive activity, comparable with labor, capital, energy, or raw materials. And it is a possession of which more may not necessarily be better. If information cannot be moved at will, analyzed, stored securely and economically, recalled at will and condensed, its worth diminishes. The last thing overworked executives and bureaucrats need is bigger "in boxes" for the uncritical gathering of information.

Who owns information? More important, how can ownership be exercised in a world of computer networks? Those basic but tantalizing questions came to the fore in the aftermath of the Milwaukee hackers' admission that they had electronically entered supposedly secure systems. The opportunities for hackers, and the problems they present, stem from the proliferation of nationwide networks of data, such as Telenet and Tymshare. Anyone with a personal computer and a modem (an inexpensive device that converts the digital signals of a computer into the analog form that is necessary for transmission over telephone lines) can legally hook into a data network by dialing the appropriate number, which is often available on the public record. Once dialed into the network, the personal computer owner, whether hacker or legitimate user, can try to plug into any of the large business, university, and military computers in the net. All that is generally needed is a three-digit area code, a two- or three-digit code that specifies the computer, and a password—which, hackers assert, is nearly always easy to guess. Once inside the system, the hacker can roam at will, finding out how the system operates, calling up data, and possibly altering the information stored in the system. In one case a hacker who entered a Columbia University computer caused the loss of data valued at $25,000.[18]

The catch is that information technology, and the ability to abuse it, have far outdistanced the law's ability to deal with it. Entering computers, removing or altering information in them, and even causing the systems to go out of service are not illegal in several states. When police authorities in Orange, Connecticut, discovered that an auxiliary employee was using the Police Department's computer to check records for his full-time employer, they could not charge him with a crime; no appropriate law was on the books of the state. Even when laws are available, the long-distance nature of hacking makes it difficult to prosecute the cases because of the uncertainty about precisely where the crime was committed. If certain forms of information were understood to be commodities and classified as "property," there would be no question as to the nature of the hacker's crime: it would be theft.

If hackers can gain access to large computers so readily, can international and industrial spies be close behind? Specialists discount the thesis of *War Games*, a movie in which a young computer hacker enters the U.S. military network and almost starts World War III. (The same week that *The New York Times* was quoting experts attesting to the implausibility of the plot of *War Games*, the *Times* recounted the story of the entry of the 414s into the Los Alamos computer!) However, the experts do concede that there are enough electronic leaks in military networks to make it profitable for Soviet-bloc computer scientists to put forth the effort. And as with hackers, so it is with spies: every effort to secure a computer network presents not a barrier but merely an intriguing challenge to the outsider determined to break and enter the system. We do know, of course, that extensive crime has been perpetrated via computer systems. What we *don't* know is just how much. The nature of computer crime is such that the machines can be programmed to cover up a theft long after it has taken place, often from a great distance—even another country!

Less threatening, but no less bothersome to authorities, is the piracy of television signals. In the early 1980s a number of television stations in Caribbean and Central American countries started to intercept television signals beamed via satellite that were intended for cable viewers in the U.S. According to the Motion Picture Association, television stations in the Bahamas, Belize, Costa Rica, the Dominican Republic, Haiti, and Jamaica, among others, were transmitting U.S. news and entertainment programs without permission. Film industry spokesmen complain that the piracy could seriously cut into the industry's profits. The government-owned broadcasting company in Jamaica, for example, showed pirated broadcasts of *Poltergeist, Victor/Victoria,* and *Rocky III,* among other movies, before they had been released to Jamaican theaters by the owners of the films! Yet stopping such electronic eavesdropping is difficult if not impossible, because international laws involving copyrights on satellite transmissions are virtually nonexistent.[19]

New Legal Questions: Copyright Ownership

The question of information ownership, brought to such prominence by the 414s, points to a great many other thorny legal issues. For example, how do we define one's legal right to information ownership? Do the "0"s and "1"s of computer language constitute a work that may be legally copyrighted, like a work of literature? What is the real nature of copyright?

The instrument that brought the issues to national headlines is the videocassette recorder (VCR), a machine whose rate of growth in the 1980s rivaled that of television sets a quarter of a century earlier. In October 1981 the Ninth Circuit Court of Appeals in San Francisco astonished the information industry, and much of the rest of the U.S., by ruling that the makers and distributors of VCRs are liable for copyright infringement when private citizens use their machines to record programs from television. An appeals court overturned the verdict, but the issues had by then become politically charged. Do owners of VCRs have the right to build up large libraries of normally copyrighted material without paying any royalty tax? Do moviemakers have the right to prevent them from doing it? Ultimately the question went before the Supreme Court, which ruled in essence it would not prohibit activities for which no laws were yet written. Until the lawmakers chose to take up the issue, home taping would be legal. The question had clearly burst on a legal system that seemed scarcely equipped to handle it.

Another copyright issue was settled less controversially. In September 1983 a federal appeals court in Philadelphia decided that software for personal computers, including software embedded on silicon chips inside the machine, deserves the same copyright protection as any literary work on a printed page. Franklin Computer Corporation had copied fourteen operating system programs—the basic instructions that police traffic through a computer—from the Apple Computer Company's Apple II model and had used the programs in its Ace 100 machine, which resembled the Apple II but sold more cheaply. Franklin's lawyers argued that programs embedded inside computers were parts of the machine and thus not subject to copyright law. A lower court agreed with Franklin, but the appeals court did not concur.[20]

Reactions to the decision were predictably diverse. Supporters of Apple argued that the decision had saved the U.S. software industry; without copyright protection, wrote William Gates of the Microsoft Corporation, "companies like Apple could not afford to advance the state of the art." Franklin, by contrast, saw the decision as supporting high-technology monopolies and inevitably costing the consumer more in the long run. What is most disturbing from a public-policy point of view is that, just as in the AT&T breakup, policy vital to the nation's use of high technology was made in the courts.

Unlike the other major problems that I discuss in this book, with the exception of biogenetics, the dilemmas of information technology do not represent situations in which a basically sound policy process has gone awry. Rather, they point to a flawed policy apparatus that is entirely unprepared to deal with these issues.

In what ways might copyright laws be changed? Can copyrights be protected and the full benefits of information technology be enjoyed? Are these ends compatible?

Invasion of Privacy

A different set of issues is raised by a process that in some ways reverses computer hacking. That is the use of computerized data on private citizens by governments and other institutions for purposes unrelated to the original reason for gathering the data. The U.S. government has long kept all kinds of files on its citizens. What the explosion of information technology makes possible is the ability to combine all the data on individuals that have been collected in the computers of different government agencies, as well as in those of businesses. The fear arises that the government is able to learn far more about its citizens than is compatible with the ideas of a free democracy.

Two cases in 1983 caused particular concern to civil libertarians. In one it was revealed that the Selective Service System cross-checked lists of draft registrants with records from the Social Security system and state motor vehicle departments to identify young men who had failed to register for the draft. In the other the Internal Revenue Service started a test to determine whether computerized records on the life-styles of Americans could be used to identify individuals who failed to pay their income taxes. "The idea is, we'll take a list of individual households and their estimated income and match it against a computerized list of all taxpayers," explained Walter Bergman of the IRS. "If the check suggests a family hasn't paid [taxes], we'll make an enquiry to find out why."[21]

Illustrating the proliferation of information that is available in computers, the IRS insisted that the sources of the data it planned to use were all openly available. They included telephone books, automobile-registration files, and statistical information about the average incomes of families living in different regions, the latter compiled and published by the Census Bureau. "The IRS experiment is very troublesome," said Robert Ellis Smith, publisher of *Privacy Journal*. "While I am quite sure that it does not violate the law, it graphically demonstrates the growing links between government and private computers. National lists of households and their incomes are obviously accurate enough for soliciting business, but that doesn't mean they are precise enough to trigger investigations."[22]

What protection do citizens need from government's surveillance of them? How can workers be protected from inadvertent disclosure to employers of their medical or financial status, by way of computer networks? Neither question is really new. But both have become matters of immediacy as a result of the rapid advances made in information technology, which accelerates and broadens the potential for large-scale abuse.

Personal privacy can be threatened quite unintentionally through the offshoots of information technology. A report distributed by the Knight News Service in 1979 told an alarming story:

A bank had installed automated teller machines to let its customers bank at all hours. The bank discovered, by reading its computerized records, that an unusual number of withdrawals were made every night between midnight and 2:00 A.M. Suspecting foul play, the bank hired detectives to look into the matter. It turned out that customers were withdrawing cash on their way to the local red light district! The article observes that "There's a bank someplace in America that knows which of its customers paid a hooker last night."[23]

Citizens who were committing no crime at the bank machines had nevertheless left themselves vulnerable to exposure. In many other instances, information collected for legitimate purposes opens up enormous potential for abuse. Banks, credit companies, insurers, hospitals, retail stores, and government agencies carry detailed profiles on millions of citizens. One would have to be a kind of hermit—self-employed and self-sufficient, paying for everything by barter or in cash, owning little in the way of personal property—to escape from inclusion in the massive computer data banks.

Must we sacrifice privacy for the conveniences of modern life? How can such personal data be thoroughly protected and controlled? And how can such control be restored to the individual citizen? We created the technology behind massive information banks; can we not also create the technology—and the public policy—that will effectively restrict its dissemination of their contents?

On the flip side of that coin, we must recognize when data collection is for the public good. The Reagan administration proposed in 1983 that the Census Bureau be allowed to share with other statistical agencies the demographic data it collects.[24] It was not a matter of whether those other agencies were entitled to the information; they were already gathering identical information on their own. It was simply a matter of eliminating redundant effort and making government more efficient. Late in 1983 the plan was killed in Congress, basically for fear of privacy intrusions. What savings might have accrued to the taxpayer if this overlapping information collection were eliminated? Who benefited from this congressional decision?

▷ I first ran into this problem in 1963. I went to see President Kennedy's budget director, Kermit Gordon, who (as a Williams Professor) had been my outside Honors Examiner in Economics at Swarthmore. I told him a little about computers (it is hard today

346

to realize just how new all this was at that time) and said that I felt it would make sense to have one central statistical bureau in the government with a large computer data base, so that each agency could draw on the data as needed, thereby eliminating a whole army of people who were at the time laboriously compiling duplicate statistics. Twelve years earlier, as a student intern in what was then the Economic Cooperation Administration, I had spent a summer compiling trade statistics and, by the end of the summer, had a good firsthand feeling for the wasteful and duplicative process of gathering statistics from many government agencies and processing them.

Kermit thought this a fine idea and suggested that I go to see Ewan Clague, then commissioner of labor statistics. While I was a bit apprehensive (I had made some comments Clague interpreted as critical in a *Harvard Business Review* piece on productivity data that I had written ten years earlier), I nonetheless had lunch with Clague, the man I had viewed in school as the legendary head of BLS. To my surprise he reacted very emotionally to my idea. The reason became obvious. Robert Kennedy had been pressing Clague to allow the Justice Department to use some of the data BLS had been gathering for compilation of their indexes. Clague was adamant that any violation of his agreements with the suppliers of the data as to secrecy of the source would destroy their validity, and he told me he would resign his post if the attorney general prevailed. I am sure he was right, and I only then began to understand at least one aspect of the problem!

"Haves" and "Have-nots"

Another potential point of vulnerability caused by information technology arises in education. According to a National Science Foundation report issued in September 1983, "ominous inequities" were appearing in U.S. students' opportunities for familiarizing themselves with computers. Wayne N. Welch and Robert E. Anderson of the University of Minnesota determined that opportunities to study computers and computing depended on social status, gender, and geographic location. Instruction in computer programming at the time was limited mainly to males attending large-city, computer-rich schools.[25] That report, and similar studies in more limited areas, conjured up the grim possibility of generations of computer illiterates, untrained and unable to cope with the demands of living full lives in a computerized world.

At a time when increasing numbers of colleges and graduate schools are requiring students to own personal computers as a condition of enrollment, will computers in the schools become symbols that differentiate the "haves" from the "have-nots"? Will educational software be slanted more toward male than female interests? How do we guarantee the enormous benefits computers can bring to the educational process? Will society create two new classes of people—computer literates and computer illiterates? If society tolerates inequality in computer learning, what spillover can we expect in our nation's industrial competitiveness and economic well-being?

If we look at the same issue of "haves" vs. "have-nots" on a global scale, we realize that we are living in a world in which information is increasingly recognized as power. Successive World Administrative Radio Conferences (WARCs) have set the stage for international infighting over who owns the frequencies in which countries can send and receive data signals. On a less adversarial note, two countries have made deliberate efforts to transfer information "power" to Third World countries: France's World Center, the brainchild of Jean-Jacques Servan-Schreiber, was formed with the idea of bringing low-cost microcomputer technology to developing countries; Japan, through its Institute for the Information Society, has initiated a kind of "computer peace corps" with similar purposes. Think of all the opportunities that exist for similar and yet more imaginative institutional innovations in every field and country!

The idea that knowledge is power is not new. What *is* new is the escalation of that power that information technology makes possible. Japanese visionary Yoneji Masuda, with whom I invariably have stimulating conversations whenever we are both in Europe or the States, has outlined two possible futures for the world: one, the Orwellian nightmare, in which information is controlled by the few, and the other, an *information democracy*, in which information technology is used to increase the participation in government by average citizens.

As a simple example of the latter, Masuda suggests that interactive videotex technology will allow each citizen to cast votes on important issues through home computer terminals or specially equipped TV sets. In this latter scenario the individual's control over his or her destiny would be heightened, and society would witness the ultimate in the individual's self-realization: "information society may be termed as a society with highly intellectual creativity, where people may draw future designs on an invisible canvas and pursue and realize individual lives worth living."[26]

While I am too much of an optimist to believe that Orwell's vision of 1984 was anything more than a warning, as opposed to a forecast, I am also enough of a realist to know that even the "information democracy" raises troubling questions. We need to encourage high-level debate on the issues posed by an information society. How will interactive videotex change the nature of the democratic process? Will information technology define the criteria for wealth and power, authority and repression, dictatorship and democracy? Who will control such a mighty tool? Does the individual citizen have an inherent "right" to information? If information is a human right, is access to information technology also a right? On what terms? How does one balance the right to know against the right to privacy? In what ways do we build consideration of such questions into our policy process?

Employment Issues

While the most profound social impacts of information technology lie ahead, the present impacts of the technology on our national and international economies are real. How will increasing "informatization" influence people's jobs?

Certainly, the fear that robots will displace people from the job market is, in my view, exaggerated. The Japanese, who lead the world in the application of robot technology, have experienced over-all increases in employment. One need only compare that picture with the high unemployment in Great Britain, which has applied fewer robots than any industrial country, if one draws a connection between robots and employment. (In reality, the situation is far too complex for any such comparison to be meaningful.)

This is not to say that robots do not displace workers. However, for today's heavy-manufacturing industries there is no alternative: they must automate or perish. The real issue is how to ease the problem of technology-related job dislocation for the worker. There must be mechanisms to facilitate labor transitions from "sunset" industries to the high-technology "sunrise" industries (Chapter 8 of this book is devoted to this subject). Otherwise the problem of technology-related dislocation always falls squarely on the worker's shoulders—in the form of unemployment.

Regarding the future impacts of information technology in jobs, I will raise two points at this juncture. The first is brought to mind by a familiar quotation attributed to John F. Kennedy: "A rising tide lifts all boats." Information technology stimulates a healthy economy by improving industrial and office productivity, ultimately creating more new jobs. The task will be to retrain workers for the new labor requirements of an information age and to promote corporate incentives for the deployment of information technology, especially in heavy manufacturing. I believe that imaginative and thoughtful uses of information technology will spur an increase in jobs over the next few decades.

Information technology is becoming increasingly the key to national economic well-being, affecting virtually every industry and service. One would be hard pressed to name a business that does not depend on the effective use of information: to design products and services, to track and respond to market demands, or to make well informed decisions. Computers and communications constitute a tool to manipulate that information. Particularly in the information-intensive industries—banking, publishing, direct-mail marketing—information technology is revising the conditions of competition as it transforms products, services, and markets. So dramatic are these transformations that the very definitions of these industries must be called into question. An official of Citibank was quoted as saying that his company "no longer considers itself a bank" as it moves aggressively into new electronic services.[27] In publishing too, as electronic text and graphics on home television screens gradually displace paper as the medium of communication, electronic prowess is emerging as a determinant of viability and survival.

What's more, the combination of computers and communications is creating wholly new industries, thereby further shaping the evolution of our economy. As noted earlier, the video-game industry, virtually nonexistent in the late 1970s, mushroomed into a giant three times the size of the movie industry in less than half a decade. Personal calculators not only displaced the slide rules of engineering students but became first a status symbol and then an everyday tool for the average citizen. Only a few years ago, some schools forbade the use of hand-held calculators; now some colleges and graduate schools deny admission to students without powerful personal computers! As new industries based on information technology are formed, their technological advances are incorporated into existing industries. Products from toys to machine tools to automobiles are now marketed on the basis of the "intelligence" made possible by microelectronic components.

Whether it's the sleek desk-top word processor, the integrated manufacturing process control system, the colorful graphic displays of computer-aided design, or the executive's decision support system, computers are increasingly the key to working better and working smarter. How many American institutions were prepared for these far-reaching changes in our economy? Who might have foreseen that our heavy-manufacturing, or "smokestack," industries would today depend on sophisticated electronics and robotics for their very survival? Given the potential of information technology to boost productivity and make U.S. industries and services second to none, can we not find some institutional medium to promote the technology—through tax policy geared to the special needs of R&D and to the capital-intensive nature of silicon chip development, faster depreciation write-offs, and other incentives? What signals is our government sending to industry?

My second point requires looking beyond the next few decades. I believe that information technology will be responsible for dramatically different patterns of work and leisure in the years ahead. The technology will have progressed to the point that, by the early part of the next century, many more types of jobs, especially those that are boring or dangerous, will be offloaded to tireless robots, while humans are freed for more creative tasks. An executive, for example, will be able to tell a voice-activated computer to turn down an invitation to deliver a speech: the **351** computer will automatically generate a polite response based on previous letters stored in its memory, stating in the executive's personal style and tone that he or she holds the requesting organization in highest regard but simply cannot attend its meeting because of previous engagements, and so forth. (I know a scientist who is well along in the development of this particular device, and he expects it to be on the market before the end of the century—a decade or so from now!) If secretaries are required in such an environment, I suspect that their jobs will demand much more of their creative potential than typing and dictation.

Will we see a world in which so many types of jobs are assumed by computers and robots that it won't be necessary for people to spend a third of their lives working? Mr. Masuda believes so. He envisions a society in which there are simply fewer jobs for humans, demanding a rethinking of the way we structure work and leisure hours. He further speculates that people may work only part of the year and pursue their own interests—what he calls "self-realization" —the rest of the year. This, to my mind, recalls the charming image of the Victorian gentleman, one who pursued intellectual interests from botany to poetry at his own leisure. Although we are nowhere near attaining this condition for most of humankind, I am full of optimism for what the future holds. For unlike the Victorian Age, this new computer-based "leisure class" would not be confined to the privileged few.

I somehow think that there will always be workaholics, who work seven days a week—individuals perhaps like myself, who are fortunate to pursue work that interests them —and there will always be those who avoid activity of any kind, whether it be labor or leisure. Yet I cannot help but feel tremendous optimism about the ways information technology will restructure one's work life. The patterns of work and leisure that developed in the Industrial Age will not be appropriate to the Information Age. Should we not begin now to consider the nature of those changes, and steer them toward a spectacular new Renaissance—in which human intellect and self-worth achieve new prominence?

Think of the impact of these changes on virtually all aspects of our governmental policies regarding employment. Is anyone thinking of this? How should our policy process be adjusted to ensure such thinking? Through publicly funded Institutes of the Future (see Chapter 3)?

Straws in the Wind

Can the United States adapt its policy machinery to cope with the realities of information technology—its unique characteristics, its rapid rate of change, the presence of subsidized foreign competition, and its ubiquity in our daily life—without stifling the initiatives that have brought the technology to its present position? We certainly have a long way to go in the U.S. at the national policy level, and we can learn a great deal from studying many models from both at home and abroad. Yet I see some evidence that institutions can adapt to the entirely new problems of this advanced technology.

The COMSAT experience is uniquely American. After a period of rapid progress in the development of communications satellites in the 1950s President John F. Kennedy forged a policy to make U.S. technological leadership in communications a government mandate. His vision was lofty. "I invite all nations to participate in a communications satellite system, in the interest of world peace and closer brotherhood among peoples throughout the world," he declared in July, 1961.[28] He favored private ownership and operation of the U.S. portion of the system but with the explicit condition that technological progress would be rapid and would be aimed at commercially viable offerings. The Communications Satellite Act was passed in 1962, and the Communications Satellite Corporation was formally established in 1963. COMSAT is now a very successful enterprise that continues in world technological leadership and is increasingly involved in competitive and profitable ventures. The cost to the taxpayer has been nominal, and the entire world has benefited.

While the conditions of the industry today are not identical to those in the early 1960s—and I would not in any case favor a government corporation for information technology —the COMSAT initiative does illustrate the success our government has enjoyed with big national projects, steered by a lofty vision and presidential leadership. The government could do the same thing today: sponsor a national high-technology project on the order of the *Apollo* moon-landing program, one that captures public imagination while making dramatic progress toward a stated technological goal.

So many areas of American life are ripe for the application of information technology as part of a nationwide project, and at the same time hold out the prospect of much wider and more practical benefits than did the Apollo moon landing. Education is one such area. Computer technology is now being introduced into the schools on a piecemeal and uncoordinated basis. Yet, as I discuss in Chapter 5, computers open the possibility of teaching and learning in fundamentally new ways. Some private firms, notably Control Data Corp., have done extensive research in computer-aided instruction, but much more will be needed to achieve the kind of widespread and judicious application that will make a real difference in the quality of education.

Great Britain took the national project approach when it instituted in 1982 an Information Technology Year, as a theme for many interrelated events. Intended as a national public awareness campaign, it rallied public and private interest in promoting new applications of computers and communications technologies. Before the "IT Year" was established, an opinion poll revealed that only 17 percent of the population knew the meaning of information technology. At the end of the year, that figure had jumped to more than 62 percent. The U.S. could take the same approach on a national, state, or local level, possibly in collaboration with private industry. The result could be research and development of new applications of information technology.

While no model project of nationwide or even statewide magnitude has yet been proposed, I see some positive signs that we are, on a societal basis, coming to grips with some of the problems posed by the new era—even if on a reactive, rather than proactive, basis. New policies on joint ventures and moves to create more secure networks are two examples.

New Policies on Joint Ventures

There are positive signs today that the U.S. government realizes the hampering effect of rigid antitrust rules on U.S.

progress in information technology. In fact, the Reagan administration started in 1983 to encourage small numbers of companies in the same field to combine their R&D resources in projects designed to boost U.S. competitiveness in world markets. Legislation proposed by the White House in the fall of 1983, for example, was intended to "remove unnecessary deterrents and protect the rights of innovators to their legitimate financial rewards." The proposed National Productivity and Innovation Act had four major purposes:

▷ Removing legal bars against joint ventures among U.S. firms by requiring the courts to weigh the competitive benefits of such arrangements against any anticompetitive purposes.
▷ Limiting damages in suits in which firms were found to be operating illegal joint R&D efforts to actual damages, rather than the triple damages that had prevailed previously.
▷ Providing more freedom to license patents, copyrights, trademarks, and other innovations for development and marketing without fear of legal suits.
▷ Strengthening protection of patents concerning improvements and innovations in manufacturing.[29]

Current law does not entirely ban cooperative research and development, and creative interpretation of legislation on the books has enabled groups of companies to combine their scientists' and engineers' skills in development projects. Soon after Ronald Reagan announced the National Productivity and Innovation Act, for example, Attorney General William French Smith invoked what one Justice Department lawyer termed "a lost provision of the law" to allow eight small high-technology companies in New England to participate in a joint R&D program on electronics without fear of lawsuits. The Small Business Technology Group, Inc., was granted antitrust immunity to pool resources and compete primarily for defense contracts. The reassurance proved possible under some rather obscure terms of the Small Business Act.[30]

Another joint venture, the Center for Magnetic Recording Research at the University of California at San Diego, is **355** supported by IBM, Kodak, and a score of other companies and is the country's first pooled research effort in magnetic storage technology.[31] However, the most promising example of new initiatives in information technology is the Microelectronics and Computer Technology Corporation (MCC), a consortium of thirteen major U.S. computer companies, whose object is to formulate an American response to the growing overseas threat in information technology. MCC was the inspiration of my friend William Norris, chairman and founder of Control Data Corporation. To create the institution he had to go through a management version of the labors of Hercules. First he had to convince a group of CDC's major competitors in the computer market—including Motorola, Honeywell, NCR, and National Semiconductor (IBM declined to participate)—that it was in the national interest and their own joint interests to link up in the venture. Next Norris had to persuade the government that the new organization should not be tied up in the red tape of antitrust legislation. Finally, having secured the necessary assurances from Washington, Norris had to put the venture into practice by overseeing the selection of its top personnel.

A key decision was the choice of Vice Admiral Bobby Inman, former deputy director of the CIA, to head MCC. Inman was specifically charged with steering MCC through the difficult straits of antitrust legislation. With a staff of executives on loan from the participating companies, Inman moved quickly to establish MCC as a positive force for driving American information technology. The company settled on Austin, Texas, with its reservoir of qualified scientists and engineers from the University of Texas, as the location of the venture and decided to aim for major leaps rather than gradual improvements in technology. With initial funding of $350 million, Inman's team of executives and scientists-on-loan targeted four initial research projects, all of them directed at countering the Japanese fifth-generation computer challenge. They are:

▷ Advanced systems of computer hardware designed to support the expert systems—which act in much the same way as human experts in specific subjects—and to enable humans to communicate with computers without need to learn computer language.

▷ Improvements that will hasten the development and quality of programs for advanced computers.

▷ Computer-aided design and manufacturing methods for the silicon chips that are the guts of modern computers.

▷ New methods of packing and linking together chips in order to take best advantage of the "shrinkage of real estate" in computers that improved chip technology makes possible.[32]

Clearly, MCC is no magic wand that will automatically ensure that the long U.S. dominance of information technology built up in previous generations of computers will continue. However, the fact that the institution has been allowed to come into existence, destroying a tradition of government opposition to joint R&D ventures, indicates a possible change in attitudes that had increasingly hampered U.S. efforts to compete in a tough international market filled with government-supported firms.

If the MCC project is successful, it could provide the fundamental and applied knowledge necessary to keep the U.S. at the cutting edge of information technology and maintain the steady advance of that technology in creatively improving the lives of all of us. My only concern is that future presidential administrations might not be as favorably disposed to joint ventures as is Reagan's. How do we ensure consistent policy regarding antitrust and joint ventures from one administration to the next?

Most importantly, how do we fashion a consistent information technology policy that will last beyond current political and technological realities, and serve us in the years of rapid change to come?

Toward More Secure Networks

In spite of the shocking revelations of information-network vulnerability that surfaced in the computer hacking stories, the phenomenon served at least one positive aim: to alert company executives and society to the potential vulnerability of information networks. (I know my own firm's clients were much more receptive, after the 414 case, to taking some of the computer security precautions we had long been advocating!) That awareness in turn sparked the search for creative new means of thwarting the computer criminals.

In part, securing computer systems involves relatively simple methods, such as introducing less than obvious codes and passwords and erecting electronic fences around computer memories to partition off the memories from outside access. Another protective technique in growing use by banks and other corporate users of information technology is the call-back. Instead of gaining immediate access to a computer system, would-be users check in and then wait for the system to call back their numbers, which are stored in the system. Plainly, only authorized users will be able to receive such a call-back. More elaborate methods are under study to enable computers to check the origins of incoming calls and immediately ascertain whether such numbers are authorized to use the systems.

Computer scientists are developing methods of scrambling sensitive data before it enters computer networks. Security personnel are also paying more attention to the human factor. For even if a system is mechanically and electronically immune to break-ins without the use of authorized codes and passwords, there is no guarantee that insiders will not pass them on to other users. "It is much cheaper to bribe somebody than it is to count on the very small probability of breaking a code," explains Tim Korb, professor of computer sciences at Purdue University. Plainly, the possibility of information theft and abuse by hackers and others will never be entirely absent; but the recent publicity will guarantee that that possibility features prominently on the agenda of the information industry.

Posing Questions

While positive developments in network security and joint ventures give much cause for optimism, I am painfully aware that I have raised many more questions regarding information technology than I have answered. Throughout this book, with the exception of this chapter and the one 358 following, I have closed each chapter with a selection of case examples illustrating positive moves toward addressing the problems I raised. In information technology, however, the policy machinery is either nonexistent or woefully inadequate to the task. In many ways our policy makers are not even asking the right questions. And one thing is certain: We will never arrive at the right answers until we first pose the right questions! My intent has been to raise the level of debate regarding this technology and possibly help policy makers and society pose those proper questions.

X

Technology Outrunning Policy: The Bio-Revolution

Research in genetics and many areas of practical medicine is advancing so rapidly that it is outpacing society's ability to deal with it on a legal and moral basis. Scientists and physicians are creating—and facing—ethical problems that cannot be solved by applying the existing academic code and the Hippocratic oath, and the repercussions of these problems go far beyond the research profession. And while many of these problems are not entirely new, they are exacerbated by the rapidity and scale of recent developments. Institutions and individuals with no relationship to science or medicine are encountering entirely new dilemmas.

Case:
New Life Forms

Molecular biologists were the first to express fear that experiments made possible in the early 1970s by advances in genetic manipulation could perhaps create new forms of life that might endanger public health and the environment. Visions of monsters and mutants began to create a public panic. The concerns were originally restricted to the community of researchers actually working in the arcane area of genetics. But as scientists realized what Robert Sinsheimer of the University of California at Santa Cruz called the "great and terrible power" of their techniques, they opened up the debate to the general public. Major meetings in California and Washington attracted a wide range of scientists, activists, journalists, and policy makers.

The basic issue was that of human safety: How should the public be protected from danger as a result of research in recombinant DNA technology, as the scientific pursuit was known? (DNA is deoxyribonucleic acid, the fundamental material of life. When geneticists "recombine" pieces of DNA, they link together genes in combinations that do not necessarily occur in nature.) No existing institution was capable of the task. There were few role models for the job. So researchers, lawyers, policy makers, and others involved, however indirectly, in the process of public protection started to hammer out guidelines for minimizing a perceived threat that had not even existed five years previously.

Inevitably the process pitted interest groups and constituencies against one another. Researchers actually working with DNA contended that they alone had the expertise to understand the real nature of the threats that their experiments might present inside and outside the laboratory. Furthermore, by bringing public attention to the possible danger—in effect blowing the whistle on themselves—they had demonstrated a remarkable sense of public responsibility. Thus, their argument went, they should take the major role in regulating use of the powerful new genetic techniques.

Environmental activists and a number of maverick molecular biologists disagreed. Whatever responsibility the research community had shown in bringing the dangers of recombinant DNA to public notice had largely been self-serving, they contended. If allowed to control the regulatory process for the technology, the researchers would inevitably bend the rules to their own advantage; public safety would take a back seat to pressure for scientific —and possibly commercial—advancement.

Other interest groups added their own unique contributions to the growing argument. Laboratory technicians, for example, argued that they should have a major voice in regulating experiments, because they stood just as close to danger as did the scientists who designed the procedures. Some local officials used the controversy as the opportunity to resurrect long-simmering town-versus-gown struggles.

Eventually the constituencies all agreed that, for the moment, regulatory authority should be lodged in the National Institutes of Health, the arm of government that supported research in recombinant DNA technology. That approach, however, created almost as many new problems as it solved old ones. Should the NIH mandate regulation standards or merely suggest guidelines? How could it enforce its regulations? What should it do about commercial laboratories, which received no government grants? What criteria should the NIH use to decide whether or not a specific experiment posed a danger to the public? The NIH appointed a Recombinant DNA Advisory Committee (RAC) to set up guidelines for research in the controversial area of biomedicine. In 1976 the RAC issued its first guidelines, which set out the types of precautions that it expected for particular types of experiments, and banned entirely certain experiments, such as those involving the transfer of drug resistance and viruses implicated in cancer.

Not surprisingly, the guidelines were greeted with dismay by both recombinant DNA scientists and environmental activists. The researchers saw the guidelines as an unnecessary extra layer of red tape with which they had to cope before carrying out crucial experiments. "They have put every recombinant DNA scientist in jeopardy of making trivial paper violations that in no way create a safety problem but that can draw serious penalties on him and his institution," complained NIH researcher Wallace Rowe. "This was probably the first time in history that the incendiaries formed their own fire brigade," countered Erwin Chargaff, a Columbia University molecular biologist opposed to recombinant DNA work and to the principle that researchers should have the main input into guidelines for their own area of research.[1]

The arguments over the research continued into the 1980s, when they started to cool down because of evidence that the experiments probably weren't as dangerous as had initially been feared. In fact, human tinkering with bacteria now seems far less menacing than what the bacteria are doing on their own. But the controversy showed the difficulty that can arise when research that may present hazards to the public outstrips the ability of public institutions to respond to it.

Case:
Kidneys for Sale

Is the profit motive inconsistent with medical matters? The question appeared in sharp focus in 1983 when Virginia physician

Dr. Barry Jacobs announced that he had formed a new organization, International Kidney Exchange, to buy healthy kidneys from human beings and sell them to patients seeking kidney transplants. The need for the scheme arose, according to Jacobs, because of remarkable advances in the ability of the medical profession to carry out successful transplant operations. A new drug, cyclosporine, discovered in the late 1970s, largely overcame the problem of rejection that had dogged the earliest efforts to transplant organs among humans. Use of the drug at Stanford University Medical Center had completely turned around the survival statistics of heart transplant patients. For example, whereas in the early 1970s only 20 percent of patients who received a new heart survived at least a year, by 1983 about 80 percent of the heart recipients were living for at least two years after the operation.

Cyclosporine removed one limitation on transplant operations, only to have it replaced with another. The drug opened up the possibility of successful organ transplants to thousands of Americans with heart, lung, liver, and kidney ailments. But only a small proportion of the patients could take advantage of the opportunity because of the shortage of donated organs. Less than 1 percent of all Americans die under circumstances and at ages that leave their organs viable for transplant, and even among the 1 percent, not all of the organs become available. In 1982, for example, more than 10,000 Americans were waiting for kidneys suitable for transplant. But during the year only 5358 kidney transplants were actually performed.

Dr. Jacobs' concept was to apply the profit motive to the procedure. International Kidney Exchange would buy healthy kidneys from people in need of ready cash—including people in Third World countries—and sell them to patients seeking transplants who could not find an appropriately matched kidney among relatives.

The medical establishment objected to the scheme on two counts. First, explained Dr. David Ogden of the National Kidney Foundation, the plan could not be justified medically. The success rate of kidneys transplanted from cadavers was just as high as that of kidneys from living donors unrelated to the kidney recipient; both types of organ donation had an appreciably lower success rate than that of kidneys from close relatives. More important, stated Ogden, "It is immoral and unethical to place a living person at risk of surgical complication and even death for a cash payment to that person." To do so "would make a travesty of informed consent, by introducing the temptation and bias of a cash award for consent."[2]

Nevertheless medical officials saw no legal method to prevent Dr. Jacobs, and any other entrepreneurs who might decide to enter the transplant business, from buying and selling organs. They had to concede that little progress was being made in reducing the shortage of organs for transplantation. Efforts to encourage hospital staff to alert transplant teams to the death or imminent death of brain-damaged patients with perfectly healthy hearts, livers, and kidneys had resulted in only minimal success. Medical staff showed an understandable resistance to talking about organ donation to the bereaved families of the newly deceased.

Certainly Jacobs' scheme showed some hints of opportunism. The physician had actually been convicted of mail fraud in a case related to Medicare billing, had spent ten months in jail, and had had his license to practice medicine in Virginia revoked. This criminal record obviously shed an unfavorable light on Jacobs' concept. Nevertheless his proposal showed up the shortcomings of the voluntary system traditionally relied on by the medical establishment to acquire human artifacts, from blood to transplantable organs.

The ethical questions raised by the for-profit sale of human organs are quite new. Somewhat similar questions were raised more than a decade ago with respect to the most basic of human artifacts: human blood.

What are the lines to be drawn—can indeed any lines at all be pragmatically drawn—if human blood be legitimated as a consumption good? To search for an identity and sphere of concern for social policy would thus be to search for the non-existent. All policy would become in the end economic policy and the only values that would count are those that can be measured in terms of money and pursued in the dialectic of hedonism. Each individual would act egoistically for the good of all by selling his blood for what the market would pay. To abolish the moral choice of giving to strangers could lead to an ideology to end all ideologies.[3]

Before the medical discovery of cyclosporine, organ transplants were largely unsuccessful, and Jacobs' scheme would simply not have been commercially viable. The creation of this single drug raised new issues that caught our medical and legal institutions off guard.

Case:
Commercialization of Biomedicine

Edward Whitehead made $400 million in stock and cash when he sold Technicon Inc., the laboratory instruments company that he had founded with his father, to Revlon Inc. His troubles started when he tried to give away a third of that amount. Duke University, his first choice for receiving the donation, refused the gift. The Massachusetts Institute of Technology debated long and hard over the conditions that Whitehead had set for the donation—conditions that a number of faculty members regarded as incompatible with the principles of academic freedom.

The problem focused on the nature of the work that Whitehead wished to fund. By 1981, when the controversy arose, genetic research had become a lightning rod for public and academic controversy. Visions of alien bugs escaping from the laboratories, in best B-movie style, mingled with scenarios of unethical professors using public funds to make fundamental discoveries, which they promptly exploited commercially for their own use. For almost a decade biomedicine had featured as a major source of scientific disagreement in the press and academia.

To opponents of the commercialization of biomedicine Whitehead's proposals represented the ultimate threat to the ivory tower philosophy. To supporters of the industrialist his largesse provided an example of the best and most creative type of philanthropy. Whitehead planned to give MIT an immediate gift of $7.5 million to use as it pleased. That amount was conditional on MIT's acceptance of another offer of more than $120 million—to house, endow, and fund research for the Whitehead Institute, an independent facility for research in biomedicine whose scientists would become members of the MIT faculty.

Supporters of the plan among the MIT faculty saw it as an opportunity to continue fundamental research at a time when normal sources of funding were drying up. "I think it's a very appropriate thing for universities to expand by establishing independent entities that can operate on their own and don't put universities further and further at the jeopardy of government," declared David

Baltimore, a Nobel laureate in medicine who was chosen as the first director of the Whitehead Institute. Opponents painted the plan as an industrial Trojan horse. "It threatens to change the nature of higher education," contended biologist Sheldon Penman. "It promises to open the door to people coming in with a lot of money to throw around."

The argument also focused on the academic morality of rapid profit making by researchers as a result of their basic studies—a possibility that many scientists working in fundamental biomedicine had quickly realized. Should professors be allowed to patent the fruits of their research when that research was heavily funded and supported by a large academic institution? And if those patents are used by a professor in establishing a commercial enterprise, should the university get a share in ownership of the or in its profits?

Supporters of the Whitehead Institute argued that it would act as a kind of buffer; by providing stable funding for basic research, it would enable MIT to ignore offers of grants from industrial sources more interested in commercial results than in extending the boundaries of human knowledge. Critics, by contrast, contended that the distinction between basic research and commercial applications had already become so fuzzy that any center of biomedicine backed by industrial money would inevitably fuel the rush to marketable products.

But perhaps the major source of controversy, as MIT's faculty debated Whitehead's offer, concerned the jealously guarded freedom of universities to appoint their own faculty members without even a hint of outside influence. According to Whitehead's offer, twenty scientists hired for the Whitehead Institute would become members of MIT's biology faculty, which numbered forty at the time. The danger, admitted MIT Provost Francis Low, who nevertheless supported the plan for the new institute, was that "the research direction would not be set by our own existing biology department."[4]

Whitehead's offer was finally accepted. Nevertheless a vague sense of uneasiness remained and a suspicion that an important barrier around the ivory tower had been breached. And within the public apprehension surrounding biomedical research, there still were large questions as to whether Whitehead's money would serve the general good of society.

While the proper relationship between academia and industry is **366** not a new issue, it is exacerbated by the introduction of new fields of research, such as biomedicine, which are associated with grave new fears of the unknown. Questions of business ethics and academic ethics are now inextricably complicated by issues of societal responsibility—questions that concern the average citizen.

Molecular biology and medicine present to public policy the same dichotomy as does information technology: on one hand the realized promise of scientific insights applied through extraordinary technologies that can give our advanced technological civilization a new level of quality and abundance in food, health, and life; and on the other the larger-than-life controversies surrounding this application. And our policy machinery is as ill equipped to deal with biomedicine as it is with information technology. Advances in science are happening too fast for our legal, political, and social institutions to cope with them.

Scientists, doctors, administrators, and the proverbial man in the street now face moral dilemmas unthinkable even in the recent past. Should research scientists be allowed to probe the fundamental pieces and processes of life, given the small but finite possibility that their research will lead to organisms dangerous to humans and the environment? Should medical teams make heroic efforts to preserve the lives of individuals who can, at best, survive as vegetables? What criteria should guide medical teams in deciding whom to treat when the medical resources are scarce? Many old questions are enlarged by the availability of heroic and costly life-preservation methods. We must face up to the problem we would all like to avoid but the one for which we agree to implicit but flawed solutions, namely, assigning a value to human life.

The moral questions may seem greater in the case of biomedicine than in that of computers only because the extent of the information-technology revolution is not yet understood. They both present new problems and amplify older ones. For example, can scientists apply their talents to academic research and simultaneously work for profit-making companies? What conflicts arise? How can they be resolved? How do we stimulate the research that leads to new cures and how can we learn to apply this knowledge **367** rapidly and safely? How can university and other basic research laboratories join with industry—the natural, efficient, economic distributor and transfer institution for technology, via products and services? How do we preserve the integrity of the university and the basic research laboratories and yet make partnerships attractive to businesses —the institutions that play a vital role in transforming the knowledge of science into products and services when and where they are needed, to the practical benefit of individuals.

Again, we face the question of why the United States is the world leader in this extraordinarily important new field. How do we maintain or enhance the conditions that led to our being ahead? I suspect that the reasons are somewhat the same as for information technology, though perhaps more attributable to funding of research in basic science in biogenetics, and that the policies for staying ahead, while having some specialized aspects, may not be too different. The role of the private sector is as vital here as in the case of information technology.

Again, all of these conundrums are not entirely new. Microbiologists and toxicologists have spent many years dealing with dangerous viruses and bacteria. Doctors have long faced decisions concerning life, death, or limbo. Electronics researchers who created the Route 128 complex around Boston in the late 1950s and early 1960s walked a thin line between academia and industry. And the pursuit of medicine almost automatically implies the need for triage.

What has changed is not only the science and technology, but also their speed of progress and depth of applicability. Today the ability of molecular biologists to manipulate strands of DNA and the skill of doctors in fighting off the specter of death have surpassed the expectations of all but the most optimistic science fiction writers of past decades. Even the concepts of bacteria programmed to produce endless amounts of specific medications, and of surgical procedures carried out on fetuses in the womb, were scarcely imagined just fifteen years ago.

The remarkable speed of advance in biomedicine has left regulatory institutions far behind. The general public has fared even worse. Faced with the sudden emergence of new

368

biomedical methods, rapidly followed by public protests against those developments, the typical lay person has generally reacted with a mixture of amazement and concern. The public's rather unfocused fear about what the brave new world of biomedicine will bring has all too often been encouraged by the advocacy of pressure groups morally and theologically opposed to the development of biomedicine along its present tracks.

Risk-Benefit Struggle

A controversy over the release of genetically engineered microbes designed to protect plants from frost damage illustrates the complexity of the risk-benefit struggle over genetic experiments. The initial guidelines on recombinant DNA technology published by the National Institutes of Health prohibited the deliberate release of any organism containing recombinant DNA, for fear that the organism might somehow harm the environment or living things. Intensive research during the second half of the 1970s, however, indicated that the original fears about the hazards of genetically altered bacteria and other organisms were probably unfounded. The guidelines were slowly relaxed, enabling researchers and industrialists to move their products increasingly into the public domain.

Pharmaceutical products such as insulin and human growth hormones made by genetically altered bacteria started to compete on the market with the natural pharmaceuticals—often at a small fraction of the cost of the real thing. That opened the way to wider uses of gene splicing, as the over-all technique is known. One major area of opportunity was agriculture.

▷ As a graduate student, Steven Lindow of the University of California at Berkeley had discovered that a great deal of frost damage to plants arises through the presence of "ice-nucleation active bacteria." Clustering on plant leaves, the microscopic bacteria enhance the formation of ice crystals and hence the freezing of the plants. Lindow and his colleagues then managed to isolate the genes that gave the bacteria the ability to promote **369** the formation of ice crystals. Using recombinant DNA technology, they excised those genes, to create apparent ice-nucleation active bacteria that in reality couldn't do their job. The hope was that when such bacteria were applied to plants, they would replace the real nucleation bacteria, thereby reducing frost damage to the plants.[5]

Early tests were successful. But to prove the true efficacy of the ersatz bacteria, the team couldn't rely on work in the greenhouse; it had to test the bugs under real, outdoor conditions. Hence Lindow and his group applied to the National Institutes of Health for permission to release his new strain of bacteria deliberately, in an outdoor field test.

The Recombinant DNA Advisory Committee of the NIH was favorable to the trial. However, a group headed by author and activist Jeremy Rifkin filed suit against the experiment. Rifkin's complaint was that the NIH had failed to comply with the National Environmental Policy Act, which requires an assessment on the environmental impact before release of any new substance that could alter an area's ecology. Rifkin's supporters, who consisted of four small activist groups, argued that, in the worst possible case, the frost-preventing bacteria might rise into the upper atmosphere and disrupt the natural formation of ice crystals, thereby affecting global climate. Researchers involved with the project pointed out that Rifkin's group lacked scientific qualifications and stressed their own arguments that small-scale studies had shown minimal possibilities of risk from the release of the new organisms. Nevertheless the fact that Rifkin's suit was supported by affidavits from some eminent ecologists suggested that the concerns were not entirely unworthy.[6]

The major difficulty faced by the courts that heard the case was that of deciding how valid were the objections to an entirely new technology. Indeed, biomedical technology has raised, as never before, the question of how society decides, through its courts, the rights and wrongs of complex technology whose mysteries are fully understood only by a small priesthood.

Working on the side of caution is the long lead time and potential and perhaps unforeseeable side effects or chain reactions. Decades may pass before the environmental changes can be learned, given our present state of knowledge in this highly complex field.

The New Eugenics

Theologians have seen a long-term threat in recombinant DNA technology. "Eugenics"—a word coined by Charles Darwin's cousin, Sir Francis Galton, to mean the genetic manipulation of an organism or species—would now be possible on a massive scale through advances in molecular biology. If scientists can alter genes in bacteria, the theologians have argued, will they not soon be able to do the same thing with humans? And will not human experiments in genetic engineering inevitably lead to efforts to manipulate the germ-line cells—the sperm and the egg—to engineer specific genetic traits into future generations? As MIT biologist Ethan Singer warned, recombinant DNA research "is going to bring us one step closer to genetic engineering of people. . . . Last time around, the ideal children had blond hair, blue eyes, and Aryan genes."[7]

The plea to prohibit genetic engineering of human germ-line cells was the gist of a resolution drafted by Jeremy Rifkin and signed by fifty-five religious leaders, including Moral Majority head the Reverend Jerry Falwell, Roman Catholic bishops, and Jewish leaders. "We are lifting our voices of caution, even protest," explained Bishop Finis A. Crutchfield of the United Methodist Church. "We are opposed to the creation and manufacture of new forms of life, not talking about repairing physical defects in individuals."[8]

But the wording of the theologians' resolution, which was presented in June 1983, suggested a very definite confusion concerning the potential use of recombinant DNA techniques to repair genetic defects and its abuse in altering the human species. In fact, the complexity of the issue seemed to overwhelm not only the theologians who signed the resolution presented to them but also those molecular biologists who dismissed any possibility that their work might be applied to harm the human race.

As is typical with new technologies, biotechnology brings risks as well as benefits. However, both dangers and benefits in this case are profound, as they are likely to impact all future generations. Is there any institution—medical, scientific, academic, religious, political—that is equal to the task of diverting biotechnology from the dangerous path that leads to Aldous Huxley's vision of a "brave new world"? There is no turning back on this technology. Who will direct its outcome?

New Legal Issues

On an entirely different level of complexity, the emergence of recombinant DNA technology gave courts of law a totally new issue to consider. The question was: Can processes involved with the creation of life be patented? The first case came from industry. Using genetic techniques that resembled but did not completely mimic recombinant DNA technology, General Electric Company scientist Ananda Chakrabarty designed a bacterium whose function was to digest oil. Chakrabarty's theory was that his newly created bugs could be used to mop up oil spills. When General Electric applied for a patent on the bacterium, the company was told that it was probably impossible to patent a living organism.

Pressure from the recombinant DNA scientists grew quickly, however; in particular, Stanley Cohen of Stanford University and Herbert Boyer of the University of California, San Francisco, applied for patents on their basic developments of the techniques that made the whole technology possible. The two researchers had discovered how to open up, at specific points, the stretches of DNA that make up genes, insert fresh genes into the exposed regions, and close up the strands of DNA in such a way that the inserted genes could operate just as if they were in their natural surroundings. Those techniques, and the General Electric bacteria, were finally awarded patents, as the courts abandoned their previous position that new forms of life were beyond their realm of authority.

The need for patents indicated the strong commercial potential of recombinant DNA technology. That potential also brewed a major storm in the academic world where university researchers used their fundamental discoveries as the springboards for launching companies to sell genetically engineered products resulting from the discoveries.

Two Masters

Can academic researchers realistically serve two masters—their university, which demands progress toward the traditional goal of advancing human knowledge, through assembly of a team containing senior faculty and graduate students, and a commercial company, whose requirements center far more around the bottom line of profit? Biomedical researchers, perhaps more than any others, have tried to straddle the fence between academia and industry. Some have succeeded, others have failed; but no academic institution has yet come up with a policy that answers all the questions raised about academic freedom, scientific accountability, and the control of the direction of research.

At the basis of the controversy is the need of universities for fresh funds in an era of government budget-paring and the ever-present though today heightened need for a transfer mechanism—the business enterprise—to bring the benefits of rapidly changing science to everyone. Traditionally, the federal government has funded basic research in molecular biology through the National Institutes of Health. But as universities received indications from Washington in the early 1980s that such funds would dwindle, they sought replacements from the obvious sources: chemical and drug companies wishing special consideration in applying the results of fundamental research to moneymaking products.

▷ DuPont gave the genetics department of Harvard Medical School $6 million.

▷ Yale University received $1.1 million from the Celanese Corporation for enzyme studies and $3 million from Bristol-Myers for the production of anticancer drugs.

▷ W. R. Grace presented MIT with more than $8 billion for developing commercial applications of the institute's work in microbiology.

▷ Monsanto gave Washington University $23.5 million for research on the medical uses of proteins and peptides, and Rockefeller University $4 million for studies of photosynthesis, the process by which plants convert sunlight to food—or why grass is green.

373

Then there were individual examples of entrepreneurship. In 1980 University of California, San Francisco, molecular biologist Howard Goodman approached the West German firm Höchst A.G., a major chemical company, with a proposal that the company fund him and selected colleagues in exchange for the opportunity to license and develop discoveries resulting from the research. Höchst pledged $70 million, which Goodman took to Massachusetts General Hospital when UCSF's bureaucratic procedures proved too impenetrable for him to deal with.[9] Walter Gilbert, a Nobel laureate at Harvard, became scientific director of the multinational company Biogen S.A., which he had helped to found. David Baltimore, before he became head of the Whitehead Institute, held more than 300,000 shares of stock in Research Inc., a company for which he had frequently acted as consultant.

Plainly, the links between industry and universities, and between industry and individual researchers, represented potential conflicts of interest. Companies, after all, determine the direction of research done on their behalf differently from the way in which the federal government, until recently the predominant funding body for biological research, does. Company researchers jealously guard industrial secrets; academic researchers more freely interchange ideas (although it was surprising how many Harvard faculty members were tight-lipped about giving us suggestions for case examples for this book, presumably because they were working on their own books!). On another level of concern, Tennessee Congressman Albert Gore, Jr., has questioned whether companies indulge in a sophisticated way of skimming the cream produced by decades of government-supported research when they sign agreements with university faculty and departments.

Despite the potential for conflict of interest, however, it does not necessarily mean that such conflicts exist. Most university agreements with industry involve clauses permitting the academic researchers the normal freedom of communication and publication that they enjoy when their research is supported by government or university funds. And, as Harvard University President Derek Bok reminds

us, "The quality of disinterestedness has never been universally achieved in practice. Even Galileo tried to sell his inventions for money."[10]

Harvard itself found the limit of disinterestedness when it insisted that Walter Gilbert give up either his tenured professorship or his executive post with Biogen. Harvard's dilemma was a complex one: Is it better for a university to tolerate a "brain drain" as its best professors leave for industry positions—taking with them knowledge learned at the university's expense—or should it insist on purist distinctions between research for profit and research for the pursuit of knowledge? Can the university ethically do both —retain the professors and claim a share in their profits as their research is commercially applied? Gilbert chose business over academia, closing the possibility for further debate in this case.

Other research institutions have reacted in a variety of ways to the perceived problems of faculty members' working for industry and academe. The University of California, Berkeley, for example, forced three professors to end or alter corporate-sponsored contracts in 1983 because of the dangers of conflict of interest.[11] MIT and the Massachusetts General Hospital, by contrast, held firm in the belief that contracts with outside companies signed by their own biological faculty members minimized the dangers of conflict of interest.

Plainly, the surge of biomedical research in recent times has shaken the ivory tower. Academic scientists are examining their consciences as never before. But to my mind the growing links between corporations and research institutions offer more positive than negative elements. Stimulation of targeted research is desirable, as long as the process does not exclude more fundamental research entirely. And the involvement of industry in academic research will guarantee that the results will find early application.

The Artificial Heart

The application of research in medicine has almost as much potential for disagreement as biotechnological studies. One major example was the implantation of an artificial heart in retired Seattle dentist Barney Clark in December 1982 by surgeons at the University of Utah Medical Center. Clark was the first person to be kept alive by an entirely mechanical heart for an extended period. He survived a hundred and twelve days attached to a large air compressor that actually powered the artificial organ. For much of the time he was in great pain.

In the aftermath of the experiment some physicians questioned whether the University of Utah team had selected the right patient for the pioneering implantation and whether the group had taken enough time to examine the implications of the revolutionary procedure that it had pioneered.[12] Is there a danger that zealous medical teams will move too rapidly to apply to human patients procedures developed in animal experiments?

The issue of potential financial conflict of interest also surfaced. The artificial heart implanted in Clark was supplied—free—by Kolff Medical Inc., a company in which both the University of Utah and Dr. William DeVries, the surgeon who performed the implantation, owned shares. (Dr. Robert Jarvik, president of Kolff Medical and inventor of the heart used for Clark, was a member of the surgical team.) Should members of surgical teams with influence over the use of artificial hearts or other devices be allowed to own shares in companies that are likely to profit from the use of those devices in human patients?

University and medical center administrations have been forced to face those issues through the rapid development of medical miracles. Just as in the case of recombinant DNA technology, they can find no easy answers. Again, our institutions are not yet set up to deal with such complex questions.

Organ Transplants and Medical Anarchy

The implantation of artificial organs is still in its infancy. However, transplantation of human hearts, as well as lungs, kidneys, and livers, is becoming an established medical procedure. In this latter case, the dilemma stems from the shortages of transplantable organs. The fact that Dr. Barry Jacobs could envision a commercial scheme for kidney transplants is instructive. Kidneys come in pairs in the human body; a person can live a healthy life with a single kidney. In theory, therefore, it should not be extraordinarily difficult for kidney patients needing transplants to obtain donated organs. Nevertheless the number of patients greatly exceeds the kidneys available.

Hearts, livers, and lungs are different, since the human body has no "backup system" for these parts. Obviously, a donated heart or liver can come only from someone who has died—and died recently, given the medical imperative of maintaining the health of the organ until the transplantation procedure. The heart, for example, must be transplanted within four hours of removal from the donor's body; the liver must be transplanted within eight hours of removal. Agencies in the U.S. that try to match donors and recipients of organs report that there is no real shortage of donatable organs. Part of the problem is that medical staffs are often slow to suggest to grief-stricken families of accident victims that they offer the organs of their deceased loved ones.

The result is a kind of medical anarchy. Within the past few years, in particular, parents of children with serious liver disease have had to resort to extreme measures to secure liver transplants. In October 1982, for example, Charles Fiske of Boston went before a televised meeting of the American Academy of Pediatrics to seek help in finding a liver for his dying daughter Jamie, a victim of biliary atresia. Fiske, a former priest, had waged a dogged media campaign by personally contacting every radio and TV station in the region, national TV networks, more than five hundred pediatricians, hospitals, insurers, Senator Edward Kennedy, Speaker of the House Thomas O'Neill, and many others. In fact, he was granted time to speak before the pediatrics academy only because of the promise of media attention.

Fiske's televised plea struck a chord in the hearts of a Utah couple, Laird and LeAnn Bellon, who had a baby son the same age as Jamie. Six days later their son lay brain-dead at Salt Lake City's Primary Children's Medical Center; a car driven by his mother had collided with a train. Upon a doctor's request, the couple agreed to an organ donation, although they could not remember Jamie Fiske's name—and staffers at the hospital were unable to identify the girl the Bellons had in mind or any other potential recipient. Clearly there was an institutional void in making such arrangements. It was only through the personal persistence of a social worker that the connection was finally made.

Thus, through a stubborn media campaign and a large measure of luck, Jamie Fiske eventually had her liver and her transplant operation. Other parents also took to the airwaves with public appeals for their own children. The media approach, however, ignored most of the forty to fifty children who, according to Donald Denny of the University of Pittsburgh, need a liver transplant each day. "The only reason we got what we needed for Jamie is that we manipulated the system," Fiske said. "To me, that's an indictment of the system. Should every family that's in need of decent health care have to figure out how to deal with the media, insurance companies, and other obstacles? Or should they have a right to expect it?"[13]

To Mr. Fiske's questions I would add these: Why, indeed, was it necessary to attract media attention to save the life of a child? Why was there not an effective medical information network in place, an electronic bulletin board on which medical practitioners could post notices about available and needed organs? And why is there not a registry system for potential donors of all ages, similar to the system associated with drivers' licenses?

Some European countries have adopted a policy whereby, in the event of death, a citizen's organs automatically become the property of the state, so there will be no delays in supplying organs to those who need them. A cadaver's organs are thus automatically available for transplant without seeking the family's permission. Should such a policy be adopted in the U.S.? If our society prefers instead to maintain freedom of choice, I see no reason why parents could not be asked to sign papers, on the birth of each child, granting permission for doctors to transplant their child's organs in the event of the child's death. Such a system could be a regular part of hospital procedure and could be renewed by the child on reaching a predetermined age and at regular intervals throughout his or her life.

Resource Allocation and the Cost of Life

In terms of allocation, should the "squeakiest wheel" always get the oil first? In the Fiske case, the Bellons had stipulated that their son's liver go specifically to the girl they had seen in the televised story, although they could not recall her name. Is media attention the best determinant of who is first in line for an organ transplant? Or should the choice hinge on who has been waiting the longest, or should it be decided by lottery?

Western culture has always looked on human life as priceless and therefore worth the application of all available resources to preserve it. However, this ethic will be sorely tested as medical resources—including skilled physicians, available organs, and health insurance funds—are stretched to their limits. The question of resource allocation will be heightened as more and more medical choices are opened to us. Will our society be forced to make hard decisions about who is most deserving to live? And, if so, what will be our criteria—youth, intelligence, contributions to society? For example, will a mentally retarded citizen "deserve" a complex life-saving procedure less than a normal citizen? Will a sixty-year-old be entitled to less health insurance, for purposes of a liver transplant, than a young child? Who will make these choices?

And what of the sheer cost of staying alive? A liver transplant and related fees may cost anywhere from $50,000 to $200,000. No doubt we will soon see more exotic procedures in the future, with far more exotic price tags. Million-dollar procedures seem not too distant. How much is society willing to pay for human life? In market terms of supply and demand, we are faced with a situation of insatiable demand. And the price mechanism, as a regulator of market demand, has worked all too imperfectly in the past.

Paul T. Menzel, in an intriguing book titled *Medical Costs, Moral Choices*, states, "The monetary value of life can be measured by the amount one is willing to pay to reduce the mere risk of death."[14] Will life, then, be worth what the market is willing to bear? Will a J. Paul Getty's life be "worth more" than that of an ordinary janitor, schoolteacher, or plumber? And if health insurance becomes the great equalizer, guaranteeing the latest medical advances to all, will the patients be allowed to make the decisions on how much health care they want to buy? The very poor, for example, might prefer to receive aid in cash —and use it to provide for their families rather than to prolong their own lives a few years. "Even if others are paying for their care," Menzel asks, "why should [the poor] be required to take that assistance in the form of health care when they would rather use the resources for other needs?" [15]

Unwanted Treatment

Other moral dilemmas have surfaced recently in which medical technology is available but unwanted. In Knoxville, Tennessee, for example, a state appeals court judge ruled that a twelve-year-old girl suffering from potentially fatal bone cancer should receive chemotherapy even though the girl and her parents did not wish to accept the treatment. The family belonged to a fundamentalist church that objects to the use of medicine. Should the girl—through her parents—have the freedom to refuse medical treatment that might improve her chances of living?

The court decided that she should have the treatment, and the child began chemotherapy. Early results indicated that her condition was improving, but the parents attributed her progress to prayer, not medication. Nevertheless the questions raised in this case remain open: Does an individual have a right to decide which treatment is best—even if that treatment is only prayer? As medical science creates new options in prolonging life, whose right will it be to exercise those options? What will be the limit of state intervention in mandating medical care? The case raises fundamental issues of individual freedom. Orders by the state that patients must receive specific forms of medication carry overtones of Big Brother in this year of 1984.

The twelve-year-old in Knoxville at least had the opportunity to speak for herself. That's not the case with infants suffering severe birth defects who can potentially be saved from early death by modern miracles of surgery. The development of sophisticated new forms of treatment has given new hope to thousands of families. But it has presented countless other parents and medical staffs with unprecedented moral questions. Should medical teams make heroic efforts to save the lives of infants doomed to live lives as near-vegetables? Is there ever a justification for denying simple medical treatment to defective babies who could live long but empty lives following minor heart or intestinal surgery?

▷ "Baby Jane Doe" was born in Long Island with a terrible variety of disorders, including spina bifida—the failure of her spinal column to close fully—and excess fluid on the brain. Her condition was partly repairable. Doctors agreed that an operation could enable Jane Doe to survive into her twenties, although seriously retarded. Without the operation her life expectancy was no more than two years. After talking with doctors, counselors, and clergymen, the infant's parents decided against giving permission for the operation. But a court-appointed guardian argued that parents had no right "to bring about their children's death by deliberate medical neglect."[16]

The court system decided in the parents' favor. But the question of whether such an issue should be settled in court remains a troubling one. Once again, the medical profession's ability to perform near-miracles has superseded society's ability to deal with the moral issues arising from the technology.

One final controversy, related to other medical issues, involves the right of individuals to refuse all medical intervention. Do patients, in other words, have the right to die? And do physicians have the right to withhold life-saving measures from dying patients? In the past, medical staffs have made such decisions in fear and trembling and sometimes in opposition to official hospital policy. Now hospitals and medical centers recognize that dying patients and their families should have the choice to forgo life-saving therapy when the quality of life that will be saved is extremely poor. Such recognition still places an immense burden on doctors, nurses, patients, and their families, as they seek to define "hopeless" medical cases in an era of medical miracles.

The right-to-die question was played out in the headlines in 1983 when a California woman, a victim of cerebral palsy and a paraplegic, went to court to fight for her right to die. **381**

In her mid-twenties, the woman decided that the quality of her life was "over" and that her strength had deteriorated to the point that she would have committed suicide if she were physically capable. She sought the help of a hospital staff in terminating her life, but a court ruling ordered that she be force-fed, if necessary, to keep her alive.

What if this woman offered to donate her heart to a patient in urgent need of a heart transplant? Fortunately the situation never came to this—and I am in no way supporting the idea of euthanasia. Indeed, the woman later reversed her decision to commit suicide. Yet I cannot help but wonder: Will our society always unconditionally opt for life over death? Or will we seek out humane measures to weigh the quality of the life we save? How will our society define and constantly redefine the boundary between life and death?

Medical researchers continuously revise the definitions of life and death. No doubt there will come a time when science can prolong life indefinitely, and that new age is beginning now. Even the prospect of cryogenic storage, which science fiction used to call "suspended animation," may well become a reality. We are placing the powers of life and death in human hands. Will we learn to use those powers wisely, fairly, humanely? Will we ever arrive at a philosophy that appoints a proper time and framework for death, and then accepts and even embraces death when that time comes?

Life Before Birth

The ability to practice medicine on the human fetus raises further questions about the boundaries of life and death. Surgeons at the University of California, San Francisco, and the University of Colorado Medical Center, among others, have devised means of operating on fetuses inside the womb. In a small number of operations carried out in the early 1980s, medical teams managed to alleviate the build-up of fluid in the brains and bladders of fetuses by inserting miniature tubes to drain it off. In one spectacular example, the UCSF team actually drew a male fetus outside the womb to operate and then returned him to the comfort of his natural surroundings. (The boy died shortly after birth of causes independent of the surgery.)

Operations of that type seem to offer nothing but good for society and for individuals. But bioethicist John Fletcher of the National Institutes of Health has warned that the techniques are not without dubious social consequences. The fetus is a patient within another patient, the mother. And it is possible that the best interests of the two patients might not be identical. Imagine, says Fletcher, that the mother does not want to undergo a fetal operation that medical staff deem best for her unborn child.[17] Should the mother be subject to compulsion or allowed to make the final decision? What if that final decision is to abort the child? Will our society maintain that the fate of the fetus rests solely with its mother (as the Supreme Court seems to have concluded by upholding a woman's right to choose an abortion)? Again, this phenomenon is not entirely new, as doctors and midwives have long faced the agonizing choice between saving the life of a newborn infant and that of the mother. Indeed, the choice has often been placed in the hands of the husband/father, and even in the hands of the clergy. Yet as medical breakthroughs continue to open new prospects for vastly complex measures to save the life of a fetus, will our society once and for all be forced to prioritize—the mother's interests vs. the unborn child's?

There is also a broader social issue. As fetal therapy and other marvels of modern medicine save the lives of children with genetic defects, those medical techniques encourage the spread of defective genes from one generation to another. Carriers who in past times could not live long enough to have children can now pass on their unfortunate genetic heritage to fresh generations. Thus the medical profession comes close to eradicating the process of natural selection —"survival of the fittest"—among human beings. The dilemma has overtones of eugenics, but nevertheless it is one that must eventually be addressed.

An Institutional Void

As we have seen, the "bio-revolution" poses a broad set of fundamental problems that have so far defied institutional efforts to solve them. Unfortunately no mechanism exists, **383** inside or outside the scientific community, for evaluating the claims and counterclaims of scientists, medical experts, policy makers, and other interested parties. True, the National Academy of Sciences often undertakes studies of controversial subjects for the federal government. But its conclusions are often regarded as politically contaminated. For example, when a National Academy panel determined that exposure to low levels of radiation present only a minor threat to human health, some panel members argued that even that evaluation had overestimated the danger!

In the mid-1970s Arthur Krantrowitz, chairman of Avco Everett Laboratories, suggested a "science court" to resolve scientific and technological issues with a bearing on public policy. As envisioned by Krantrowitz, the court would behave something like a court of law, with attorneys for each side of an issue—supporting and opposing continued research in recombinant DNA, for example—questioning the "experts" pro and con. A panel of scientists chosen for their impartiality in the issue would then decide which side's arguments had greater merit.

Nothing came of the idea, for a variety of reasons. The scientific community in general felt that legal procedure was not appropriate to eliciting scientific truth. Further, many issues are controversial precisely because the relating measurements and statistical data are unknown, and may never be known—a situation that no adversary procedure can solve.

The search continues for an institution to clarify scientific findings and review issues of public concern. For the time being, a mystified public can only accept that it will be subject to a variety of different interpretations of technical issues that directly influence daily life.

Positive Developments

I don't wish to appear too pessimistic about the achievements of biotechnology and medicine. They are making possible successes that only the most farsighted among us could have imagined just a few years ago.

▷ Made-to-order vaccines are now possible by scrambling the DNA in smallpox vaccine to create vaccines for virtually any infectious disease. By inserting a gene from another virus—herpes, hepatitis, influenza—into the smallpox vaccine virus, the smallpox vaccine expresses a trait of the patched-in virus and effectively arms the body against the disease.[18]

▷ Genetic engineering on plants will produce "supercrops" by the year 2000, including shorter cornstalks loaded with ears, and square tomatoes for easy packing, according to a study released in December 1983 by the consulting firm of William Teweles and Company. With the new technology, many crops will produce a higher yield, resist pests and disease, grow in adverse weather conditions, require little or no fertilizer, and be more nutritious, the report said. The promise of more abundant and more nutritious food, produced at a lower cost, opens new hope for eliminating world hunger.[19]

▷ Treatment of patients with genetic defects, such as sickle-cell anemia, promises to become commonplace. Research published in the *New England Journal of Medicine* in the fall of 1982 describes a drug treatment that strips hemoglobin-producing genes of chemicals that repress their activities, allowing them to switch on again. This genetic manipulation is a step toward scientists' goal of using recombinant DNA technique to perform genetic "surgery" in damaged cells.[20]

▷ The most hopeless cases of the past can now take some measure of hope. "David," a boy born without the ability to fight off germs, spent the entire twelve years of his life in a sterile plastic bubble. Although he did not survive the treatment that doctors hoped would free him from his condition—bone marrow transplants—his brief life made possible years of research that may make future victims of severe combined immune deficiency (SCID) syndrome the beneficiaries of a normal life.

Certainly modern biomedicine has created new social and moral pressures, which so far have defeated the efforts of institutions to deal with them. But I detect a few straws in the wind to suggest that institutions are recognizing the problems and are slowly learning to cope with them. The creation of hospices in which the terminally ill are treated with loving care and unconventional pain relief, such as **385** marijuana therapy, provides one example of a positive institutional response to a major medical problem. The formation of academic committees to oversee the use of recombinant DNA and to protect patients undertaking experimental medical procedures shows that another community is ready to acknowledge the new realities.

Two new institutions give me real cause for hope that we can deal with the problems created by the rapid advance of biomedicine. One is the growth of a network of organ-procurement agencies around the U.S. to deal with the unsatisfied demand for organ transplants. About one hundred and ten agencies of this sort seek to match patients in need of kidneys, livers, and hearts with potential donors. And the North American Transplant Coordinators Organization supplies taped telephone messages listing the organs required by transplant centers around the nation. Furthermore, the agencies are gradually publicizing their work and making medical staffs aware that dying accident victims can leave a precious heritage in the form of transplantable organs. It is at least possible that, in the future, parents of children needing new organs will not have to rely on the television networks to state their cases.

Information and its dispersion to medical staffs and families of potential organ donors provide the key to success for the organ-procurement agencies. The spread of information also plays the major role in an ambitious new program that should help the general public to deal in a more confident and informed way with some of the dilemmas raised by medical practice. In Des Moines, Iowa, the Public Agenda Foundation launched a broad campaign to keep the public fully informed about everything relevant to its good health. Hospitals, medical societies, universities, the local chamber of commerce, area businesses, unions, churches, schools, and other community organizations banded together in a massive effort to tell the public in detail about the medical issues that affected them, from the medical technology available to methods of buying medical insurance. Television, radio, and newspapers joined in the effort, on the principle that an informed public is a public best able to make realistic decisions on social issues affecting it. The early results of the experiment suggested that Des Moines residents were indeed better informed. (A more detailed account of the Public Agenda Foundation's work appeared at the close of Chapter 3, "Short Time Horizons.")

Providing this type of service in the future won't guarantee that controversies will no longer arise over biomedical progress. But it may well enhance the level of debate and lead to more rational decisions on how best to use the technology available through research.

Final Questions

The reason for exploring both molecular biology and information science in this brief space is to demonstrate the point that quite new problems as well as great amplification of older ones are the inevitable by-products of two of the most socially valuable fields of scientific research of our age. The same is true of other and quite different fields of research, but the two I have chosen should suffice as examples, and they are the fields in which I have had firsthand experience.

The processes by which, and framework within which, we handle many everyday problems of health and safety are being changed at the same time. While our prospects are greatly enhanced by the advances in biological sciences, it is my objective in both this chapter and the one previous to point out a few of the new questions these fields pose regarding the way we organize and operate the institutions of our society.

Throughout this book I have offered case examples at the closing of every chapter to illustrate positive moves toward solving the problems outlined. In this chapter and the previous one on information technology we are dealing with situations in which the institutional problems are quite new and the examples of institutional change are sparse. I therefore hope that the questions raised in this chapter will serve as a springboard to further questions and enlightened discussion in this area.

XI

A Guiding Vision

Perfecting the structure, functioning, and interrelationships of institutions, while necessary, won't be sufficient without a generally accepted overarching vision of what it is our society wants. Without such a vision, and without the leadership to articulate that vision, we will be left with nothing more than mere craft or technique to steer our efforts, building what, by past standards, can only be judged as molehills. Might not the task of making our institutions work become the theme for at least an interim guiding vision?

When I began this book, I felt that the only point I could make in this final chapter was this: Even if we are successful in making appropriate changes in structure, function and process in all the areas I describe in previous chapters, it will not be enough unless we can match it with our own age's equivalent of the kind of unifying vision Professor Elting Morison described so well in his *From Know-How to Nowhere:*

> The last great scheme for organizing the energies of men conformed to many of the requirements for good working vision. This was the concept of Progress that dominated the Western world for a century from the defeat of Napoleon at Waterloo to the pistol shot at Sarajevo in 1914.[1]

Far be it from me to have the temerity to suggest the next great unifying idea! Yet as I have developed my ideas on getting right the processes of making our society work, I have begun to wonder whether this itself might not serve at least as an interim guiding vision. If we do not succeed in making our immediate future livable, let alone the society we leave to our children, we face the very real prospect of an authoritarian government of either right or left—which, of course, is where much of the world already lives—and the guiding vision will be George Orwell's nightmare.

Professor George Lodge of Harvard writes:

> If our leaders and their institutions ignore what they must do, they can expect the worst: an increased alienation from them and all that they represent, a surge in violence, and a drift toward anarchy. Already it is possible to see the coalition of revolution in America: the underclass, chronically unemployed, many members of minority communities, and intellectuals with no place to go. We can hear their complaint and anticipate their battle cry: "exploitation of the poor by the rich, who control a careless and corrupt government in league with self-centered corporations, which conspire to sustain the pursuit of suicidal military superiority."[2]

The more I wrestle with the problem, the more its obviousness has overcome my temerity at suggesting that, unless we succeed at making our institutions work, we need not worry about a more grand and sweeping guiding vision. But let me first examine the last great idea—Progress—even if, as Professor Morison says, "the thing has been overdone."

Progress—a vision that holds that humankind is advancing ever forward from some darker, more primitive past, perhaps toward a "Golden Age"—has been the great synthesizer of human energies for centuries. With an eye to progress and a few simple tools our forebears in the nineteenth century forged the great railroads across a hostile and uncharted landscape while entire nations were transplanted from farms to factories. What heroic vision! What have we today to match the scale and grandeur of such works? Instead, the signs of stagnation and even regression are everywhere:

▷ The troubled United Nations, an institution that is "united" in name only. The international body is increasingly viewed as nothing more than a glass house in which poorer countries cast stones at richer countries—particularly at the U.S.—and hurt, rather than help, the cause of world peace. Rather than fulfilling its mandate to promote cooperation, it has itself become the battleground for what U.S. Ambassador Jeane Kirkpatrick calls a "version of class war." [3]

▷ The rise of cultism. Nearly one thousand Americans left their homeland, like modern-day pilgrims, to devote their lives and fortunes to a bizarre cult of death in Jonestown, Guyana. The members of the People's Temple were missing something in their lives, and they were willing to seek it as far away as the jungles of Guyana. It was more important to them than their homes, their life's earnings, their families. The proliferation of this and other weird do-it-yourself religions and personality cults—the Hare Krishnas, the Moonies, Synanon, Children of God—poses serious questions about our society's most basic institutions: religion, family, community.

▷ The divided Common Market. On December 6, 1983, a summit meeting of the Common Market in Athens failed and collapsed, threatening the survival of the world's largest trading bloc. "We were not able to come to any agreement on any single issue," Greek Prime Minister Andreas Papandreou told reporters after the critical two-day meeting.[4] The community has of late been suffering from a crisis of leadership which is the worst in its history.

▷ Western ideology on the defensive. Margaret Thatcher appeared in Ottawa to deliver to the Canadian Parliament a speech that might have been much more appropriate at the Athens summit. In it she exhorted the Western nations, in essence, to get their act together if they hoped to stand up to the Soviet Union: "We must constantly proclaim our ideals, to our own young at home, to young countries who have yet to choose, to those who live in the shadow of tyranny. It is time for freedom to take the offensive." [5]

What prevents the countries of the European Community from recognizing their common interests? What causes the free nations, including the U.S., to "take the offensive" only

against themselves or each other? What causes large segments of our population to become so disenchanted with our society's most basic institutions that they seek out astrologers, gurus, cults, and fanatics? As Professor Robert Nisbet points out, in his *History of the Idea of Progress*, "The result of ceasing to believe in God is not that one will then believe nothing; it is that one will believe anything."[6]

Nisbet joins Professor Morison in his conclusion that the idea of progress is on the wane (although Nisbet traces the idea back more than twenty-five hundred years). Nisbet defines progress as a dogma—from the Greek root meaning "seems-good"—and dogma as the spring of human action, will, and ambition:

> The idea of the slow, gradual, inexorable progress of mankind to higher status in knowledge, culture and moral estate is a dogma. . . . Everything now suggests, however, that Western faith in the dogma of progress is waning rapidly in all levels and spheres in this final part of the twentieth century.
>
> The reasons . . . have much less to do with the unprecedented world wars, the totalitarianisms, the economic depressions, and other major political, military, and economic afflictions which are peculiar to the Twentieth Century than they do with the fateful if less dramatic erosion of all the fundamental intellectual and spiritual premises upon which the idea of progress has rested throughout its long history.[7]

What are those premises on which this sustaining vision has rested? Nisbet defines five foundation stones in the history of the idea which have endured from the times of the ancient Greeks to this century: belief in the value of the past; conviction of the nobility, even superiority, of Western civilization; acceptance of the worth of economic and technological growth; faith in reason and in the kind of scientific and scholarly thought that can come from reason alone; and finally, belief in the ineffaceable and intrinsic worth of life on this earth.

It is certainly not true that nothing but good has flowed from these premises. Racial exploitation and the politics of power have often moved under the banner of progress. Yet it is also true that all the magnificent accomplishments of the Western world are intimately connected with the idea of progress.

Ironically, as Nisbet tells us, the dogma is taking root most tenaciously in those countries that present the greatest threat to Western culture and civilization:

> In those nations, faith in the past (Marxism, of course), in the nobility of their own civilization, in the worth of economic and technological advancement, in knowledge (undergirded by Marxian writ), and of the supreme importance of life and work on this earth, reigns.
>
> Such, one must record in melancholy tones, is not the case in Western civilization at the present time. Disbelief, doubt, disillusionment and despair have taken over—or so it would seem from our literature, art, philosophy, theology, even our scholarship and science.[8]

Compare these signs of disillusionment with the exuberance and confidence of Cuba's leader, Fidel Castro, in his funeral homage to the Cuban soldiers killed in Grenada in 1983:

> Imperialism is bent on destroying symbols. . . . It wanted to destroy them in Grenada, and it wants to destroy them in El Salvador, Nicaragua, and Cuba. But symbols, examples, and ideas cannot be destroyed. When their enemies think they have destroyed them, what they have actually done is made them multiply. In trying to wipe out the first Christians, the Roman Emperors spread Christianity throughout the world. Likewise, all attempts to destroy our ideas will only multiply them.[9]

That Marxism, "the god that failed," should still provide at least the articulated central focus for billions of human beings—despite the daily demonstrable dimensions of its failure in the struggling economies and crumbling morale of those countries that espouse it—is more reflective of the power of an idea than any of the specifics of Marxism/Leninism. Perhaps the sheer colossal scale of the failure will yet give us a chance to formulate around freedom a construct of a workable society that succeeds.

Progress, and its reincarnation in Marxism, have been the two great guiding visions of recent history. But what do we have to replace them? Where to proceed for a new guiding vision? Professor Morison's thoughts are instructive.

> Nobody really knows the truth in these matters. We have just begun to think about the situation. But it may be suggested to the thinkers that the problem before us is only partly biological or economic. It is part artistic. One half of art is finding the proper structures—whether the sonata form or frame of government—within which the raw data of existence may be processed—made intelligible. Given such a context—neither so vague as anarchy nor so specific as a procrustean bed—the imagination, which abhors the steady set, may proceed, perhaps indefinitely, to novel combinations and interpretations of the data. Indeed the proper frame for its exercise, it may turn out to be the one inexhaustible resource that we have.[10]

Would it be too narrow to suggest that making our society work, and getting its structures and its institutions right—whether the "sonata form or frame of government"—is the place from which to proceed toward a new guiding vision? If, as I suspect, progress lies in *process*, our best hope is to find the right "how" that will lead us to the right "what." The task before us is to loosen old mind sets and encourage institutional innovation and experimentation.

There are no shortcuts to institutional rebuilding, and justly so. As Professor Ronald Müller wisely admonishes: "The new framework will not supplant or ride roughshod over the nation's traditional beliefs and values. . . . In fact, it is the very need to preserve our most cherished beliefs and values that makes the political challenge of the 1980s so crucial."[11]

Perhaps the proper place to begin in this delicate task of divining a new guiding vision of society is in leadership that will formulate and articulate that vision.

The Context of Leadership

Leadership—today an abused concept, outmoded by those who feel it should be replaced by collective conscience—must transcend today's obsession with celebrity and charisma. Social historian Barbara Goldsmith writes,

393

The line between fame and notoriety has been erased. Today we are confronted with a vast confusing jumble of celebrities: the talented and the untalented, heroes and villains, people of accomplishment and those who have accomplished nothing at all, the criteria for their celebrity being that their images encapsulate some form of the American dream, that they give enough of an appearance of leadership, heroism, wealth, success, danger, glamour, and excitement to feed our fantasies. We no longer demand reality, only that which is real seeming. . . .

Our inability or lack of concern in questioning the qualifications of people to be celebrated represents an increasingly pernicious phenomenon, for it is axiomatic of a society that we are who we celebrate.[12]

And today's political "leaders" are among these celebrities and image masters. They do no more than look behind themselves with market-research techniques to see which way the troops are going and then rush to get to the front of the line. As Winston Churchill once wrote regarding the responsibility of a political leader: "Nothing is more danger-ous than to live in the temperamental atmosphere of a Gal-lup Poll, always taking one's . . . political temperature. . . . There is only one duty, only one safe course, and that is to try to be right."[13]

Leadership of substance, of quality, must relate to the elements essential to making today's world work.

▷ Wider and more meaningful application of the techno-logical fruits of science, from artificial intelligence to neuro systems linked to man-made information systems.

▷ Management structures that attract and retain creative people, from scientists to writers to opera singers—and make them more productive.

▷ Coupling entrepreneurial drive with the worldwide func-tions of multinational corporations in ways that enhance each.

▷ Learning how to involve everyone who wishes to be in decision making where it will contribute to the quality of the decision yet enhance rather than detract from the direction and dynamics of the enterprise.

▷ Achieving enough unity of purpose to allow prioritization among the many alternatives rather than dithering, vacillating, and wasting resources while taking stabs in many divergent directions.

▷ Finding ways of considering the longer-term implications of current decisions in both the public and private sectors and continually reviewing results against expectations of decisions and policy updates.

▷ Learning how to balance protection of individual rights against the arteriosclerosis of excessive litigation.

▷ Creating an environment conducive to constant change and one in which the individuals themselves encourage innovation knowing they will benefit and not suffer from it.

I am aware of the magnitude of what I am suggesting. Yet I am a businessman—I deal in what is possible, otherwise I go broke. I have degrees in engineering and economics, and these are some help in evaluating what is possible—what the mathematicians and technicians of my firm tell me, what the learned books and papers say. Ten years ago artificial intelligence was good business for science fiction publishers. Today my company is looking at the application of artificial intelligence to management-information systems.

Today we are faced with entirely new questions and choices that make leadership a dangerous—some would say impossible—business. Sir Winston Churchill warned that "the dark ages may return on the gleaming wings of science." On the other hand, humankind can use its vast new stores of knowledge to achieve what Huxley called "higher levels of mental or psychological activity." Global destruction or a new golden age: Which will direct our choice?

It is in the context of new and basic questions that leadership must be addressed in this transitional period in humankind's history. It is our selection of means and ends, of structure and process, that will either call forth our essential nobility or plunge us into ignominy.

An Absence of Leadership

Perhaps, as some suggest, remarkable circumstances are the necessary cauldron from which, as if magically, remark-   **395** able leaders emerge. Washington, Jefferson, and Adams presided over the birth of a nation. Lincoln persevered over forces that threatened to tear our country apart. Roosevelt carried the country through a great and terrible war. I have no doubt that the magnitude of crisis has the effect of magnifying human greatness, summoning forth strength and courage when they are most needed.

Yet it is not always so; the times do not always make the leader. John F. Kennedy inspired a nation to explore the new frontier of space while tackling world poverty through the Peace Corps—at a time when the U.S. had emerged from a decade of peace. Martin Luther King was not a mere by-product of change but an architect of change, challenging the nation's complacence and double standards with a powerful crusade for racial equality. And the most memorable leader and visionary of all times—a young Jew from Nazareth—came forth in an era of history that was singularly unremarkable.

The absence of Maos and Gandhis in recent times is due partly to the absence of followers—an unwillingness on the part of the general public to embrace anyone as leader or hero. In recent years the principal social movements in this country seem to have coalesced not around great individualists but around concepts: feminism, environmentalism, self-improvement. The U.S. public seems generally mistrustful of power and those who wield it, as if another Watergate, some great lie or deception, were lurking just around the corner. Religious cultists are, of course, a notable exception, yet I do feel that their weird brand of "leadership" is much more indicative of a larger leadership void in our society.

One of the great difficulties, I think, in being a modern-day leader lies in the multiplicity of constituencies that demand representation. The Machiavellian notion of a leader as a conquerer—traditionally male, aggressive, white, privileged—is running out of steam, and new coalitions are seeking new role models. Women are tiring of male leaders who, at best, view half the human race as an "issue" or a "problem" and, at worst, ignore women in their policy making altogether. Demanding acceptance as coequal citizens, women's groups press for female candidates for President

and Vice-President in the 1984 election year. At the same

time, the Reverend Jesse Jackson steps forth as the first black presidential candidate, promising to represent a "rainbow coalition" of the underprivileged.

At one time America's many coalitions represented the strength of pluralism, the great American melting pot. Today the situation is one of fragmentation and *dissensus*. Should we conclude that the age of leadership has passed away, in favor of collectivism, power sharing and participatory rule? Or should we simply look for leaders from new sources and nurture new images of strength and character?

Clearly a key element of leadership is going to be the ability to reconcile seemingly disparate objectives. Richard Bolling reminds us that this is neither new nor impossible:

No doubt many have forgotten or never known about the remarkable period during which the important and effective policies of the late 1940s—which gave us two decades of economic growth—were made. . . .

To establish these policies the Truman Administration drew on a coalition of the "unlike"—Democrats, Republicans, business people (especially), and other special-interest groups. The results were the Marshall Plan, the Employment Act of 1946, and the modernization of the federal government through the first Hoover Commission. These groups together represented enlightened self-interest at its best. . . .

There is no way to get the job done without a new consensus on policy, which the past indicates can be achieved only by a coalition of the unlike, by a coalition of interest groups behind policies that will work for the country and that each finds acceptable.[14]

Management vs. Leadership

When I speak of leadership, I am not talking about management skills, although these figure into it. As Machiavelli noted, leadership combines the inspirational and the managerial, and his description of King Ferdinand of Spain illustrates this concept:

And thus he was always planning great enterprises, which kept the minds of his subjects in a state of suspense and admiration. And these enterprises followed so quickly one upon the other, that he never gave men a chance deliberately to make any attempt against himself.

It is also important for a prince to give striking examples of his interior administration . . . when an occasion presents itself to reward or punish any one who has in civil affairs either rendered great service to the state, or committed some crime, so that it may be much talked about. But above all, a prince should endeavor to invest all his actions with a character of grandeur and excellence.[15]

The crisis of leadership that cost Jimmy Carter his re-election in 1980 was widely attributed to his inability to arouse "suspense and admiration" among the American people, although he fared much better at "interior administration." He was competent and hardworking, but he was viewed as a President without passions, without "fire in his belly." His failure was not so much that he himself was passionless but that he failed to stir passions; it was not so much that he was weak but that he failed to communicate strength.

The Carter presidency serves as a reminder that a great leader must be a great communicator, and in today's world the presidential podium is television. One of the interesting and unintended side effects of our limitations on presidential campaign spending was the new prominence of television in the campaign. Buttons, placards, bumper stickers, and other traditional campaign paraphernalia are all but extinct. The candidates must save their limited funds for the most strategic medium: television.

As a communicator, Carter was a study in contrasts. On one hand, he won the 1976 election by conveying the right image—honest, benign, Christian—the good shepherd who would lead us from Watergate to safer pastures. In fact, it is inconceivable that any candidate could be elected to the nation's highest office without the right television presence. Lincoln's coarse and bearded face would have fared poorly under the bright lights of the TV studio. Theodore H. White, in his lively study of the American presidency, called Carter a master of the medium, skillfully parlaying television time into votes in 1976: "Carter learned television fast. His smile went on as soon as the camera's red light flashed, as if he were plugged in. . . . There could have been no Carter presidency without television."[16]

On the other hand, conducting a successful public relations campaign may be enough to win an election, but it was not enough to carry candidate Carter through the vicissitudes of office. The Oval Office demands another kind of communicator: one who can convey not just an "image," in the Hollywood sense, but a vision, a sense of our country's mission and purpose. If Carter had any conception of a guiding vision of American society before he entered the White House, he surely lost it once he was elected. He approached the magnitude and complexity of his task by becoming more an administrator and less a leader.

It is a problem that applies not just to the presidency but to Congress as well. I believe our elected officials spend far too much time on administrative details when they should be setting broad-brush policy approaches and constructing a national consensus. For example, it is insane to have our congressional leaders fussing over appropriations for every bill or weighing and cross-checking technical data, when their focus should be political choices. "Ineffectiveness in Washington is not new," writes Ted Sorensen. "Our recent presidents are not the first to find their authority diminished and their proposals impeded. The country has survived this kind of Washington power outage in previous eras. But this time the national problems not being adequately addressed, are so deep-seated and far-reaching that the irreversible consequences of continuing drift could drastically alter our national future."[17]

President Reagan seems to have taken the right approach to the management-versus-leadership question. He has won praise as a masterful delegator, doling out administrative duties and concentrating instead on being the country's foremost spokesperson: a communicator. It is not my purpose to judge the substance of what he communicates; history alone can be the judge of whether his policies did ill or good. My concern here is with an essential quality of leadership: communication. It is a quality needed not only in the presidency, but in the Congress as well.

A major problem with our leaders is the process by which we elect them. The skills that qualify someone to succeed in an election campaign may be quite different from those needed in the elected office. Is there not some way by which we might more closely match the talents that surface in a campaign with those required in public service?

The media could make a real difference here. The media might abandon their focus on opinion polls and surveys, designed to calculate who's ahead and by what margin—as if the race itself were the issue. In fact, this focus on polls has the dangerous effect of discouraging people from voting for strong candidates who are behind in the polls: if a candidate seems unlikely to win, such a vote would be considered a "throwaway" vote. Instead, the electronic and print media could offer us detailed comparisons of the candidates' backgrounds, records of achievement, statements on major issues—in short, solid information on the candidates. Thus our election criteria might be based on reasoned political discourse, unlike the present system, which more closely resembles betting on racehorses.

There is a Chinese proverb that was also quoted by one of my Harvard teachers, John Glover, and which seems to me entirely appropriate to the character of leadership needed today. Roughly paraphrased, it states that a leader is one who, when the battle is won, leaves behind the conviction that the people did it themselves. True leadership, then, has the appearance of being effortless, even superfluous. It is for this reason that defining leadership qualities is often so illusory.

Some have suggested that the world has grown too complex for anyone to be a successful leader, that the job of U.S. President has grown too big for any one person to do it well. This is tantamount to saying that the age of leaders is over, and I am too much an optimist to believe that. Yet leadership has clearly become enormously difficult and complex. Ted Sorensen characterizes it thus:

> What political leader, in this period of economic transition and readjustment, will explain to a worker in an aging industrial plant that protectionism will not prevent that worker's lifetime skills from being rendered obsolete by a single microchip performing one million operations per second? Who will change the popular tax and credit laws that encourage borrowing and consumption at the expense of U.S. savings accumulation and capital formation, which, as a

percentage of gross national product, have declined to one of the lowest levels in the industrialized world. Who will accept the domestic political pressures involved in galvanizing the industrialized nations into harmonizing their economics, monetary, trade, credit, subsidy, exchange rate and development assistance policies? [18]

Yet I feel that this is a time of transition for leadership values, and it will be some time before we arrive at a new consensus of what we expect of our leaders. I have already suggested that some of the old icons of leadership are crumbling—the white, male, aggressive "conquerer." While such an image still wins substantial support, it is not enough to sustain a public increasingly alarmed by the threat of global annihilation in a nuclear war.

I have some suggestions as to how we might begin the slow process of arriving at a new consensus on leadership values. First I will address the much larger aspect of the leadership question which goes beyond the qualities of any individual: that of an overriding societal vision.

A Guiding Vision

"Where there is no vision, the people perish." So goes the ancient admonition from Proverbs 29:18.

Far from being merely an abstract or supernatural concept, the idea behind the much quoted phrase is a down-to-earth observation. It says that humans need purpose—individually and collectively. Without a sense of purpose the individual is not only lost but will rapidly disintegrate. Without purpose there is no motivation, no direction, no way to focus the physical and mental faculties of the human. What is true of the individual is even more true of the collective—be it the tribe, the nation, the corporation, the union. What holds the body politic together is the communality of purpose.

When we say "vision," however, we mean more than a commitment to do now what must be done now. Vision implies a purpose beyond the moment, a view of the future, a dreaming and thinking ahead. A vision suggests the imaginative conceptualization of a future that is not inconsistent with the present but that will move the present to something nearer to the ideal.

At various points in this exploratory discourse, we have referred to the importance of setting priorities as a way to overcome "vetoes" and to balance "trade-offs." Priorities will differ, of course, for any two individuals. And the same is true for any two or more institutions within a society. But if a society is to survive and surpass, it requires priorities that are consistent with a vision that can inspire, enthuse, arouse, pull together the many diverse elements in a nation or in a civilization that embraces many nations. Without some such vision, a people—a singular word with plural meaning—shall perish.

Great Visions

History is replete with visions that have guided people in great numbers over great spans of time. Sometimes the vision was put into words so that its advocates could say "It is writ." At other times the vision was unstated but so deeply etched in the minds or the mode of the people that it lasted longer than the written word. Sometimes the vision was wide-lensed, encompassing the total relations of a society; sometimes it was narrowly focused, a clearly defined project. But always the vision became the great energizer —the way for humankind to be more than what was demanded at the moment. Let us consider some of the great visions, stated and unstated, all-embracing and narrowly specific.

There was Cain, recorded in history as a villainous character because he killed his brother. Biblically, no doubt, that was intended to be a morality play on man's inhumanity to man. But what Cain did to Abel, progress has done to those who did not progress, since the beginning of time: "Abel, the shepherd, was a child of nature. The farmer forces nature, and the history of our civilization begins with Cain, the first farmer. Agriculture, whatever its origin, made a stable society both possible and necessary. Husbandry not only provided more food and did it more reliably, but above all it furnished a sort of food, grain, which could be stored in pits for a long time to tide the society over those months when nothing else was available. Thus agriculture became and remained the foundation of civilized life."[19] Ever since Cain, the "farmer" (the civilized man) has been pushing out the "shepherd." Put more generally, those who have learned to dominate nature have established their dominance over those who have been the children of nature, living always at the mercy of the elements.

The very idea that man could, would, and should make nature his servant is a "guiding vision," a notion of the relationship of humans to the universe, a concept so deeply rooted in Western civilization that those who live under its spell assume that the spell is merely the nature of nature itself. In due time this dogma grew to be so seemingly self-evident that it became definitional. Progress would come to mean mankind's increasing control of the environment.

Agriculture—the root of civilizations—meant more than the application of certain tools and techniques to soil. It modified human thought. As Professors Garraty and Gay put it:

> The change to agriculture meant also a mental change. Man began to correct nature, and he did so with his eye on the future. Every techne, as Aristotle says, requires the idea of a result before the material realization of that result can be achieved. . . . The agriculturalist worked not for today, not even for tomorrow, but for a distant and uncertain objective which was very remote when he planted a tree. The future had become for him a far off yet foreseeable time. Symmetrically, the Past became valuable. Today was now a station on the long road from the Past to the future.[20]

The word "vision" now took on its futuristic connotation. It was necessary to see daily deeds in the longer light of a lifetime and of generations. Time per se had to enter the calculus of creation.

Another collection of visions was expressed in the law, as stated in the written word. It is in Exodus and Deuteronomy that Moses hands down the Decalogue he received from God, together with many other commandments on what is right and what is wrong. The laws, engraved on the tablets of Sinai, were of course not the first ordinances on human behavior. Out of the mores of many tribes derived the morality that, without the written word, had guided cultures.

But as society became more complex and as people sought justice in judgment, it became necessary to reduce law to a code, to a series of "thou shalt nots" and "thou shalts." The Ten Commandments were, of course, to be followed by other sets of laws. The 282 articles of the Hammurabic Code (about eighteen centuries B.C.) laid down the law for ancient Mesopotamia. In subsequent centuries there was Roman law, common law, the Napoleonic Code, and the corpus juris of many nations. Underlying each of these compendia for human conduct was a philosophy of justice, a vision of what the good society should be.

Not all visions have been enacted into laws enforced by governments. The Sermon on the Mount is a prescription for Christian behavior which goes far beyond items customarily litigated by attorneys. To "turn the other cheek" was a precept of another order, a vision of human behavior to which man might aspire if he sought to approach the perfection of the divine. It was—it is—a vision that has inspired generations, a guide to what man might be even if he never quite achieves it.

Sometimes a vision appears as a specific project in the form of such epic undertakings as China's Grand Canal and Great Wall, Egypt's pyramids, and Britain's Stonehenge. Although these and such others as the Taj Mahal and the Temple of Solomon are generally looked on as exploitative acts of self-glorification by egomaniacal rulers, there is reason to believe that each of these incredible works served as a dramatically visible vision to motivate a people.

A striking insight into the role of these "projects" in the total context of a culture is offered by Professors Garraty and Gay in their discussion of the pyramids.

> Modern man may ask whether the capital and labor expended in erecting the enormous funerary complex centered on the royal pyramid could not have been better devoted to low-cost housing. The same question, however, can be asked about Gothic cathedrals or the Temple of Jerusalem.
>
> The first need of any social system is to create incentives to make people do more work than that required by their immediate wants. . . . In earlier and poorer societies religion provided the incentive for works of economic supererogation; it raised common labor to the dignity of a ritual gesture. The

Sumerian king is represented carrying on his head a basket with bricks for the foundation of a temple. When men of Lagash had to repair a canal it was the canal of their god Ningirsu.[21]

The pyramids were not in themselves a vision. Rather, they were an expression of a vision that assumed it was the will of the gods to build them. The monument became the visible symbol of the vision—an impressive way to convey a theological abstraction to the great mass, a means to stir collective creativity.

Throughout history wars have played a similar role, without necessarily involving any deities, although more often than not a war was fought in the name of one god or another. Wars draw the nation together; if the war is won, the victory is remembered by following generations as proof of national virility and virtue. Recurrently the metaphor of war is invoked for nonbellicose crusades, such as the war against poverty, the war against disease, the war against illiteracy, and even the war against war. "War" is an ever reiterated "guiding vision" because it identifies a common foe, sets a societal goal, suggests sacrifice by individuals for the general welfare.

A vision may be simple or complex. For Moses it was simple. It was his mission to lead his people out of slavery and into the Promised Land. His source of authority for this audacious act was Jehovah—the one and only. For Marx, the vision was equally simple: to have the proletariat seize power and establish the classless society. His source of authority was science, as he read it. For James Madison the vision was complex: to create a nation not only free of foreign domination but also free of domestic tyranny, even the tyranny of the majority. To that end he sought a scattering of power, with checks and balances, and he advocated a collection of so many diverse elements that no one enclave of opinion would be a majority by itself. His source of authority was "we, the people." For Jean Monet the vision was ever more complex. It was to unite the historically warring nations of Europe into one confederation, the Common Market, without dissolving the national sovereignty of any of these powers. His source of authority was Ananke, the Greek god of necessity. Each in his own way—Moses

405

and Marx, Madison and Monet—had a vision that was to become the vision of peoples.

The association of individual names with the great visions of humankind comes naturally. It is a proper assumption that when something happens, someone made it happen, especially if that something has to do with humans and the cultures they create. What we remember—that is, what Clio records—is the epic act that finally dominates the social scene. What is too often unrecognized and unrecorded is the struggle that preceded the final outcome.

At decisive moments in history there are many notions—visions—in conflict with one another. Which way shall we go? The outcome is not always predictable, even if in retrospect commentators choose to portray the end result as inevitable. It may well be that some good ideas lost out and that some very mean notions won. In either event, it is useful to be aware that human beings—individuals and movements—are active agents of history, that the wish and the will shape societies.

As one case, consider the visions in conflict in the Age of the Warring States in China from the fifth to the third centuries B.C. The background was the collapse of the Chou Dynasty under attacks of Ch'in in a struggle that endured over several centuries. "The deterioration of the old order encouraged speculation about ways in which the imagined golden age of antiquity could be restored, about other and better forms of government, and the purpose of existence."[22] The disorder in the political world spurred a search for reorder in the intellectual world. Many visions were brought forward.

There was the Confucian view that man is good and that vice is an aberration introduced by evil masters and institutions. Through education and moral example man could recapture the goodness that was his in the olden age of Chou. There were the Legalists, who believed that man was essentially evil and that what he needed were stringent laws enforced by stern masters. They wanted a state run by efficient bureaucrats. There were the Moists—pacifist, universalist puritans—who looked down on ceremony, music, and ornamentation; who abhorred war; who sought a solution through universal love. Internally, they were run by dictators. Externally, they kept intervening regularly on the side of the underdogs, thereby—contrary to their best intentions—becoming the finest military experts of their day. There were the naturalists who propounded the principle of complementary opposites: Yin, the passive female, and Yang, the active male. Opposites not only attracted each other, they needed each other—as night needs day, as summer needs winter.

Finally, there were the Taoists, who believed that underlying all seeming difference and conflict was a unifying principle that could be perceived only intuitively. Unlike the other four schools that proposed man's active engagement in the economic and political life of his time, the Taoists preached disengagement—a state of surrender to the material world that would bring spiritual fulfillment, a vision of man gradually and naturally attaining Nirvana.

With the unification of China for the first time in 221 B.C., the Legalists won out. It can be argued—in retrospect—that they were the right people for the first time. To hold a great and diverse nation together and run the country required stringent laws, stern masters, and appointed officials (trusted bureaucrats) instead of hereditary nobles. But it may very well be that it was the vision of the Legalists that made the unification possible.

Very much aware of the power of ideas—visions—in shaping societies, a Legalist minister issued an edict in 213 B.C. to burn all heretical books. He was selective, however, exempting books on agriculture, medicine, pharmacy, and divinations, on the apparent assumption that they were ideologically neutral. Despite this tough line, the Legalists and their patron Ch'in did not last for eternity. Upon the death of the king, civil war broke out again and a new dynasty moved in. In 191 B.C. the Book Burning Edict was rescinded.

Now Confucianism was in, but it was a reformed body of thought that had eclectically drawn on all other schools for words, wisdom, and political ways. Of course "the more Confucius was enshrined as universal sage, the more his followers departed from his teaching."[23] But the vision— man is good and will someday liberate himself from corrupting evil—continued as a unifying inspiration. Confu-   **407** cianism also served to legitimize authority: the king rules with the consent of heaven, and if the ruler turns immoral, heaven will remove him.

Visions are man-made. There is no one vision for all time nor for all mankind. Visions compete with one another, influence one another, adapt to circumstances. Visions also differ in their size: some are planets, others solar systems, still others like the Milky Way, although they all tend to think of themselves as universal in their application. For instance, the concept of progress was a huge universe.

A Century in Transition

Visions don't die easily. For America World War I itself was part of a progressive process: "the war to make the world safe for democracy." For Wilson this was a moment to establish a league of nations—a most ambitious vision that was rejected by the U.S. Senate. For the Bolsheviks the end of the war was the beginning of the proletarian revolution that they hoped and expected would soon sweep the planet. William Randolph Hearst hailed that overthrow of the czars as the crown jewel in the democratic diadem of Europe. In Germany the Weimar Constitution shone brightly as the essence of the democratic concept in a land once controlled by Prussian militarism. In 1924 the Locarno Pact was signed outlawing war. Even the Great Depression in the United States did not entirely extinguish the light of progress as Franklin Delano Roosevelt introduced his New Deal and moved to overcome the depression and master the "business cycle."

What shook the world was the rise of fascism, especially under Hitler in Germany. In the home of Goethe, Schiller, Lessing, Beethoven, and the Weimar Constitution atavistic passions were to crack through the delicate veneer of civilization. The alliance of the Communists with the Fascists in the early years of World War II made a mockery of the notion that these were irreconcilable forces. A deep cynicism took root in the world.

It was an age when Freud would rewrite the story of humankind with a new set of characters: the savage id, the raging superego. The dark side of humanity was revealed.

Freud's probing of the psyche uncovered a richly complex world that lost a great deal in translation as it entered popular lore. Vision, as a societal motivator, would be supplanted by calculated, pseudoscientific explanations for our actions. There was a "reason" why humankind waged wars and committed crimes. There was a psychology behind everything, from a simple act of friendship to the writing of a poem.

Psychoanalysis would become a full-fledged movement among the intelligentsia. Scholars would evaluate literary works in terms of the neuroses of their writers: Faulkner's Oedipus complex or William Blake's "obvious" images of castrating woman. Psychoanalysis in some respects even supplanted morality: a would-be assassin of President Reagan was "innocent" by reason of the "explanation" of poor psychological health. It was as if the American justice system no longer demanded its citizens to choose between right and wrong—only to act in accordance with one's childhood experience.

A deeper cynicism was evoked in the world by the explosions of atomic bombs in Hiroshima and Nagasaki. Human progress was no longer inevitable. In fact, with the continuing buildup of even more terrible bombs and the threat of nuclear annihilation within sight, even a societal retrogression seemed possible. Dire predictions from the Club of Rome et al. further fostered a sense of human limitations, as if the resources of the planet were about to be utterly extinguished.

In some respects the present age resembles the Age of the Warring States in China some two and a half millennia ago. At that time multiple views of the world "created an intellectual ferment which is singular in the history of China."[24] Similarly, our present age of uncertainty is likely to stir a comparable ferment. It would be tempting to predict the outcome of that ferment and suggest my own vision of how the world should be. To do so would be presumptuous. Besides, a great societal vision is not proposed or planned or voted on, like just another statute. It is an evolution of human thinking from which, at some advanced point, a great leader emerges—as if from nowhere—to articulate to society a view of the world that by that time appears quite natural.

Yet, might we not try consciously to approach such a vision, or at least an interim vision? Far be it from me to suggest so fundamental an alternative for society in the next century, but would it be too small a concept to suggest making the society work? If we are not to court authoritarian governments, we had better get right the framework and the processes of our society. And as I have tried to demonstrate in this book, that is neither a trivial matter nor is it going to happen without a considerable job of public education and communication worthy of real leadership.

Creatures of Habit

How do we proceed in finding the new framework, the new sonata forms that Professor Morison described so eloquently? Old mind sets do not die easily, as an example from ancient Egypt illustrates:

▷ The ancient Egyptians were surprisingly good mathematicians. But they were enmeshed in a system of arithmetic notation that made it impossible for them to write a fraction like seven-eighths by the simple symbol $\frac{7}{8}$. They would have to write $\frac{1}{2}$, $\frac{1}{4}$, $\frac{1}{8}$. It was a system of unitary fractions in which the numerator had to be one.

It took many centuries before someone or some other culture devised a more effective way of expressing fractions to make it possible for latter day mathematicians—or school children—to solve problems without having to write $\frac{1}{40}$, $\frac{1}{224}$, $\frac{1}{488}$, $\frac{1}{610}$ to represent $\frac{2}{61}$.[25]

The Egyptians had become the intellectual prisoners of their own artifact. They had invented certain signs to represent numbers and the relations between them, and these persisted for a long time. Indeed, as late as the seventeenth century certain Russian documents are said to have expressed one-ninety-sixth as a "half-half-half-half-half-third."[26] In due time the system of notation became a given. "It is remarkable," notes James Newman, "that the Egyptians who attained so much skill in their arithmetic manipulations were unable to devise a fresh notation and less cumbersome methods. We are forced to realize how little we understand the circumstances of cultural advance; why societies move—or is it perhaps jump—from one orbit to another of intellectual energy, why the science of Egypt 'ran its course on narrow lines' and adhered so rigidly to its clumsy rules."[27]

How much more liberated are we from our systems of "notation"? Consider the calendar. We have four months with 30 days, seven with 31 days, and one with only 28 days —except, of course, when it has 29. Every time we want to recall how many days there are in a month, we run through an ancient nursery rhyme—somebody else's concoction— "Thirty days hath September . . ." The Egyptian notations and our own calendar suggest a pattern of societal structuring in which an invention becomes a social convention imposing its compulsion on the members of a society. Why has mankind put up with this most subtle form of tyranny for these many millennia?

A strong impetus behind convention is survival. Homo sapiens has "made it" so far not because he is the strongest, the swiftest, or the fiercest of all beasts but because he has a "social instinct" that allows him to construct societies for survival in all kinds of circumstances—in deserts and forests, polar and tropical zones, on mountains and in valleys, as a nomad and an urbanite, under kings and presidents. This "social instinct"—the compulsion to go with the herd —requires two basic conventions: first, words (another one of those inventions) to make communication possible between members of the "herd," and second, institutions (another set of inventions) to define the relationships among the members of the tribe (clan, city, polis, polity, nation).

We know that both language and institutions change over time, although they do so very slowly. When a conquering nation tries to impose its language on a conquered people, the conversion is difficult, painful, and never fully successful, as the evolution of the English language irrefutably attests. Institutions do change more readily than language but never easily: first, because man fears the unknown, and second, because there are always those who are the "in" party in the present institutional arrangement, and they fear that in another arrangement they may be the "outs." As should by now be quite clear to any reader of this book, I am not limiting the term "institutions" to governmental bodies: Laws, courts, parliaments, military, police, elections, agencies. There are far more extragovernmental institutions: family, church, corporations, unions, clubs, teams, markets, associations, professions, street gangs, organized crime, networks, and old school ties. They are the cement of societies.

Even when some social arrangement is uncomfortable for people, they are likely to put up with the discomfort rather than risk adjustment to the new. Fundamentally, this is instinctive, the reflex of humans, creatures of habit, who seek certainty in the consolation that tomorrow will not be too unlike yesterday. Life would be quite unbearable if suddenly some morning the sun rose in the west or if putting one leg ahead of the other caused us to fly vertically one day, stand still on another, and just collapse in a pratfall on a third day. To avoid disruption of existing arrangements is also the "prudent" thing to do. As the Declaration of Independence, that great revolutionary document, put it: "Prudence, indeed, will dictate that governments long established should not be changed for light and transient causes; and accordingly all experience hath shewn that mankind are more disposed to suffer, while evils are sufferable, than to right themselves by abolishing the forms to which they are accustomed."

Both habit and prudence—perhaps they are children of the same parent, *the search for security*—dictate the conservative course: Look and look again before you leap! And yet, while all history relates man's reluctance to change, it also, paradoxically, relates man's restless impulse to change, either because necessity forces invention or because vision reveals a better way or—as most commonly happens—because necessity and vision coincide.

If man had not repeatedly broken the mold of ideas and institutions into which he was born we would all still be living in caves or trees. Social invention—the idea that becomes institutionalized—brought man from the Neanderthal period to the present. If someone had not challenged the unitary fraction, most people still would not be able to do simple arithmetic. If someone had not challenged the scientific truth that an atom is the smallest possible particle of matter, we would not have opened up the universe of power that exists within the atom. If someone had not challenged the "divine right" of kings, self-government would still be unknown. If someone had not invented an imaginary "i"—the square root of minus 1—modern physics and engineering would have been impossible.[28] We have moved ahead because nothing in human history is more constant than change.

Changes in societal arrangements are really nothing more than the inevitable expression of humanity's cultural adaptability. Its evolution, as chronicled in recorded history, is not a physical but a social progress, embodied in the changing nature of societies. Sometimes the changes are slow and incremental; sometimes they are sudden and explosive. To use Newman's terms, sometimes societies "move" and sometimes they "jump." We generally refer to the former as "reform" and to the latter as "revolution."

Reform and revolution are not the only alternatives for an institution—be it a nation, a business, a church, or a union —that is confronted with external or internal challenge. Ruin is the third possibility—and the pages of history are strewn with such rubble. Gibbon chronicled the decline and fall of the Roman Empire. Oswald Spengler forecast the "decline of the West." Arnold Toynbee, in *A Study of History*, recorded the birth and death of so many civilizations that one almost surrenders to the notion that no nation ever escapes its doomsday fate. Shelley's poem to Ozymandias is a reminder of the once great whose works now lie in unremembered dust:

And on the pedestal these words appear:
"My name is Ozymandias, king of kings:
Look on my works, ye Mighty, and despair!"
Nothing beside remains. Round the decay
Of that colossal wreck, boundless and bare
The lone and level sands stretch far away.

It seems to be fairly certain that all institutions are slated for extinction and early extinction if they do not have the capacity for self-renewal—a self-renewal that is almost impossible without self-reexamination. For most social organizations such insight to develop a new outlook does not come easily. Although logic strongly suggests that action should be taken before things break down, history is replete with instances of great actions undertaken only in times of great crises. And usually such action is associated with the name of some one leader: Christ, Mohammed, Luther, Churchill, Napoleon, Lenin, Mao Tse-tung, Gandhi. Where are such leaders today?

The recurrent question is whether the leader is a product of his times or whether the times are a product of the man. The question probably has no answer. If there is a great leader saying the right thing at the wrong time, he will have no followers and will go to his grave unmourned, unnoted, and unknown. Recall Homer's fate: "Seven wealthy towns contend for Homer dead,/Through which the living Homer begg'd his bread." Conversely, the times may have cried out for a great leader but, in his absence, things went from bad to worse. There have been many, too many, such occasions for countries, companies, and political coalitions. What makes societies viable, what results in institutions that *do* work, is the coming together of the moment and the man, things and thoughts, necessity and invention.

When De Tocqueville visited the United States in 1835 and again in 1840 he was turned off by the puny stature of the statesmen, especially as contrasted with the preceding giants such as Washington, Jefferson, Adams, Franklin, Hamilton. De Tocqueville suggested that perhaps the years of war, liberation, and writing of the Constitution had brought out the best in the best men. The crisis did not create greatness, but it had allowed human greatness to come forward. What we will never know, however, is how many crises were avoided because people of vision, foreseeing the danger and envisioning a brighter future, acted in time.

A New Ball Game

Today's world, of course, is much more complex than that of Jefferson and Washington. An instructive metaphor for modern times comes from Ralph Siu, a scientist, philosopher, government bureaucrat, management consultant. It is a game of his invention called Chinese baseball. Siu describes the game as follows: It is played exactly like American baseball, but "there is one and only one difference. And it is this: after the ball leaves the pitcher's hand and as long as the ball is in the air, anyone can move any of the bases anywhere."[29] Those are the moving parts in a game that must continue.

In our time many "bases" move during play. Technology changes. The population—age, sex, educational level—changes. Old values yield to new. New products disrupt markets. Faraway wars throw homelands into turmoil. Old authorities fall into disrepute and new idols are erected. Currencies fluctuate, ownership shifts, governments intervene, terrorists explode, prices zoom out of sight, crime runs rampant. In short, the bases move right in the middle of the play.

It is a world seemingly out of control, and all our advanced technologies for processing and disseminating information only seem to make things worse. We are overwhelmed with so much contradictory information that it becomes nearly impossible to make responsible choices. Professor Müller describes the situation well: "Political paralysis and lack of consensus reflect an electorate and its political leaders who are bombarded by contradictory 'facts,' as well as ideas and opinions. We are in an era of 'information overload.' "[30]

Where We Agree

How do we arrive at a new consensus for a guiding vision of society when the bases are moving, the rules are changing, and conflicting signals confound us?

I think the key to arriving at a common understanding of our society's goals is information—not more of the same "information overload" but thoughtfully prepared, quality information. I believe that policy makers greatly underestimate the ability of the American public to make sacrifices and work together toward long-range goals. If the public were carefully apprised of the risks and benefits associated with government and corporate actions that affect their lives, they would be in a better position to participate responsibly in the decision-making process.

To give a very simple example—but one I think many people can identify with—each week the newspapers seem to report on new "evidence" about substances that are dangerous to our health. Caffeine has been linked over the years with cancer, heart disease, birth defects, high blood

415

pressure, stress, insomnia—you name it. Sprinkled among those reports with almost equal regularity are others telling about its beneficial effects: it gives you a healthy lift, it relaxes you, it energizes you. I think the normal reaction to these conflicting reports is to throw your hands up in exasperation, ignore the "experts," and go along as you would have if you had never had the benefit of the advice. If it becomes impossible to make informed decisions on something as simple as your morning cup of coffee, how can we even begin to approach the *critical* issues of our time?

Again I will say that the key is not more information but quality information. Democracy depends on an informed citizenry, and public education is the precious oil our democracy needs to get its gears running anew. I am very pleased to be involved with an organization that is founded on just that principle. In an earlier chapter ("Short Time Horizons") I described the work of the Public Agenda Foundation, which was established by Cyrus Vance and Daniel Yankelovich. That chapter dealt with a highly successful public education campaign in Des Moines, Iowa, in which the citizens of that community received an intensive course over several weeks on health care.

More recently Public Agenda has embarked on a vitally important and highly ambitious campaign to inform the public on the nuclear arms debate. As Cyrus Vance wrote:

> No question has raised more confusion than what role the public can and should play. Our premise is that the answer to this question is clear: the public should have a say on those aspects of the nuclear arms race that raise questions of fundamental human values, as distinct from technical matters or questions of military tactics or geopolitical maneuvering.
>
> The main task is to grapple with the alternative policies that may be forged and their respective costs and consequences. Such a public debate is essential if the nation is to reach a cogent and broadly accepted policy on nuclear arms.[31]

At the moment I write, this important project is in the planning stages. Its approach would be, first, to conduct a broad study to identify public concerns on this issue. Second, it would identify, analyze, and assemble a variety of nuclear defense choices that can form the basis of public debate. Third, the group would communicate with the public through a variety of formats and media—television, newspaper supplements, brochures, film, radio, and so on —designed to present choices on nuclear defense clearly and accessibly to the average citizen. Beginning with a three-month campaign in one demonstration site, the project would become the nucleus of a "public affairs network." Public Agenda would also provide opportunities for the public to share their conclusions with their leaders, partly by including a briefing book for presidential candidates and other officials designed to illuminate and interpret the public's state of mind.

Might not such an intensive, reasoned, thoughtful approach to public education serve as a model for national debates on other vital issues? Might not the wealth of computer and communications technology in this country— technology that now channels more verbiage and redundant data than useful information—be put to responsible and constructive use in the building of a new "information democracy"? Already we have seen national information networks, such as The Source, serve as electronic forums for political debate. Videotex technology offers additional opportunities for interactive debate over home television screens. I would stress, however, that the use of these technologies to promote public participation in decision making becomes truly meaningful only with the kind of thoughtful preparation and educational underpinnings that Public Agenda has pioneered. I strongly suspect that the public, when given clear choices on complex issues, would arrive at conclusions that reveal a great deal more communality than *dissensus*.

The Next Vision

The British philosopher Alfred North Whitehead tells us, "The vitality of thought is in adventure. Ideas won't keep. Something must be done about them."[32] Democracy is such an idea. And the "adventure," as far as this particular idea is concerned, is in innovation and experimentation. "When existing theory fails, the older American way was experimentation," wrote Arthur Schlesinger. "That is, after all, not a bad way to arrive at theory."[33]

In the preceding pages I have given numerous examples of institutional inventing and innovation: new relationships between business and government, such as the Business Roundtable; new prospects in public services, from street cleaning to public schools, made possible by privatization experiments; new ways in which corporations are responding to changing values and a complex social and political climate; my own proposal for Institutes of the Future, to create the conditions for longer-range thinking and planning; alternative legal institutions, to cut away the underbrush of obstacles and delays in the judicial process; and organizational inventions, such as the Public Agenda Foundation, to meet entirely new challenges in public education on complex modern issues. I have also described new categories of institutional problems associated with information technology and biomedicine—fertile grounds for additional institutional inventing.

There is no paucity of ideas from which our new vision of society will ferment, and I am painfully aware that I have only scratched the surface of them. Nor can I hope to do more than guess at what the next great vision of society will be. Perhaps it will not be merely national but global in character. Ever since the first photographs of the planet earth were beamed back to us from space, we gained a perspective on our commonality unprecedented in human history. Interdependence is a theme that binds many smaller visions of society, from those of environmentalists to multinational corporations to poets. Moreover, it is hard to imagine that the next great vision will not be, to some degree, technology-based. Just as the steam engine defined the Industrial Age, I suspect that information technology will be the indispensable tool of the next great visionaries— or perhaps some technology that is beyond present human reckoning.

MIT Professor Frank Davidson enriches the theme of technological vision in his recent important study *Macro*. Giant hydroelectric projects, transatlantic tunnels, new pathways sliced across the Rocky Mountains, electromagnetically levitated subways—these large-scale engineering projects, says Davidson, are the stuff of human progress.

His proposal is not technology for technology's sake but bigger and better systems to promote human cooperation and improve the quality of life. "The different sectors of our society," he says, "can cooperate and even devise new instrumentalities whenever a novel public need is perceived and articulated, and when enough people are convinced that a stated objective is worth attaining. . . . We are entering a new age of technological diplomacy."[34] Whether they are technological or artistic or religious or some other, I would concur that large-scale projects that enlist the minds and energies of broad populations will be the turning points on which our future vision will hinge. It is my hope to stir the imaginations of countless others who will unabashedly "think big."

My own determination to "think big" led to the writing of this book, in the hope of designing a more livable future for all of us. Getting right the processes and structures by which we work, govern, and live is a "big" task indeed, and perhaps big enough to serve as at least an interim vision that will guide us toward the next great unifying idea.

Clearly we are not going to succeed in the necessary reshaping of our future unless we adopt new relationships and new roles in many of our most fundamental institutions. The relationships among universities, basic research, industry, private sector and public sector and the interface among these elements is where real action is going to take place.

Identifying process, institutional relationships, and the need for new institutions and political mechanisms plus a shift in government focus to policy and away from delivery of service—no small order. Might this not suffice as our own next order of business when it comes to an overarching vision?

When I look back to the original inspiration for this book —my April 1980 Trueman Wood Lecture before the Royal Society of Arts in London—I am reminded of an idea that was first enunciated on the same podium from which I spoke. That idea was the Crystal Palace Exhibition, which played a crucial role as a focal point for realizing the momentous scope of achievement in the nineteenth century. It signaled the arrival of a new era.

I would like to suggest the importance of focal points in   **419** any important societal change: bright signals that engage the human imagination and announce that a new world has begun. There is so much room for experimentation, so much that needs to be done if we are to make our institutions and society work. Such efforts could go a long way toward closing the gap between what our society can achieve—and what we do achieve.

Notes and Selected Bibliography

Notes

Chapter 1
Why Things Don't Work Anymore, And What We Can Do About It

1. Suzanne Daley, "First Cars for IRT Made by Japanese Fail 30-Day Tests," *New York Times*, February 26, 1984.
2. Daniel Yankelovich and John Immerwahr, *Putting the Work Ethic to Work* (New York: Public Agenda Foundation, 1983), p. 26.
3. Statistics provided in a telephone interview by the Road Information Program, Washington, D.C.
4. "Pull New York Out of Its Ruts," Editorial, *New York Times*, April 1, 1984.
5. See Peter Salin's *The Ecology of Housing Destruction* (New York: New York University Press, 1980).
6. Michael Levitt and Barbara Lloyd, *UPSET: Australia Wins the America's Cup* (New York: Workman Publishing, 1983), p. 188.
7. James Reston, "Discussing the Bugs in the Machinery," Q&A: David A. Stockman, *New York Times*, April 12, 1984.
8. Abraham Lincoln, from two pages of autograph manuscript in the Pierpont Morgan Library, New York.
9. Elting E. Morison, *From Know-How to Nowhere: The Development of American Technology* (New York: Basic Books, 1974), p. 176.
10. Charles Schultze, quoted from "New Rules and Opportunities for Business," keynote speech by John Diebold, Third Tri-Annual International Productivity Congress (Vienna), p. 5 (quoted from Schultze, "Politics and Economics of Public Spending" [Washington, D.C.: Brookings Institution, 1969]).
11. Theodore C. Sorensen, *A Different Kind of Presidency* (New York: Harper & Row, 1984), pp. 23-24.
12. Robert Nisbet, *History of the Idea of Progress* (New York: Basic Books, 1980), p. 9.

13. Charles E. Lindblom, *Politics and Markets: The World's Political-Economic Systems* (New York: Basic Books, 1977), pp. 344–345.
14. See Gerard K. O'Neill's *The Technology Edge: Opportunities for America in World Competition* (New York: Simon & Schuster), p. 272.
15. Alexander Hamilton, *Papers on Public Credit, Commerce and Finance*, ed. Samuel McKee, Jr. (New York: Columbia University Press, 1934), p. 276.
16. Charles Schultze, "Industrial Policy: A Dissent," *Brookings Review*, October 1983.
17. Committee for Economic Development, "Strategy for U.S. Industrial Competitiveness" (New York: 1984), manuscript pp. 1, 6.

Chapter 2
Vetoes and Priorities

1. Peter Gwynne, "Piping Coal to the Southeast," *Technology Review* (Oct. 1982), p. 14.
2. Ibid.
3. Matthew L. Wald, "Seabrook Cost May Burden New Englanders," *New York Times*, April 4, 1984.
4. Paul Lewis, "In Europe It's Still Full Speed Ahead for Nuclear Power," *New York Times*, Dec. 4, 1983, p. E18.
5. Charles E. Lindblom, *Politics and Markets: The World's Political-Economic Systems* (New York: Basic Books, 1977), p. 347.
6. Mark Shields, "Who Would Vote for TVA Today?" *Washington Post*, Sept. 24, 1982.
7. George Will, *Statecraft as Soulcraft* (New York: Simon & Schuster, 1983), pp. 49–50.
8. John Gardner, "Toward a Pluralistic but Coherent Society," Aspen Institute Executive Seminar Readings, 1983, Second Week, Day 6, p. 7.
9. James Madison, *The Federalist*, No. 10, ed. Jacob E. Cooke (Middletown, Conn.: Wesleyan University Press, 1961), p. 58.
10. Gardner, "Toward a Pluralistic Society," p. 8.
11. Ibid., p. 9.
12. Ibid.
13. Adam Smith, *The Wealth of Nations* (New York: Modern Library, 1937), p. 66.
14. Ibid., p. 128.
15. Ibid., p. 126.
16. Ibid., p. 250.
17. Thomas Sowell, *Knowledge and Decisions* (New York: Basic Books, 1980), p. 110.

18. Baron Nathaniel M. V. Rothschild, "Coming to Grips with Risk," *Wall Street Journal*, March 13, 1979, p. 22.
19. Elting E. Morison, *From Know-How to Nowhere* (New York: Basic Books, 1974), p. 176.
20. Ibid.
21. Sowell, *Knowledge and Decisions*, p. 82.
22. See "Industries and Environmentalists Developing Common Policies in an Area of Controversy: The National Coal Policy Dispute," Diebold Corporate Issues Program, Case Study III.4 (New York: Diebold Group).
23. See Garry Wills, *Inventing America: Jefferson's Declaration of Independence* (New York, Doubleday, 1978).
24. Based on a press release on the Public Education Fund dated Sept. 22, 1983, and on information submitted to the board of directors of PEF at its first grant-giving meeting.
25. See Alfred D. Chandler, Jr.'s *The Visible Hand: The Managerial Revolution in American Business* (Cambridge, Mass.: Harvard University Press, 1977).
26. See "Resolving Environmental Disputes Through Mediation," Diebold Corporate Issues Program Case Study III.3 (New York: Diebold Group).
27. Briefing paper on Social Security at conference sponsored by Senator Bill Bradley, Nov. 23, 1982, p. 3.

Chapter 3
Short Time Horizons

1. Edward A. Feigenbaum and Pamela McCorduck, *The Fifth Generation* (Reading, Mass.: Addison-Wesley, 1983), p. 196.
2. Thomas Sowell, *Knowledge and Decisions* (New York: Basic Books, 1980), p. 95.
3. Osbert Sitwell, *Left Hand, Right Hand!* (Boston: Little Brown, 1944), p. xiii.
4. Patricia McCormack, "Educator Says Limits on Doctors Will Bring Better Health Care," UPI wire, Dec. 8, 1983, 7:36 P.M. EST.
5. Michael Ledeen, "Learning to Say 'No' to the Press," *The Public Interest* (Fall 1983), p. 113.
6. Nelson Smith and Leonard J. Theberge, eds. *Energy Coverage—Media Panic*, Media Institute (New York: Longman, 1983), p. xi.
7. Ibid., p. xii.
8. Quoted in ibid., p. 105.
9. Ibid., p. 152.
10. Pat Choate and Susan Walters, *America in Ruins: Beyond the Public Works Pork Barrel* (Washington, D.C.: Council of State Planning Agencies, 1981), p. 87.

11. Proceedings, New York Conference on the Infrastructure, New York Academy of Sciences, Dec. 5–7, 1983.
12. Derek C. Bok, "Student Aid and the Public Interest," *Harvard Magazine* (May–June 1982), p. 79.
13. George Will, *Statecraft as Soulcraft* (New York: Simon & Schuster, 1983), p. 36.
14. Ibid., p. 37
15. Arthur C. Clarke, *Profiles of the Future: An Inquiry into the Limits of the Possible* (New York: Harper & Row, 1958), pp. 2, 9–10.
16. Ibid., p. 8.
17. Lord Rothschild, *Meditations of a Broomstick* (London: Collins, 1977), p. 156.
18. Frederik Pohl, in an interview with John Diebold.
19. Clarke, *Profiles of the Future*, p. 15.
20. Theodore C. Sorensen, *A Different Kind of Presidency* (New York: Harper & Row, 1984), p. 89.
21. "Strengthening the Federal Budget Process," statement by the Research and Policy Committee of the Committee for Economic Development, 1983.
22. Interview by David Ewing, "Monsanto's 'Earling Warning System,' " *Harvard Business Review* (Nov.–Dec. 1981), p. 108.
23. Robert Pear, "GM Agrees to Pay $42 Million to End Case on Job Bias," *New York Times*, Oct. 19, 1983.

Chapter 4
The Misrule of Law

1. George Vecsey, "A Judge Ends the Agony," *New York Times*, Aug. 19, 1983, p. 22.
2. Steven Brill, "What to Tell Your Friends About IBM," *American Lawyer* (April 1982), p. 11.
3. David Margolick, "Burger Says Lawyers Make Legal Help Too Costly," *New York Times*, Feb. 13, 1984.
4. Ronald F. Pollack, "Lawyers for the Poor," *New York Times*, June 17, 1983, p. 27.
5. Derek Bok, "A Flawed System," *Harvard Magazine* (May–June 1983), p. 40.
6. Quoted in Jethro K. Lieberman, *The Litigious Society* (New York: Basic Books, 1981), p. 178.
7. James Stewart, Jr., Jill Abramnson, Ward Sloane, and Alissa Ruben, "Endless Litigation," *American Lawyer* (July 1982), p. 46.
8. James Cramer, "Boston's Slow Court," *American Lawyer* (August 1981), pp. 79–80.
9. Bok, "A Flawed System," p. 40.
10. Ibid., p. 41.

11. Russell Baker, "Lawyers for Cars," *New York Times*, June 8, 1983, p. 27.

12. Marlene Adler Marks, *The Suing of America* (New York: Seaview Books), p. 4.

13. See Marks, *Suing of America*, p. 3.

14. Ibid.

15. Kathleen Sylvester, "A New Term, an Old Case," *National Law Journal*, Oct. 17, 1983, p. 13.

16. Elizabeth Drew, *Politics and Money* (New York: Macmillan, 1983), p. 89.

17. Thomas E. Silfen, "When a Trial Lawyer Is on a Jury," *Washington Post*, Aug. 26, 1983, p. 11.

18. Stephen Breyer, *Regulation and Its Reform* (Cambridge, Mass.: Harvard Univ. Press, 1982), p. 1.

19. Peter Megargee Brown, "Misguided Lawyers," *New York Times*, Dec. 6, 1983, p. A31.

20. John Keker and Lloyd Cutler, "Megafirms Aren't the Answer," *American Lawyer* (July–Aug. 1983), p. 7.

21. McGlynn opinion in the Fine Paper class action, March 1983.

22. OPM Leasing report by the bankruptcy trustee, 1983.

23. *Wall Street Journal*, Oct. 11, 1983, p. 1.

24. Steven Brill, "End Charity to the Future Rich," *American Lawyer* (Oct. 1981), p. 5.

25. James Lardner, "The Way We Train Lawyers Is a Crime Against Society," *Washington Post*, Oct. 9, 1983, p. 1.

26. See "Xerox Reduces on the Robert Banks Diet," *American Lawyer* (Apr. 1982), p. 33.

27. Irving Kaufman, "Utopia Without Lawyers?" *New York Times*, Aug. 14, 1983, Op-Ed page.

28. Lieberman, *The Litigious Society*, p. 186.

29. CPR Legal Program Proceedings (New York, Feb. 1983), p. 2.

30. Larry Lampert, "Arbitration Proves Its Value in Complex Construction Case," *Legal Times* (June 6, 1983), p. 1.

31. Charles F. McCoy, "Federal Legal-Aid Cuts Spur the Bar to Increase Free Work for the Poor," *Wall Street Journal*, March 30, 1984, pp. 1, 16.

32. Ibid., p. 16.

33. Ellen Joan Pollock, "The Alternative Route," *American Lawyer* (Sept. 1983), p. 70.

Chapter 5
Unleashing Innovation in Public Services

1. E. S. Savas, *Privatizing the Public Sector* (Chatham, N.J.: Chatham House, 1982), pp. 24–25.

2. See Suzanne Daley, "Westchester Bus Shops Arouse Kiley's Interest," *New York Times*, Feb. 23, 1984, p. 4.
3. From untitled story, no by-line, on UPI wire of Jan. 24, 1984, 2:07 P.M. EST.
4. Savas, *Privatizing*, p. 25.
5. See Reporter at Large, "Kate Quinton's Days," *New Yorker*, Nov. 21, 1983, pp. 72, 75.
6. E. S. Savas, ed., *Alternatives for Delivering Public Services* (Boulder, Colo.: Westview Press, 1977).
7. "Public-Private Partnership: An Opportunity for Urban Communities," statement by Research and Policy Committee of Committee for Economic Development (Feb. 1982), p. 62.
8. Savas, *Privatizing*, p. 72.
9. Denis Gulino, "Commission Chief: Taxpayers Equal 'Suckers,' " UPI wire, Jan. 12, 1984, 4:12 P.M. EST.
10. Tom Hazlett, "What Ever Happened to Proposition 13?" *Reader's Digest* (Oct. 1981), pp. 124–127.
11. Savas, *Privatizing*, p. 26.
12. Brad Pokorny, "Dover's Plan to Hire Private Firm to Fight Fires Sparks Firemen's Anger," *Boston Globe*, July 3, 1983, p. 17.
13. Arthur Harrigan, "Commentary," *New Challenges to the Role of Profit*, 3d. Ser., John Diebold Lectures at Harvard (Lexington, Mass.: Lexington Books, 1978), p. 64.
14. Ibid.
15. R. Scott Fosler and Renee A. Berger, *Public-Private Partnerships in American Cities* (Lexington, Mass.: Lexington Books, 1982), pp. 116–127.
16. Quoted in John Diebold, *Private Enterprise and Public Policy* (New York: Diebold Institute for Public Policy Studies), p. 42.
17. John Williams, "UPS Delivers Profits by Expanding Its Area, Battling Postal Rates," *Wall Street Journal*, Aug. 25, 1980, p. 1.
18. *Education, Technology and Business*, No. 1 in series of analyses and positions of Diebold Group, based on address by John Diebold at Swarthmore College (New York: Praeger, 1971), p. 3.
19. Ibid., p. 5.
20. Charles F. Silberman, *Crisis in the Classroom* (New York: Random House, 1970), cited in *Education, Technology and Business*, p. 33 (n. 13 above).
21. Quoted in Diebold, *Private Enterprise*, p. 42.
22. Theodore Gage, "Cops Inc.," *Reason* (Nov. 1982), pp. 23–25.
23. Ibid., p. 27.

24. Ibid., p. 28.
25. Ibid.
26. Alice Noble, "Business Computerizes Rural Iowa Community," UPI national wire, Nov. 25, 1983, 6:37 A.M., "*Horizons, Living Lifestyle*" section.
27. Jon A. Stewart, "The Falck Organization: A New Model for Delivering Social Services?" *Transatlantic Perspectives* (Feb. 1982), p. 11.
28. Ibid., p. 13.

Chapter 6
Talent as Capital
1. Daniel Yankelovich, *New Rules* (New York: Random House, 1981), p. xv.
2. Sharon Frederick, "Why John and Mary Won't Work," *Inc. Magazine* (April 1981), pp. 70, 73–74.
3. UPI wire, Jan. 16, 1984, 8:36 P.M. EST.
4. C. Wright Mills, "Work," essay in *White Collar* (New York: Oxford, 1953), p. 236.
5. Gene Gregory, "Japan's Education Edge," *World Press Review* (Feb. 1984), p. 27.
6. Pehr Gyllenhammar, *People at Work* (Reading, Mass.: Addison-Wesley, 1977), p. 4.
7. Letter from Sidney Harman to John Diebold, Dec. 19, 1983.
8. Frederick, "Why John and Mary Won't Work," p. 73.
9. Shoshana Zuboff, "The Work Ethic and Work Organization," an essay in *The Work Ethic: A Critical Analysis* (Madison, Wis.: Industrial Relations Research Association, 1984), p. 157.
10. Yankelovich, *New Rules*, p. 42.
11. Keith Sward, *The Legend of Henry Ford* (New York: Rinehart, 1948), p. 32.
12. Quoted in Zuboff, *The Work Ethic*, p. 165.
13. Daniel Yankelovich et al., *Work and Human Values* (New York: Public Agenda Foundation, 1983), p. 6.
14. Gus Tyler, "The World of Work Gets Wider and Wilder," *The Future of Business Annual Review, 1980/81* (New York: Pergamon Press, 1980), p. 15.
15. Juanita Kreps, ed. *Women and the American Economy: A Look at the 1980's* (Englewood Cliffs, N.J.: Prentice-Hall, 1976), p. 9.
16. Seymour L. Wolfbein, "Planning for a U.S. Labor Force of the 80's," *National Productivity Review* (Spring 1982), p. 231.
17. Sar A. Levitan and Clifford M. Johnson, "The Survival of Work," essay in *The Work Ethic*, p. 6.
18. Wolfbein, "Planning for a U.S. Labor Force," p. 232.
19. Ibid., p. 237.

20. Ibid.
21. Tyler, "The World of Work," pp. 2–3.
22. Wolfbein, p. 231.
23. Tyler, p. 6.
24. Wolfbein, p. 230.
25. Levitan and Johnson, "The Survival of Work," p. 7.
26. Ibid.
27. Tyler, p. 7.
28. Ibid.
29. Levitan and Johnson, pp. 13–14.
30. Ibid., p. 19.
31. *Survey of Working Conditions* (Univ. of Michigan: Survey Research Center, 1971), p. 406.
32. Yankelovich, *Work and Human Values*, p. 151.
33. Ibid., p. 7.
34. Daniel Yankelovich and John Immerwahr, *The Work Ethic and Economic Vitality* (New York: Public Agenda Foundation, 1983), p. 5.
35. Ibid., p. 5.
36. Ibid.
37. Daniel Yankelovich and John Immerwahr, *Putting the Work Ethic to Work* (New York: Public Agenda Foundation, 1983), p. 19.
38. Yankelovich and Immerwahr, *Putting Work Ethic*, p. 14.
39. Ibid.
40. *A Guide to Worker Productivity Experiments in the United States 1971-1975* (Scarsdale, N.Y.: Work in America Institute, 1977), p. 64.
41. Ibid.
42. Ibid., p. 67.
43. Ibid., p. 74.
44. Ibid., p. 77.
45. Ibid., p. 99.
46. Halcyone Bowen, *Corporate Employment Policies Affecting Families and Children* (Aspen Institute for Humanistic Studies, 1982), p. 24.
47. Ibid., p. 25.
48. Ibid., pp. 89–90.
49. *Productivity Through Work Innovations*, ed. Jerome M. Rosow and Robert Zager (Scarsdale, N.Y.: Work in America Institute, 1983), p. 75.
50. *The Future of Work* (Washington, D.C.: AFL-CIO, 1983).
51. Erik Larson and Carrie Dolan, "Large Computer Firms Sprout Little Divisions for Good, Fast Work," *Wall Street Journal*, Aug. 19, 1983, p. 1.
52. Ibid., p. 17.

53. Catherine Marenghi, "Will Telecommuting Take Hold?" *PC Week* (March 20, 1984), p. 39.
54. See ibid., p. 38.
55. William Foote Whyte et al., *Worker Participation and Ownership* (Ithaca, N.Y.: ILR Press).
56. Ibid.
57. Ibid.
58. "The Company That Stopped Detroit," *New York Times*, Aug. 21, 1982, cited by Michael P. Rosow and Robert Zager, *Productivity Through Work Innovations* (New York: Pergamon Press, 1982), p. 49.
59. "Quality Circles Boost Productivity in North Carolina's State Offices," *World of Work Report*, Vol. 6, No. 9 (Sept. 1981), p. 65.
60. Ibid.

Chapter 7
Managing for Sociopolitical Change

Most of the research on which this chapter is based was conducted over a period of several years by the Diebold Group, Inc., as part of its Diebold Corporate Issues Program. The following are outside references.

1. Jim Drinkhall, "IBM Settles Stolen-Data Suit With Hitachi, Wins Right to Inspect Firm's New Products," *Wall Street Journal*, Oct. 7, 1983, p. 2.
2. "Japan's High-Tech Spies," *Newsweek* (July 5, 1982), p. 53.
3. Franklin Lindsay, Jerome Rubin, and Richard Cohen, "People and the New Technologies: An Issue for Managers," paper prepared for Public Agenda Foundation, New York, 1983.
4. See Robert Reich, *The Next American Frontier* (New York: Times Books, 1983), p. 143.
5. Robert H. Hayes and William J. Abernathy, "Managing Our Way to Economic Decline," *Harvard Business Review*, (July/Aug., 1980), p. 67.
6. Pamela G. Hollie, "Humanizing Corporations," *New York Times*, Oct. 21, 1983, p. D1.
7. Robert Sangeorge, "National Toxic Waste Cleanup Program Readied," UPI wire, April 1, 1984, 11:08 P.M. EST.
8. Ibid.

Chapter 8
Labor in Transition: Facilitating Change in Jobs

1. "Fort Wayne Mobilizes to Aid Those Left Jobless by Truck Plant's Closing," *New York Times*, July 16, 1983, p. 5.
2. Labor Relations Report, No. 787 (Washington, D.C.: Bureau of National Affairs, 1975), 53:571.

3. Jay Mathews, "Math Quiz Showed Most Were Ill Equipped for Course," *Washington Post*, Nov. 8, 1983, p. A1.

4. Barry Bluestone and Bennett Harrison, *Capital and Communities: The Cases and Consequences of Private Disinvestment* (Washington, D.C.: Progressive Alliance, 1980), pp. 78–82.

5. A. F. Ehrbar, "Grasping the New Unemployment," *Fortune*, May 16, 1983, p. 112.

6. Ibid., p. 111.

7. William Diebold, *Industrial Policy as an International Issue* (New York: McGraw-Hill, 1980), pp. 80–81.

8. "Education, Technology and Business," No. 1 in series of analyses and positions of Diebold Group, based on address by John Diebold at Swarthmore College (New York: Praeger, 1971), p. 28.

9. Ibid., p. 29.

10. Ehrbar, "Grasping the New Unemployment," p. 110.

11. John P. Davis, *Corporations* (New York: Capricorn Books, 1961), p. 145.

12. Gus Tyler, *The Political Imperative* (New York: Macmillan, 1968), p. 61.

13. Tyler, *Political Imperative*, p. 61.

14. From *Memorials of London*, cited by Davis, *Corporations*, p. 170.

15. Rosalind Williams, "The Machine Breakers," *Technology Illustrated* (July 1983), p. 60.

16. Cited by Gus Tyler, *The Labor Revolution* (New York: Viking Press, 1967), p. 118.

17. Alexander Hamilton, *Papers on Public Credit, Commerce and Finance*, ed. Samuel McKee, Jr. (New York: Columbia Univ. Press, 1934), p. 202.

18. *Labor Relations Report* (1983), 53:721.

19. Ibid.

20. LRR, No. 787 (1975), 53:571.

21. Ibid.

22. LRR (1971), 53:578

23. Ibid., 53:573.

24. Ibid.

25. Ibid., 53:574.

26. Ibid., 53:572.

27. LRR (1981), 65:231.

28. Ibid.

29.–32. LRR (1983), 53:1.

33. Ibid., 53:44.

34. William Serrin, "Where Are the Pickets of Yesteryear?" *New York Times*, May 31, 1981, C:2.

35. *Automation and the Work Place*, Washington, D.C., Office of Technology Assessment (March 1983), pp. 38–39.
36. Ira C. Magaziner and Robert B. Reich, *Minding America's Business* (New York: Vintage Books, 1983), pp. 272–273.
37. Ibid.
38. Ibid., p. 274.
39. Ibid., p. 346.
40. Markley Roberts, AFL-CIO, "Technology and Labor," July 27, 1982, ptd. in *Automation and the Work Place*, p. 93 (see n. 35 above).
41. Richard Madden, "Connecticut Moves to Aid Workers Affected by Plant Closings," *New York Times*, June 5, 1983, p. 50.
42. Magaziner and Reich, *Minding America's Business*, p. 274.
43. Markley Roberts, "Technology and Labor," p. 94.
44. William Batt, "When Plants Close, Rhône-Poulenc Tries Job Creation," *World of Work Report* (Sept. 1981), p. 71.
45. "Ford to Test Lifetime Guaranteed Jobs," *New York Times*, June 3, 1982, D:4.
46. Adam Smith, "If Smokestack America Shrinks, Can Psychology Cure the Depression?" *Esquire*, April 1984, p. 68.

Chapter 9
Technology Outrunning Policy: The Information Age

1. Bruce Nussbaum, *The World After Oil* (New York: Simon & Schuster, 1983), p. 166.
2. Harry Freeman, "If America Were Allowed to Sell Its Services to the World," *Washington Post*, Jan. 25, 1983, Op Ed page.
3. Quoted in Glenn Flanagan, "Bank Proposes Canada–U.S. Pact on Computer Services," UPI wire, Nov. 7, 1983, 7:17 P.M. EST.
4. Dena Kleiman, "Hospital in City Reports Computer Tampering," *New York Times*, Aug. 19, 1983, p. 1.
5. William D. Marbach, "Beware: Hackers at Play," *Newsweek*, Sept. 5, 1983, p. 42.
6. Jeffry Beeler, "Hacking: Mark of Genius or Plain Theft?," *Computerworld*, Sept. 12, 1983, p. 8.
7. Gerard K. O'Neill, *The Technology Edge: Opportunities for America in World Competition* (New York: Simon & Schuster, 1983), p. 276.
8. *Stimulating Technological Progress*, A Statement of the Research and Policy Committee of the Committee for Economic Development (January 1980), p. 10.
9. Gina Kolata, "Japanese Borrow Plan from U.S.," *Science* (May 1983), p. 584.

10. Andrew Pollack, "The Birth of Silicon Statesmanship," *New York Times*, Feb. 27, 1983, p. 30.
11. Gene Bylinski, "The Japanese Chip Challenge," *Fortune*, March 23, 1981, p. 116.
12. Jack Robertson, "Large U.S. RAM Losses Tied to Japanese Policies," *Electronic News*, Feb. 7, 1983, pp. 1, 13.
13. Ed Scannell, "Fujitsu Runs 256K RAM Chip on New Micro," *Computerworld NCC Daily!*, May 17, 1983, p. 3.
14. John Diebold, *Automation: A Management Classic Reissued* (New York: AMACOM, 1983)—rerelease of Van Nostrand, 1952, edition in its original form, with new introduction, p. 111.
15. John Tilton, *International Diffusion of Technology: The Case of Semiconductors* (Washington, D.C.: Brookings Institution, 1971), p. 94.
16. John Diebold, "The Information Technology Industries as a Case Example of International Trade Policy Issues in High Technology in the 1980's," prepared for the Institute for International Economics, New York, June 25, 1982, p. 30.
17. Ibid.
18. [No by-line] "Laws in U.S. Called Inadequate to Block Abuse of Computer," *New York Times*, Sept. 18, 1983, p. A42.
19. Peter Kerr, "Foreign 'Piracy' of TV Signals Stirs Concern," *New York Times*, Oct. 13, 1983, p. 1.
20. Victor F. Zonana, "Appeals Court Rules Apple Software Is Subject to Copyright Law Protection," *Wall Street Journal*, Sept. 2, 1983, p. 2.
21. David Burnham, "Private Computers' Income Data to Aid IRS in Hunt for Evaders," *New York Times*, Aug. 28, 1983, p. 88.
22. Ibid.
23. Jacques Vallee, *The Network Revolution* (Berkeley, Cal.: And/Or Press, 1982), pp. 180–181.
24. David Burnham, "U.S. Urges Census Bureau to Share Its Census Data," *New York Times*, Nov. 20, 1983, p. 32.
25. See Wayne W. Welch and Ronald E. Anderson, "Computer Inequities in Opportunities for Computer Literacy," a report released in September 1983 and based on a study funded by the National Science Foundation.
26. Yoneji Masuda, *The Information Society as Post-Industrial Society* (Tokyo: Institute for the Information Society, 1980; rptd. Bethesda, Md.: World Future Society, 1981), p. 3.
27. Robert A. Bennett, "Changing Ways at Citibank," *New York Times*, April 21, 1983, p. D1.
28. Herbert Schiller, "The Sovereign State of COMSAT," *The Nation*, Jan. 25, 1965, pp. 71–72.

29. Norman Sandler, "Antitrust Proposal," UPI wire, Sept. 12, 1983, 5:23 P.M. EST.
30. Unsigned piece on joint ventures, UPI wire, Sept. 20, 1983, 7:37 P.M. EST.
31. Thomas Moore, "Embattled Kodak Enters the Electronic Age," *Fortune*, Aug. 22, 1983, p. 128.
32. Jake Kirchner, "MCC Finalizes Plans for $350 Million in R&D," *Computerworld*, Sept. 26, 1983, p. 116.

Chapter 10
Technology Outrunning Policy: The Bio-revolution

1. See Sheldon Krimsky, *Genetic Alchemy* (Cambridge, Mass.: MIT Press, 1982); and Barbara Goldoftas, "Recombinant DNA: The Ups and Downs of Regulation," *Technology Review* (May/June 1982), p. 29.
2. Walter Sullivan, "Buying of Kidneys of Poor Attacked," *New York Times*, Sept. 24, 1983, p. 9.
3. Richard M. Titmuss, *The Gift Relationship: From Human Blood to Social Policy* (New York: Pantheon Books, 1971), p. 12.
4. Sharon Begley, "A $127 Million Gift Horse," *Newsweek*, Oct. 12, 1981, p. 87.
5. Michael Rogers, "Gene Splicing Leaves the Lab," *Newsweek*, Aug. 15, 1983, p. 63.
6. [No by-line] "Groups Seek to Halt Release of Bacteria with Altered Genes," *New York Times*, Sept. 15, 1983, p. A17.
7. "The Theological Letter Concerning the Moral Arguments Against Genetic Engineering of the Human Germline Cells," June 8, 1983 (distributed by the Foundation on Economic Trends, Jeremy Rifkin, director, Washington, D.C.), p. 6.
8. Kenneth A. Briggs, *New York Times*, June 9, 1983, pp. A1, A19.
9. Katherine Bouton, "Academic Research and Big Business: A Delicate Balance," *New York Times Magazine*, Sept. 11, 1983, p. 62.
10. Derek Bok, *Beyond the Ivory Tower: Social Responsibilities in the Modern University* (Cambridge, Mass.: Harvard Univ. Press, 1982), p. 151.
11. David Sanger, "U. of California Puts Limit on Private Research Pacts," *New York Times*, Aug. 21, 1983, p. 22.
12. Lawrence K. Altman, M.D., "The Artificial Heart Mired in Delay and Uncertainty," *New York Times*, Oct. 25, 1983, C:1.
13. Harry Stein, "The Saving of Jamie Fiske," *Esquire* (Nov. 1983), p. 69.

14. Paul T. Menzel, *Medical Costs, Moral Choices* (New Haven: Yale Univ. Press, 1983), quoted in Herbert Stein, "The Price of Health" (book review), *Fortune*, Oct. 31, 1983, p. 203.
15. Ibid.
16. "Baby Jane Doe" (editorial), *Wall Street Journal*, Nov. 23, 1983.
17. John C. Fletcher "Healing Before Birth: An Ethical Dilemma," *Technology Review* (Jan. 1984), pp. 26–36.
18. Claudia Wallis, "Made-to-Order Vaccines," *Time*, Oct. 31, 1983, p. 82.
19. Don Mullen, "Genetically Engineered Super Crops by 2000, Study Predicts," UPI wire, Dec. 6, 1983, 2:08 P.M. EST.
20. [No by-line] "Genetic Fix," *Time*, Dec. 20, 1982, p. 72.

Chapter 11
A Guiding Vision

1. Elting E. Morison, *From Know-How to Nowhere: The Development of American Technology* (New York: Basic Books, 1974), p. 167.
2. George C. Lodge, *The American Disease* (New York: Alfred A. Knopf, 1984), pp. 272–273.
3. " 'As UN Tries to Regulate Just About Everything—,' " *U.S. News and World Report*, April 25, 1983, p. 43.
4. Brooke W. Kroeger, "Common Market Summit Collapses in Failure," UPI wire, Dec. 6, 1983, 8:47 A.M. EST.
5. "The Right Stuff" (editorial), *Wall Street Journal*, Sept. 30, 1983, p. 30.
6. Robert Nisbet, *History of the Idea of Progress* (New York: Basic Books, 1980), p. 351.
7. Ibid., p. 9.
8. Ibid., p. 318.
9. Fidel Castro, farewell address delivered at Revolution Square, Havana, Nov. 14, 1983, ptd. in *New York Times*, Nov. 20, 1983, pp. 60–61.
10. Morison, *From Know-How to Nowhere*, p. 186.
11. Ronald Müller, *Revitalizing America* (New York: Simon & Schuster, 1980), p. 234.
12. Barbara Goldsmith, "Celebrity," *New York Times Magazine*, Dec. 4, 1983, p. 74.
13. Quoted by Theodore C. Sorensen in *A Different Kind of Presidency* (New York: Harper & Row, 1984), p. 93.
14. Richard Bolling, "The Tyranny of Special Interests," review of Mancur Olson, *The Rise and Decline of Nations* (New Haven: Yale Univ. Press, 1983), *Harvard Business Review*, Nov.–Dec. 1983, pp. 90–94.

15. Niccolò Machiavelli, *The Prince* (New York: Washington Square Press, 1963), p. 99.
16. Theodore H. White, *America in Search of Itself* (New York: Warner Books, 1982), pp. 193, 195.
17. Sorensen, *A Different Kind of Presidency*, p. 29.
18. Ibid., pp. 41–42.
19. John A. Garraty, Peter Gay, et al., *The Columbia History of the World* (New York: Harper & Row, 1972), pp. 51–52.
20. Ibid.
21. Ibid., p. 124.
22. Ibid., p. 115.
23. Ibid.
24. Ibid.
25. James Newman, "The Rhind Papyrus," *Mathematics* (San Francisco: W. H. Freeman, 1979), p. 11.
26. Ibid.
27. Ibid.
28. Ibid., p. 3.
29. R. G. H. Siu, *The Master Manager* (New York: John Wiley, 1980), p. 33.
30. Müller, *Revitalizing America*, pp. 231–232.
31. Cyrus Vance, letter of July 12, 1983, to John Diebold.
32. Alfred North Whitehead, *Dialogues of Alfred North Whitehead*, as recorded by Lucien Price (Boston: Atlantic Monthly Press, 1953), p. 100.
33. Arthur Schlesinger, Jr., *Wall Street Journal*, June 5, 1979, p. 22, quoted in Ronald E. Muller, *Revitalizing America* (New York: Simon & Schuster, 1980).
34. Frank P. Davidson, *Macro* (New York: William Morrow, 1983), pp. 19–20, 25.

Selected Bibliography

America's Competitive Challenge: The Need for a National Response. Report to the President of the U.S. from the Business-Higher Education Forum. Washington, D.C., 1983.

Anderson, Dean. *President at the Creation.* New York: W. W. Norton, 1969.

Arnold, Thurman. *The Folklore of Capitalism.* New Haven: Yale Univ. Press, 1937.

Aron, Raymond. *The Elusive Revolution: Anatomy of a Student Revolt.* New York: Praeger, 1969.

Artz, Frederick B. *The Development of Technical Education in France, 1500-1850.* Cambridge, Mass.: MIT Press, 1966.

Ash, Brian. *Faces of the Future: The Lessons of Science Fiction.* New York: Taplinger, 1975.

Backman, Jules, ed. *Entrepreneurship and the Outlook for America.* New York: Free Press, 1983.

Beenstock, Michael. *The World Economy in Transition.* London: Allen & Unwin, 1983.

Berg, Ivor. *Education and Jobs: The Great Training Robbery.* New York: Praeger, 1970.

Berlin, Isaiah, and Henry Hardy, eds. *Personal Impressions.* New York: Viking, 1980.

Bernal, J. D. *The Social Function of Science.* Cambridge, Mass.: MIT Press, 1967.

Bloom, Murrary Teigh. *The Trouble with Lawyers.* New York: Simon & Schuster, 1968.

Bluestone, Barry, and Bennett Harrison. *Capital and Communities: The Cases and Consequences of Private Disinvestment.* Washington, D.C.: Progressive Alliance, 1980.

Bok, Derek. *Beyond the Ivory Tower: Social Responsibilities in the Modern University.* Cambridge, Mass.: Harvard Univ. Press, 1982.

Bolling, Richard, and John Bowles. *America's Competitive Edge*. New York: McGraw-Hill, 1982.

Boorstin, Daniel, J. *The Americans: The Democratic Experience*. New York: Random House, 1973.

Bower, Joseph L. *The Two Faces of Management—An American Approach to Leadership in Business and Politics*. Boston: Houghton Mifflin, 1983.

Breyer, Stephen. *Regulation and Its Reform*. Cambridge, Mass.: Harvard Univ. Press, 1982.

Briggs, Asa. *Iron Bridge to Crystal Palace, Impact and Images of the Industrial Revolution*. London: Thames and Hudson, 1979.

Bronowski, J. *A Sense of the Future*. Cambridge, Mass.: MIT Press, 1977.

Brooks, Harvey. *The Government of Science*. Cambridge, Mass.: MIT Press, 1968.

Bundy, McGeorge. *The Strength of Government*. Cambridge, Mass.: Harvard Univ. Press, 1968).

Burnet, Sir Macfarlane. *Genes, Dreams and Realities*. New York: Basic Books, 1971.

Burns, James MacGregor. *Presidential Government: The Crucible of Leadership*. Boston: Houghton Mifflin/Riverside, 1965.

Caldwell, Lynton Keith. *Environment: A Challenge to Modern Society*. Garden City, N.Y.: Natural History Press, 1970.

Capron, William, ed. *Technological Change in Regulated Industries*. Washington, D.C.: Brookings Institution, 1971.

Carovillano, Robert L., and James W. Skehan, S.J., eds. *Science and the Future of Man*. Cambridge, Mass.: MIT Press, 1970.

Chandler, Alfred D., Jr. *The Visible Hand: The Managerial Revolution in American Business*. Cambridge, Mass.: Harvard Univ. Press/Belknap, 1977.

Chase, Allan. *The Biological Imperatives: Health, Politics and Human Survival*. New York: Holt, Rinehart & Winston, 1971.

Choate, Pat, and Susan Walters. *America in Ruins: Beyond the Public Works Pork Barrel*. Washington, D.C.: Council of State Planning Agencies, 1981.

Clarke, Arthur C. *Profiles of the Future: An Inquiry into the Limits of the Possible*. New York: Harper & Row, 1958.

Committee for Economic Development. *Public-Private Partnership: An Opportunity for Urban Communities*. Statement by the Research and Policy Committee of Committee for Economic Development, Feb. 1982.

Committee for Economic Development. *Stimulating Technological Progress*. A Statement by the Research and Policy Committee of the CED, January 1980. New York and Washington: CED, January 1980.

Committee for Economic Development. *Strengthening the Federal Budget Process*. Statement by the Research and Policy Committee of Committee for Economic Development, June 1983.

Crozier, Michel, Samuel P. Huntington, and Joji Watanuki. *The Crisis of Democracy*. Report to the Trilateral Commission on the governability of democracies. New York: NYU Press, 1975.

Dahrendorf, Ralf. *Life Chances: Approaches to Social and Political Theory*. London: Weidenfeld & Nicolson, 1979.

Daniels, George H. *American Science in the Age of Jackson*. New York: Columbia Univ. Press, 1968.

Davidson, Frank P. *Macro*. New York: William Morrow, 1983.

Davidson, William H. *The Amazing Race—Winning the Techno-rivalry with Japan*. New York: John Wiley, 1984.

Davis, John P. *Corporations*. New York: Capricorn Books, 1961.

De Sola Pool, Ithiel, ed. *The Social Impact of the Telephone*. Cambridge: Mass.: MIT Press, 1977.

Deutsch, Karl W. *The Nerves of Government*. New York: Free Press, 1966.

Diebold, John. *Automation*. New York: Van Nostrand, 1952.

Diebold, William. *Industrial Policy as an International Issue*. New York: McGraw-Hill, 1980.

Dorf, Richard C., and Yvonne L. Hunter, eds. *Appropriate Visions: Technology—The Environment and the Individual*. San Francisco: Boyd & Fraser, 1978.

Drew, Elizabeth. *Politics and Money*. New York: Macmillan, 1983.

Drucker, Peter F. *The Age of Discontinuity: Guidelines to Our Changing Society*. New York: Harper & Row, 1969.

———. *Managing in Turbulent Times*. New York: Harper & Row, 1980.

Enthoven, Alain L., and K. Wayne Smith. *How Much Is Enough? Shaping the Defense Program*. New York: Harper & Row, 1971.

Esposito, John C. *Vanishing Air*. The Ralph Nader Study Group Report on Air Pollution. New York: Grossman, 1970.

Fagen, M. D., ed. *Impact: A Compilation of Bell System Innovations in Science and Engineering Which Have Helped Create New Industries and New Products*. Bell Laboratories, 1971.

Feigenbaum, Edward A., and Pamela McCorduck. *The Fifth Generation*. Reading, Mass.: Addison-Wesley, 1983.

Fellmeth, Robert. *The Interstate Commerce Omission: The Public Interest and the ICC*. Ralph Nader Study Group Report on the

Interstate Commerce Commission and Transportation. New York: Grossman, 1970.

Final Report, President's Task Force on Communications Policy, Dec. 7, 1968. Washington, D.C.: U.S. Government Printing Office.

Fosler, R. Scott, and Renee A. Berger. *Public-Private Partnerships in American Cities*. Lexington, Mass.: Lexington Books, 1982.

Frank, Isaiah, ed. *The Japanese Economy in International Perspective*. A supplementary paper of the Committee for Economic Development. Baltimore: Johns Hopkins Univ. Press, 1975.

Friedman, Benjamin M., ed. *New Challenges to the Role of Profit: The Third Series of the John Diebold Lectures at Harvard*. Lexington, Mass.: Lexington Books, 1978.

Gabor, Dennis. *The Mature Society*. New York: Praeger, 1972.

Gee, Edwin A., and Chaplin Tyler. *Managing Innovation*. New York: John Wiley, 1976.

Gilder, George. *Wealth and Poverty*. New York: Basic Books, 1981.

Gimbel, John. *The Origins of the Marshall Plan*. Stanford, Cal.: Stanford Univ. Press, 1976.

Grace, J. Peter, chairman. *President's Private Sector Survey on Cost Control: A Report to the President*, January 15, 1984, Vol. I & II.

Gregg, Pauline. *Modern Britain: a Social and Economic History Since 1760*. New York: Pegasus, 1967.

Gyllenhammar, Pehr. *People at Work*. Reading, Mass.: Addison-Wesley, 1977.

Harris, Richard. *Justice: The Crisis of Law, Order and Freedom in America*. New York: Dutton, 1970.

Hartwell, R. M. *The Industrial Revolution and Economic Growth*. London: Methuen, 1971.

Haskins, Caryl P. *The Scientific Revolution and World Politics*. New York: Harper & Row, 1964.

Hayes, Frederick O'R., and John E. Rasmussen, eds. *Centers for Innovation in the Cities and States*. San Francisco: San Francisco Press, 1972.

Heilbroner, Robert L. *The Future as History*. New York: Harper & Bros., 1959.

Hobsbawm, E. J. *Industry and Empire: The Pelican Economic History of Britain. Vol. 3: From 1750 to the Present Day*. Harmondsworth, Eng.: Penguin Books, 1969.

Holland, Stuart. *The State as Entrepreneur: New Dimensions for Public Enterprise: The IRI State Shareholding Formula*. London: Weidenfeld & Nicolson, 1972.

442

Hunnius, Gerry, G. David Garson, and John Case, eds. *Workers' Control: A Reader on Labor and Social Change.* New York: Random House, 1973.

Jennings, Eugene E. *An Anatomy of Leadership: Princes, Heroes, and Superman.* New York: Harper & Bros., 1960.

Jewkes, John. *Government and High Technology,* Third Wincott Memorial Lecture, London School of Economics. October 31, 1972. London: Institute of Economic Affairs, 1972.

de Jouvenel, Bertrand. *On Power: Its Nature and the History of Its Growth.* Boston: Beacon Press, 1962.

Kanter, Rosabeth Moss. *The Change Masters—Innovation for Productivity in the American Corporation.* New York: Simon & Schuster, 1983.

Katzmann, Robert A. *Regulatory Bureaucracy: The Federal Trade Commission and Antitrust Policy.* Cambridge, Mass.: MIT Press, 1980.

Kellner, Peter, and Norman Crowther-Hunt. *The Civil Servants: An Inquiry into Britain's Ruling Class.* London: MacDonald, 1980.

Kirzner, Israel, Leslie Hannah, Neil Mckendrick, Nigel Vinson, Keith WicKenden, Sir Arthur Knight, Sir Frank McFadzean, P. D. Henderson, D. G. MacRae, and Ivor Pearce. *The Prime Mover of Progress: The Entrepreneur in Capitalism and Socialism.* London: Institute of Economic Affairs.

Kohlmeier, Louis M., Jr. *The Regulators: Watchdog Agencies and the Public Interest.* New York: Harper & Row, 1969.

Kreps, Juanita, ed. *Women and the American Economy: A Look at the 1980's.* Englewood Cliffs, N.J.: Prentice-Hall, 1976.

Krimsky, Sheldon. *Genetic Alchemy.* Cambridge, Mass.: MIT Press, 1982.

Kuhn, Thomas S. *The Structure of Scientific Revolutions.* 2d ed. Chicago: Univ. of Chicago Press, 1970.

Landes, David S. *The Unbound Prometheus: Technological Change and Industrial Development in Western Europe from 1750 to the Present.* Cambridge, Mass.: Cambridge Univ. Press, 1969.

Lerner, Max. *America as a Civilization: Life and Thought in the United States Today.* New York: Simon & Schuster, 1957.

Levitt, Michael, and Barbara Lloyd. *Upset: Australia Wins the Americas's Cup.* New York: Workman, 1983.

Lieberman, Jethro K. *The Litigious Society.* New York: Basic Books, 1981.

Lilienthal, David E. *The Journals of David E. Lilienthal. Volume I: The TVA Years, 1939-1945.* New York: Harper & Row, 1964.

Lindblom, Charles E. *Politics and Markets: The World's Political-Economic Systems.* New York: Basic Books, 1977.

Lodge, George, C. *The American Disease: Why the American Economic System Is Faltering . . . and How the Trend Can Be Changed with a Minimum of Crisis.* New York: Alfred Knopf, 1984.

Logsdon, John M. *The Decision to Go to the Moon: Project Apollo and the National Interest.* Cambridge, Mass.: MIT Press, 1970.

Lukacs, John. *Outgrowing Democracy: A History of the United States in the 20th Century.* New York: Doubleday, 1984.

Machiavelli, Niccolò. *The Prince.* New York: Washington Square Press, 1963.

McKee, Samuel, Jr., ed. *Papers on Public Credit, Commerce and Finance by Alexander Hamilton.* New York: Columbia Univ. Press, 1934.

Magaziner, Ira C., and Robert B. Reich. *Minding America's Business.* New York: Vintage Books, 1983.

Maier, Pauline. *The Old Revolutionaries: Political Lives in the Age of Samuel Adams.* New York: Knopf, 1980.

Maine, Sir Henry Summer. *Popular Government.* Indianapolis: Liberty Classics, 1976.

Mantoux, Paul. *The Industrial Revolution in the Eighteenth Century.* New York: Harper & Row, 1961.

Marks, Marlene Adler. *The Suing of America.* New York: Seaview Books, 1981.

Marx, Leo. *The Machine in the Garden: Technology and the Pastoral Ideal in America.* New York: Oxford Univ. Press, 1964.

Mason, Edward S., ed. *The Corporation in Modern Society.* Cambridge, Mass.: Harvard Univ. Press, 1960.

Mason, Otis T. *The Origins of Invention: A Study of Industry Among Primitive Peoples.* Cambridge, Mass.: MIT Press, 1966.

Masuda, Yoneji. *The Information Society as Post-Industrial Society.* Tokyo: Institute for the Information Society, 1980; rptd. Bethesda, Md.: World Future Society, 1981.

Mathias, Peter. *The First Industrial Nation: An Economic History of Britain.* New York: Scribners, 1969.

————. *The Transformation of England: Essays in the Economic and Social History of England in the Eighteenth Century.* New York: Columbia Univ. Press, 1979.

Maurizi, Alex R. *Public Policy and the Dental Care Market.* Washington, D.C.: American Enterprise Institute, 1975.

Menzel, Paul T. *Medical Costs, Moral Choices.* New Haven: Yale Univ. Press, 1983.

Mintz, Morton, and Jerry S. Cohen. *America Inc.: Who Owns and Operates the United States.* New York: Dial Press, 1971.

Mishan, E. V. *Technology and Growth: The Price We Pay*. New York: Praeger, 1970.

Moore, Thomas Gale. *Trucking Regulation Lessons from Europe*. American Enterprise Institute/Hoover Institution Policy Study 18, Jan. 1976 (Hoover Institution Studies 54). Washington, D.C.: AEI, 1976.

Morison, Elting E. *From Know-How to Nowhere: The Development of American Technology*. New York: Basic Books, 1974.

Moynihan, Daniel Patrick. *Loyalties*. New York: Harcourt Brace Jovanovich, 1984.

Muller, Robert. *Revitalizing America*. New York: Simon & Schuster, 1980.

Munzer, Martha E. *Valley of Vision: The TVA Years*. New York: Knopf, 1969.

Mutti, John, and Peter Morici. *Changing Patterns of U.S. Industrial Activity and Comparative Advantage*. Washington, D.C.: National Planning Association, 1983.

Myrdal, Gunnar. *Beyond the Welfare State*. London: Gerald Duckworth, 1960.

Nisbet, Robert. *History of the Idea of Progress*. New York: Basic Books, 1980.

Noble, Trevor. *Modern Britain: Structure and Change*. London: B. T. Batsford, 1981.

Nussbaum, Bruce. *The World After Oil*. New York: Simon & Schuster, 1983.

Olson, Mancur. *The Rise and Decline of Nations: Economic Growth, Stagflation, and Social Rigidities*. New Haven: Yale Univ. Press, 1982.

O'Neill, Gerard K. *The Technology Edge—Opportunities for America in World Competition*. New York: Simon & Schuster, 1983.

Ong, Walter J. *Morality and Literacy—The Technologizing of the World*. London: Methuen, 1982.

Ouchi, William. *Theory Z: How American Business Can Meet the Japanese Challenge*. New York: Avon Books, 1982.

Packard, Vance. *Our Endangered Children—Growing Up in a Changing World*. Boston: Little, Brown, 1983.

Parker, Donn B. *Crime by Computer*. New York: Scribners, 1976.

Pascale, Richard Tanner, and Anthony Athos. *The Art of Japanese Management: Applications for American Executives*. New York: Simon & Schuster, 1981.

Pauwels, Louis, and Jacques Bergier. *The Morning of the Magicians*. New York: Stein & Day, 1964.

Peters, Thomas J., and Robert H. Waterman, Jr. *In Search of*

Excellence: Lessons from America's Best-Run Companies. New York: Harper & Row, 1982.

Peterson, Peter G., chmn. *Foundations, Private Giving, and Public Policy.* Report and recommendations of the Commission on Foundations and Private Philanthropy. Chicago: Univ. of Chicago Press, 1970.

Pierson, Frank C. *The Minimum Level of Unemployment and Public Policy.* Kalamazoo, Mich.: W. E. Upjohn Institute for Employment Research, Kalamazoo, 1980.

Price, Harry Bayard. *The Marshall Plan: Its Meaning.* Ithaca, N.Y.: Cornell Univ. Press, 1955.

Pryke, Richard. *Public Enterprise in Practice: The British Experience of Nationalization over Two Decades.* London: MacGibbon & Kee, 1971.

Ramo, Simon. *Cure for Chaos: Fresh Solutions to Social Problems Through the Systems Approach.* New York: David McKay, 1969.

Ramsey, Paul. *Fabricated Man: The Ethics of Genetic Control.* New Haven: Yale Univ. Press, 1970.

Rees, Merlyn. *The Public Sector in the Mixed Economy.* London: B. T. Batsford, 1973.

Reich, Robert. *The Next American Frontier.* New York: Times Books, 1983.

Revel, Jean-François. *Without Marx or Jesus.* New York: Doubleday, 1970.

Reynolds, Morgan O. *Power and Privilege—Labor Unions in America.* New York: Universe Books, 1984.

Ritterbush, Philip C., ed. *Scientific Institutions of the Future.* Washington, D.C.: Acropolis Books, 1972.

Rohatyn, Felix G. *The Twenty-Year Century—Essays on Economics and Public Finance.* New York: Random House, 1983.

Rosow, Michael P., and Robert Zager. *Productivity Through Work Innovations.* New York: Pergamon Press, 1982.

Rothschild, Baron Nathaniel Mayer Victor, Lord. *Meditations of a Broomstick.* London: Collins, 1977.

Ruzic, Neil P. *The Case for Going to the Moon.* New York: Putnam's, 1965.

Sait, Edward McChesney D. *Political Institutions: A Preface.* New York and London: Appleton Century, 1938.

Sale, Kirkpatrick. *Human Scale.* New York: Coward, McCann & Geoghegan, 1980.

Salins, Peter. *The Ecology of Housing Destruction.* New York: New York Univ. Press, 1980.

Savas, E. S. *Privatizing the Public Sector.* Chatham, N.J.: Chatham House, 1982.

Sayre, Wallace S., and Herbert Kaufman. *Governing New York City: Politics in the Metropolis.* New York: Russell Sage Foundation, 1960.

Schooler, Dean, Jr. *Science, Scientists, and Public Policy.* New York: Free Press, 1971.

Schumacher, E. F. *Small Is Beautiful: Economics as if People Mattered.* New York: Harper & Row, 1973.

Schumpeter, Joseph, A. *Business Cycles, A Theoretical, Historical, and Statistical Analysis of the Capitalist Process,* Vol. I and II. New York: McGraw Hill, 1939.

Searle, G. R. *The Quest for National Efficiency: A Study in British Politics and British Political Thought 1899–1914.* Oxford: Basil Blackwell, 1971.

Selznick, Philip. *Leadership in Administration: A Sociological Interpretation.* Evanston, Ill.: Row, Peterson, 1957.

Shanks, Michael. *The Innovators: The Economics of Technology.* Baltimore: Penguin Books, 1967.

Silberman, Charles F. *Crisis in the Classroom.* New York: Random House, 1970.

Sitwell, Osbert. *Left Hand, Right Hand!* London: Macmillan, 1952.

Siu, R. G. H. *The Master Manager.* New York: John Wiley, 1980.

Skolnikoff, Eugene B. *Science, Technology and American Foreign Policy.* Cambridge, Mass.: MIT Press, 1969.

Smith, Adam. *The Wealth of Nations.* New York: Modern Library, 1937.

Smith, Nelson, and Leonard J. Theberge, eds. *Energy Coverage —Media Panic.* Media Institute. New York: Longman, 1983.

Sowell, Thomas. *The Economics and Politics of Race: An International Perspective.* New York: William Morrow, 1983.

———. *Knowledge and Decisions.* New York: Basic Books, 1980.

Steffens, Lincoln. *The Autobiography of Lincoln Steffens.* New York: Harcourt Brace Jovanovich, 1968.

Stein, Bruno, and S. M. Miller, eds. *Incentives and Planning in Social Policy: Studies in Health, Education, and Welfare.* Chicago: Aldine, 1973.

Steiner, Gilbert Y. *The State of Welfare.* Washington, D.C.: Brookings Institution, 1971.

Stewart, James B. *The Partners: Inside America's Most Powerful Law Firms.* New York: Simon & Schuster, 1983.

Sward, Keith. *The Legend of Henry Ford.* New York: Rinehart, 1948.

Tilton, John. *International Diffusion of Technology: The Case of Semiconductors.* Washington, D.C.: Brookings Institution, 1971.

Titmuss, Richard M. *The Gift Relationship*. New York: Random House, 1971.

Toynbee, Arnold. *The Industrial Revolution*. Boston: Beacon Press, 1956.

Tullock, Gordon. *Private Wants, Public Means: An Economic Analysis of the Desirable Scope of Government*. New York: Basic Books, 1970.

Turvey, R., ed. *Public Enterprise*. Harmondsworth, Eng.: Penguin Books, 1968.

Tyler, Gus. *The Labor Revolution*. New York: Viking, 1967.

——. *The Political Imperative*. New York: Macmillan, 1968.

U.S. Industrial Competitiveness: A Comparison of Steel, Electronics, and Automobiles. Office Technology Assessment, U.S. Congress. Washington, D.C., 1981.

Vallee, Jacques. *The Network Revolution*. Berkeley, Cal.: And/Or Press, 1982.

Walters, A. A. *Noise and Prices*. Oxford: Clarendon Press, 1975.

Westin, Alan F. *Privacy and Freedom*. New York: Atheneum, 1967.

White, Theodore H. *America in Search of Itself*. New York: Warner Books, 1982.

Whyte, William Foote, et al. *Worker Participation and Ownership*. Ithaca, N.Y.: ILR Press, 1983.

Wiener, Martin J. *English Culture and the Decline of the Industrial Spirit, 1850–1980*. Professor of History at Rice University. Cambridge and New York: Cambridge Univ. Press, 1981.

Will, George. *Statecraft as Soulcraft*. New York: Simon & Schuster, 1983.

Wills, Garry. *Inventing America: Jefferson's Declaration of Independence*. New York: Doubleday, 1978.

Yankelovich, Daniel. *New Rules: Searching for Self-Fulfillment in a World Turned Upside Down*. New York: Random House, 1981.

——and John Immerwahr. *The Work Ethic and Economic Vitality*. New York: Public Agenda Foundation, 1983.

——, et al. *Work and Human Values*. New York: Public Agenda Foundation, 1983.

vonAuw, Alvin. *Heritage and Destiny: Reflections on the Bell System in Transition*. New York: Praeger, 1983.

INDEX

Abbott Laboratories, 257
Abernathy, William, 255
Action for Rational Transit, 43
activists, 246, 250, 253, 361–62, 370
  corporations' cooperation with, 24, 60–62, 258, 264, 267
Adams, John, 63, 109, 396, 414
Addams, Charles, 20
Adenauer, Konrad, 36, 85
adversary process, 61, 126–27, 130
Afghanistan, war in, 92, 103
AFL-CIO, 228, 293, 296
Agee, William, 239–40
Agricultural Extension Service, 30
agriculture, 102, 104–5, 285
  biotechnology and, 369–70, 385
  climate and, 83, 98, 104
  development of, 30, 402–3
  in Soviet Union, 30, 99, 104
airline industry, 105, 224, 251, 309
Alice in Wonderland (Carroll), 96
Alternatives for Delivering Public Services (Savas), 162

America in Ruins (Choate and Walters), 96
"American Century," 16
American Film Festival, 116
American Lawyer, 121, 122, 138
America's Cup, 17–18
Anderson, Robert E., 347
antiauthoritarianism, 212–14
antinuclear protest, 47, 92
antitrust legislation, 57–58, 81–82, 124–26, 133, 135, 242, 311–13, 329, 334, 355
AP (Associated Press), 92
Apollo, 88–89, 97, 354
Apple Computer, 231, 343–44
arbitration, 72–73, 139–40, 146, 238
Argyris, Chris, 233
Aristotle, 214, 403
Arizona, water supply in, 83
Army Corps of Engineers, U.S., 45, 72
Asbell, Bernard, 181
Aspen Institute, 213, 219, 227
AT&T, 81–82, 124, 173, 179, 246, 311–13, 324, 339, 344
Audubon Society, 47
Australia, 17–18, 310
Autobiography of Lincoln Steffens, The (Steffens), 41
Automation (J. Diebold), 336–37

449

automobile industry, 29, 94, 98, 118–19, 193–94, 203, 211, 240, 250, 272, 279, 294, 300–301, 317
  in Japan, 35, 94, 130, 234

"baby boom," 76, 213
"Baby Jane Doe," 132, 381
Backus, Robert, 48
Bacon, Roger, 112
Baker, Russell, 130
Ball, George, 90
Baltimore, David, 365–66, 374
banking, 93–94, 224, 265–66, 308–9, 318, 345–46, 350
Bank of America, 265–66
Bank of England, 63
Banks, Robert, 141
Bardeen, John, 81
Barr, Tom, 124–25
baseball:
  Chinese, 414–15
  lawsuits in, 122–23, 126, 131
Bates, G. Wallace, 143
Battelle Laboratories, 44
BBC, 58, 195
Beasley, Howard, 237
Bell, Griffin, 130, 143
Belli, Melvin, 130
Bellow, Laird and LeAnn, 377–79
Bell System, 81–82, 225, 311–13
Bendix Corporation, 239–40
Bergman, Walter, 345
Bethlehem Steel, 301–2
Bible, 401–5
"big bang" theory, 81
Bill of Rights, U.S., 52
biotechnology, 321, 360–87
  agriculture and, 369–70, 385
  education and, 365–66, 373–75
  environmentalists and, 361–362, 370
  importance of, 316
  information technology and, 306–7, 320
  legal system and, 134, 370, 372, 380–84
  life-and-death issues in, 132, 363–64, 375–83, 386
  profit motive in, 362–64, 376
Black Mesa Line, 45–46
Bliss, Russell, 99
Boeing, 105, 120–22
Bok, Derek, 97, 128, 129, 374–375
Bolling, Richard, 397
Boyer, Herbert, 372
Brattain, Walter, 81
Brazil, 309, 329
Brett, George, 122, 123
Brill, Steven, 125, 138
Bucy, Fred, 339–40
bureaucracy:
  incentive structure of, 159–60
  need for defeat of, 25, 28, 40, 168
Burger, Warren E., 126–27, 138–39
Burke, J. E., 258
Burn, Joe, 293
Bush, Vannevar, 110
Business Roundtable, 134, 245, 261, 328, 418
Byrom, Fletcher L., 65

Cabbage Patch Kid dolls, 131
caffeine, 415–16
California, Proposition 13 in, 169–70
Carey, Hugh L., 43
Carson, Rachel, 88, 239
Carter, Jimmy, 98, 103, 398–99
Cary, Frank, 125
Castro, Fidel, 103, 392
Center for Public Resources, 143–44
CETA, 277
Chakrabarty, Ananda, 372
Chandler, Alfred D., 66
Chaplin, Charlie, 196, 276, 337
Chargaff, Erwin, 362
Chen Chiu, 313–14
China, Age of Warring States in, 406–8, 409
China, People's Republic of, 41, 100, 213

Chinese baseball, 414–15
Choate, Pat, 96
Churchill, Sir Winston, 36, 110, 394, 395
CIA (Central Intelligence Agency), 111
Clague, Ewan, 347
Clamshell Alliance, 47
Clark, Barney, 376–77
Clark, Ramsey, 125
Clarke, Arthur, 110, 112
Clean Air Act, 62
Clean Sites, Inc., 266–67
climate, unpredictability of, 83, 98–99, 104
Club of Rome, 111, 409
coal, 45–46, 59, 61–62, 86, 99
Cohen, Richard, 254
Cohen, Stanley, 372
COLA (cost-of-living adjustments), 75, 76
Cole, Robert, 234
Coleco, 131
Coleridge, Samuel Taylor, 111–112
Colorado River, 83
Committee for Economic Development, 33, 67, 166, 325
Common Market, 390, 405
communications industry, 311–313, 316–17, 319, 324, 339, 350, 353
competitiveness, 228, 317
  decline of, 16, 31, 33
  in public services, 21, 162, 167
computers, 37, 79–80, 81, 95, 101, 107, 108, 140, 160, 195, 201, 221–22, 224, 230–233, 276, 277, 308–59
  criminal use of, 313–16, 341–342, 357–58
  education and, 168–69, 181–182, 189–90, 281–82, 347–348, 354
  see also information technology
COMSAT, 353

Confucius, 406, 407–8
Congress, U.S.:
  machinery of, 19, 24, 27, 38, 66–67, 114–15
  power of, 56, 67
  voting patterns of, 60, 95
Congressional Budget Act, 66–69, 114
Congressional Budget Office, 67–69, 113, 114–15
Constitution, U.S., 49, 51, 62, 66, 114
consumerism, 246, 249, 262, 264
Control Data Corporation, 189–191, 259–60, 282, 354
Convergent Technologies, Inc., 230–32
Coons, John E., 183
copyrights, 133, 342–43
Cormick, Gerald W., 72–74
Corporate Security, Inc., 187
corporations:
  acquisition of, 236–37, 239–40
  activists' cooperation with, 24, 61–62, 258, 264, 267
  creativity in, 20, 193, 196, 205, 206, 232
  evolution of, 65–66
  management of, 236–69
  multitrack, 204–5
  post-multinational, 39, 198–99
  short time horizons of, 93–95
  spying by, 237–39
Costle, Douglas, 267
Cox, Archibald, 143
Cravath Swaine & Moore, 124–126
"creative forgetting," 31
"creative misunderstanding," 234
Crisis in the Classroom (Silberman), 181–82
crisis management, 15–16, 18, 55, 84
Cronkite, Walter, 91
Crutchfield, Finis A., 371
Cuban Missile Crisis, 103
cults, 390, 396

Cunningham, Mary, 240
Cunningham, William, 188
Cuomo, Mario, 96
Cutler, Lloyd, 135

Dade County, Fla., 144–45, 161
DARPA (Defense Advanced
    Research Projects Agency),
    338
data transfer, 308–10
Davidson, Frank, 418–19
Davis, Karen, 154
Decker, Gerald, 61–62
Declaration of Independence,
    53, 412
de Gaulle, Charles, 85
Delaney amendment, 247
"demand pull," 158, 163, 174
Deming, W. Edwards, 233
democracy, 24, 27, 43, 52, 416
    information, 348–49, 417
    limits of, 49, 53
Denmark, public service in,
    191–92
Denny, Donald, 378
Depression, Great, 56, 408
Des Moines, Iowa, public-
    education campaign in, 117,
    386, 416
DeVries, William, 376
Diebold, William, 32, 33, 279–
    280
Diebold Corporate Issue
    Program, 61–62
Diebold Group, 281, 317
Diebold Institute for Public
    Policy Studies, 160–62, 330
Diebold Research Program, 101,
    222
dioxin, 99
"discretionary effort," 220–22
DNA, 307, 361–62, 369–72, 384–
    385, 386
    see also biotechnology
"Don't rock the boat"
    syndrome, 20, 28, 151, 193
Doriot, Georges, 90, 197
Dow Chemical Company, 61–62
drugs, 39, 248, 257, 369, 373

Du Pont, 246–47, 262, 267, 373
dust bowl, 102, 112

Eastern Europe, economy of,
    35, 41
Edelstein, David, 124–26
Edison, Thomas A., 110
education, 85, 89, 103, 154–56,
    216, 219, 249
    biotechnology and, 365–66,
    373–75
    computers and, 168–69, 181–
    182, 189–90, 281–82, 347–
    348, 354
    extension of, 200–202, 280–82
    innovation in system of, 64–
    65, 168–69, 180–83, 201,
    280–82
    job training as, 38, 118, 201,
    272–73, 277, 278, 282–83,
    289–90, 299, 350
    of public, campaigns for, 60,
    117, 386, 416–17
    tax-deductible, 38, 201, 299
    technology and, 96–98, 168–
    169, 180–82, 189–91
    vouchers for, 182–84
Egypt, ancient, 410–11
Einstein, Albert, 306
Eisenhower, Dwight, D., 23, 63,
    103, 110, 114, 338
electric power, 48, 50, 70–71,
    86
Electronic Data Services, 263
electronics industry, 81
English common law, 59
environmental concerns, 60, 69,
    98–100, 102, 105, 112–13,
    241, 242, 246–47, 249, 262,
    266–67
    biotechnology and, 361–62,
    370
    coal and, 45–46, 61–62, 99
    dams and, 50, 71–74, 104
    Dow Chemical Company and,
    61–62
    nuclear power and, 47, 100
    toxic wastes and, 99–100,
    117, 131, 266–67

TVA and, 50
Westway and, 45
EPA (Environmental Protection Agency), 47, 62, 135, 237, 262, 266–67
ETSI (Energy Transportation Systems, Inc.), 45–46
eugenics, 371
"European disease," 18
Evans, Daniel, 72
"expressivism," 213
Exxon Corporation, 107, 267

Falck, Sophus, 191–92
Falwell, Jerry, 371
family, changes in, 214–18, 223, 226, 227
Fanning, Larry, 287
FBI (Federal Bureau of Investigation), 238, 314, 315
FCC (Federal Communications Commission), 311–13, 329
featherbedding, 284
federal budget, 66–68
federalism, 62
Federalist, The (Madison), 51
Federal Register, 134
Federal Reserve System, 63
Feigenbaum, Ed, 82
Feldstein, Martin, 278
Ferdinand V, King of Spain, 397–98
Fernandez, Louis, 266–67
Fifth Generation, The (Feigenbaum and McCorduck), 82
Fiske, Charles and Jamie, 377–79
Fletcher, John, 383
fleximodes, 223–28
Food and Drug Administration (FDA), 39, 247–48, 257, 264
food industry, 24, 247, 264–65, 317–18
Food Safety Council, 264–65
Ford Motor Company, 202, 211, 240, 294, 300
France, 35, 48, 85, 165, 296, 297, 299–300, 316, 330, 348

Frankel, Marvin, 143
Franklin Computer Corporation, 343–44
Frazee, Rowland, 310
Freeman, Harry L., 310
Freud, Sigmund, 408–9
Friedman, Lawrence, 139
Friendly, Fred, 92
From Know-How to Nowhere (Morison), 22, 388
Fuchs, Victor, 154
"Future of Work, The," 293

Gallen, Hugh, 47
Galton, Sir Francis, 371
Gardner, John, 53–55
Garlinghouse, Mark, 124
Garraty, John A., 403, 404–5
Gates, William, 344
GATT (General Agreements on Tariffs and Trade), 280, 310
Gay, Peter, 403, 404–5
General Accounting Office, 83, 115
General Electric, 184, 207, 225, 246, 260, 372
General Motors, 17, 106, 131, 202, 246
employees of, 40, 118–19, 154, 193–94, 272, 280, 294
genetic engineering, 371, 385
Germany, Federal Republic of (West Germany):
business in, 29, 35, 84, 93, 97–98, 198, 203, 223–24, 230, 278, 295, 297, 298, 310, 328
information technology in, 309, 316–17, 339
Pershing missiles in, 92
Germany, Nazi, 60, 408
Gibbon, Edward, 413
Gilbert, Walter, 374, 375
Glass-Stigal Act, 94
Glover, John, 400
Goddard, Robert, 97
Goldsmith, Barbara, 393–94
Goodman, Howard, 374
Gordon, Kermit, 287, 346–47
Gore, Albert, Jr., 374

government:
  decentralization of, 55
  industrial policy of, 31–35
  process in, 49–50
  role of, 29–31, 37–41, 54, 185–
    186, 299
  see also specific branches
Grace, Peter, 168, 171
Grand Coulee Dam, 27
Great Society, 103
Green, Eric, 148
Greene, Harold, 313
Greenspan, Allan, 64
Grenada, 392
"gridlock," 24
Gyllenhammar, Pehr, 202

hackers, 314–16, 341–42,
    357–58
Haldane, J. B. S., 111
Hall, Robert, 189
Hamilton, Alexander, 32, 285,
    414
Hanley, John, 117
Hanson, John K., 189–91
Hardin, Garrett, 104–5
Harley-Davidson, 94
Harman, Sidney, 203–4
Harrigan, Arthur, 170–71
Harvard Business Review, 240,
    347
Harvard Law School, 138
Hathaway, Stan, 46
Hayek, Friederich A., 163
Hayes, Robert, 255
health, threats to, 58–59, 99–
    100, 117, 131, 275, 361–62,
    365, 384, 415–16
Health and Human Services
    Department, U.S., 89
health care:
  commercialization of, 362–66
  cost of, 40, 89, 116–17, 153–
    154, 174, 175–76, 224, 226
  lawsuits relating to, 132, 370,
    372, 380–84
  see also biotechnology
Hearst, William Randolph, 408
heart, artificial, 376–77

Heineman, Ben E., 237
Henry, James, 144
Henry VI (Shakespeare), 137
History of the Idea of Progress
    (Nisbet), 26–27, 391
Hitachi, 201, 238
HMOs, 174
Homer, 414
Hooker Chemical Corporation,
    99–100
housing, 17, 29
Hughes, John, 188
Humphrey, Hubert, 106
Hungary, trading companies of,
    39, 41
Huxley, Aldous, 372, 395

IBM, 95, 127, 128, 183–84, 202,
    231, 238, 276, 313, 324,
    328, 356
  U.S. antitrust case against,
    124–26, 334
Independent Petrochemical
    Corporation, 99
*Industrial Policy as an
    International Issue*
    (W. Diebold), 279–80
industrial revolutions:
  first, 26, 85, 199–200, 220,
    336, 418
  third, 41
infant mortality, 17
inflation, 48, 75
influenza, 58
information democracy, 348–49,
    417
information explosion, 280–81
information technology, 37, 81,
    140, 208–9, 277, 281–82,
    308–59
  biotechnology and, 306–7, 320
  importance of, 316, 350, 417
  in Japan, 79, 80, 238, 310,
    316, 326–27, 330, 331–34,
    348
  joint ventures in, 355–57
  legal disputes about, 124–26,
    238, 342–44
  privacy vs., 344–47

in West Germany, 309, 317,
339
see also computers
infrastructure, decay of, 17, 95–
96
Inman, Bobby, 356
In Search of Excellence (Peters
and Waterman), 94
instant gratification, 29
interest groups, 51–55, 61
interest rates, 48
International Association of
Machinists, 294
International Harvester
Company, 270–71, 294
International Paper Company,
260–61
international trade, 16, 30, 38–
39, 279–80, 285, 309–10,
331–34
"intrapreneurship," 230–31
Inventing America (Wills), 62–63
"invisible hands," 56–57, 172
Iowa, education in, 117, 189–90,
386, 416
Iran, hostages in, 103
IRS (Internal Revenue Service),
38, 299, 345
ITT scandal, 240, 241, 250

Jackson, Jesse, 397
Jacobs, Barry, 362–64, 376
Jaime, Irma, 147
Janson, R., 225
Japan:
atomic-bomb attack on, 48,
409
automobile industry in, 35,
94, 130, 234
business in, 29, 30–31, 34–35,
39, 84, 87–88, 93, 198, 201–
202, 203, 206, 233–34, 240,
280, 295–96, 297, 298, 300,
326–27, 328, 349
culture of, 31, 35, 87–88, 130–
131, 280
information technology in, 79,
80, 238, 310, 316, 326–27,
330, 331–34, 348

legal system in, 129–31, 309–
310
Meiji Restoration in, 30–31
nuclear power in, 48
Jarvik, Robert, 376
Jefferson, Thomas, 56, 63, 396,
414
Jencks, Christopher, 182
Job Training Partnership Act,
277–78, 302
Johnson, Clifford M., 217
Johnson, Lyndon B., 56, 103
Johnson & Johnson, 252, 258
Justice Department, U.S., 132,
347
antitrust suits of, 81, 124–26,
311–13, 329, 334

Kahn, Herman, 103, 107
Kansas City Royals, 122–23
Kansas-Nebraska Act, 53
Katz, Milton, 105
Kaufman, Irving, 142–43
Kelsey, Frances, 248
Kennedy, Edward M., 377
Kennedy, John F., 27, 45, 46,
90, 103, 287, 350, 353, 396
Kennedy, Robert F., 347
Kenyon, Jack, 170
Keynes, Lord John Maynard,
137
kidney transplants, 362–64,
376–77
King, Martin Luther, 396
Kirkland, Lane, 76–77
Kirkpatrick, Jeane, 390
Koch, Edward, 43, 82
Kokotovich, Mike, 300
Korb, Tim, 358
Korea, economy of, 206, 330
Krantrowitz, Arthur, 384

labor:
alienation of, 209–10
declining standards of, 16–17,
94, 95, 194–95
dehumanization of, 196, 210–
211
future of, 33, 273

labor (*cont.*)
  incentive structure for, 16–
    17, 29, 170, 211–12, 224–25
  job mobility of, 35, 270–302
  job training for, 38, 118, 201,
    272–73, 277, 278, 282–83,
    289–90, 299, 350
  motivation of, 204–5, 211–12,
    219–20, 223–24
  QWL of, 228–29
  shortage of, 20, 88, 273
  talented, 198–99, 205–6, 208
  see also unemployment;
    unions; salaries
Lavelle, Rita, 266
lead and lag times, 85–86,
  88–89
leadership, 393–401
  absence of, 395–97
  as abused concept, 41, 393–
    394
  defined, 41
  management vs., 397–401
  source of, 414
Ledeen, Michael, 90
Legal Services Corporation, 127
legal system, 120–48
  biotechnology and, 134, 370,
    372, 380–84
  changes needed in, 105, 126–
    127, 139–48
  history of, 403–4
  information technology and,
    124–26, 140, 238, 342–44
  in Japan, 129–31, 309–10
  statistics on, 129, 135
Legal Times, 144–45
Legislative Reference Service,
  115
Lempert, Larry, 144
Levitan, Sar A., 217
Liberty, 18
Lieberman, Jethro, 143
Likert, Rensis, 198, 233
Lilienthal, David, 51, 160
Liman, Arthur, 128
Lincoln, Abraham, 21, 30, 53,
  56, 396, 398
Lindblom, Charles, 28, 49

Lindow, Steven, 369–70
Lindsay, Franklin, 254
Lindsay, John V., 43
Linowitz, Sol, 144
Lloyd, Kent, 155
Lockheed Aircraft Company,
  101, 240, 250
Lodge, George, 389
Long Island Lighting Company,
  48
Love Canal, 99–100, 240
Lovett, Robert, 103
Low, Francis, 366
Luce, Henry, 16, 29

Macaulay, Thomas, 26
McCarthy, Jane, 72, 73
McCloy, John J., 36, 108
McCorduck, Pamela, 82
McDonald, Denny, 190
McGee, George, 27
McGlynn, Joseph, 135
Machiavelli, Niccolò, 396,
  397–98
McNamara, Robert, 159
Macro (Davidson), 418
Madison, James, 51, 54, 405
Magaziner, Ira C., 296
Magna Carta, 49, 214
Magregor, Douglas, 233
mail, 177–80
  electronic, 178–79, 224
Mainstream Access, 301–2
Mallory, George, 314
Marshall, John, 18
Martin, Billy, 122
Martin-Marietta, 239
Marx, Karl, 209–10, 405
Marxism, 392, 405
Maslow, Abraham, 223
Massachusetts, legal and
  government procedures in,
  27–28, 129, 141–42, 169,
  188
Masuda, Yoneji, 348–49, 352
Mathews, Jay, 272–73
Matthofer, Hans, 276
Mayo, Elton, 212
Mazzocchi, Anthony, 292

456

MCI Communications, 179, 311, 313
media, 89–93, 116, 195, 251, 252–53, 312, 348, 386, 417
  manipulation of, 60, 250, 264
  organ transplants and, 377–79
  in presidential campaigns, 398–99
  role of, 21, 29, 58–59, 90, 335, 400
  see also newspapers; television
Media Institute, 91
"media panic," 91
mediation, 72–74, 140, 267
Medical Costs, Moral Choices (Menzel), 379
Medicare, Medicaid, 153–54, 263
"me first" generation, 29
Meiji Restoration, 30–31
Memorial Sloan-Kettering Cancer Center, 314
Menzel, Paul T., 379–80
metric system, 107
Mettler, Ruben, 226
Mianus River Bridge, 17, 96
Michels, Allen, 231
Michigan, environmentalists, in, 61
Microelectronics and Computer Technology Corporation (MCC), 356–57
Mill, John Stuart, 284
Miller, Irwin, 257–58
Mills, C. Wright, 199–200
Missouri, toxic wastes in, 99
Missouri Compromise, 53
MIT (Massachusetts Institute of Technology), 365–66, 373, 375
MITI, 34–35, 316, 338
Mitsubishi, 238
Mitterand, François, 316
Mobil, 253
modems, 341
Modern Times, 196–97, 276, 337
Monet, Jean, 405
Monsanto, 117–18, 266–67, 373

Morison, Elting E., 22, 59–60, 388–89, 391, 393, 410
Moss, Larry, 62
movie industry, 132–33, 318, 342–43
Müller, Ronald, 393, 415
"multitrack organizations," 204–5
MX missile, 64

National Academy of Sciences, 86, 115, 384
National Aeronautics and Space Administration, 88–89, 329
National Coal Policy Project (NCPP), 61–62
National Commission on Excellence in Education, 156, 180
National Commission on Social Security, 76–77
National Health Service Corps, 138
National Institutes of Health (NIH), 361–62, 369, 370, 373
National Science Board, 281
National Security Council, 63–64
National Semiconductor Corporation, 238, 356
Nazism, 60, 408
NCPP (National Coal Policy Project), 61–62
NEC, 201–2
New England Coalition on Nuclear Pollution, 47
New Hampshire, nuclear power plant blocked in, 46–48
Newman, James, 410–11, 413
newspapers, 90, 195, 271, 287–289
  see also media
Newton, Sir Isaac, 306
New York City:
  condition of roads in, 17, 43
  homeless in, 17
  public transit in, 16, 44, 151–153
  school system in, 156

New York City (*cont.*)
  water supply in, 82–83
  Westway dispute in, 43–45
New York *Daily News*, 271, 287–
  288
New Yorker, 20, 159
New York Times, 16, 90, 135,
  142, 271, 287–88, 342
  on Pine Tar dispute, 123
  on Westway, 44
New York Yankees, 122–23
Nisbet, Robert, 26–27, 391–92
Nixon, Richard, 56, 103, 158
nonadversarial process, 61–62
Norris, William, 189–90, 259,
  356
North Carolina, quality-control
  circles in, 234–35
North Eastern Pharmaceutical
  and Chemical Corporation,
  99
Northwest Industries, 236–37
Norway, 309
NRC (Nuclear Regulatory
  Commission), 47
nuclear-arms race, 92, 338, 409,
  416–17
nuclear power, 46–48, 58, 73,
  86, 91, 100, 111, 134
Nussbaum, Karen, 221

Oakes, John B., 44
Office of Environmental
  Mediation, 72
Ogden, David, 363–64
Ohio, police in, 186–87
Ohio pipeline, 45–46
oil prices and shortages, 46, 48,
  99, 101, 106–7, 111
O'Neill, Gerard K., 316
O'Neill, Thomas "Tip," 377
O'Neill, William, 296
Ontario Hydro, 70
OPEC (Organization of
  Petroleum Exporting
  Countries), 111
OPM leasing scandal, 136
organs, human:
  artificial, 376–77
  transplanted, 362–64, 376–78,
    386
Orlando (Woolf), 124, 320
Orwell, George, 335, 348, 349,
  389
"Ozymandias" (Shelley), 413

PACs (political-action
  committees), 67
Papandreou, Andreas, 390
"paper entrepreneurialism,"
  255
Parliament, 67, 110
Parsons & Whittemore, 144–45
Patman, Wright, 278
Patrick, Neil, 314
"Peanuts," 18
PEF (Public Education Fund),
  65
penicillin, 59
Penman, Sheldon, 366
Penzias, Arno, 81
People at Work (Gyllenhammar),
  202
Pershing missiles, 92
Peters, Thomas J., 94
Peterson, Peter, 29
pharmaceutical industry, 39,
  248, 257, 369, 373
Pilder, Richard, 301
Pine Tar dispute, 122–23, 126
pluralism, 51–55
"Pogo," 18
Pohl, Fred, 111
polarization, dangers of, 92, 116
police, privatization of, 161, 186–
  189
"political gridlock," 24
"political inventing," 25, 30, 59–
  60, 62–67, 114
Politics and Markets
  (Lindblom), 28, 49
pork barrels, 44, 95
Postal Service, U.S., 177–80
"post-crisis decisions," 103
"post-multinational
  corporations," 39, 198–99
power plants, 70–71, 105
  nuclear, *see* nuclear power

PP&L (Pennsylvania Power and Light Co.), 70–71
PREP (Productivity Research and Extension Program of North Carolina State University), 234–35
presidency:
    campaigns for, 398–400
    power of, 55–56, 67, 114
    terms of, 113–14
    veto power of, 49, 52
presidential commissions, 64
President's Private Sector Survey on Cost Control, 168, 171
Privatizing the Public Sector (Savas), 152–53
process, as concept, 49–50, 393
productivity, 31, 203, 206, 208–209, 228, 233–35, 243–44, 288
    measurement of, 208
Profiles of the Future (Clarke), 110, 112
profit motive, 170–71, 172, 174, 176–77, 244
    in biotechnology, 362–64, 376
progress, 26–27, 29, 286, 388–393, 403, 408
    declining belief in, 27, 391
protectionism, 279–80, 285
PSNH (Public Service of New Hampshire), 46–48
Public Agenda Foundation, 16, 93, 115–17, 213, 219, 221, 222, 254, 386, 416–17
public-education campaigns, 60, 117, 386, 416–17
Public Interest, The, 90
public services, 151–92, 216
    competition in, 21, 162, 167
    in Denmark, 191–92
    privatization of, 20–21, 162, 166–67, 186–92
public transit, 16, 44, 151–53

quality-control circles, 233–35
QWL (quality of work life), 228–229

railroads, 46, 86
RAM (random-access memory) chips, 79–80, 331–32
R&D (research and development), 81–82, 84
    obstacles to, 38, 39, 62, 82, 97–98
"ratchet effect," 164
Reagan, Ronald, 165, 399, 409
Reagan administration, 76, 97, 103–4, 132, 134, 146, 184–185, 245, 266, 346
recessions, 198
Regional Plan Association, 44
regulatory agencies, 57–58, 134–135, 241, 245–50, 257
Rehnquist, William, 122
Reich, Robert B., 255, 296
Reilly, William, 267
Reinhardt, Uwe, 154
"Report on Manufacture" (Hamilton), 32, 285
retirement, 29, 36, 168, 200, 212, 291
    see also Social Security
Reuther, Walter, 276
Rhône-Poulenc, 299–300
Rifkin, Jeremy, 370, 371
rights, individual, 24, 27, 38, 52, 53
Rising Star Industries, 232–33
risk taking:
    in biotechnology, 369–70
    government regulation and, 246–49
    social values and, 58–59
Rivlin, Alice, 69
robots, 188–89, 274, 349, 351
Rockefeller, Nelson A., 43
Roosevelt, Franklin, 56, 112, 396, 408
Rothschild, Lord Nathaniel, 58, 111
Rowe, Wallace, 362
Rowen, Henry, 93–94
Rowse, Payton, 305
Rubin, Jerome, 254
Ruckelshaus, William, 267
"rule of reason," 61–62

Russell, Bertrand, 111
Rutherford, Ernest, 111
Rutkowski, Chris, 232–33
Ryan, Sylvester, 121

saccharin, 247
salaries, 57, 75, 181, 208, 211–
    212, 226, 278, 279, 297
  guaranteed, 290
  quality of life and, 20, 223
  quality of work and, 16–17,
    194, 196, 205, 211, 288
Salines, Peter, 17
Sanders, Matt, 231
Savas, E. S., 152–53, 156, 162
savings rates, 29, 36, 40
scapegoats, 74
Schlesinger, Arthur M., Jr., 418
Schless, Phyliss, 227
Schleyer, Hanns Martin, 328
Schultze, Charles, 23, 32
Scowcroft, Brent, 64
Seabrook nuclear power plant,
    46–48
Seacoast Anti-Pollution League,
    47, 48
Sears, Roebuck, 134, 246
Seattle, dam controversy in,
    71–73
Securities and Exchange
    Commission, 93
semiconductor industry, 79–80,
    206, 231, 317, 327–28, 331–
    332, 338
"senior boom," 76
Servan-Schreiber, Jean-
    Jacques, 348
services, service economy, 215–
    216, 220–21, 310
Sessions, Robert, 160
Shakespeare, William, 137
Shanker, Albert, 175
Shapiro, Irving, 247
Shelley, Percy Bysshe, 413
Sherman Antitrust Act, 57–58
Shields, Mark, 50–51
Shockley, William, 81
Silberman, Charles, 182

Silent Spring (Carson), 237
Simpson, John D., 151
Singer, Ethan, 371
Singer, Hutner, Levine &
    Seeman, 136
Sinsheimer, Robert, 360
Sitwell, Osbert, 88
Siu, Ralph, 414–15
slavery, 53
Smith, Adam, 56–57, 172, 177
"Smith, Adam " (George
    Goodman), 302
Smith, Nelson, 91
Smith, Robert Ellis, 345
Smith, William French, 355
Snoqualmie-Snohomish Basin,
    71–73
Snow, C. P., 307
socialism, pluralism absent in,
    52
Social Security, 36, 64, 69, 74–
    78, 88, 89
Sony Corporation, 132–33
Sorenson, Ted, 24, 113–14, 399,
    400–401
Southern Pacific Railroad, 46
Soviet Union, 103, 198, 339–40,
    408
  agriculture in, 30, 99, 104
  economy of, 35, 41, 111, 171
Sowell, Thomas, 58, 60, 87
space shuttle, 88–89
space travel, 88–89, 97, 110,
    158, 185, 353, 396
Spengler, Oswald, 413
Staats, Elmer, 50, 113
Statecraft as Soulcraft (Will),
    53
State Department, U.S., 64
steel industry, 38, 279, 301
Steffens, Lincoln, 41
Steinmetz, Charles, 207–8
Stewart, Jon, 192
Stimulating Technological
    Progress, 325
Stockman, David, 19
Study of History, A (Toynbee),
    413
Sturz, Herb, 159

Summerdale Public
    Participation Project,
    70–71
"sunrise" industries, 33, 350
Supreme Court, U.S., 121–22,
    132–33, 134
Sutton, Willie, 137
Sweden, 220, 295, 296, 297,
    298, 309, 339

Taoists, 407
taxes, 20, 345
    cutting of, 103–4, 169
    deductions from, 38, 201, 299
    Social Security and, 69, 75,
        77–78
Taylor, Frederick, 211
teachers:
    burnout of, 155
    glut of, 89
    new roles for, 182
    salaries of, 181
technofix, 18
technology, 22, 158, 196, 215
    agriculture benefited by, 30
    dehumanizing effect of, 275–
        277, 293
    discretionary effort and,
        221–22
    education and, 96–98, 168–
        169, 180–82, 189–91
    entrepreneurship and, 254
    schizophrenic attitude toward,
        250
    unemployment and, 35, 273–
        275, 335
    unions and, 284, 288, 292–93
    see also biotechnology;
        information technology
Technology, 86
Technology Review, 46
Telecredit, in minitrial with
    TRW, 147–48
telephone service, 81–82, 311–
    313, 324
television, 116, 181, 195, 281,
    312, 335, 342, 417
    influence of news coverage
        by, 91–92

organ transplants and, 377–79
    in presidential campaigns,
        398–99
    see also media; video
        technology
Ten Commandments, 403–4
textile industry, 34, 279, 284,
    285, 299
thalidomide, FDA and, 248
Thatcher, Margaret, 165, 390
Theberge, Leonard, 91
Three Mile Island, 48, 58, 91,
    134
"time horizon," 87
Timex, 231
Tocqueville, Alexis de, 35, 321,
    414
Toland, Karen, 231
"Toward a Pluralistic but
    Coherent Society"
    (Gardner), 53–54
toxic wastes, 99–100, 117, 131,
    266–67
Toynbee, Arnold, 413
Trade Adjustment Assistance
    Program, 278, 279
trade-off mechanisms, 59–62,
    185
    defined, 43
Tragedy of the Commons, The
    (Hardin), 104–5
transistors, 81, 82, 311
Transportation Department,
    U.S., 107
Truman, Harry S, 50, 397
TRW, 226
    Telecredit in minitrial with,
        147–48
TVA (Tennessee Valley
    Authority), 50–51
Tylenol scare, 252
Tyler, Gus, 214

UAW (United Auto Workers),
    118, 193–94, 272, 289–90,
    294, 300
unemployment, 285–86
    current trends in, 273

unemployment (*cont.*)
  historical changes in
    consequences of, 222–23
  innovative programs for,
    290–98
  misguided programs for,
    277–78
  nature of labor force masked
    by, 227
  Social Security reform and,
    75–76, 89
  technological change and, 35,
    273–74, 279, 335
unions:
  class strife and, 284–86
  history of, 282–86
  lobbying efforts of, 296–97
  public confidence in, 244
  role of, in job transitions,
    292–94
  technological change and,
    284, 288, 292–93
  work innovation and, 228–29
United Kingdom, 63, 67, 97,
    105, 110, 140, 339
  business in, 26, 29, 165, 195,
    220, 285, 295, 297, 329,
    349, 354
United Nations, 49, 389–90
United States:
  in 1920s, 29
  in 1930s, 29, 56
  in 1940s, 16, 233
  in 1950s, 216
  in 1960s, 16, 29, 32, 97, 198,
    199, 213, 249
  in 1970s, 29, 32, 61, 89, 198,
    215, 216, 240, 244, 245, 249
  in 1980s, 61, 89, 198, 216
  cultural characteristics of, 35
  decline of, 16–17, 29, 198,
    203
  Founding Fathers of, 26, 51–
    52, 85, 414
  goals and planning for, 23–25,
    106–10
  income in, 17, 218
  literacy in, 17
  longevity in, 17

postwar, 16, 63–64, 67, 212–
    214, 408–9
  roads in, 17, 43, 107
Univac, 101
Universal Studios, 132–33
UPS, 177–78
*UPSET: Australia Wins the
    America's Cup* (Levit and
    Lloyd), 17–18
urban blight, 29
U.S. Synthetic Fuels
    Corporation, 106–7
utilities, 70–71

Vance, Cyrus, 93, 113, 115, 146,
    416
Van Gemert, William, 120–22,
    126
Velsicol Chemical Corporation,
    236–37
vetoes, 19, 24, 43–78
  democratization of, 49
  multiple, 51
  time limit for, 50
video technology, 133, 224, 318,
    319, 343, 351, 417
Vietnam War, 101, 103, 213
Visible Hand, The (Chandler),
    66
voucher concept, 182–83, 278,
    297–98

Wall Street Journal, 90
Walters, Susan, 96
War Games, 342
wars, national unity through, 55,
    405
Washington, D.C., public
    transit in, 152
Washington Post, 50, 90, 133,
    139, 272
Watergate, 56, 101, 241
Waterman, Robert H., Jr., 94
water supply, 46, 82–83, 102,
    104
Watson, Thomas, 258
Watts, Glenn, 293
Wealth of Nations, The (Smith),
    57, 177

weather prediction, 83, 98–99, 104, 184–85
Weber, Max, 210
Weimar Republic, 60, 408
Weinberger, Caspar, 339
Welch, Wayne N., 347
Wessel, Milton, 62
West Germany, *see* Germany, Federal Republic of
Westway, 43–45
"What Price Health Care?," 116
White, Gilbert F., 83
White, Theodore, 398–99
Whitehead, Alfred North, 417
Whitehead, Edward, 365
"white knights," 239–40
Wilcox, Clair, 334
Will, George, 53, 109
Williams, Spencer, 238
Wills, Garry, 62
Wilson, Robert, 81
Wilson, Woodrow, 56, 408

Winnebago Industries, 189–90
women, changing role of, 214–219, 227, 396
Woodside, William S., 44
Woolf, Virginia, 124, 320
word processing, 140, 221
Work and Human Values, 213
work ethic, 210, 219–21
Work in America Institute, 228
"World of Work, The" (Tyler), 214
World War I, 408
World War II, 214, 226, 231, 408–9
Worthington, Robert, 190
Wyoming, coal-slurry pipeline project in, 45–46

Xerox Corporation, 95, 141, 273

Yankee ingenuity, 35, 321
Yankelovich, Daniel, 93, 116, 213, 220, 243–44, 416

465